The New Spymasters

The New Spymasters

Inside the Modern World of Espionage from the

Cold War to Global Terror

STEPHEN GREY

St. Martin's Press New York

THE NEW SPYMASTERS. Copyright © 2015 by Stephen Grey. All rights reserved. Printed in the United States of America. For information, address St. Martin's Press, 175 Fifth Avenue, New York, N.Y. 10010.

www.stmartins.com

The Library of Congress Cataloging-in-Publication Data is available upon request.

ISBN 978-0-312-37922-3 (hardcover)
ISBN 978-1-4668-6713-0 (e-book)

St. Martin's Press books may be purchased for educational, business, or promotional use. For information on bulk purchases, please contact the Macmillan Corporate and Premium Sales Department at 1-800-221-7945, extension 5442, or write to specialmarkets@macmillan.com.

First published in Great Britain by Viking, an imprint of Penguin Random House.

First U.S. Edition: July 2015

10   9   8   7   6   5   4   3   2   1

To Sophie and Daniel

Contents

Contents

Glossary

Modern spying terms

Analyst Someone employed to examine secret and open-source intelligence and draw conclusions.

Betrayal In order to gather human intelligence, a spy must inevitably betray someone.

Case officer An employee of an intelligence service who recruits and manages secret agents. Such operatives typically object to being called spies, since it may imply betrayal.

Clandestine action Secret political or military action abroad.

Cover or **legend** The fictional identity, biography and/or purpose of an intelligence officer or secret agent, created to allow them access to certain individuals or places.

Covert action Political or military action by a secret service, the sponsoring country of which remains hidden and unacknowledged.

Dangle A walk-in (*see below*) sent to a secret service by an enemy as a plant or double agent in order to provide false information or otherwise cause damage.

Dead drop A pick-up place for an agent to leave secret intelligence he has stolen.

Debriefing Questioning a source, agent or captive; can also be a euphemism for harsh interrogation.

Diplomatic cover Most intelligence officers travel abroad under cover as diplomats. This provides them with immunity from being prosecuted for spying.

Double agent A secret agent working for one master who is persuaded to work for another too.

False flag A trick used by a secret service to make a secret agent think he is being recruited by another country's service.

Handler The term for a case officer who manages or 'runs' a secret agent. Keeping the agent alive and sober is hard.

HUMINT Intelligence from all kinds of human sources including spies and ordinary contacts. This may also include intelligence from debriefings and interrogations.

Illegal The exception: an intelligence officer who works without diplomatic cover and carries out spying. In the US, illegals are known as NOCs: Non-Official Covers.

Informer Someone who provides tip-offs to secret services or a law enforcement agency, but who may not be under their active control.

Intelligence officer A staff employee of a secret service. He may, among other roles, be a case officer or analyst.

Laws . . . are to be obeyed at home and broken abroad. Spying is illegal in every country of the world, even for diplomats.

Requirement (also known as 'tasking') Instructions from a secret service's political masters to collect specific intelligence on a target or subject.

Secret intelligence Vital information that is kept secret: i.e. is protected in some way. Protected government information is usually marked as such: e.g. labelled Top Secret, NOFORN (i.e. 'no foreign national') or Official.

Secret intelligence service A government agency whose function is to gather intelligence and carry out secret tasks, whether recruiting spies, gathering SIGINT (*see below*), analysing secret intelligence or carrying out covert and/or clandestine actions.

Secret police A secret service that identifies, watches and may secretly arrest and interrogate alleged enemies of the state. (A security service like MI5, with no power of arrest, is not in this sense a secret police.)

SIGINT Signals intelligence: i.e. intercepting electronic signals, including from communications systems, radar and weapons systems. The great seductive rival of human intelligence.

Spy or **Secret agent** Any person who steals secret intelligence and then passes it on to a government agency, in their own country or abroad.

Sub-agent or **Sub-source** An agent working for another agent, providing hearsay intelligence.

Targeter An analyst who locates targets for assassination or capture.

Triple agent A double agent who is 're-doubled' to betray his new master and work for his original master.

Glossary

Walk-in A volunteer for a spy agency who may literally walk into an embassy or contact the secret services by email, telephone, letter or some other means.

Secret agencies and their role

United States

Central Intelligence Agency (CIA) Includes both a clandestine service (the National Clandestine Service), which handles spy operations, and a larger intelligence division, which analyses the product from multiple sources of intelligence, including open sources. The main CIA customer is the US president, who must also authorize its covert actions.

Defense Intelligence Agency (DIA) Part of the Department of Defense; similar in structure to the CIA, with a clandestine service and with analytical and science and technology directorates, all providing military-related intelligence.

Federal Bureau of Investigation (FBI) Self-tasking agency which functions generally as a federal police but has counterintelligence, counterterrorism and national security divisions that carry out domestic secret intelligence work: e.g. running spies inside violent extremist groups. Also responsible for investigating any crimes against US persons or interests abroad.

National Security Agency (NSA) Huge agency that collects SIGINT globally.

United Kingdom

Defence Intelligence (DI) Similar to the American DIA; provides all-source intelligence and analysis of a primarily defence and strategic nature.

Government Communications Headquarters (GCHQ) British equivalent of the American NSA; single-source agency with a focus on SIGINT.

Joint Intelligence Committee (JIC) The main customer and coordinator for UK intelligence. It provides intelligence assessments, covering all sources, and sets requirements for SIS and GCHQ.

Secret Intelligence Service (SIS) Also known popularly as MI6 (a cover-name that was used in the 1930s and the Second World War); the foreign intelligence service and the rough equivalent of the CIA's clandestine service; single-source (HUMINT) agency. Analysis is mainly handled by other departments in the British government, including the JIC and DI. All significant operations require ministerial approval.

Security Service (MI5) Domestic intelligence service. It is still referred to generally by its designation in the First World War, MI5, and called the BSS (British Security Service) by US agencies. It carries out secret security work, targeting violent extremist threats (mainly terrorism) to the UK. It runs agents and interrogates sources, but, unlike a police force, has no power of arrest. MI5 is self-tasking.

France

Direction Générale de la Sécurité Extérieure (DGSE) Foreign intelligence service.

Direction Générale de la Sécurité Intérieure (DGSI) Internal intelligence service, created in May 2014 and replacing the **Direction Centrale du Renseignement Intérieur (DCRI)**, itself the result of a merger – in July 2008 – of the **Direction de la Surveillance du Territoire (DST)**, the former domestic intelligence service, and the **Renseignements Généraux (RG)**, the former police intelligence service.

Germany

Bundesamt für Verfassungsschutz (BfV) Domestic intelligence service, which, due to memories of the Nazi-era Gestapo, operates at a state level only and with restricted powers.

Bundesnachrichtendienst (BND) Foreign intelligence service of modern federal Germany.

Stasi Nickname for the Ministry for State Security (**Ministerium für Staatssicherheit** or **MfS**), the secret service of the former communist-run East Germany (GDR). Its foreign spy service was called the Main Reconnaissance Administration (**Hauptverwaltung Aufklärung** or **HVA**).

Glossary

USSR/Russia

Committee of State Security (KGB) Secret service of the USSR, which, among other names, was first called the Cheka (1917–29), then the MVD, NKVD (1934–46), MGB (1946–53) and finally the KGB (1954–91). Only a small elite division of the KGB, the First Chief Directorate, handled spying operations abroad.

Federal Security Service of the Russian Federation (FSB) Domestic secret service of post-Soviet Russia.

Foreign Intelligence Service (SVR) Replaced the First Chief Directorate as Russia's foreign intelligence service.

Main Intelligence Administration (GRU) All-source Soviet and then Russian foreign military intelligence agency.

Middle East

Countries in the Middle East generally have either one intelligence service, the Mukhabarat, handling both foreign and domestic intelligence and reporting to the country's head of state, or a Mukhabarat and a separate domestic secret police, usually under the direction of the Ministry of the Interior. For example:

EGYPT

The **State Security Investigation Services (SSIS)** or Mabahith Amn ad-Dawla reports to the interior minister. The **Mukhabarat (EGIS)**, the foreign service, reports to the president.

JORDAN

The **General Intelligence Directorate (GID)** handles both domestic and foreign intelligence, and reports to the king.

SAUDI ARABIA

The **General Directorate of Investigation (GDI)** is the umbrella department that oversees the **General Security Services (GSS)** or Mabahith, which is the domestic intelligence service and secret police. The **General Intelligence Presidency (GIP)**, also known as Mukhabarat al-Ammah or al-Istikhbarat al-Ammah, is the main foreign intelligence agency, but it also coordinates the dissemination of all Saudi intelligence and reports directly to the king.

Timeline of Major Events

1909: The British Secret Service bureau is founded. Two years later, it is divided into what became the domestic Security Service (MI5) and the foreign Secret Intelligence Service (SIS).

1914–18: First World War.

1917: The Bolshevik party, a communist faction, seizes power in Moscow and St Petersburg and founds the Soviet Union. Its intelligence service, created by Felix Dzerzhinsky, is known first as the Cheka and later, among other names, as the NKVD and KGB. From 1920 its headquarters are in Lubyanka Square, Moscow.

1939–45: Second World War. The UK founds the Special Operations Executive (SOE) for secret operations behind enemy lines in 1940 and in 1942 the US founds the Office of Strategic Services (OSS).

1947: The CIA is founded, replacing the Central Intelligence Group (CIG), established a year before.

1955: The Soviet army withdraws from Austria.

1961: The construction of the Berlin Wall.

1962: The Cuban Missile Crisis.

1979: The Soviet Union invades Afghanistan.

1982: Israel invades Lebanon.

1987: First Intifada (uprising) of Palestinians against Israeli occupation starts.

1988: Soviet troops begin withdrawing from Afghanistan.

1989: The Berlin Wall is breached. The 'Iron Curtain' collapses. Massacre in Tiananmen Square, Beijing.

1990: Iraq invades Kuwait, beginning the first Gulf War. Nelson Mandela is released from prison in South Africa.

1991: The Soviet Union is dissolved. Iraq is defeated in Gulf War by US and allied troops. Somali government is toppled, leading to a bloody civil war and decades of lawlessness.

1992: Bosnian War (until 1995). US troops enter Somalia (remaining until 1994). A military coup in Algeria prevents Islamist movement gaining power; beginning of Algerian Civil War (until 2002).

1993: Oslo Accords end the First Intifada and establish Palestinian self-rule in the West Bank and Gaza territories.

1994: Rwanda genocide. First Chechen War (to 1996). CIA officer Aldrich Ames is exposed as a KGB spy. Britain's SIS 'comes out' and is affirmed in a new law. Ceasefire by Northern Ireland's Irish Republican Army (IRA).

1995: Algerian militants launch bomb attacks on the metro in Paris, France.

1996: IRA violence resumes in Northern Ireland.

1998: Osama bin Laden's al-Qaeda organization declares war on the US and organizes bomb attacks on US embassies in Kenya and Tanzania. Good Friday Agreement ends war in Northern Ireland. Kosovo War (to 1999).

1999: Second Chechen War (to 2009).

2000: Second Intifada begins (to 2005).

2001: 11 September (9/11) attacks in US. Afghan War begins (ongoing).

2003: Second Gulf War: invasion of Iraq, followed by civil war from 2004 (ongoing).

2004: Madrid train bombings. Orange revolution in Ukraine.

2005: 7 July (7/7) attacks on the London Underground and bus network.

2006: London Plot to use 'liquid bombs' on transatlantic planes.

2008: Israeli troops enter Gaza (remaining until 2009). Russia–Georgia War.

2009: Jordanian secret agent kills seven CIA employees in Afghanistan.

2010: Arab Spring begins with political protests in Tunisia; spreads to Libya, Egypt, Bahrain, Yemen and Syria (ongoing).

2011: Osama bin Laden killed.

2013: Edward Snowden, a private contractor, releases classified documents on the National Security Agency.

2014: Russia annexes the Crimea region of Ukraine. A new 'Islamic State' seizes swathes of territory in Syria and Iraq.

Author's Note

The following account is based, in part, on numerous interviews conducted not only over five years researching this book but also over two decades of covering security as a journalist. Quotations from people are based on those conversations or correspondence with myself or my researcher. Since many of these interviewees are or were active in the secret intelligence world, for reasons of discretion they are frequently quoted anonymously and no further information is provided about the interview. If the quotation is from another source, this is indicated in the text or by a note, with details of that source provided at the end of the book. If any attribution is missing or incorrect, or you have any other comments, please contact me via my website (www.stephengrey.com) so I can make any necessary changes in future editions of the book.

Please also note that I sometimes refer to individuals by their first given names; this should not imply any partiality but is done simply for clarity. Also, for ease of read, I refer throughout to a spy as 'he', but of course spies are men and women.

The New Spymasters

Introduction: The Exploding Spy

'When the heart speaks, the mind finds it indecent to object'

– Milan Kundera, *The Unbearable Lightness of Being*[1]

On 31 December 2009, a Jordanian doctor opened the door of a pick-up truck and prepared to greet officers of the Central Intelligence Agency for the first time. There were eight people waiting. They had even made a birthday cake for him. The CIA and the White House had high hopes for this day. The doctor was a spy, a man who had driven to this US base in Khost, Afghanistan, from the wild tribal zone of neighbouring Pakistan. They hoped he could lead them to the al-Qaeda leader, Osama bin Laden.

Wrong. The doctor was working for the other side, for al-Qaeda. He reached into a pocket, pressed a detonator switch and blew himself up. Seven people from the CIA were killed: the base chief, Jessica Matthews, four other officers and two security guards. The eighth victim was a Jordanian intelligence officer; the ninth an Afghan driver. Matthews had made the birthday cake. She had been searching for bin Laden for years. Perhaps that made her desperate to believe in the doctor. But she had mis-read the signs. She had been one of the world's leading experts on al-Qaeda. One commentator suggested her death was the intelligence 'equivalent of sinking an aircraft carrier in a naval war'.[2]

The doctor had been a double agent, maybe a triple agent. Here was the first real hope of getting a spy next to bin Laden, a genuine lead. He had seemed to be the perfect New Spy: a mole inside America's biggest adversary since Soviet Russia. And then it all was blown away.

His name was Humam al-Balawi. He was a Jordanian national but by descent he was a Palestinian, the people who were in conflict with America's close ally, Israel. Having worked at refugee camps, he had seen the victims of what he saw as Israel's aggression and he had every reason to be furious with a United States that financed Israel. And he had proved his hatred, writing a blog on the Internet that advocated war on the

Americans. He was an obvious man to attack the CIA. He was also a perfect man to spy for the CIA.

It was a brilliant cover story. If al-Balawi really was working for the CIA, then he would have been one of their greatest ever spies. He was such an unlikely spy – and therefore so right for the job.

It was not to be. If only they had checked. They had never met him before. Yet when he came to the base, he wasn't even searched. Jessica had not wanted to offend him. She had wanted to accord him 'respect'. But as a last testament that al-Balawi recorded on video made clear, he had been playing the American and Jordanian spy services for weeks.

On a marble wall back at CIA headquarters in Langley, Virginia, they carved seven more stars. Seven more of their comrades killed in the field of action. Since the terror attacks of 11 September 2001, twenty-five stars had been added.[3]

Welcome to the deadly world of spycraft.

'To work in intelligence is to live with perpetual failure,' said a former leading figure in the British secret service.[4]

By any measure, the al-Balawi mission in Khost was a tragic, wretched and careless venture. But the operation was also an audacious act: a dance into the unknown and a proof-of-life signal that, despite the careless blunders of those days, the spy game was not over.

This book is an inquiry into the modern secret agent and his employer, the spymaster. Our subject is what the novelist and sometime intelligence officer Graham Greene called 'the human factor', the business in which a real walking, talking person like al-Balawi sets about gathering 'intelligence', by which I mean some secret or protected information.

In the trade, the use of a human being, a spy, to gather intelligence is known as *human intelligence* (HUMINT) collection. There is obviously a dark side to our subject. Spying is the art of betrayal. Almost inevitably, to gather secrets a spy must betray his country, or at least betray the trust placed in him by those who have given him access to the secrets.

While it showed that the spy game continued, did the debacle of Khost show that the spymasters were now incompetent? The CIA's potential secret agent had been 'grotesquely mishandled', said a military historian, Edward Luttwak, among other critics.[5] Or was it that using human spies against al-Qaeda leaders was just too difficult?

In these pages, I address the state of human intelligence and do so by seeking to answer three questions. First, how has spying changed in the twenty-first century? Second, when can spying still be effective? And third – the essential question posed by Khost – what kind of spying is needed and will help deal with the specific threats of today and the future?

Given the incredible things that can be divined in the twenty-first century by stealing a copy of someone's electronic mail or listening to their phone, for instance, the idea of taking the word of an old-fashioned human source may seem rather questionable. Spying has been called the world's second-oldest profession, but it can also seem to be an anachronism.

As the Khost mission showed, spying carries tremendous risks. Spies must betray the secrets of the country or group they target. But betrayal can be addictive. Spies can, in turn, also betray those who recruit them. Since spies must survive by telling lies, it can be hard to know when they are telling the truth.

The discovery of a spy operation can trigger diplomatic rows, sow discord and, at worst, be a pretext for war. By contrast, the use of spy satellites or the bugging of conversations – technical methods of getting intelligence – can seem a far safer way to gather information. A former CIA operative described being told by an analyst colleague, 'Please give us a great agent. Satellite photos don't tell us where the missile is aimed or who can fire it.' But Admiral Stansfield Turner, a CIA director under President Jimmy Carter, declared that technical spying 'all but eclipses traditional, human methods of collecting intelligence'.[6] After the 1990 Gulf War he again summed up what became a dominant, if often unspoken, view that the US should not depend on old-style spies:

> The litany is familiar: We should throw more and more human agents against such problems, because the only way to get inside the minds of adversaries and discern intentions is with human agents. As a general proposition that simply is not true . . . Not only do agents have biases and human fallibilities, there is always a risk that an agent is, after all, working for someone else.[7]

But despite the risks that Turner described, hardly a month goes by without a new spy being unmasked. At the time of writing, the United States was being accused by Germany of recruiting a spy inside its defence department and another in its secret services. In response, the CIA's

Berlin chief of station was expelled, with the German chancellor, Angela Merkel, declaring that the Americans had 'fundamentally different conceptions of the work of the intelligence services'.[8] And yet for governments whose secret services or law enforcement agencies employ spies like these, the potential benefit of having a 'spy in the enemy camp' is frequently too seductive, even if the 'enemy' is actually a close ally.

Spies, then, are a persistent feature of modern states. But do they make much difference, in particular against the biggest threats that nations face today?

Good specific human intelligence is still critical. It might arguably have permitted action to thwart the attacks of 11 September 2001, in which 2,753 people died,[9] or the tribal massacres in Rwanda, East Africa, in which 800,000 people died in just 100 days in 1994. But bad intelligence suggesting that Iraq had weapons of mass destruction also helped lead to an invasion of that country which cost the lives of up to 500,000 people.

Espionage is an old and elemental human art, susceptible to endless permutations, which is why it is always hard to generalize about spying, though the motivations for betrayal – ideology, religion, money, blackmail etc. – tend to remain unchanged. As I once heard a former chief of British intelligence say, 'There have been no new motives since the Mesopotamians.'

This book is not a comprehensive survey. It reflects the experiences of those I have met while working primarily in the western hemisphere and dealing mainly with the security services of the United States and Britain, with some additional contacts in Germany and France and across the Middle East and South Asia. It omits huge developments in eastern Asia, South America and Africa.

Just as the Cold War finished, I began a career as a journalist and writer. In the years that followed, working mainly abroad, and particularly reporting on national security, I have been privileged to meet spies, and the spymasters who recruit and run them, everywhere from cigar rooms in Washington, tea rooms in London, beer gardens in Germany and coffee shops in Cairo and Beirut, to military bases in Iraq and Afghanistan and walled compounds in Pakistan. Some of them worked for secret services and some for other agencies in the military and law enforcement that also practise espionage.

In this sense, I have grown up with a new generation of spies, watching as they redefined their enemies and raison d'être, and changed their character too. I was fortunate that this occurred at a time of greater openness, when someone such as myself – with only modest connections – was able to find a window into this world.

While sharing the experiences and insights of the spies and spymasters I have met, I have also tried to maintain the critical distance that is lacking from most official publications or books written by retired spies, who, even if they do not say so, must submit their accounts for approval by the secret services.

In addition, I have included experiences of the spied-upon: the violent militants or radical activists who come up with new strategies on a daily basis to escape attention. At a conference in Oxford, a former chief (known as 'C') of Britain's Secret Intelligence Service introduced me in a wary tone to the panel as 'someone who has actually met al-Qaeda'.

Spying is an old habit. There are spies mentioned in the Bible and in the records of ancient China and Egypt. There were spies in ancient Mesopotamia and even documents marked 'Top Secret'. From the twentieth century, spies have featured so often in books and films that it is easy to think we know the subject backwards. But much of what is said is confused, wrong or based around myths.

One of the reasons spying can seem rather dated is that so many of the popular conceptions about it derive from the role played by spies in the confrontation between the former Soviet Union and the West. The spy game was central to the Cold War: the KGB and its allies on one side, the CIA and its partners on the other. While the military stood poised for action but remained largely motionless, the spy wars were real.

For those like me who grew up in this time of confrontation, who can forget the spy stories in the news, in literature and in the movies? As children we played spy: we put on false moustaches, tailed our enemies across the playground, learned to write in code and passed messages in invisible ink. The problem was that in the excitement over espionage's trappings – its intrigue, dangers and gadgets – underlying questions about its success or failure were rarely posed.

The first part of this book takes us back to the Cold War and the origins of the modern secret service. I want to explain not only the nuts and bolts of spying, but also why the assumptions that many people make about spying, based on our understanding of this period, are often dubious.

When operations like Khost are criticized by old-timers, it is worth knowing, for instance, that there never really was a past golden age of espionage.

History can give us direct and positive lessons for the present. For example, while the fight against terrorism would come to dominate intelligence work, this was not a new concern for secret services. The real story of Britain's secret espionage fight against the Irish Republican Army in Northern Ireland, for example, is only just emerging. And it provides a template for how spying against terrorists can work, even if modern terrorists are different in important ways.

With the second part of the book we enter the uncharted period after the Cold War, when the spymasters confronted ill-defined or unfamiliar adversaries and had to find new targets for their spies. Initially, there was even some suggestion that spymasters and spies were no longer relevant. Sir Colin McColl, the chief of SIS at the end of the Cold War, recalled being treated by 'intelligent, knowledgeable people' like a long-forgotten uncle and asked, 'Are you still here?'[10] Years later, following new wars and colossal attacks by terrorists, few doubted the need for intelligence. But the debate continued as to whether, with improvements in technology, human spies were still valuable. In a little-noticed discussion, some argued that spies were useful to spy on governments but useless against modern targets such as radical Islamists and their suicide bombers. Some highly experienced spymasters argued that human intelligence was a 'dying art' and would play at best a secondary, if not negligible, role compared to technical methods.

I had to establish if this was true before I could consider what kind of spies we really need. Could a spy get close to such ruthless, chaotic enemies, and do so without stirring up the proverbial hornet's nest and thereby making those enemies more dangerous?

The road to the failure of human intelligence collection in Khost started with the tearing down of the Berlin Wall in 1989. As the Soviet Union disbanded two years later, debate began about whether the end of superpower rivalry would lead to a 'peace dividend', a scaling back of defence and intelligence spending. According to the *New York Times* in an editorial on 9 March 1990, there was 'a fabulous fortune to be amassed' by such budget cuts. Within a decade, it predicted, up to $150 billion a year could be saved. Others argued that intelligence services should be cut back too.

Bills were introduced in the US Congress to emasculate and even abolish the CIA. Congressman Dave McCurdy told the House of Representatives in 1992, 'With the demise of the Soviet Union, that threat has been substantially reduced . . . the governmental organizations which have been primarily focused on the Soviet Union must . . . be re-evaluated. This process has begun for the Armed Forces, and it must be undertaken for our intelligence agencies as well.'[11]

William Pfaff, an influential opinion writer, said what others were thinking. In an article entitled 'We Need Intelligence, Not Spies', he asked, 'What are spies for? They recruit one another to betray their respective services, but what positive things do they accomplish?' Pointing to numerous CIA operations that had damaged the US government's reputation, he went on, 'the CIA, as it has existed for the last 47 years, is at the end of its useful life'.[12]

While the idea that the ancient craft of spying could be allowed to wither away completely was but a brief delusion, the secret services still required years of lobbying to maintain their status – and their budgets. And even though they managed to survive, it was often at the expense of the human intelligence side of their work.

One reason to doubt the need for secret activities such as spying was a new sense of transparency and openness. Even if nuclear-armed Russia remained a threat, the end of the Iron Curtain meant so much less information was hidden. Closed lands were opened. People had more freedom to speak. It was much harder to explain why you needed spies to collect information. In the now ex-communist countries, secrets were spilling out. Even the former KGB, whose communist masters had been deposed, opened its archives for a short while to the press and public (often for cash). Former agents were being unmasked.

Spy agencies in the West also had their perestroika and 'came out' – but not because of any change of heart. The spies showed their faces because they were looking for new roles. They needed public support to protect their budgets and, above all, they needed something or someone to replace the old 'Main Enemy', as the Soviet Union was known in the CIA. Spymasters argued that they should use their skills to fight major gangsters (or 'organized crime'), the drugs trade and even illegal immigration.

In a democracy, secret services should take orders from elected politicians, not lobby for new or different orders. But internal documents from Britain's domestic security service (MI5) give a glimpse of how such agencies manoeuvred in secret in the 1990s to preserve their role. In one example, MI5 directors worried that if a ceasefire by the IRA in Northern Ireland held and counterterror work by the Service, as they called themselves, declined they would be faced with the following choices:

1. Do nothing and accept significant reduction in size of the Service; or
2. Move towards acquisition of new work. E.g. in Organized Crime, by one of two routes:
   – Big Bang (immediate and overt bid for an expanded role)
   – Incremental, undisclosed approach.[13]

MI5 chose the last option: secret campaigning. Most of its staff were not even told, let alone Parliament or the public. Speaking notes by Stephen Lander, then the director general, concluded, 'Service's strategy will become visible in part through pushing at the edges – but *it will fail if complete intentions are revealed* prematurely – therefore essential that SMG [Senior Management Group] does not disclose this agenda to any other staff at this stage' (my emphasis).[14]

Although the arguments made by the secret services were self-serving, they did have some merit. With the Berlin Wall gone, the world had become more chaotic. While the chance of a Red Army invasion was now zero and the possibility of a nuclear holocaust was at least reduced, the likelihood of smaller-scale atrocities or conflicts had increased. For all its high stakes, the Cold War had temporarily suspended many serious national and regional conflicts. Among other things, global superpower confrontation in the Third World had in effect suspended the process of decolonization. Subsidies from superpowers had sustained dictators in nations whose borders bisected tribal divisions and where elite, unrepresentative social classes frequently held sway. Without the subsidies, the struggle for power in those countries could resume. The world, the intelligence agencies argued, had thus suddenly become more dangerous.

Writing in 1996, a former military intelligence officer, Michael Smith, summed up the spy community's view:

The demise of the Warsaw Pact, which many saw as signalling the end for the spy, and indeed the spy writer, has only increased the need for intelligence as fragile new democracies threaten to plunge back into totalitarianism, weapons-grade nuclear materials are traded on the black market,

8

and Third World countries that were previously kept in check by their superpower mentors turn into dangerous mavericks.[15]

These arguments, together with a combination of bloody events and liberal thinking, would end up preserving the secret services. Events started even before the Soviet Union had been dissolved, with the invasion of oil-rich Kuwait in 1990 by a former Western ally, Iraq. There followed the tragic bloodletting in Somalia in 1991, the massacres of the Bosnian War – beginning in 1992 – and ethnic genocide in tiny Rwanda in the summer of 1994.

The advent of this 'new instability' gave Western political leaders a reason to love their secret services once more. The same liberals who had viewed the military and secret services as tools for repression, Cold War sabre-rattling and neo-imperialism now asked them to help stop human rights abuses and massacres.

This new interventionist viewpoint was championed by US president Bill Clinton, who took office in 1993, and later by British prime minister Tony Blair, when he came to power four years later. Clinton was a slow convert. He had run for office on a 'peace dividend' manifesto, promising to focus as president not on foreign events but on domestic growth. 'It's the economy, stupid' became his campaign slogan. When in office, however, he responded to a growing popular sense that, without the danger of a Soviet reaction, the US had a freer hand and even a responsibility to intervene, particularly after tragic events like the genocide in Rwanda. For Blair, this duty to respond to foreign evils became an article of faith. 'We cannot turn our backs on conflicts and the violation of human rights within other countries,' he said in a pivotal 1999 speech in Chicago, 'if we want still to be secure.'[16] This pre-emptive 'Blair doctrine' needed to be built around good intelligence. Intervening early, without waiting to be attacked, required precise and accurate forewarning.

So, with all the new threats and pressure for global intervention, the secret services had secured for themselves a breathing space. But while politicians had come to realize that they still wanted and needed intelligence, they were in disarray about how to collect it, and were wary of using real spies.

In the 1990s, the introduction of electronic mail and mobile telephones for consumers offered two new forms of communication that were enticingly easy to steal and bug. Such technical methods of spying were particularly attractive in this new period of post-Cold War friendly international relations. From bitter prior experience, politicians knew that recruiting secret agents even among declared enemies always risked causing a scandal, but it was much worse in peacetime. The discovery of a spy or an attempt to recruit one was never seen as a friendly act. It could jeopardize the peace. Interception of communications, by contrast, was seen as risk-free: as long as no one found out, you could spy as easily on your friends as on your enemies. That is why signals intelligence, as such interception was called, always carried the highest kind of security classification, way above Top Secret.

Time and again, US politicians who controlled the purse strings debated the right mix between human and technical means of collecting secrets, particularly after the latest, greatest 'intelligence error'. It was never really an either-or question; it was always about calibrating the balance between the two approaches. But in a cautious era, advocates of human intelligence methods often seemed to lose the argument. In 1994, Brent Scowcroft, a former US national security adviser, argued the contrary position. He suggested that post-Cold War, 'we need a new kind of intelligence, a different kind of intelligence that is less directed at technical collection, where we are good', and he suggested a move 'back to human intelligence, where we don't do as well'.[17] But those who disagreed ultimately carried more weight because technical methods offered swifter results with less risk. Budgets for spying were cut back and – perhaps more decisively – risky or potentially embarrassing operations were not authorized.

Then came the attacks of 11 September 2001. There had been plenty of warnings about terrorist plots to strike within the United States, but this was on a bigger scale than most imagined possible. Amid the recriminations that followed, there was much debate about whether the secret services had lost their way. There were promises of reversing spending cutbacks and reviving spycraft. But there were also some sharper questions.

Was it really so hard to get inside al-Qaeda? *The Economist* magazine asked provocatively in 2002:

Al-Qaeda, America's spymasters tried to claim, was peculiarly difficult to infiltrate, since it was open only to kinsmen of members. That notion was blown apart by the appearance of John Walker Lindh, a Californian airhead, in Osama bin Laden's trenches. As one former CIA boss puts it, 'Al-Qaeda was an evangelical organization: it wanted members. We never suggested any.'[18]

As one old-time CIA spymaster argued shortly after 9/11, the problem in the spy world was always one of focus. Recruiting spies required a sustained and directed effort of many years and, before 9/11, that effort could not be mustered. 'If only,' he told me, 'we'd had a man on the rock beside Osama bin Laden, learning of his thoughts, learning his plans.' The spy you really needed was someone in the inner circle who was close enough to gather real secrets. That did not mean he had to be a senior figure, but the spy had to be trusted, to be physically close to bin Laden. Without such a spy, the CIA had gathered widespread rumours of an imminent attack on American soil, but there had never been the kind of useful specifics that could have stopped the 9/11 attacks. 'We never had anyone close enough,' he said.

This was the conversation that inspired me to write this book and try to answer the three questions I had posed. Given the difficulties involved, could such a 'man on the rock' be the epitome of the twenty-first century spy? Would such a spy be as effective and useful as, say, the information from intercepts and surveillance? And was this the type of spy we really needed to protect us against the biggest threats to our security? With a new 'war on terror' just launched, I set out in subsequent years to follow attempts to recruit such a man.

The spymaster had explained that on the seventh floor, the executive level of the old building at the CIA headquarters at Langley, they had held regular 'hard target' meetings to discuss the main threats to the US. By the late 1990s, al-Qaeda was on the list. The problem was that, until it was too late, al-Qaeda was never top of the list. This meant that, unless a volunteer spy – a 'walk-in' – came knocking, the CIA had almost no chance of getting an agent into the upper echelons of the organization. There was no serious targeting.

After the attacks, however, it was all supposed to be different. The intelligence game was back on, with a strict focus on finding and countering the terrorists. The third part of the book and the conclusion take us through from 2001 until near the present day, a period in which the direction of intelligence activity became, once again, clear. Al-Qaeda – and Osama bin Laden himself – became the Western powers' new 'Main

Enemy', replacing what had been the Soviet Union in the Cold War. It was a call to arms. In the weeks after 9/11, the CIA received 150,000 CVs from eager would-be recruits.[19] Those few who were selected for duty were thrown into battle against Al-Qaeda. By 2011, it was estimated that 70 per cent of Western intelligence resources were being devoted to combating terrorism.[20]

Recruited into the CIA's first case officer class after 9/11, T. J. Waters recalled what his instructors told him: 'If you learned nothing else on September 11, at least know this: Satellites, telephone intercepts, and hidden microphones are all well and good, but they're no substitute for knowing what someone is thinking, what they are planning in their heads. All the billions we've spent on advanced technology and nobody knew about September 11.'[21] But for all the talk, traditional human spy work did not become the focus of attack against al-Qaeda. Instead, the secret services were frequently sidetracked from HUMINT by rival methods.

Officers who work for secret services may be involved not only in spying or recruiting spies but also in trying to exert influence by covert action – the instigation of an event by a sponsor who remains concealed and can therefore deny responsibility. (In spy-speak, 'clandestine action' is slightly different: the action itself is a secret.) Covert action includes paramilitary work, such as organizing coups d'état or supporting guerrilla movements like the mujahideen in Afghanistan. It may mean disruptive measures, such as emptying an adversary's bank accounts. It may also come in the form of support work for other agencies, such as helping the police to conduct surveillance or planting bugs for the US signals intelligence agency, the NSA.

In the first years after 11 September, the focus of secret services was the struggle against terrorism, and within counterterrorism the main weapon was covert action, not recruiting spies. This covert action consisted in the first instance of liaison work with the intelligence services of other countries (places like Egypt, Jordan, Yemen and Pakistan, where al-Qaeda was present) and secondly of the handling of prisoners. In the war on terror, the CIA worked with the US military and foreign agencies to round up hundreds of Islamic militants and members of al-Qaeda's leadership. As described in my book on rendition, *Ghost Plane*, the CIA's business became the capture, transport and interrogation of terrorism suspects.[22] All this activity was, in effect, not spying but global secret police work. Espionage had a far lower priority than this programme of transferring people from country to country and holding them in secret jails.

What the CIA defined as HUMINT now included the product of prisoner interrogations; soon the majority of HUMINT was to be from such 'debriefings', as George Tenet, the CIA director, announced. Defending torture techniques like the near-drowning experience of waterboarding, he said, 'I know this program alone is worth more than the FBI, the Central Intelligence Agency, and the National Security Agency put together have been able to tell us.'[23] Former vice-president Dick Cheney further claimed that the interrogation of just one suspect, the alleged 9/11 architect Khalid Sheikh Mohamed, surpassed all: 'There was a period of time there, three or four years ago, when about half of everything we knew about al-Qaeda came from that one source. So, it's been a remarkably successful effort. I think the results speak for themselves.'[24]

Yet, as some veterans warned, these paramilitary and police methods all came at the expense of traditional spy work. This meant that opportunities for recruitment were missed. Tyler Drumheller, European division chief of the CIA in the period after 9/11, complained that the emphasis on prisoners had sapped resources, attention and brainpower away from the hard business of recruiting and running spies. 'We are an intelligence service, an espionage service,' he said. 'Not jailers, not policemen, not interrogators. We debrief people; we don't interrogate them.'[25]

According to other veteran spymasters, it was not only that the money, as well as the best and brightest talent, was shifted into counterterrorist direct action; it was that politicians lost their enthusiasm for the long game of the careful nurturing of sources. In their desperation to prevent the next bloody terrorist attack (and to avoid being held responsible for failing to take all possible measures to do so), these leaders had little of the patience or willingness to accept the risks that spy running required.

The lengthy wars fought by the US military and its allies, including Britain, in Afghanistan from 2001 and Iraq from 2003 were another diversion. As thousands of troops became embroiled in bloody civil wars, the CIA established enormous, heavily protected bases in both countries. Britain's SIS was deployed too in smaller numbers. The agencies were under great pressure to provide any kind of intelligence or take any action that could save lives. 'Everything that the military didn't want to do or felt uncomfortable doing ended up in the lap of the CIA,' said Drumheller.

With its troops in combat, the military wanted quick results; again, there was little patience. The rapid response to demands for more HUMINT was to interrogate more prisoners, or collect a report from a local partner. Liaison and prisoners were again the default. It was not a good environment for recruiting your own spies.

Later in the 2000s, at the close of the Bush presidency and continuing after the election of Barack Obama in 2008, the American covert action programme established a third pillar. Moving beyond liaison with other secret services and the handling of prisoners, the most important tactic became an assassination programme that involved killing Islamic militants with bombs and missiles from drone aircraft. Some in the business believed it was yet another distraction. Once again, intelligence officers were being recruited not to run spies but to assist with covert action, this time to help produce targets for assassination.

So, were the old methods destined for burial? Were spies just a sideshow, at best the handmaidens of an anti-terrorist killing machine: useful but expendable gofers who could be dispatched to run around, say, the badlands of Pakistan, to plant bugs or tracking devices, as some did, to give the drones better targets?

Not only were secret services distracted but, against new enemies, HUMINT was having an existential crisis. In the intelligence community, given the relative effectiveness of other methods, the value of spies against the modern state's most potent enemies was still in question. The West might continue to find traditional spy techniques effective against traditional enemies such as the Chinese Communist Party or Russia's Kremlin, it was argued, but would find them fruitless for penetrating what politicians considered the main threat, namely the modern Islamic terrorist group.

Sir Richard Dearlove, who served as chief of SIS from 1999 to 2004, made just such a case. Infiltrating the IRA had been hard enough, he argued in a public lecture in London in 2008, but terrorist groups like al-Qaeda were different. He challenged the optimistic view that it was possible to run a spy on the inside, to have a 'man on the rock'. Al-Qaeda had now become disparate, 'like a flock of birds', according to Dearlove. And even if you got an agent inside, the information they discovered might be valuable for only a few days, or even hours. With clear guidance already given publicly by al-Qaeda leaders about permitted targets and methods, there was often little need to share details of a planned attack within a network in advance. Al-Qaeda-style terrorists were not the only threat, and more traditional efforts at recruiting secret agents could be continued against these other threats, he maintained; but beating the terrorists required mass surveillance.

Sir David Omand, a former head of GCHQ, Britain's signals intelligence agency, and intelligence coordinator at No. 10 Downing Street, took a similar view. What mattered for dealing with current threats, he said, was less the kinds of secrets governments keep and more 'access to the data flows'. He meant access to people's communications, to confidential information held by banks and to movements through examining airline databases. This type of intelligence, he argued, was more valuable now to counter an organization such as al-Qaeda, as it allowed terrorists to be tracked and their networks uncovered.[26]

So had the quest for a 'man on the rock' been superseded? The attack in Khost – being duped by al-Balawi in the one operation to get so close to senior al-Qaeda leaders – seemed to suggest not. HUMINT had been squeezed, not squashed. When it had the chance, the CIA was as enthusiastic as ever to plant a spy inside. But, as Khost indicated, such opportunities were rare. And the operation's outcome demonstrated why no one was counting on the spies: HUMINT was no longer centre stage. The operation had been the CIA's best shot in the spying game and the White House had been watching. It failed in spectacular fashion.

The CIA went back to its high-tech methods and continued the fight. The main weapons were the killer drones, unmanned aircraft controlled from the US that fired missiles into Pakistan's north-western frontier. The CIA became more accurate in its aim. The drones were hitting fewer civilians and the CIA's surveillance network was showing its resilience. Two and a half years after the failed Khost mission, US intelligence got its most important target. The CIA directed Special Forces into Pakistan to kill Osama bin Laden. In the streets of Washington, DC, a triumphant crowd shouted 'CIA! CIA!' It was not something agency veterans ever expected to hear. The US and the CIA had prevailed.

As an official account of the killing emerged, there were no early indications that bin Laden had been betrayed by a spy. Instead, the manhunt illustrated very well the techniques of global covert policing. This was 'new intelligence' at work: reams of intelligence analysis and spidery network diagrams, prisoner 'debriefs' and endless all-seeing surveillance.

It was from this new high-tech world that, in June 2013, a whistle-blower emerged – a contractor from the NSA with administrator-level access to its computer systems, Edward Snowden. The thousands of highly classified documents he made available to journalists showed the power of the surveillance toolkit available to Britain and the United States. GCHQ, he revealed, wanted 'to exploit any phone, anywhere, anytime'.[27]

No wonder the value and efforts of human spies sometimes appeared meagre. Yet the secret agent was not dead – far from it. For all his faults, attempts to write off the agent were misguided and misinformed. As will become clear, the nature of spies, and the value of human intelligence, had been misunderstood from the beginning.

First rule of intelligence: forget everything you know.

PART ONE

The Cult of Intelligence (1909–89)

Chapter 1
The Secret Agent

'Spies in the British service commonly take up their dangerous duty
out of sheer love of adventure'

– Captain George Hill, British secret service officer in Moscow[1]

Captain Francis Cromie – thirty-six years old, tall and strongly built, a commander in the Royal Navy and bearer of the Distinguished Service Order – reached into the consul's drawer and pulled out a revolver.[2] It was 31 August 1918, a day when Russia was at a crossroads in its history. It was also Cromie's last day alive. He was in the British Embassy in wartime Petrograd (St Petersburg) and it seemed that the 'Red revolution' of workers and peasants' communism was in jeopardy.

A day earlier, Moisei Uritsky, the local chief of the new secret police, the Cheka, had been murdered in cold blood. Now word came through that, 400 miles away, the leader of the Reds, Vladimir Ilyich Lenin, had been shot too. He was in bed in the Kremlin with two bullets inside him, one in his chest and one in his neck, and surgeons were unclear if he would survive.

Further north, British and other allied troops had landed on 4 August in the town of Archangel to join the White Army – the combined anti-revolutionary forces. Though this allied force consisted of only 5,000 men, more were expected, and the Bolsheviks feared that they would be marching south. There was word too that inside the city foreigners were conspiring with ultra-left revolutionaries and former tsarists to mount a counter-coup against the new revolutionary government.

These rumours were true and one of the plotters was Captain Cromie, a man of action and an intelligence officer. With other British secret servants then in Russia, he was tangled up in the West's first trial of strength with the new communist power. The events of those epic days, and the errors made, would define modern espionage.

Just after 4 p.m., witnesses at the embassy heard shouts and the slamming of car doors in the yard outside. The Cheka had arrived. Cromie was busy holding a council of war in the chancellery with fellow diplomats and several spies and hangers-on. But he had been betrayed. Two of his trusted contacts in the room, Lieutenant Sabir and Colonel Steckelmann, who claimed to be part of the tsarist White Russian forces, were in fact Cheka agents.

In another part of Petrograd, a British intelligence officer – the man the public would later know as 'the ace of spies', Sidney Reilly – was waiting to meet Cromie. He was hoping that a coup against the Reds he had fomented was about to be launched.

According to an eyewitness, as recorded in the British National Archives, a member of the Red Guards – the armed volunteers of the Bolshevik revolution – approached the chancellery door with a revolver. Cromie turned to his companions and said, 'Remain here and keep the door after me.' He then opened the door, levelled his gun and shouted, 'Clear out, you swine', before heading down the passageway, pushing the Red Guard before him. No one saw what happened next, but during an exchange of fire in the corridor two of the raiders were shot.[3]

Cromie sprinted down the corridor and out on to the chandeliered grand staircase. As he leapt down its carpeted steps, the Cheka agents, already upstairs, chased after him, firing down from the balcony. Two bullets penetrated the back of his skull and he fell in a heap at the bottom of the stairs. He groaned softly, his blood draining into the carpet.[4]

Captain Cromie had become involved with fellow British spies in a bid to overthrow the Bolsheviks, but they had been outwitted and compromised. He was perhaps the first man to die because of a blunder by officers of His Majesty's Secret Service.

These were the early days of what became British intelligence. In 1909, the Secret Service bureau (referred to simply as SS) had been founded as the world's first intelligence agency in response to a media-led campaign of panic about imperial Germany's supposed espionage activities. (The CIA did not follow for another thirty-eight years.) The bureau's foreign section was founded two years later, with an annual budget of a mere £7,000 (the equivalent of just under £300,000 in 2014 prices).[5] During the

First World War it was absorbed into the War Office and known as department MI1c, but for most of its existence it has been officially called the Secret Intelligence Service (SIS), and is known to insiders simply as the Service. By the late 1930s it would become popularly known by one of its cover names, MI6.

From its inception until 1923, SIS was led by an eccentric, Captain Mansfield Smith-Cumming, who went by Cumming or 'C'. He insisted on signing his letters with a big capital 'C' in green ink – the initial and green ink still being used today by the current chief – and his men were a collection of mostly upper-class, ruthless mavericks.

It was the era of amateurs and audacity. After a preliminary interview in the Whitehall attic that Cumming had made his lair, his new recruits were dispatched abroad with little or no training and with few instructions.

Cumming's agency was a break with tradition. For centuries Britain's greatest spies had not been part of a separate bureaucracy. Certainly, intelligence networks were not unknown – whether Sir Francis Walsingham's informers in Tudor England, or Prime Minister William Pitt the Younger's all-source intelligence organization, established in the 1790s to combat French-inspired revolutionaries in Europe, or more recently British India's security apparatus.[6] But politicians believed that the British public had come to abhor such things, except as an expedient in an emergency. 'Nothing is more revolting to Englishmen than the espionage which forms part of the administrative system of continental despotisms,' wrote Erskine May in the second volume of his 1863 *Constitutional History of England.*[7] The spies who were respected had been the nation's explorers and adventurers who learned foreign tongues, mixed in with the 'natives' and revelled in all the danger (and, more often than not, in the loot). Even as Cumming plotted a new order, there were men like T. E. Lawrence (Lawrence of Arabia) in Jordan and the future Saudi Arabia, as well as the intrepid Gertrude Bell in Iraq, who continued that tradition. Before them there were spy-diplomats like Captain Arthur Conolly of the East India Company (beheaded in Bukhara, in modern-day Uzbekistan, for spying in 1842) and Captain Sir Alexander Burnes (murdered in Kabul in 1841). Both had trekked over the mountain passes of the Hindu Kush, playing their part in the so-called 'Great Game' made famous by the writer Rudyard Kipling. Mostly volunteers, they were hardly 'secret agents'. While many operated under a flimsy disguise – as surveyors, for instance – their activities were neither secret nor discreet. As a more recent 'incremental' (to use one term for such a person) put it to me, 'I was recruited before I was even born.' But they were still spies. In the Great Game, they were gathering information about the extent of Russian encroachment and trying to elicit details of the secret intrigues between Russian envoys and local tribes.

Spying from the start of the twentieth century was more closely defined. Article 29 of the 1907 Hague Convention was clear that spying involved skulduggery:

> A person can only be considered a spy when, acting clandestinely or on false pretences, he obtains or endeavours to obtain information in the zone of operations of a belligerent, with the intention of communicating it to the hostile party. Thus, soldiers not wearing a disguise who have penetrated into the zone of operations of the hostile army, for the purpose of obtaining information, are not considered spies.

In this new era, the mostly aristocratic, mainly amateur and adventurous tradition of spying did linger on in Cumming's new agency. But the bureau's early experiences showed the need to reinvent methods.

In the First World War, the secret service had not proved itself a great success. While the navy had cracked the German cipher codes, Cumming had been unable to recruit any agents inside Germany, with the notable exception of a Dutch-based itinerant naval engineer, Dr Karl Krüger. The service's main success, instead, had been in the Netherlands and Belgium, with a network of train-spotter agents who tracked the movements of troops and supplies and helped describe the German order of battle. A post-war history of intelligence on the western front records 'the bulk of the work of the Secret Service in occupied territory was devoted to train watching'.[8] After the war, Britain made the mistake of authorizing the issue of medals or other honours to over 700 Belgian agents, putting them all in danger when the Germans invaded again in 1940.[9]

It was in revolutionary Russia, after the fall of the Tsar in 1917, that British intelligence not only found an enemy that would obsess it for decades but also took on a new shape. Stories of the derring-do of the men involved – people like Cromie and, in particular, three of his comrades in secret intelligence who then operated in Russia, Sidney Reilly, Paul Dukes and George Hill – have been told before in many colourful ways. But what the storytelling typically omits is just what failures their operations were, and how these failures demonstrated why espionage needed to adapt. Against an emerging modern state like the early Soviet Union, these missions established what worked and, more critically, what did not.

Despite their failures, Cromie and his generation also helped to establish the myth of espionage. Their amateur-style, action-man heroics created a potent, enduring and largely false idea of the intelligence officer as a 'master spy'. It was a myth that endured – and still does – partly because it was useful. It has been exploited ever since to recruit spies and expand budgets.

Lenin's tightly knit Bolshevik party, the communist faction that had taken over in the October Revolution of 1917, was a worthy foe, along with their intelligence outfit, the Cheka.[10] After years of organizing secretly against the repressive regime of the tsars, the Bolsheviks were masters of conspiracy. Not only did they watch all foreigners and undertake intense surveillance of suspected spies, they also introduced double agents and provocateurs, and made use of elaborate ruses. In this high-pressure world of spy versus spy, Western intelligence had to rethink its approach, become professional and – contrary to the myth – outsource the actual spying to others.

A spy intrigue that is blown open to public scrutiny is known by American intelligence as a 'flap'. In Britain's first ever flap, in 1918 Petrograd, the protagonists, Captain Francis Cromie and Lieutenant Sidney Reilly, were rather different characters.

Born in Ireland in 1882, the son of a British Army officer and diplomat, Cromie had a commanding but slightly aloof bearing. He joined the Royal Navy Submarine Service at the age of twenty-one and in 1915 torpedoed and sank the German cruiser *Undine*, for which he was awarded the Distinguished Service Order the following year. He was dispatched to Russia in 1915, leaving behind a young wife and child. His task was to command a flotilla of British submarines that patrolled and fought in the Baltic, and he was decorated a number of times by Tsar Nicholas II. After the Revolution, when the imperial Russian navy withdrew from the war and disbanded, Cromie's initial role ended, but in January 1918 he was reassigned to the embassy in Petrograd as naval attaché. He may have engineered this, as one admiral later put it, because of a 'romantic interest': a young aristocrat, Sophie Gagarin, became his lover.

Cromie's new role was primarily in intelligence. His boss was Admiral Sir William 'Blinker' Hall, the Royal Navy's legendary chief of intelligence (then by far the most powerful of the Empire's mushrooming secret services). Among Hall's functions was the running of the navy's message decryption service, which was named Room 40 after its original base at the Admiralty. When Cromie began his job in January he still had naval assets to protect, but as the German army drew closer, he arranged the scuttling of the Royal Navy's six submarines and blew up supplies. And by the start of the summer that year he engaged himself – with others in British intelligence – in a far more grandiose scheme: to subvert Bolshevik power.

In August 1918, two men, Jan Buikis and Jan Sprogis, walked into the embassy in Petrograd. This was just after British troops had landed to the north in Archangel. The visitors claimed to be officers from an elite Lettish regiment that formed the praetorian guard of the Soviet leadership (Latvians were then called 'Letts'). Buikis and Sprogis told Cromie that their comrades did not want to fight the British; instead they wanted help to change sides and cross to the British lines.

Cromie sent the men on to Moscow and it was there that the Lettish defectors met Bruce Lockhart, Britain's first official envoy to the Bolshevik government, and were introduced to the man who worked as agent ST1 of the British secret service: Sidney Reilly. The Letts knew him as 'Mr Constantine'. With Reilly, the Letts went from talking of defection to plotting an armed counter-coup. Meanwhile, in Petrograd, Cromie was equally involved in conspiracies. Many of his objectives were purely military: with the Germans now only 100 miles away, he hatched a plan with tsarists to find a way to blow up Russia's Baltic fleet, by then under the control of the Bolsheviks and based in nearby Kronstadt, to avoid its being captured by the Germans and to destroy bridges ahead of German advancing columns.[11] But, along with Reilly, he also had hopes of something more. As he telegraphed to London in June 1918, 'Intervention on a thorough scale is the only thing that will save the situation and Russia.'[12] A fellow diplomat in Russia noted, 'Cromie wished to unite the large number of Russian organisations to work together under British instruction.'[13]

At this time Britain was still embroiled in the Great War, with thousands dying daily on the western front. In August 1918, the British suffered 80,000 casualties, and on one day alone – 8 August – 6,500 Allied soldiers were killed.[14] The Bolsheviks, meanwhile, had made peace with Germany, signing the Treaty of Brest-Litovsk on 3 March 1918. This gave the Western Allies an interest in confronting the Bolsheviks and supporting the pro-tsarist White Russian forces, who rejected the peace deal.

As Britain moved closer to outright war with the Bolsheviks, Cromie knew that he was under close scrutiny. The Cheka followed him around and, after his flat was turned over, he moved to a 'safe house'. He had to abandon this – escaping over the rooftops in his pyjamas – after another Cheka raid one night.[15] He then moved into the embassy compound, along with Sophie Gagarin.

Cromie still believed that there was a chance of influencing the course of history. He kept in close touch with the two men he knew as 'Tsarist officers', Steckelmann and Sabir, who had promised to help him. Both claimed to be Russian White Guards based in nearby Finland. On the morning of Cromie's death, Steckelmann had sent a message to the embassy before he came in person, saying that the 'time for action is ripe and cannot be delayed'.[16] In fact, as the British were to discover later, he and Sabir were secret agents of the Cheka.

The Cheka had come to believe, correctly, that Cromie was plotting against them and this may be why he was killed. As the *Times* correspondent George Dobson, who was present in the embassy, reported soon afterwards, Cromie 'was evidently regarded by the raiders as the arch-conspirator amongst all the plotters . . . He often said that he would never be taken alive by the Bolsheviks, and [the] pointing of their revolvers at him was a provocation which he naturally resented.'[17]

That day, unaware that Lenin had been shot and of the growing jeopardy of his own situation, Sidney Reilly had made his way to Petrograd. While all the drama at the embassy was taking place, Reilly was waiting for Cromie in the flat of the MI1c station chief, Commander Ernest Boyce. After hearing of the shoot-out, Reilly slipped quietly away to Moscow on a sleeper train.

While the story of Cromie and his death in Petrograd was quickly forgotten, Sidney Reilly's activities came to be regarded as probably Britain's most famous tale of espionage. It was first publicized in 1931 in a posthumous – and largely fictional – 'autobiography' written with his wife and was then published as a book and a limited edition of the *London Evening Standard*.[18] Further accounts of his life were published, including some by former intelligence officers. Together they created a popular icon for SIS that persisted. Strange, then, that he really had little in common with what the agency became.

Reilly did epitomize some of the qualities of a master of espionage. An arch-con man, he was a gifted linguist able to blend in almost everywhere, with the beguiling ability to move intransigent minds, make friends and steal secrets. He was also, along with his friend and successor in Russia, Sir Paul Dukes, one of the last intelligence officers sent into Russia in order to spy themselves. In SIS, lone operators like him were a short-lived phenomenon, and perhaps the fact that his story was an aberration explains why he and the so-called Lockhart Plot merited only a handful of lines in the agency's official history.[19]

Reilly was born in 1873 into a Jewish family near Odessa, Ukraine, as Shlomo Rosenblum. After moving to London in the 1890s, he married an Irish woman and took her maiden name. From then on, as he turned into a businessman and professional con man, he claimed to be Irish. Travelling frequently to Russia over subsequent years, Reilly mainly seems to have acted as a freelance agent, stealing or gathering information that he could sell to another party. He gave the British information about oil prospects in the Caucasus and stole Russian defence plans that he sold to the Japanese during the Russo-Japanese War. He was also involved in selling war materiel – from buying large amounts of gunpowder in Japan to organizing the purchase of munitions in New York for the Russians. His last pre-revolutionary appearance in Russia was in the summer of 1915.[20]

Shortly after the October Revolution in 1917, Reilly asked to join the British military. He had been in New York, working on war contracts, and after enlisting in Toronto in the Royal Flying Corps, he arrived in London on 1 January 1918.

According to his most recent and thorough biographer, Andrew Cook, Reilly was probably pursuing a path to get him back to Russia for private motives: 'He hoped to recover a fortune that he had left behind in St Petersburg.' Reilly had left paintings and valuables in the country and he was looking for a chance to repatriate them.[21]

SIS's original files on Reilly demonstrate that even before he was hired and dispatched to Russia on 18 March 1918, Cumming had no illusions about Reilly's character. Background checks by MI5 had reported he was a confidence trickster, and a telegram from the SIS station in New York said, 'We consider him untrustworthy and unsuitable to work suggested.' An SIS officer called Norman Thwaites also quoted a banker who described Reilly as a 'shrewd businessman of undoubted ability but without patriotism or principles and therefore not to be recommended for any position which requires loyalty'.[22]

But 'C', whom Reilly visited on 14 March, thought he was the man for the job and recorded in his diary: 'Scale introduced Mr Reilly who is willing to go to Russia for us. Very clever – very doubtful – has been everywhere and done everything. Will take out £500 in notes and £750 in diamonds which are at a premium. I must agree tho' it is a great gamble as he will visit all our men in Vologda, Kiev, Moscow etc.'[23]

Only after Reilly set sail did MI5 discover and inform SIS that, in contradiction to what their new officer claimed, there were no records of his birth in Clonmel, Ireland.[24]

No one ever called Reilly handsome. A telegram from 'C' to operatives in Russia described him as a 'Jewish-Jap type, brown eyes very protruding, deeply lined sallow face, may be bearded, height five foot nine inches'.[25] But he proved attractive to women and did little without the aid of scattered mistresses. In Moscow, he had two: Elizaveta Emilyevna Otten, an actress, and Olga Starzheskaya. According to their later testimonies, they never knew he was anything but a Russian.

Though ably promoted by his friends, Reilly was hardly the 'master spy'. He was, it is true, gifted at living undercover and adopting different guises. As a polyglot and native Russian speaker, he came to be known in Petrograd as Konstantin Markovich Massino, a Turkish merchant. In Moscow, he was Mr Constantine, a Greek businessman. Elsewhere he boldly called himself Sigmund Rellinsky, a member of the Cheka's crime investigation department. But while Reilly had mastered disguise, he lacked the detachment of a reliable observer – someone who could quietly merge with the shadows. His instinct was always to act, to provoke, to interfere, and in this he was impetuous. He lacked sound judgement.

Though he was not born an Englishman, Reilly had the gifts and the flaws of the stereotypical upper-class Brit. He was brave, far too persuasive for his own good, successful with the opposite sex, but also dim to the point of incompetence.

Landing first in Murmansk in April 1918, Reilly went to Petrograd for a month. He did not waste time in forming a judgement. He telegraphed 'C': 'We have arrived at critical moment when we must either act immediately and effectively or abandon entire position for good and all.'[26]

On 7 May, Reilly reached Moscow. At first he was brazen with the Bolsheviks. He marched into the Kremlin and demanded to see their leader, Vladimir Lenin. He got as far as an aide, General Vladimir Bonch-Bruevich, who immediately complained about him to Lockhart, then the official British liaison to the Soviets.[27]

After that, Reilly went undercover and began scheming with those plotting to block Bolshevik power. Among the leaders of opposition to Lenin was a General Boris Savinkov, a former minister in the first revolutionary government, which had been led by Alexander Kerensky. That regime had replaced the Tsar but been overthrown in turn by the Bolsheviks, with their slogan 'All Power to the Soviets' – committees of workers and peasants. Both Lockhart and Reilly met Savinkov's underground group, and the French gave Savinkov money. According to a later official Soviet account, Savinkov, who returned to Moscow in 1924 and surrendered, admitted that he had supplied a weapon to Dora Kaplan, the woman who shot Lenin. Judging by their other inventions, that claim was probably a lie, but even Britain's minor support to Savinkov demonstrated to the Cheka that the Western powers were their mortal enemies.

History, it is said, is told by the victorious. In the case of the Soviets, it was particularly distorted. But while Britain's role as a conspirator was deliberately exaggerated, there was no question that the British secret service was plotting to destroy the Bolsheviks.

After seeing Cromie in Petrograd, around 15–16 August the two Lettish officers, Buikis and Sprogis, went to see Lockhart. He, according to a Soviet account, told Buikis, 'Your first and most important task is to arrest and kill Lenin. Yes, yes, kill him because if he escapes that will be the end of the cause.' Lockhart denied fomenting any such violence. His official reports suggested that he approved of Reilly's plan to get the Lettish regiments to change sides, but 'when he referred again to the necessity of a movement in Moscow [i.e. an attempted coup] we all demurred and pointed out there was nothing to gain by this'.[28]

Lockhart did give the Letts a laissez-passer to cross the British lines. But, he said, it wasn't until Reilly started getting involved that a conspiracy developed. He claimed at one point to have warned Reilly to have nothing to do with 'so dangerous and doubtful [a] move' as a coup attempt.[29]

But, whether with official backing or not, Reilly, as an employee of SIS, took matters into his own hands. He began to develop a much more elaborate plot, hoping to use the Lettish regiments to take on Soviet power in both Petrograd and Moscow. Reilly later told Soviet interrogators, 'From passive intelligence work, I, like other members of the British mission, gradually switched to a more-or-less active fight against Soviet power.'[30] Lockhart recorded in his official report:

> After my release I discovered from Captain George Hill, R.F.C., who was Reilly's assistant in Moscow, that the Bolshevik accusations were substantially true and that in spite of the advice of [the French general] Lavergne, myself and the other Allied representatives a coup d'état had been planned . . . The charges of bridge and railway destruction were also true.[31]

Reilly even started preparing a list of the new ministers he wanted in power, many of whom were old cronies of his. The Lettish officers, Buikis and Sprogis, were now joined by a Lieutenant-Colonel E. P. Berzin, the commander of the Lettish regiment guarding the Kremlin, to give their tale credibility. Reilly's deputy in Moscow, Captain George Hill, recorded that Berzin had suggested 'that men like Trotsky and Lenin should be assassinated' but Reilly had opposed the idea, not wishing to 'make martyrs of the leaders'.[32]

By 17 August, Reilly was meeting Berzin alone. He gave him 1.4 million roubles to carry out the plot. Lockhart wrote in a telegram that they had agreed to give Berzin financial support and to leave the money with Reilly, 'who is an extremely able man and in my opinion by far the cleverest of our agents in Russia'.[33] The plan was that all British diplomats should be evacuated, but the two secret service officers in Moscow, Reilly and Hill, should stay behind. They could shoulder the blame for whatever happened. 'In the event of failure and our being found in any plot, Reilly and myself should have simply been private individuals and responsible to no one . . . the whole brunt would have been borne by us.'[34] That message was reinforced in Petrograd by Commander Boyce, the secret service chief of station, who told Reilly that his Lettish coup plan was 'extremely risky but . . . worth trying, and that failure of the plan would drop entirely on the neck of Lt Reilly'.[35]

On 3 September, three days after the raid on the British Embassy, the Bolsheviks announced the shocking details of what they called the Lockhart Plot, claiming that the British had conspired to overthrow Lenin. Soviet newspapers and pamphlets described the discovery of a 'sensational plot' to overthrow their government: 'Allied complicity in counter-revolutionary plot proved,' screamed one bulletin.[36]

Much of the detail – eagerly repeated by pro-Soviet writers in the years ahead – was invented. As the Bolshevik revolution descended into terror, the plot became Exhibit A of conspiracy. In truth, the Letts never did plan to revolt. Evidence of a connection between what Reilly, Lockhart and Cromie had been plotting and the shootings of Lenin and Uritsky was tenuous. And the reason for that was that the British secret service had been entirely tricked: almost all of the British contacts proved to be provocateurs – agents of the Cheka. As Lockhart discovered when confronted in his cell by the Bolshevik chief of counter-revolution, Yakov Peters, when the Lettish officers had first come to him they had been acting on Peters's instructions.[37]

For British spying it was a disaster. They had tried to plot and, unluckily for Reilly, there had been many witnesses. He had wanted to capture Lenin and defeat the Revolution. But the men they recruited for their mission were all in the pay of 'Iron Felix' Dzerzhinsky, founder and chief of the Cheka. In a farce of the first order, a fictional plot – spun together by British agents and Cheka provocateurs – had been overtaken by a real plot, so that the shootings of both Uritsky and Lenin came as a genuine surprise.

The aftermath of the fake and real plots was terrible. The shooting of Lenin was followed directly by the events of the Red Terror, in which tens of thousands were to perish. On 1 September, the Red Army journal *Krasnaya Gazeta* declared, 'Without mercy, without sparing, we will kill our enemies in scores of hundreds. Let them be thousands, let them drown themselves in their own blood. For the blood of Lenin and Uritsky . . . let there be floods of blood for the bourgeois – more blood, as much as possible.' The same day the Bolshevik Commissars for Justice and Internal Affairs issued a decree stating, 'It is absolutely essential to safeguard the rear by means of terror.' *Isvestia*, the Bolshevik party's newspaper, printed a letter from Joseph Stalin demanding 'open, mass, systematic terror'. His orders were carried out and between 50,000 and 200,000 people were executed.[38]

Although the British secret service's bungled intrigues added to Bolshevik paranoia and provided useful propaganda, it is hard to imagine that they really made much difference to the scale of this terrible revenge. Certainly, the active plotting against the Bolsheviks gave the Cheka an excuse to raid the embassy and sealed Cromie's fate. And if Reilly, Cromie and their friends had succeeded in their bolder plans and had, for instance, managed to kill some Soviet leader, then that could have led to further dire consequences. But with hostile troops on their territory, the Russians had plenty of reasons already to distrust the British. As Winston Churchill wrote later, this was a time of confrontation: 'Were they [the Allies] at war with Russia? Certainly not; but they shot Soviet Russians at sight. They stood as invaders on Russian soil.'[39] But despite their clearly opposed interests, the Bolsheviks' foreign policy was intrinsically pragmatic. The discovery that Britain's diplomats were prepared to finance the assassination of Bolsheviks – proof of malicious intent – may have helped to sway their calculations, encouraging the view that negotiation was pointless and convincing them that Britain was hostile.

London neither sanctioned nor gave advance approval for Reilly's plots. SIS files provide no indication that Cumming knew that his agents were fomenting such schemes. Reilly and the others were sent to perform espionage, not organize coups. But this was not the age of micromanagement. His Majesty's agents, just like his ambassadors, were expected to think for themselves. When Reilly returned, Cumming gave no sign that he disapproved of his actions. Instead, Reilly was given the Military Cross and dispatched, within a month, to spy on the Soviets again (this time working with White Russian forces in the Ukraine).

Reilly was not dismissed from the secret service until 1921. Within twelve months, Cumming was advising his Vienna station that the 'master spy' was now in the cold: 'You should certainly not appear to be hiding anything from him or show a want of frankness, but at the same time be careful not to tell him anything of real importance.'[40]

For the next few years, Reilly continued his scheming, mostly for profit. Then, in 1925, he was lured back to Russia by Soviet agents, only to be captured and executed by the Cheka on 5 November. He had confessed to being an intelligence operative but – Russian archives revealed later – he did not name any of his comrades.[41]

So, what impact did all these escapades have on the nature of spying?

Actual spying in Russia, it was soon clear, would become nigh on impossible for foreigners like Reilly, even if they had been born there. The adventurer-spy Reilly had epitomized was rapidly becoming an anachronism – or at least under the sort of closed regime that the communists ran. Probably the last of such agents was Reilly's friend Paul Dukes, who entered Russia and continued to work undercover until 1920. He left unscathed and received a knighthood. Of all SIS's early spies, he was the most successful. A fluent Russian speaker who, as a music student, had a genuine reason for being in Petrograd, Dukes infiltrated local Bolshevik groups, worked in munitions factories and even joined the Red Army as a soldier (where he deliberately blew up the wrong bridges). But George Hill, in his report to British intelligence on his activities in Russia, spelled out in a very down-to-earth way the difficulties of performing secret work in the growing security state. For a start, there were simple practical problems. The telephone system was suspended or was monitored, so 'it was quite impossible to give warnings or to ring up to find if the coast was clear'. Finding accommodation was equally impossible, because 'house committees' were established that checked the identity of anyone renting a room, and the new 'servants' league' offered rewards to servants who helped to 'impeach their employers as enemies of the people'. Anyone's house was subject to search 'without writ or order' and a cover story was hard to come by since so many professions were on a blacklist. Hill had bought an antiques-cum-chemist's shop as a cover, but now it was illegal to sell medicines without a licence and antiques were protected as 'national treasure'. It was also hard to keep account of payments to agents. While they needed to be superbly 'over-paid' to stop them earning more by betraying you, or turning to blackmail, none would sign a receipt.

As Hill explained, 'It should be noticed that today in Russia not a single agent will put his name to any piece of paper or receipt, so that if in future agents are to be employed by us in Russia, any hope of establishing control by the old system of voucher must be abandoned.' Just getting hold of money – with the banks in revolutionary hands – was one of the 'greatest difficulties of the Russian SS [secret service] work'.[42]

Summing up the nature of the profession in his memoirs, Hill described how British spies 'commonly take up their dangerous duty out of sheer love of adventure'. But he hinted at the shift away from that and towards an activity defined by the hiring of others – towards, at its worst, renting a pair of second-hand eyes:

British spies have slipped through the Khyber Pass disguised as Afghans, or loitered in Eastern bazaars in the dress of native traders, but it is difficult for a man, however much he has tarried amongst them, to imitate with fault-less exactitude the accent, habits, ways of thought of an alien people, and for that reason the espionage agent finds himself again and again compelled to resort to the employment of nationals. It is because of this part of his work, because of the necessity imposed on him of associating with traitors, that a certain odium has come to be attached to the name of spy.[43]

Whatever that odium, in the light of the experience of early Soviet Russia, modern spying came to depend on the employment of traitors. A government hired an intelligence officer working for an intelligence agency, and then that officer and agency hired a local person, usually an amateur, to actually do the spying and to betray their country's secrets.

The point is not that British or American officers never did any real spying themselves, but that stealing secrets was no longer their main job. Instead, others – be they stooges or fully informed recruits – were hired or cajoled to grab the secrets on behalf of the professionals.

In the spy game after Reilly and Dukes, intelligence officers typically also handled these local recruits from a safer vantage point. For most of the interwar years, SIS officers retreated into the protection of British embassies. From 1919, the agreed primary cover of the SIS officer was as a 'passport control officer' in the consular section. While this would not have protected Cromie, it was a compromise that usually gave Cumming's emissaries a degree of safety and also an excuse to be in the country (although not formal diplomatic immunity). It also kept spying at some distance from regular diplomacy. (Profits from issuing passports and visas to Britain also provided a secret additional subsidy for SIS that supplemented the 'secret service vote', which was passed annually in Parliament in an open session.[44])

British soldier-adventurers continued to be sent in wartime to spy behind enemy lines. During the Second World War, swashbuckling types such as Fitzroy Maclean parachuted into German-held Yugoslavia to link up with the partisans, and fellow irregular Neil 'Billy' McLean went into occupied Albania.

But after the Second World War, officers from almost all foreign services, including both SIS and the newly formed CIA, returned to embassy work. This time they worked undercover while fully accredited as diplomats, thus claiming immunity from prosecution for their activities under the Vienna Conventions. The drawback was this required them to exhaust themselves doing two jobs: both working for the spy service and performing their 'cover tasks' – for example, by doing consular jobs.

The intelligence world had turned such a complete circle that to even call an intelligence officer a spy at the close of the twentieth century was seen as offensive and certainly inaccurate. In the official language of espionage, they were not even secret agents.

In 1978, the chief counsel of the US House of Representatives' Select Committee on Assassinations introduced the next witness, a Mr John Clement Hart, as 'a career agent with the CIA, having served approximately twenty-four years'. He was to offer evidence on the interrogation of a KGB defector, Yuri Nosenko. After he swore the oath, Hart just had one point of clarification:

> Thank you, Mr. Chairman, gentlemen. Before I begin my statement, I would like to make a prefatory remark on a technical aspect of what was said about me . . . I was not and never have been what is called a career agent with the CIA. I bring that up only because that term happens to have a technical meaning in the Agency. I was what you would call an employee or an officer of the Agency. And I would like to have that made part of the record.[45]

In the jargon of the modern spy agency, those directly employed on the staff of the 'service' were 'operations officers', 'case officers', 'operatives', 'handlers' and 'spymasters' – many things, but not agents. At the CIA in particular, they liked this to be clear. In a 2004 talk, another former senior CIA operative, Howard Hart (no relation), made the point emphatically: 'We are *not* spies, we run spies. We recruit spies.'[46] The CIA elaborated on its website: 'A spy is someone who provides classified information about his country to another country.'[47]

The same point of view could be heard in Britain. A former leading officer of British intelligence, interviewed in a quiet corner of England, was quite particular: 'I take it rather badly to be called a spy. I would prefer you refer to me as a spymaster.' And this is what became of the secret service.

At the root of spying, such men knew, was a grubby act of betrayal. As Hill had hinted, the shift from spying directly to hiring others had made spying synonymous with treachery, and far less glorious. Spies could be liked but never fully trusted. Fundamentally, spies were not *our people*. They were and are – as 'C' called Reilly – 'very doubtful'.

While in the real world the all-action 'master spy' may have become a rare beast, he lives on in the popular imagination, as James Bond and other heroes of popular fiction demonstrate. For a fiction writer, it was certainly far more exciting to merge the now distinct roles of intelligence officer and secret agent. It was also expedient to blend the role of peacetime secret agent with wartime military intelligence work.

Ian Fleming, who wrote the Bond novels, got a taste of espionage when, in the Second World War, he worked as assistant to the director of naval intelligence. Here he had ample chance to meet the different elements of Britain's wartime secret state. In addition he got to know Colonel 'Wild Bill' Donovan of the US Office of Strategic Services (OSS), who went on to found the CIA. In 1942, Fleming became involved in setting up a unit of commandos whose special mission was to make shock raids to gather intelligence. No wonder Fleming said the Bond character he invented was 'a compound of all the secret agents and commando types I met during the war'.[48]

In the case of Bond, there is some indication that Fleming was also influenced by the Reilly legend, in particular through a friend, the same Bruce Lockhart, then head of the 'black propaganda' political warfare executive, who had been Reilly's co-conspirator in Russia. One of Fleming's former colleagues at the *Sunday Times* claimed that Fleming 'once told me he invented the character of James Bond after reading about the exploits of Sidney George Reilly in the archives of the British intelligence service'.[49] This may be fanciful but, as Andrew Cook puts it:

> Like Fleming's fictional creation, Reilly was multi-lingual with a fascination with the Far East, fond of fine living and a compulsive gambler. He also exercised a Bond-like fascination for women, his many love affairs standing comparison with the amorous adventures of 007. Unlike James Bond, though, Sidney Reilly was by no stretch of the imagination a conventionally handsome man. His appeal lay more in the elusive qualities of charm and charisma. He was, however, equally capable of being cold and menacing.[50]

Whether or not the influence was direct, Bond was in the Reilly mould. And while the real world of spying may have diverged, these stories firmly maintained a myth of spying that has suited agencies like SIS and the CIA. The fictional heroic deeds of their intelligence officers, their virtual invincibility and huge importance were a lure for recruits and intelligence sources. While the truth of intelligence was a classified secret, the myth was the attractive bright light.

One reason why myth is so important is that most good spies started as volunteers knocking on the door of agencies like the CIA and KGB. Their motives were driven by myth. And the false image has been relentlessly exploited. In a speech in 2004 after his retirement, James Pavitt – until then deputy director for operations at the CIA – conjured up an image of the modern spy business as a worthy successor to its forebears. 'I would like to borrow the words of an Englishman from another time who – better than any spy novel – captured the spirit and ethos of the clandestine service,' he said. And then he spoke these lines:

> From time to time, God causes men to be born who have a lust to go abroad at the risk of their lives and discover news – today it may be far off things, tomorrow, of some hidden mountain, and the next day of some nearby men who have done a foolishness against the state. These souls are very few; and of these few, not more than ten are of the best.[51]

Pavitt was quoting from a spy novel, Rudyard Kipling's *Kim*, the story of the 'child of the world' during the Great Game of the British Empire. It was the tale of a young man of another age, at ease with every language and custom of the Hindu Kush region, who could pass unnoticed and collect information. He was the spy the British had always wished they had, a more innocent version of Reilly. But the modern-day intelligence officer, as Pavitt knew, was not some updated version of Kim or Reilly.

There were some exceptions of course. There is always a danger in any description of this highly varied business in being too emphatic. 'I like to think I did some *spying*,' said one former SIS officer, who was particularly known for his unilateral – and at times very dangerous – exploits.

At the SIS training base in the eighteenth-century Fort Monkton near Gosport, new recruits have been taught for decades by retired army sergeant majors how to handle a pistol. But in truth the agency became a very cautious place, much less gung-ho than its American cousins, and almost entirely focused on the simple business of running spies: protecting their identity and keeping them alive. While some of these agents perished, at the time of writing insiders said that not a single SIS career officer had been killed in action since the Second World War.

But the myths established by Kipling, Reilly and Bond had a life of their own, one that was particularly important because they established a virtuous circle. According to one former SIS officer, Britain had created a 'cult of intelligence' that would serve it well, ensuring 'invitations to the top table' of world affairs, even as it lost its empire and declined as a world power. 'We created the impression that intelligence was something we were very good at.'

And was that impression justified?

'Yes, we were good at it.' Just because the public had a false idea of how human intelligence worked, that did not mean it wasn't working. Britain, he said, became adept at running spies, at being spymasters.

The spy war that had begun after the 1917 Bolshevik Revolution would see a stunning series of intelligence coups: spies employed for years by the Soviet Union, for example, who worked inside the most sensitive jobs in the West, as well as spies employed by the US and Britain with access to the most sensitive of Soviet secrets.

The question that lingered, however, said the same former officer, was whether spying really had any effect and made all those sacrifices worthwhile.

Chapter 2
The Best-Ever Liars

'Imagine a locker room full of guys and each of them trying to tell how many girls they've screwed – that's sort of the recruitment thing . . . "Man, I got one" '

– Milton Bearden, former CIA officer[1]

In August 1940, a year into the Second World War, an event of some significance in the history of espionage took place. A Cambridge University-educated journalist from *The Times* was taken up the carpeted stairs to the fourth floor of St Ermin's Hotel, Caxton Street, in Victoria, London. A guard stood by in the corridor.

'Take a good look at Philby, because he is now going to be one of us,' said the officer of Britain's secret intelligence service.[2]

He had just introduced and vouched for a Soviet penetration agent, newly recruited to Section D (sabotage and black propaganda) of SIS. The agent was inside.

Kim Philby had been working for Soviet intelligence for the last six years under the code names Stanley or Söhnchen (little son).[3] Vetting of new officers was then so lax that no one had discovered his left-wing past, not least his dissolved marriage to a German communist, Litzi Friedmann. Within three years of his appointment at St Ermin's, Moscow was pleased to find he had progressed further. He secured a position at SIS headquarters at 54 Broadway, around the corner from St Ermin's, and a job in Section IX, the counter-Soviet division. Moscow told Philby to 'do everything, but *everything*' to become head of section; he did and succeeded.[4]

It was 'a masterstroke', as spy historian Professor Christopher Andrew would declare. Philby and the rest of the so-called 'Cambridge Five' were 'the ablest group of British agents ever recruited by a foreign power'.[5] Andrew regards Philby as one of the greatest liars in history. Perhaps so. But his success was also testament to the arrogance of the British ruling class at the time. They had been trapped by their assumption that no one with such a background could ever betray their country.

The story of Philby is one that British intelligence would rather forget, one that damaged its credibility for decades. Even so, it remains an essential case study on the nature of spying – and what spying can achieve.

His case poses this question: if Philby really was one of the greatest spies in history, why did he ultimately make so little difference?

Understanding why his achievements were limited, and why the actions of so few 'great spies' in the Cold War had real consequence, not only reveals that much of the effort and money spent on spying is wasted but also exposes the elemental weaknesses of the spy game. These weaknesses can sometimes be mitigated; in fact a look at past exaggerations of success and failures also provides clues about how spies can be usefully deployed.

When Philby started spying for the Soviet Union in 1934 only nine years had elapsed since Reilly's last foray into Russia. By then the advantage in the game of espionage was firmly on the Soviet side. For the West, the Soviet Union had become a sort of black box, mysterious and mostly inaccessible. But the NKVD – the successor to the Cheka and the forerunner of the KGB – was by contrast able to operate with relative ease in the much freer West. By both concealing the evils and failures of the Soviet communist system and, among other methods, exploiting concern about the rise of fascism, it had successfully recruited many spies across the West.

There was one small difficulty: much of what the best Soviet spies reported was widely discounted and disbelieved in Moscow. In the case of Philby, what he reported seemed just too good to be true.

Back at 'Centre', as the headquarters of Soviet intelligence in the Lubyanka building, Moscow, were known, his controllers were aware of British skills at deception.[6] By the time he got his job in SIS, the war was on and Philby's fellow spies had already told Moscow of the British system of 'Double Cross', by which they were feeding false plans to the Germans. Agents sent to Britain were captured and made to send back false information.

What if, Philby's controllers asked, the same kind of planted falsehoods were being deployed by the Cambridge ring against the Soviet Union?

When Philby's file was unearthed in Soviet intelligence archives after the Cold War, it revealed that the Soviets had ceased all contact with him in February 1940, thinking that he was going nowhere. They re-established contact only after they learned he had joined SIS. But they were suspicious. Soviet analysts set Philby a test in 1942. They asked him to name the agents SIS had in the Soviet Union. When Philby said that SIS had none, it was taken as proof that he was an impostor. When fellow spy Anthony Blunt confirmed Philby's report, it was taken that he too was a double agent. Philby's file, number 5581, was handed to an analyst within the NKVD, Elena Modrzhinskaya.[7] She was tasked with analysing all the information provided by Philby in order to determine whether or not he was lying. She recorded, 'Not a single valuable British agent in the USSR or in the Soviet Embassy in Britain has been exposed with the help of this group, in spite of the fact that if they had been sincere in their co-operation they could easily have done so.'[8] And she concluded, 'He is lying to us in a most insolent manner.'[9]

Modrzhinskaya was convinced the SIS must have been run by fools if Philby and Co. were genuine and their masters did not realize that so much precious information was leaking to Moscow.[10] She also complained that Anthony Blunt, who had penetrated MI5, was taking 'incomprehensible' risks by carrying original secret materials to meet his case officer. According to Soviet archives, from 1941 to 1945 he handed over a total of 1,771 documents.[11]

Phillip Knightley – the former *Sunday Times* journalist who first exposed Philby's position in SIS – concluded that Modrzhinskaya's report was 'confirmation of a theory that I have long held – that most spying is useless because the better the information a spy produces, the less likely he is to be believed'.[12] For a secret service, this was the key problem with hiring foreigners as agents. It was hard to trust them.

In 1943, the NKVD wrote to its London 'rezident' (station chief) to say that all five Cambridge spies were British moles. 'There is no other way of explaining,' wrote the Centre, 'how "The Hotel" [code name for SIS] and "The Hut" [SOE] could entrust such critical work in such responsible areas to individuals who were involved in Communist and leftist activities in the past.'[13]

But Moscow could never be sure they had been deceived, said Knightley. No one wanted to risk their careers by cutting off contact with potentially the best spies they ever had. Even if the Cambridge spies were plants, it would have been foolish to tip off the British that the NKVD knew. So they reluctantly continued to run these agents, not discovering for years that they were genuine. It meant that real gold nuggets of information were given little weight. For example, Moscow dismissed a 1943 report from their British agents providing a crucial technical detail – the thickness of armour on new German tanks. The NKVD's London residence (as the Russians call their foreign intelligence stations) was informed by Moscow the information was dubious because the report did not harm British interests.[14]

Even so, not everything Philby said was ignored. In one case, the Soviets reacted swiftly and ruthlessly. This was when Philby warned, in September 1945, that one of their intelligence officers based in Istanbul, Konstantin Volkov, was planning to defect to the West and was promising to bring news of a mole 'fulfilling the function of head of a section of British counter-espionage in London' (in other words, Philby himself). Moscow sent two hit men to murder him, which they did.[15]

There were similar Soviet blunders to Philby's case in the handling of Richard Sorge – a dashing member of the Nazi Party, a journalist and, in 1941, a part-time officer at the German Embassy in Tokyo. He was also an agent for the GRU, Soviet military intelligence.

For months, there had been rumours that Adolf Hitler was about to renege on his pact with the Soviet Union and invade the country. Stalin himself had said that war with Germany was inevitable, but he refused to accept specific warnings that it was imminent. Then on 1 June 1941, Sorge wrote, 'Expected start of German-Soviet war around June 15 is based exclusively on information which Lieutenant-Colonel Scholl brought with him from Berlin . . . [for Ambassador Ott].'[16]

His report (confirming eighty other warnings from sources[17]) was annotated in Moscow: 'Suspicious. To be listed with telegrams intended as provocations.' Stalin had rejected a previous warning as being sourced from 'a shit who has set himself up with some little factories and brothels in Japan'.[18]

Sorge was only a week off the mark. German tanks and four million soldiers started pouring across the Soviet border on 22 June, launching Operation Barbarossa.

As John le Carré wrote in 1966:

In 1941 Sorge had given to his Russian masters the exact date on which the German armies would invade the Soviet Union. At the hour of victory, this report was still rotting in a file marked 'dubious intelligence', and the two Soviet officers who had controlled Sorge's activities lay in their graves, purged as enemies of the people.[19]

The rejection of intelligence sent to Moscow by what were then the Soviet Union's top spies, Philby and Sorge, was no accident. Rather, as Knightley hints, it touches on the nature of spying.

It might be tempting, as some do, to pin the problem on Stalin and the Soviet system at the time. After all, the communists were legendary for their paranoid and conspiratorial nature, as well as the extreme caution that was engendered by the purges and show trials of the 1930s. (By 1941, three of Philby's previous controllers had been shot dead in purges.[20]) Stalin himself may have been paranoid to the point of insanity. But there were examples from the spy work of other nations suggesting that secret agents' greatest triumphs were destined, in general, to be disbelieved.

One former CIA station chief described such an episode, which has never previously been disclosed. Before the Yom Kippur War of 1973, an agent had obtained for him all of Egypt and Syria's invasion plans. He filed them to headquarters in Washington. The plans detailed the order of battle and the position of every unit. But he, and by extension his source, were not believed. The officer involved told me that CIA analysts could not accept that he had such a good agent who would provide him with these things. After the event, the station chief was a hero. It boosted his future credibility. But such opportunities were rare and too easily squandered, as they were here, because of analysts' unwillingness to believe the human source. The CIA considered this episode an example of the success of agent reporting being trumped by a failure of analysis. The ex-officer said, 'Since Pearl Harbor I have never been a great believer in assessment by analysts who are thousands of miles from the reality on the ground and just reading reports. Accurate agent reporting is fact. Intelligence analysis and estimates are guessing – educated guessing, but still guessing.'[21]

Or, back in 1909, consider an agent called Le Vengeur, a member of the German general staff, who sent French intelligence a copy of the Schlieffen Plan, which described how the Kaiser would invade France in the First World War. His disclosures were ignored, even when the plan was also stupidly published in the *Deutsche Revue*.

It becomes evident from many cases that real-life spy stories tend to end in an anticlimax. A great coup, some terrible plot discovered, but then, when the spy comes home to tell his story, it is all for nothing. Why do the efforts of spies so often come to naught? It has to reflect a number of critical weaknesses in the business.

First, spies struggle with credibility because human intelligence delivers its product in a particularly frail vessel. To obtain secrets, spies must be treacherous. They must betray their country and tell lies to those around them. Truths from a spy come delivered in a wrapping of lies. It is hard to be sure that such habitual and accomplished liars are not being deceptive about the information they are delivering. This doubt is accentuated by the way modern spy agencies depend on foreign agents, rather than using their own officers. The agencies usually deliver what is second-hand information, technically hearsay. The game has too many layers.

Second, there is the problem of what we could call truth-shock. An important revelation is something that challenges existing belief. The better the story, the harder to convince. Dull and conventional wisdom, unsurprising warnings, these all pass safely and rapidly into reports for presidents and prime ministers. But an intelligence agency that issues a surprising warning risks ridicule and inquiries if it turns out to be wrong and so will tend to agonize over such warnings, possibly until too late.

Third, there is a problem of incentives. To use the language of economics, spying, like journalism and diplomacy, can be viewed as part of the market for information, a market that is famously imperfect. It is hard to trade efficiently in information because to describe fully the product that you are selling (for example, to say that the Russian president will visit Minsk on Monday) is already to hand over the product and devalue it. Secret intelligence is even harder to trade because it is information that often cannot be verified. A plan for a nuclear missile strike may be verifiable only after it has taken place. Imperfect markets like this lead to what economists call 'perverse incentives' – a tendency to do suboptimal things. A rational spy may have an incentive to invent or exaggerate secrets that cannot be verified. And the rational spy agency may have a perverse incentive to reject information it cannot immediately verify, and to overvalue verifiable titbits.

These weaknesses – a lack of credibility, inbuilt inertia against shocking information and poor incentives – conspire to hinder spies from making a difference. Intelligence agencies have worked to counter these problems by, for example, developing a sceptical mindset to test the credibility of their agents. But, as both the CIA and the KGB found to their cost during periods of the Cold War, healthy scepticism can turn quickly into a sickly, paralysing paranoia that corrupts faith in faithful friends. Such a disease can devalue all the highly prized fruits of intelligence.

What should these inbuilt weaknesses tell us about whether or not spies can ever be effective? Generalizing from specific cases is always dangerous. Even with Philby and Sorge, the fact that during certain periods their intelligence was ignored hardly allows us to sum up the overall value of their betrayal, still less of spying as a whole. But the sheer scale of the espionage that took place during the Cold War, and the volume of detail about it disclosed publicly, do provide us with a platform from which to make a number of observations.

The first is that, in spying, activity is not the same as achievement. You don't have to take Knightley's radical view that everything about spying is useless to note that much of it was.

A secret service is rarely honest to the public about itself. In the Cold War, to justify the arms race of intelligence spending, it served the interests of both sides to aggrandize the achievements of their rivals, the enemy. But, in contrast to much of what has been said in public and made its way into the literature, this was not some golden age of spying. For most of the period, huge amounts of effort were expended recruiting spies whose main value was to provide the secret services with information about each other in what became almost an internal, private war. So, while a culture of secrecy kept the public in the dark – for example, it was illegal in the United States and Britain to publish the names of undercover intelligence officers – Soviet intelligence often had a full briefing about the inside of SIS and the CIA. In the 1930s and 1940s, the Soviets had Kim Philby in SIS and Anthony Blunt in MI5; by the 1980s they had Aldrich Ames in CIA headquarters and Robert Hanssen in the FBI. On the other side, the West was fully briefed on Soviet intelligence. They had, among others, Oleg Penkovsky and later Oleg Gordievsky in the GRU and KGB respectively.

Really valuable intelligence might have told political leaders what their enemies or potential enemies were planning or contemplating. But in all the years of superpower confrontation, both sides had a critical lack of political agents. The KGB never did have a spy in the White House. 'When people say that Soviet intelligence penetrated the higher echelons of Western government, I know that this is not true,' said Oleg Kalugin, the

Soviet general and former head of KGB foreign counterintelligence.[22] Nor did the CIA ever have a spy in the Kremlin, as William Colby, the former CIA director, admitted.[23]

By way of a caveat, Britain's star agent-in-place in the late Cold War, Oleg Gordievsky, did deliver valuable political intelligence when he was the KGB station chief in London while also working for SIS. He – and the intelligence he provided – played a pivotal role in making Margaret Thatcher believe and support Soviet president Mikhail Gorbachev's campaign of glasnost, which ultimately brought down the communist edifice. His achievement was mainly to deliver understanding, not secrets. 'No doubt he produced lots of facts to go with this understanding,' said one insider who observed these events close at hand, 'but it was in changing Western perceptions of the regime that he seems to have been most influential.'

The second observation is that spying has proved successful when it was highly focused and politically directed.

The world is so complex and the future so hard to predict that spy agencies that have tried to do everything, to have spies everywhere, have rarely achieved much, even with a large budget. Stalin, whatever his faults, took the opposite approach to intelligence. He had the gift of marshalling all the resources at his disposal towards a single objective that he defined. Such determination helped the Soviets pull off the espionage coup of the twentieth century: the acquisition of the atomic bomb.

With more than 200 Americans working as Soviet agents during and after the Second World War, and a series of agents involved at various levels within the Manhattan Project, which produced the first nuclear bombs, the first Soviet bomb tested in 1949 'was a copy of the American original tested . . . more than four years earlier', Christopher Andrew records.[24] One of those blamed for this leak of technology was a German scientist and émigré to Britain, Klaus Fuchs, who confessed to an MI5 interrogator that he had given the Russians 'all the information in his possession about British and American research in connection with the atomic bomb'.[25]

As with much spy literature, discussion on atomic espionage is often shallow, ignoring the strides taken independently by the Soviets' own weapons programme. Some research suggests the stolen intelligence was used mainly to compare results. But, even so, this would have been critical. Spying was crucial to this strategic shift.

Hans Bethe, a fellow nuclear physicist, suggested that, by his spying, Fuchs was 'the only physicist I know who truly changed history'.[26] He should also have added the creators of the nuclear bomb, Albert Einstein and J. Robert Oppenheimer.

The third observation is that human intelligence has the most effect when it is corroborated or, even better, verifiable. These are technical terms of spy-speak. Corroboration means obtaining the same information independently from other sources. Without such a backup, you are left with 'single source intelligence'. Verifiable intelligence means information that can be checked. So, for example, a secret agent's report that a bomb had been planted in a Rome hotel could be corroborated by another agent's report or by another source of intelligence, such as a bugged telephone. It could be verified if the agent gave other specific information that allowed the actual bomb to be found.

Corroboration and verification are double-checks on intelligence. And while, as mentioned, a requirement for double-checks will skew what spies provide (at the expense of uncheckable but useful truths), this double-checking has generally proved the only practical way to make human intelligence useful. Few spies have been so brilliant, or so convincing, that their intelligence was ever trusted without being backed up in this way.

Philby's story is again instructive. In trying to show why Philby's intelligence was valuable – despite Moscow's doubts – some biographers cite the case of the warnings he provided after the Second World War about a programme by the CIA and SIS to insert agents into Eastern Europe and Albania in particular. In a mission known as Operation Valuable, between 1949 and 1954, the West made successive attempts to overthrow a newly established Albanian communist leader, Enver Hoxha, and to restore the esteemed King Zog. But, as a result of tip-offs, most of the Western agents were captured as they landed on the coast or parachuted in and were executed.

Philby's role is often cited uncritically here, partly because he boasted about it. Philby became infamous, as one newspaper writer puts it, as the traitor who 'sent agents to their deaths behind the Iron Curtain'.[27] Philby himself wrote that the 'agents we sent into Albania were armed men intent on murder, sabotage and assassination . . . To the extent that I helped defeat them, even if it caused their deaths, I have no regrets.' Yuri Modin, Philby's NKVD contact in London, also claimed that Philby 'gave us vital information about the number of men involved, the day and the time of the landing, the weapons they were bringing and their precise programme of action'.[28]

But, as most historians concede, Operation Valuable was anyway penetrated from top to bottom by Soviet spies. And whatever value Philby may have delivered had credibility because it was corroborated by those other spies, and indeed by the capture of the agents when they landed. He could be trusted on Albania because he was not a solitary source. On his own, even this master spy counted for little.

There is research that questions whether Philby even provided details of the agents' landings – the central claim made by all who have built up his importance. This challenge comes from Albert Lulushi, an Albanian-American author, based on a study of declassified CIA files. Nicholas Pano, a history professor, in a review of Lulushi's work, concludes that he puts Philby in perspective:

> It demonstrates that although he was knowledgeable of the plans against Albania, he did not have access to the operational plans in Albania. Although he was a factor in the failure of this adventure in Albania, the main factors were the rivalry and divisions among the Albanian émigré groups, the leaks of operational details from these groups, the bureaucratic approach that the CIA and British planners of these operations often took, and the rivalry among different intelligence agencies with interests in Albania at the time.[29]

At the time of writing, this evidence is too fresh to be conclusive. But what it underlines is the need for caution in accepting any claim about the immense value of a particular spy, as well as the huge interest that almost everyone has in exaggerating his importance.

On the other side of Cold War spying, there was a clear example of intelligence that made a difference. While US political intelligence in Moscow was often thin, the CIA successfully stole many Russian technical secrets. This had impact because the stolen designs and science could be tested and replicated.

Adolf Tolkachev, a senior Russian aeronautical scientist who spied for the CIA between 1977 and 1985, gained access to (and was also involved in the design of) radars for the Soviet fighter programme and so helped the US defeat them. According to James Pavitt, the former CIA deputy director for operations, Tolkachev's spying saved the US billions and 'ensured us air superiority at a critical juncture of the Cold War'.[30] Dmitri Polyakov, a major general in Soviet military intelligence, was another great catch. He spied for nearly twenty years from 1961 and was described by Sandy Grimes, a CIA counterintelligence officer who helped catch Aldrich Ames, as 'our crown jewel' and possibly 'the best source that any intelligence service has ever had'. He passed on specifics of Soviet missiles and other weapons.[31] (Unfortunately, the CIA had failed to protect their agents with proper compartmentalization. The need-to-know principle was ignored and too many people knew their identity. Both were betrayed by Soviet agents – Tolkachev by Ames and Polyakov by Hanssen – and executed at the Lubyanka.)

Pavitt emphasizes the money saved by technical intelligence, but another reason such intelligence was valuable was that it could be tested. The stolen secrets triggered a research programme, not only to learn methods to counteract the Soviet weapons but also to verify that the intelligence was accurate. The cost of verification was one reason why clandestine actions to steal the actual weapons were regarded as even more important. SIS officers pulled these off in Afghanistan and the CIA in Egypt.[32]

A final observation here is that spying must be a weapon of last resort.

The benefits of successful spy missions may be outweighed by the costs of spying that goes wrong. Against all the theft of technical secrets that helped the different sides with their arms race there were many failures, not just the death by execution of so many agents – whether Volkov, Penkovsky, Polyakov or Tolkachev – but the constant atmosphere of tension and distrust that spy games could engender.

Perhaps the most instructive case was an East German operation that showed the cost of recruiting an agent without thought for the consequences. It led to the resignation of West German chancellor Willy Brandt and showed the cost of spying for spying's sake.

Günter Guillaume, codenamed Hansen, and his first wife, Christel, were officers in the East German foreign intelligence service, the HVA, who were sent in 1956 to infiltrate the West German leadership. They pretended to have escaped from East Germany and set up, with HVA money, a café in Frankfurt. Both joined Brandt's Social Democratic Party (SPD), for whom Christel became a secretary in the local headquarters. Over a number of years, Günter worked himself up the party ranks, eventually becoming chairman of the Frankfurt SPD and a member of the city council.[33]

In 1969, following Willy Brandt's election as West Germany's first SPD chancellor, and after successfully managing the election campaign of a local minister, Guillaume asked if there might be a position for him in the Chancellery. After a short time in a minor position there, he moved up to become Brandt's most trusted aide and one of the very few who accompanied him and his family on holiday. The Soviets, via the Stasi, now had direct access to Brandt's thinking, correspondence and policymaking.

By May 1973, West German counterintelligence had begun to suspect the Guillaumes of being HVA spies. Despite this, they did not alert Brandt to their suspicions and just put Christel under surveillance.[34] It wasn't until March 1974 that Günter also started to be watched, and a month later both husband and wife were arrested on suspicion of espionage.

The political scandal that resulted from this threatened to bring down the SPD coalition government. Not only had the Chancellor trusted a spy as his aide and confidant, but rumours began circulating that Guillaume had been collecting compromising information, and possibly photos, of the married Chancellor with various women, as well as information about his heavy drinking. By resigning, Brandt saved the government, but not himself.

Brandt had been the architect of a policy of East–West rapprochement that was in the interests of East Germany. As Markus Wolf, the HVA chief, later acknowledged, the operation had 'unwittingly helped to destroy the career of the most farsighted of modern German statesmen'.[35] After the fall of the Berlin Wall, he wrote to Brandt, apologizing that the HVA 'contributed to the extremely negative political events that led to your resignation in 1974'.[36]

Wolf's problem was that he became too good. Spying was used without enough thought, instead of being reserved for securing the sort of secrets that really mattered.

If the nature of the spy business is frequently portrayed wrongly, so too is the character of the Cold War's real warriors: the intelligence officers at the heart of the business. And while the profession's achievements are often aggrandized, many of its greatest characters, the top spymasters, are remarkably candid about their limitations. The best of them consider counterintuitive thinking an article of faith.

For a frontline perspective on spying's value, as well as to learn more about how Cold War spies were really recruited, it was worth spending time with some of the greats of anti-Soviet espionage. One of the most thoughtful was the former head of the CIA's Soviet section, Milton Bearden. Meeting him involved a drive out to a favourite haunt of ex-spies, the Ritz Carlton Hotel at Tysons Corner in McLean, Virginia.

Bearden was a legend whose name I had first heard mentioned in Germany in the 1990s. He was credited then for Operation Rosenholz (Rosewood), the operation that led to the CIA acquiring, as the Berlin Wall tumbled, a list of almost all the Stasi's agents abroad, winning him the Federal Cross of Merit from the German state.[37]

I learned later that Bearden, then station chief in Islamabad, Pakistan, had also been one of the key figures in running the CIA covert war in Afghanistan. When he returned to headquarters, he ran the agency's wider war as chief of the agency's Soviet section. He retired from the CIA in 1994, devastated by the discovery that one of his officers, Aldrich Ames, had betrayed them all.

By the end of Bearden's career, the CIA had ballooned, employing around 25,000 people. That included analysts and technical specialists – positions that in the UK, for example, would not come under the auspices of SIS. Officers like Bearden were part of the elite, from the clandestine service that actually ran spies and covert operations. Called various names at different times, including the Directorate of Plans, the Directorate of Operations (DO) and, since 2005, the National Clandestine Service (NCS), this section has always been the heart of the 'real CIA' and numbered no more than 6,000, including support staff.[38]

(To compare the British and American agencies, it is important to realize that the CIA's clandestine service is the counterpart of SIS, not the entire CIA. SIS, which is said by insiders to employ between 2,000 and 3,000 people, focuses entirely on running agents and field operations; analysis of its product is carried out elsewhere in Whitehall. But the CIA's DO was also far more action-orientated than SIS, with more ex-military recruits and much wider remit to engage in covert action.)

'The CIA is the DO,' said Bearden. 'The rest of it, the analysis, etc. is just Rand Corporation or the Brookings Institution with razor wire around it.'

Like many former CIA case officers I had come to know, Bearden was a big and distinctive man, not someone to blend into the shadows. 'They ordered these burgers only crocodiles can eat,' said one former officer in the BND, Germany's foreign intelligence service, recalling his contacts with US intelligence. And in the words of Jack Devine, an old colleague of Bearden and another giant of a man: 'It's no good hiding away. People have to know where to find you.'

That had been a key lesson for me. As Bearden explained, during the Cold War 'by and large, it was the job of the intelligence officer to make sure everybody knew his post office box'.

People who wrote books about spies spoke of all their training in recruiting spies, how they were taught to find people's motives and exploit them. But, at least in the Cold War, this training rarely counted for much. Almost all spies of any importance had been 'walk-ins', volunteers who chose to betray without any prompting or recruitment.

With a very few exceptions on the Soviet side, the West versus East spy game during the Cold War was 'about the skilful management of volunteers', according to Bearden. 'You've got people who defect – who defect in place – and they do it for all of the same reasons that drive man: fear, revenge, lust, sex, greed or even something like boredom occasionally. And he makes the decision – it's almost always guys – to become bigger than himself. He becomes a spy. So, if you're Russian, who are you going to spy for – China, Albania? You're going to spy for the main adversary, the main enemy.'

It is worth noting here that while other professional spymasters interviewed by the author agreed with Bearden's assessment about the scarcity of real recruits when operating against the Soviets inside the Eastern bloc (Bearden's main sphere of operations), many argued it *was* possible to make targeted recruits of softer targets in more benign environments, of which more later.

As Bearden correctly described, some of the best spies for the West were forced literally to throw themselves at their erstwhile enemy to get hired. It took Tolkachev thirteen months and six approaches in Moscow – including banging on the CIA chief-of-station's car – before headquarters authorized a meeting. That he became one of the CIA's most valuable agents was thanks only to his determination and persistence.[39]

I asked Bearden about all those how-to recruitment stories. It was 'largely bullshit', he replied. 'Imagine a locker room full of guys and each of them trying to tell how many girls they've screwed – that's sort of the recruitment thing . . . "Man, I got one".'

He then added, 'It was the middle-school, testosterone-driven thing that you have to have done it all yourself. Did I get X who was a communist to change his mind? No. All that mattered was that he provided huge amounts of intelligence.'

Was any spy in this particular battleground actually recruited deliberately? I had spent a while going through a long list of spy cases by then. On the CIA scorecard, the only one I could identify as a deliberate recruit was a Soviet diplomat named Aleksandr Ogorodnik, code-named Trigon.

'Yes,' Bearden replied. 'I'll give it. It was because an operation was run; he didn't just drop a note into the car. There weren't many others, maybe a couple of others.'

The CIA got to Trigon while he was in Columbia after discovering that he had a mistress. The mistress, who loved him, was then recruited, believing that spying would allow her to live with Trigon. After returning to Moscow and joining the Soviet foreign ministry, Trigon filed some supposedly invaluable intelligence.

'But his intelligence was not necessarily acted on or believed,' said Bearden.

Recruitment of spies, according to those involved, always required a long-drawn-out process in which access could be maintained to the target. The reason why almost all Soviet agents were walk-ins was because of, as someone else involved put it, 'the near impossibility of developing personal contact with target personnel because of the stringent defensive security measures of the Soviet state'. But if all the recruitment training that CIA officers got was thereby redundant, was the agency's campaign against the Soviets essentially incompetent?

Not at all, according to Bearden. The heart of the business was not recruiting but rather 'running spies', the handling of active agents. And there he remained fiercely proud – though oddly as proud of his comrades in the KGB.

'My point is everybody talks about the recruitment being the biggest deal. You know what? Most are volunteers. The biggest deal is being able to securely handle people in Moscow under the noses of the entire second chief directorate [the KGB's department for internal security and counter-intelligence] – like we did until they were betrayed.

'I don't think there are many modern exceptions to the rule that the only time the Soviets caught a spy was when that spy was betrayed by our side, your side [the British], or the Germans. That's pretty much a fact. It's true for us [US] too. The FBI almost never caught a spy unless someone betrayed them.'

In Moscow, huge resources were devoted to tailing US diplomats, and Soviet citizens had little freedom. Yet, even so, the CIA ran spies under the KGB's nose, which was a 'stunning accomplishment', said Bearden.

What gave tension to the spy game was that so much effort and preparation went into vital contacts that might last seconds and, if they went wrong, could prove fatal for the agent. For the CIA officers posted as 'diplomats' in the embassy in Moscow, making it work involved elaborate choreography.

Bearden explained, 'There is a scheduled brush contact – [passing a secret written message by "accidentally" brushing past someone in a public street] – or brief encounter with an agent – with Adolf Tolkachev, say – for nine o'clock on Friday night. Today is Monday. Today and tomorrow, we'll be finding out who of my four people here are looking free . . . Then you start an orchestrated thing to break someone loose – and I might not know until Thursday who's free. And then you're going to be off, make cover stops all over the place, plan your whole day to where they [the KGB] don't know you've disappeared at six o'clock – you could go black [evade surveillance] in Moscow on Friday evening, and they never caught you.'

Then it was the meet: 'You might be saying, "How are you doing? How's your son? Here's the medicine for him. This is the stuff you said you'd get, the microfilms . . . This Monday we're going to take care of that . . ." Because I'm his only contact with what he thinks is the human race at this point. In this moment he's a superman – he is above the world, that's it. This may be the most important three, four, five minutes of his life . . . they might also be his last.'

Bearden's words begin to slow. He is starting to turn inward, thinking of the ones who survived this entire saga only to be shot because of betrayal by Ames. In total there were thirty-six, including ten who were executed.[40] In court, Ames admitted compromising 'virtually all Soviet agents of the CIA and other American and foreign services known to me'.[41]

We then turned to the point of our meeting. Was it all worth it? From reading *The Main Enemy*, the book Bearden wrote with journalist James Risen, I had got the impression that in his career fighting the KGB he had collected plenty of scalps, but it wasn't clear what good really came of it.

Looming largest for Bearden was the covert CIA war against the

Soviets in Afghanistan, in which he had played such a key role when he was chief in Islamabad. 'That sped up the dissolution of the USSR greatly,' he said.

I replied that, true as this might or might not be, it did not count. I was trying to assess the value of espionage – the business of spying and betrayal – not covert action.

Ever since its formation, the CIA had always been a mix of intelligence gathering and action. What critics often missed was that it always was – and remains today – the tool of the American president. The agency did what he wanted and, by and large, each president was tempted to use the CIA to fight some secret wars. After the Second World War, the nuclear threat meant that the Soviets could not be engaged in a conventional war. But they could be confronted around the world by the secret efforts of a secret agency. Covert action gave the president a lever to pull, an option short of the kind of overt military action that could escalate into nuclear war. Even covertly, however, the CIA could do little directly behind the Iron Curtain. Instead, the opportunities lay in undecided space, the unoccupied countries of the world that might swing either way in their loyalties. That is why insiders sometimes semi-seriously referred to the CIA operations division as 'the Department of the Third World'.

So life in the CIA or the KGB was mostly not about pure spying. It was a market for influence. In any one nation, the job 'was more about making that country ours instead of theirs. It denied them that piece on the chessboard, and in the end he who had the most pieces won. It was about "country management" so that I don't get any surprises out of that country,' explained Bearden.

As to whether all this Cold War covert action did any good, much has already been said, not least in the epic study by Tim Weiner, *Legacy of Ashes*. That book – which portrayed decades of missteps, bloody failures and counterproductive actions – caused fury in the CIA, which suggested in a rare, if not unheard of, public statement regarding a book about the agency that Weiner had repeatedly distorted history: 'Backed by selective citations, sweeping assertions, and a fascination with the negative, Weiner overlooks, minimizes, or distorts agency achievements.'[42]

I shall not comment here on who is right. I only add a small criticism: that Weiner rather left the impression that bloody intervention, coup plotting and so on were all the CIA did. He forgot the business of spying: the function of the intelligence agency to recruit agents and gather protected information.

On the value of Cold War espionage, Bearden thinks the jury is still out. In the CIA versus KGB battle, 'If either one or both had decided not to play the game, would it have made any difference to the outcome? Probably not.'

What is certain, he said, was there was too much mutual obsession. The 'recruitment of intelligence officers by the KGB and CIA became easy . . . We all knew each other's phone numbers. But what we did was turn that into the main activity, into the belief that if you recruit a KGB officer he'll tell you who the spies are.'

The question he asked himself, in his sceptical way, was whether, in the history of the West, human intelligence had really been the basis for a major policy development by a president or prime minister, particularly as human intelligence was often disbelieved. His curious answer – and he was not the only one to make this case – was that, in what he called 'reverse-perverse' logic, when it came to Cold War spying's biggest achievements, it was spying against America that had made the most positive difference.

In Bearden's view, even the nuclear spies did some good. 'Stalin would have been hysterical about the American burgeoning nuclear development if he hadn't penetrated the entire Manhattan Project with a whole array of people.' Julius and Ethel Rosenberg kept Stalin from doing 'something goofy. That betrayal of the US probably saved us a huge war.'

He also mentioned the Stasi agent Topaz, real name Rainer Rupp, who was Markus Wolf's man inside NATO. When, in 1983, NATO had mobilized its forces for a ten-day pan-European exercise, code-named Able Archer, including a simulation of the highest level of nuclear alert, it was people like Topaz who convinced the octogenarian Kremlin leadership that all those military manoeuvres were not a build-up to a nuclear first strike.[43]

On the reverse side, he was not saying there were no successes. 'I still believe that, on the whole, the stuff Tolkachev gave us provided a commercial advantage to General Dynamics that meant our fighter aircraft for the next two generations performed better than anything. Because we literally sat in on the Soviet design efforts.' But so much other intelligence work was 'grossly inefficient' – a huge effort for little result.

On balance, was it worth it? It was the question Bearden said he asked himself constantly, particularly thinking about those who died. In Tolkachev's case, for instance, 'was his accomplishment worth him dying?' For now, it was a question Bearden did not want to answer.

From Philby to Tolkachev, the great spies of the Cold War illustrated some of the tremendous skills that intelligence agencies had developed to operate traitors covertly within an enemy camp. Those involved took pride in their spying coups, even as they were ashamed by the betrayals of certain colleagues and even if many, like Bearden, harboured doubts about what had been achieved.

Above all, human intelligence emerged as a frustrating business – a resource-hungry, time-consuming and usually fruitless pursuit at constant risk of backfiring. Some countries existed happily without even engaging in it. But while its impact was usually slight, occasionally, at a very crucial moment, human intelligence could provide the golden arrow, the piece of information that, if it could be corroborated and used correctly, might be decisive, as it was for Stalin with the designs he stole for the atomic bomb.

As we have seen, some of the lessons of Cold War espionage were universal, from the intrinsically fragile nature of intelligence based on human treachery to the need for corroboration or verification to set against this weakness.

There were also aspects of this period that were special, not least the totalitarian nature of Soviet society and hence the strict limits to meaningful contact between Soviet and Western citizens. These restrictions gave little opportunity for the sort of prolonged contact that might have resulted in successful recruitment, so that when agents were recruited the difficulty of control and communication meant that doubts inevitably crept in as to whether agents had been compromised or not. But, though operating in the Soviet bloc was unique, there were parallels for future spying. In the twenty-first century, as the CIA tried to recruit spies in training camps for terrorists in remote mountain areas, for instance, its officers faced the same fundamental problem of how to trust and direct spies who were barely seen and barely known.

Even if communications are good, the physical distance, cultural barriers and profusion of intermediaries that lie between the spy and the decision-maker, the person who consumes the intelligence, always make for uncertainty. Kim Philby's trouble was that his Moscow controllers, and beyond them the Kremlin, operated, mentally and physically, in a world apart. If they had known him better they would have realized that his treachery was genuine and been better able to judge the information he provided.

Even in the Cold War period, however, there were other theatres of spying where human contact was far more profound, where spies could be actively recruited and their credibility might come not through the verification of information but through a deep understanding of their motives.

Battlegrounds like this provide evidence of how spies can be run and continue to survive among even the deadliest of enemies.

Chapter 3
Friendship

'The reality is that the past is a very, very dark place for everybody'

– Martin McGuinness, former IRA commander[1]

Not all spies provide information that is disbelieved. Not all intelligence gathering has unforeseen consequences. Even during the wasteful years of the Cold War arms race, there were times when the spy agency proved its worth, when human intelligence turned out to be indispensable. Britain's military campaign in Northern Ireland, which began in 1968 and ended thirty years later, is such an example. Insiders mention the story of one of Britain's best spies, an agent deep inside one of the most successful terrorist organizations, the IRA, which struck one deadly blow after another against the British state in its campaign for a united Ireland.

A CIA officer first pointed me in this direction. 'You gotta look at Ireland. That was a matter of survival for the British, and we learned from them.' British intelligence came to believe that its HUMINT was so good that it was instrumental in eventually defeating the IRA. Two former senior officers of SIS further tempted me to investigate. 'The IRA was defeated by penetration,' said one. The other disagreed in the strongest terms. 'The IRA was never defeated,' he insisted. But he too spoke of incredible success at recruiting sources inside that group.

One particular British spy – code-named Steak Knife – was mentioned as being more valuable than any other, probably saving dozens of lives. His story, and that of the army unit that ran him, controversial though it is, is a case study in how spying really can work. And together with the wider history of how success was achieved in Britain's own secret 'war on terror', it resonates today because of the techniques required in keeping alive a spy inside a group of rebels intent on murder.

Even though terrorism has changed in the twenty-first century, the

Ireland intelligence war set the template. And the truth here is important for all to know, because if we in a democratic society choose to send spies against such deadly enemies, we should be aware of the compromises involved, and the need for society to set limits on these operations.

Steak Knife's story also illustrated something of what might be called the lost art of recruitment. In contrast to the pattern set in spying against the Soviet Union in the Cold War and described by Bearden in the previous chapter, few British spies in Ireland were volunteers. Recruitment was carried out by intelligence officers from the army, police and secret services who understood something of the elemental business of persuasion: how to grab the soul of another person and refashion it for a radically different purpose. As will become clear, the recruitment of the very best spies – those who steal secrets from the inner circles of an enemy camp and who do so and remain in place over an extended period – usually relies on a special bond of friendship, one that is established by time and patience. In the rush to respond to the next great threat, whether from the Russians or Islamic terror groups or hackers, we need to ask ourselves if we can afford the time to allow the spies we need to be recruited.

The existence of Steak Knife and allegations about his real identity have been leaked and published before. So have many inaccurate details about him. But with access to several new sources of information, I think we can attempt an account of what really happened. Due to their sensitive former positions, even years later few of the people quoted here can be identified.

It makes sense to start the story with one Freddie Scappaticci. He was born in Belfast in 1946, the son of an Italian immigrant, Daniel Scappaticci, who had arrived in the province in the 1920s. A football enthusiast, young Freddie had a trial with Nottingham Forest Football Club, but when that did not work out he became a bricklayer and later a builder. At the start of the Troubles in Northern Ireland, he joined the IRA's more militant Provisional wing – also known as the Provos or PIRA – which had broken away from the Official IRA in 1969. (The terms IRA and PIRA are often used interchangeably.) PIRA would come to lead the campaign against the British. In 1971, Scappaticci was interned without trial by the British for alleged PIRA membership.

In May 2003, reports in the press claimed that Scappaticci had in fact been a British agent code-named Steak Knife (whose existence had been revealed four years earlier in the *Sunday Times*). Shortly after his name was published, Scappaticci appeared at a press conference and issued a statement read by his lawyer. He denied that he was Steak Knife and denied that he had worked for army intelligence or ever been involved in terrorism (although he did later confirm his membership of the IRA). He attacked the media for its 'reckless and extremely damaging' articles. The press had shown 'absolutely no regard to [his] position or the harm such publication' would do to him and his family.[2]

In the light of these denials, it is best just to follow the story of a man of a similar age and description who came to the attention of the British Army and was later code-named Steak Knife (most have spelled the source's name as Stakeknife, but this is incorrect). At some point in the 1970s, according to British intelligence, this man killed a British soldier, or certainly wounded one. He then rose rapidly to become the commanding officer of the Provisionals' Belfast Brigade and was friends with a number of the IRA's rising stars, men like Gerry Adams, who went on to lead Sinn Féin, the IRA's political wing. For some reason, Steak Knife then fell out of favour with his commanders. While he retained his connections, he was relieved of his command. This slight was a weakness that made him a target for recruitment.

The use of spies by the secret services, army or police to fight terrorism is hardly new. And perhaps no country, with the possible exception of France, has more experience of this than Britain. In the UK, units to gather counterterrorism intelligence were established years before any other secret service agency. What used to be Scotland Yard's intelligence wing, Special Branch, was created in March 1883 to combat terrorist plots by Irish Republicans – Fenians as they were then called – and later also anarchists. That was more than twenty years before the Secret Service Bureau (the forerunner of MI5 and SIS) was founded to combat the German threat.

After the Second World War, as her empire began to crumble, Britain's secret services worked closely with police in fighting 'insurgencies' by rebel groups, some of whom used both assassinations and attacks on civilians among their tactics. These included the pro-Zionist Irgun and Stern Gang in Palestine, EOKA in Cyprus, the Malayan communists and the Mau Mau in Kenya.

With Britain showing no intention of relinquishing Northern Ireland (which had been formed from six out of the nine counties of the old Irish province of Ulster), the threat of Irish terrorism remained high. In 1968, the Troubles began with protests about discrimination against the Catholic population. When British troops were sent to Ulster a year later and conflict with the IRA began, British intelligence gathering was makeshift. In the early days, however, the task was made easier by the open character of the IRA. Its members were all well known in the working-class Catholic communities where it recruited.

The British Army brought over the tactics it had employed to quash colonial rebellions. Extensive use was made of casual torture such as sleep deprivation, beating and putting prisoners in stress positions – measures later judged to be torture by the European Court of Human Rights. As one former British intelligence operative told me, IRA prisoners were even taken up in helicopters and threatened with being pushed out. (Sometimes they actually were, but the trick was to hover just above the ground.) It was effective in making people talk.

But by the late 1970s both the army and the IRA had become more sophisticated. A turning point was a 1977 decision by the Provisional leadership in Ulster to break away from control by Dublin and establish a Northern Command. At the same time, much tighter security was imposed, including the creation of cell-like Active Service Units (ASUs). The IRA had gone underground.

Arrayed against the IRA were multiple British intelligence units. First, there was the province's police force, the Royal Ulster Constabulary (RUC), whose Special Branch handled the recruitment of informers. Next there was the regular army, whose regiments each had intelligence officers, in addition to a specialized intelligence corps that was attached to headquarters and handled multiple sources. Finally, there were the secret services, MI5 and SIS. As Northern Ireland was designated a home territory – that is, part of the United Kingdom – MI5 had prime responsibility there, but due to its more extensive experience, particularly in agent recruitment, SIS had been drafted in at an early stage to handle sensitive sources, primarily in the Irish Republic to the south, but also in the north. All these British units clashed constantly, even after 'police primacy' – putting the RUC in command – was instituted to restore some order.

The field of spying was already crowded, but the British decided to respond to the IRA's heightened security by, among other things, creating a new elite squad to recruit spies: the Force Research Unit or FRU (pronounced 'Frooh'). Although its activities later became controversial, it was also one of the most successful intelligence organizations ever, recruiting some of Britain's highest-placed sources in Northern Ireland.

The FRU focused on detail. They built up a picture of the IRA's command structure and then worked out how to recruit an agent to gain access to it. 'The success rate was very small, but when you had got someone it was worth the effort,' said one former member of the FRU. One of their first conclusions was that an ideal agent was someone very close to an ASU but not actually a member. Any agent who was given a place in an ASU needed to be extracted or helped to change roles quickly. Such men were dangerous because it was legally and morally too problematic. 'It was not going to last. He was just too close to the physical end and, one way or another, he could get killed or get someone else killed.'

About 40 per cent of the FRU's paid-up sources had no connection at all to the terrorists. They were what are often called access agents (as opposed to penetration agents), easily acquired 'eyes and ears' sources who picked up mood music from the street and pointed to interesting figures. The former FRU member recalled, 'The IRA was such a big deal in certain parts of the province that just by sitting in a pub you could pick up a lot.' Another FRU insider added, 'When we started, many in the RUC scoffed at the number of sources we had who had almost no connection to PIRA. That changed when they proved their value.' The pursuit of a top-level agent could be accelerated, he said, by having many lower-level agents.

The ideal source was the confidant, someone who was told everything but did very little. In the early days, that might have been the wives or mistresses. But as the male-dominated IRA tightened its security, it also began to shut out its womenfolk. One of the best early agents was a driver for an ASU commander. Officially, he had no access at all, except that the commander had what the Irish call the 'blarney'. He never stopped talking, so much so in fact that the agent heard almost everything.

It is no surprise that, when identifying recruitment targets, the FRU looked out for an individual with a weakness. As Pierre Lethier, a former officer with French foreign intelligence, put it memorably, 'We live off weakness; until we spot weakness we just sit around smoking cigars and reading the *Financial Times*.'[3]

In general, the FRU looked for the usual diseases – greed, jealousy, anger, lust, envy – as motivating factors for recruitment prospects. In order to avoid being tricked, they liked traits or weaknesses that could be corroborated. An IRA member was sleeping with another man's wife? That could be verified. And the target would undoubtedly be jealous and angry – ripe for an approach. That was one reason, said one recruiter, why they had little time for political beliefs as a motivation. 'Ideological motivations are the worst because you can't prove them. You can't prove what someone really believes. And the political situation can change and so the reason he is working for you may disappear.'

The FRU also came to reject any form of volunteer or 'walk-in', a luxury that most secret services could not afford. 'Walk-ins are absolutely the worst kind of agent. You have absolutely no reason to know who they are. It was often a test [by the enemy] to find out what we knew or see how we worked, or to feed us false information.'

The collection of intelligence on Gerry Adams, who ended up on the Provisional IRA's four-man Army Council, as well as later leading Sinn Féin, illustrated their methodology. His family, they discovered, had a major weakness: his father, the revered Gerry Adams Senior, was a paedophile.[4] It later emerged that the IRA leader's brother was too and that he had abused his own daughter.[5] The details of the extensive covert operation to exploit that weakness in the Adams family will probably become public at some point, but not here. Suffice it to say, the extent of cooperation with the British from a few immediate members of the Adams family has been a well-kept, long-term secret.

Steak Knife's weakness 'was his desire for revenge', according to someone involved. He felt slighted. After losing his position as the Belfast Brigade commander, he was disappointed and bitter – even if, for old times' sake, he retained friendly social contact with both Adams and many of the IRA's most senior leaders.

Turning Steak Knife was a deliberate operation and it began not too long after the FRU was formed. In 1978 he was arrested on a pretext and brought to a police station. FRU members remember him then as short and muscular, with 'the physique of a miner'. Over the course of many hours, they played on his emotions, telling him, 'You are a better man than they think you are.' There was a hint too that he had grown disaffected. 'He had lost faith in the cause. He was no longer a believer.' They chatted for many hours without agreement. And then Steak Knife was released.

Initial contact was one thing. The seed of betrayal could be planted. 'He carried on being a PIRA man, but there was something inside him telling him that what he was doing was wrong,' said one person involved. In this case it worked. He began to have doubts. But could he be run as an active agent?

Over the coming months, FRU recruiters found excuses to come across Steak Knife. Still a source on trial, he crossed the line towards being a fully fledged agent when he agreed to meet up with them, usually just for drinks in ordinary pubs. But it was a long process.

As a venue for espionage, the advantage of Northern Ireland over, say, Moscow or Prague was always access. Former officers in the CIA or SIS have explained, the reason Soviets were so hard to recruit was that it was almost impossible to meet them. The CIA's Milton Bearden told me it was impressive that they had been able to handle agents at all in Moscow, considering 'all the huge resources they [the KGB] put on to our people there'. In contrast, the British in Northern Ireland had multiple ways of meeting their enemy. Targets for recruitment could be arrested on a pretext and questioned at a police station or army barracks; meetings could also be arranged in cafés and pubs. If necessary, they could rendezvous in safe houses in rural areas, for example.

'There were always plenty of places to meet,' said one handler. In the north of the province, 'really you just had to get out of west Belfast [the stronghold of the IRA]. And even there you could walk and talk – there was plenty of through traffic.' The centre of Belfast was neutral and east Belfast was safe. The countryside was usually fine, except for South Armagh, which was known as 'bandit country'. There, there were 'only natives and strangers'. Everyone was noticed and 'it was hands on your weapons at all times'. In that case, the only safe way to talk to someone was to arrest them.

Just meeting the FRU was enough to compromise someone like Steak Knife. When recruiting a source, said handlers, there was no need to ram the point home. As the colonial saying goes, 'Softly, softly, catchee monkey.'

One recruiter said, 'You basically have to be a good listener. You have to come at what you want at a tangent. To talk away normally and then throw something into the hat. You have to lead them down the path.' Though a study of weaknesses would be useful to identify a source and develop a strategy, they would not necessarily be exploited overtly; sometimes they were never discussed. You had to be subtle. 'You even don't want them to say, "I want to work for you." You want them to see it's a natural path. Once they agree to meet you away from their routine, then you are halfway there. They understand the consequences. And you don't want to remind them what they are doing.'

Implicit blackmail or outright bribery was for the low-rent end of spy recruitment. The FRU tried to pride itself on paying out almost derisory low sums: 'If someone has a weakness, you want to come as their saviour; you are their new best friend who can help them overcome it. We don't say to them, "You should do this because of this and that." There is a lot of subtext; there is a lot of they know you know they know . . . but it's never discussed.'

Ultimately, things probably worked out because Steak Knife and his handlers just clicked. As someone well informed said, 'They have to like you. Steak Knife liked football; he liked drinking; he liked music. His handlers liked football, drinking and music too.'

What makes a good recruitment? No two cases were alike with either recruits or agents. But in the course of interviews conducted over more than two decades I did come to see that the image of how people became spies was frequently mistaken. Fiction has the spymaster as a cold and pitiless creature, but the recruiters from secret services I have met – and who have had, in the view of their peers, the most success – were quite the reverse. And many of them insisted that the best spies signed up for the sake of a simple thing: friendship.

One of my first such lessons came from a surprising quarter: East Germany's state security ministry, the Stasi. Despite its oppressive and blunt efforts at domestic surveillance, the Stasi had a nimble and efficient foreign service, the HVA, which was led by a man with the justified reputation as a master spy, Markus Wolf.

My experience of Wolf's service started in 2000 when, as a foreign correspondent for the *Sunday Times*, I was working in Berlin with a colleague and friend, an American writer called John Goetz. We were trying to identify the people behind a list of 100 code names we had received of those who spied for the Stasi in Britain.[6] We laboured over our detective puzzle, working through intelligence reports marked '*Streng Geheim*' (Top Secret) and plotting a matrix of which individuals could have gleaned such information. And by chatting to some of the former star performers of East German intelligence in summer beer gardens, we received a brief course in the art – or sales pitch – of betrayal.

It was true that some spies were recruited through coercion. Indeed, Wolf was famous for his 'Romeos', the sex spies who lured their adversaries into compromising situations. It was true too that there were sad cases, like the lecturers at certain British universities who still bought into the ideology. But by and large, said the former recruiters, a spy was seduced by a long process which, at its core, was the simple act of making friends with someone.

'I can think of no useful spy who was not the result of a genuine friendship,' said one Stasi officer we met.

He had identified the core issue about recruitment that concerns us. A country could always try to get spies by offering huge bags of money as a reward, and sometimes this did work, but such spies were intrinsically less reliable. But if this Stasi officer was right and friendship was the key, to establish that level of trust takes time. A recruiter would need to spend time with the would-be spy, creating bonds from shared experiences – a day drinking or visiting a show or taking a holiday together – which ultimately made him part of the other person's life. And then, regardless of political views, human nature might just stoke up the empathy needed to persuade that person to help his friend by crossing the line and betraying his country.

'The best way to recruit someone was through friendship, through a common understanding,' said another old Stasi man, who was based in London and whose code name was Eckhart. 'Recruitment is a process that takes a long time. Some people would slowly realize I was from the intelligence services. And if they continued contact with me, then I knew I could start the work.'

I heard further echoes of this theory – and its implications for the spies that a democratic society needs – when I interviewed one of the CIA's famed recruiters, a man well known in the business for having done that rare thing of convincing a Soviet diplomat to become a US agent. At first the CIA man was as tight as a clamshell. I provoked him by suggesting spying was mostly a failure and the CIA little more than an expensive programme to handle walk-ins. At this, he grew loquacious, while still insisting that his name should not be used. Let us call him 'Frank'.

'We had ways of working. It was a process and you couldn't just walk up and make an offer to a guy.' Patience with that long game seemed to be dying out, said Frank, and this is where his words carried weight. Spy agencies act on orders from political authority, and when the politicians lack statesmanship, not knowing when to act and when not to, they can handcuff the agencies. If, spurred on by pressure from a twenty-four-hour media for instant action, a government lacks strategic patience, its secret service loses tactical patience, the sort of patience required to make good recruitments. As Frank saw it, American politicians in the twenty-first century, particularly after the attacks of 11 September, had become unable to give the art of intelligence a chance. They grasped at immediate responses (such as invading Afghanistan) because they were in a rush, even if, as happened in Afghanistan, it took a decade to get out again.

In the long game that worked, said Frank, he, the recruiter, had been the point man, handling the crucial one-on-one relationship. But, contrary to the popular image, this had been a team game, with tremendous research and support from his station (the local CIA team) and from headquarters in Virginia. 'They might spot the nuances that you didn't see.' Even the most casual-looking moves were pre-planned. 'I talked it over with my boss: is he leading me along? They did detailed homework.'

Prospective spies were called 'developmentals'. They were considered 'projects' and great effort was put into thinking about how to persuade them across the line and become recruits. Only a few very rare types in the CIA could recruit through 'sheer force of will', by sitting down with someone and persuading them with unassailable arguments that betrayal was the right option.

A person needed a good reason to spy. 'There has to be a hook,' said Frank. Money worked, but 'mainly as lubrication'. There were people persuaded by noble causes, where the spying was idealistic and the recruiter could even convince them that it was 'all in the service of democracy'. But that was largely 'bullshit', he said. As another CIA veteran put it, 'Ideology basically went out in the 1930s.' What really worked was much simpler: having that 'incredibly close personal relationship with someone'. Without the skills to make those friendships, 'you are not going to succeed'.

And then you had to twist the friendship, said Frank, which was perhaps the hardest thing to live with: your interest was rarely pure. Somehow, at that point, you needed to 'pop the question', to let the person realize that you had wanted him all along for a specific role: to be your spy. You also needed a cold place inside yourself to retreat to. You had to remain independent. It was a crime in the CIA to 'fall in love' with your source, to lose objectivity, to be the one who was being played. 'At some point you have to be willing to manipulate a friendship. Not every guy can do this. It doesn't make you a great person. It's not necessarily going to make you the happiest person in the world.'

Spying was dangerous and the recruiter was potentially leading his new friend to his death. 'You are fucking with people's lives. You have a moral responsibility to these people. Then, at some point, you would have to hand them off, to a new case officer. I worried constantly about recruiting someone and turning that agent over to someone else. It's like giving a kid away,' said Frank. But he did it anyway. That was the job. And he had made sure his agents knew what they were getting into.

Steak Knife's handlers agreed that recruitment was friendship with that twist. 'They are or become your friends, but it is also something a bit one-sided. You are never going to invite them to Special Forces dinners or tell them about your girlfriend or your real life.' A handler could establish a very personal relationship with his agent, but there was an element of acting. The handler needed to preserve some separation.

The skilful bit of counterterrorist spycraft in the 1970s, 1980s and 1990s was not just signing up recruits but also steering their terrorist careers towards a useful position within an organization. In the case of Steak Knife, he was helped and persuaded to regain his confidence and ascend the IRA's ranks again. He ended up as second-in-command of the IRA's counterintelligence wing, charged with hunting the very sort of 'touts' (traitors) that he himself had become. Also known as the 'nutting squad', the unit was notorious for the kneecappings and other punishments handed out to traitors.

It was a promising place to be. Close to the IRA's leadership, he could be a sounding board for their fears and doubts, and – even if he was involved in the brutal treatment of traitors – he would not be directly involved in any terrorist attack. His role was also self-protective: he would be among the first to hear about fears of a mole in their ranks.

According to someone involved, one such occasion came in 1984. Michael Bettany, an MI5 officer, had been caught trying to sell secrets to the Soviet Embassy in London. Sentenced to jail for breaching the Official Secrets Act, he was carelessly held on remand in Wandsworth Prison alongside an IRA prisoner, Pat Magee, who was accused of planting the Brighton Bomb. Bettany had served extensively in Northern Ireland and, although he regretted it later and told MI5 what he had done, he approached Magee in the prison chapel and could not resist passing on details of the British agents he knew in the IRA. Magee in turn passed those details on to a prison visitor.

Among the leaks were details about Steak Knife himself. Luckily for him, it was Steak Knife who was handed this information and he was able to suppress it. But other sources were blown by Bettany's betrayal. Among them was Willie Carlin, agent for both MI5 and later the FRU. He was a former British Army non-commissioned officer from Londonderry. When he retired from the army, he volunteered for an intelligence mission and was sent back to get close to Martin McGuinness, then the IRA leader in the city and a member of the four-man leadership of the Northern Command. Carlin's penetration – under the code name 3007 and then Fox – was so successful that he went on to be selected as a candidate for Sinn Féin in council elections. He told the FRU he had become so involved he even helped Sinn Féin organize the rigging of elections. But, after Bettany's betrayal, Carlin had to be resettled.[7]

Steak Knife's role was a deep secret but, under the rules of police primacy, the FRU had to inform the RUC about him, and even let senior RUC officers know his identity. 'The secret was supposed to stay only with the head of the RUC's Special Branch, but of course it percolated down,' said one FRU handler. And however secret Steak Knife was supposed to be, his status did not give him a 'get out of jail' card.

At one point Steak Knife and his 'security squad' detained a suspected traitor. They blindfolded him, but the prisoner recognized Steak Knife's voice. Able to escape and jump out of a window, the man ran to a police station and accused Steak Knife of the abduction. Now a wanted man, Steak Knife fled across the border into the Republic.

During his time on the run – or 'OTR' as it was called – Steak Knife could not understand why the FRU were unable to get the RUC to drop its charges. 'He thought we were gods, untouchables,' said one insider. The truth was, even if they could have intervened, they did not want to. A spell of OTR did wonders for Steak Knife's credibility within the IRA and he also picked up wonderful intelligence from the South. (For the FRU, it meant hair-raising meetings with their agent in 'bandit country' near the border, as FRU officers were not authorized to operate in the Republic.)

The charges against Steak Knife, which were eventually dropped, illustrated the hardest part of running an agent like him: namely, how to prevent him being complicit in crime.

When Steak Knife's alleged identity as Scappaticci was first revealed, two sources went public with details of his spying. One was Peter Keeley, a retired soldier and former FRU agent who used the name 'Kevin Fulton'. The other was a disaffected former FRU member, Ian Hurst, who used the name 'Martin Ingram'. Neither had been a case officer or been even remotely involved with Steak Knife, but, from their work with the FRU, both had picked up some details of the case. Both alleged that Steak Knife had been allowed to participate in serious crimes.

In his account of the case, Hurst wrote:

> It is a fact of life that no informant inside any paramilitary organization could possibly get to the heart of that organization without committing criminal offences, and this is where the agencies who employ such inform-ants walk a fine line. They have to ask themselves how far they can allow such agents to go, and when does the cost become too much.[8]

According to Keeley, a Catholic from Newry, the British had to allow Steak Knife to take part in not only the kneecapping and torture of alleged IRA traitors, but also the murder of several of them. Keeley said Steak Knife also had advance knowledge of, and did nothing to forestall, a plot to ambush and kill two senior RUC officers on the border.

Once a soldier with the Royal Irish Rangers, Keeley had returned to civilian life and infiltrated the IRA himself, working over the years for the FRU, the RUC, British customs and MI5. He alleged the British issued instructions for their agents to take part in attacks to maintain cover: 'My handlers told me to do anything to win their confidence. That's what I did. My brief was that if I got into a situation where I couldn't get to my handlers but if I had to break the law, I was to try not to take a life.'[9]

The intelligence services had a strategy to mitigate the dangers, but Fulton said it did not always work:

> I was to shoot high or blow up a bomb prematurely. But that isn't always possible. If I f***ed up all the time, then the IRA would shoot me. Don't forget I also ran the risk of getting shot by the army and the police. I mixed explosives and I helped develop new types of bombs. I moved weapons. If you ask me, 'Did I kill anyone?' then I will say 'no'. But if you ask me if the materials I handled killed anyone, then I will have to say that some of the things I helped develop did kill. I reiterate, my handlers knew everything I

did. I was never told not to do something that was discussed. How can you pretend to be a terrorist and not act like one? You can't. You've got to do what they do. The people I was with were hard-hitters. They did a lot of murders. If I couldn't be any good to them, then I was no use to the army either. I had to do what the man standing next to me did.[10]

Keeley had his grudges and some unanswered questions remain about parts of his account. In 2013, an Irish judge, Peter Smithwick, who led an inquiry into the murder of two RUC officers and collusion allegations surrounding it, found him to be a 'very impressive and credible witness' whose 'evidence was truthful'.[11] However, others have concluded that Keeley changed his stories too frequently.

From what I learned from several interviews with people involved in espionage in Northern Ireland, the idea that the security services deliberately allowed the IRA to murder someone to protect a source in place was inconceivable. Did they allow agents to commit other crimes short of murder? Certainly. The police and intelligence operatives in Ulster even had a term for crimes they permitted: 'freebies'. And might things have gone tragically wrong sometimes? It was possible, even probable.

The issues involved were legal, practical and moral. In the 1970s and 1980s, UK law had no provision to allow an agent to commit any crime. They might turn a blind eye, but they could not sanction it. In practical terms, it was also dangerous. If an agent became involved in plotting a murder, he might himself get killed or arrested, rendering him useless. And then there were the ethics, probably the most powerful factor. No one in the British Army or RUC had any wish to be involved in anything that could lead to the murder of a fellow soldier or policeman, and even less in the killing of an innocent bystander. This was a war fought on home turf and it would have seemed unconscionable to have been involved in the killing of a comrade or neighbour. 'That would be the most horrendous thing. You cannot imagine how abhorrent that would have seemed,' said someone closely involved.

To avoid such killings, the UK put in place a sophisticated strategy, one that has often been significantly underplayed due to the sensitivity at the time of the tactics and technology involved. It involved tracking and disarming illicit bombs and firearms, as well as covert communications with agents to deal with emergencies.

The standard first tactic was to make a bomb non-functional and harmless. Special teams of covert bomb disposal technicians, controlled by MI5, would break into a home or weapons cache and tamper with the devices. If a bomb later failed to detonate it would raise little suspicion – after all, most of the IRA's devices were home-made and errors were expected.

For the sake of security, sometimes even the agents themselves had no knowledge of what had been done. They might have thought the British callous, because they did not know the secret actions being taken to mitigate the danger. 'There were agents who thought we were allowing them to plant a bomb, not knowing that we had secretly made it ineffective,' said a former bomb technician who was attached to MI5.

Although he was no longer a member of an ASU and therefore not required by the IRA to handle guns or bombs, Steak Knife often reported on the location of weapons caches or plans to mount an attack. Following such reports, guns were often secretly removed and fired at an army range so as to collect the weapon's ballistic signature. (This would be used later to work out if they were involved in any attack.)

Some rifles were also fitted with tracking devices, in a process known to insiders as 'jarking'. This was an effective and, in its time, highly advanced way of protecting Steak Knife and other agents. If the British came and seized the guns, they risked exposing the informer. But if the guns were tracked onwards through several hands, then they could be seized to prevent their use but no one would be sure who had tipped off the army.

For use in an emergency, if he was ever called to commit a murder or serious crime, Steak Knife was also issued with another clever little spy gadget. This was what they called a 'sick pill'. It looked like an ordinary aspirin and could be easily concealed. If swallowed, it would send you retching uncontrollably into the toilet. No sane terrorist would want you joining them on a mission in that state.

As a final resort, Steak Knife also had a panic button: a secret switch inside an ordinary-looking household radio in his family kitchen that would summon assistance from the army.

Despite all those measures, did the FRU avoid involvement in murder in the Steak Knife case and others? The full truth will probably never be known. While the army did what it could to save lives, agents also put their own lives on the line. For the sake of survival, as they juggled the different rules of the two worlds they lived in, there were probably plenty of crimes that agents never told their handlers about. As one former RUC officer said, 'Do you think an agent is not smart enough to realize there are things he should not share with his handler? There were times when it was in both their interests to keep quiet.'

Martin McGartland was an informer recruited by the RUC Special Branch who became an IRA volunteer. He later recounted the multiple ways his handlers helped him to thwart attacks, including impregnating Semtex bombs with special chemicals to stop them exploding.[12] However, he is an agent who has openly stated that he was forced to be complicit in the murder in east Belfast of a British parachute regiment soldier, Private Tony Harrison. It was not always possible to stop the commission of a crime.

> I knew then that I was driving to the home of a soldier whom they intended to shoot in cold blood. I wondered what I should do; I wondered if there was anything that I could now do to save the man's life. As we drove along, I prayed that Felix [cover name for his RUC handler] had been able to trace the man and have him moved from the house, but he had told me nothing of the soldier since we had first checked out the area a month before. I debated whether I should try any trick, like stalling the car or crashing it into a vehicle, as if by accident . . . I wound down the car window so that I would hear if any shots were fired. I prayed that I would hear nothing. I waited what seemed an age, but it was probably less than 60 seconds. Then I heard the shots – one, two, three, four, five – I counted them, and knew in my heart that some poor bastard had been murdered in cold blood.[13]

McGartland's loyalties were clear. He and the FRU did all they could to thwart the IRA. But elsewhere there was evidence of much greater ambivalence by the security forces when they dealt with Protestant paramilitary groups, those who had declared loyalty to the Crown, even as they were prepared to countenance nakedly sectarian murders of Catholics. As later official inquiries were to uncover, a minority of agent runners in both the RUC and the FRU had colluded in the murder of prominent Republican figures.

The danger with such conclusions – whether true or false – is that they mask the success of other FRU operations and all the lives they protected, both Catholic and Protestant. According to those most closely involved,

Steak Knife helped to foil dozens of attacks and arranged the seizure of many weapons, saving dozens of lives.

For years, Steak Knife was the rock star of Northern Irish spies. And when his existence was finally revealed, his former handlers asked why it had taken so long. After all, his identity had become far too well known in law enforcement circles for his own safety.

In the 1980s, the FRU had a special 'HQ detachment' at army head-quarters in Lisburn. It answered directly to and worked closely with the director of intelligence, the Assistant Secretary Political (ASP), who was normally from MI5. The FRU was based in a Portakabin known as 'the rat hole' and almost its entire purpose was to handle Steak Knife.

Over time, Steak Knife extended his circle. He befriended most of the IRA's leadership, certainly those in Belfast. They would drive around town chatting, not knowing that behind his car stereo was a sophisticated bug-ging device, recording every word. Steak Knife's tapes of senior IRA commanders talking in his car would become an essential showpiece of a secret tour of army headquarters that was laid on for a visiting prime min-ister or for Whitehall officials with the highest of clearances. 'Steak Knife was recruited for tactical intelligence, but over time his value became stra-tegic,' concluded one insider.

Once, when Steak Knife wanted to buy a new car, technicians from MI5 – known to the FRU for some long-forgotten reason as 'the wasters' – tried to remove the existing bug. Unfortunately, it fell down inside the chassis. To avoid its discovery, the entire car was blown up at an army range. Steak Knife was driven out to watch and was even allowed to press the detonator.

After a while, it became clear what was happening. Of the key motives for spying, 'love of the game' had taken over. 'He loved the buzz and the deceit, the intrigue, the thought of knowing something that no one else knew.'

It was said later that Steak Knife had been motivated by money, but that seems unlikely. He was paid around £300 for a meeting, said one insider. 'We used to see him about every ten or fifteen days, so maybe he got about £10,000 a year. It was hardly a fortune. He didn't do it for money. He just got to love the thrill of it.'

Contrary to honour and the rules, rival British intelligence agencies often tried to lure Steak Knife away from the FRU by offering him more money. In one case, he recounted, the RUC, who often arrested him, offered him over £250,000. But, like many Republicans, Steak Knife saw the army, as represented by the FRU, as inherently more reliable than the RUC. He said he wouldn't work for the police – or 'the peelers', as he and other Republicans called them – or even for SIS.

Though he found it thrilling, sometimes the pressure of living on the edge got to Steak Knife. That was why, at one point, the army sent its top general in Northern Ireland, Major-General John Wilsey, for a secret thirty-minute meeting in a car park to thank and reassure him. But living a dangerous lie for years on end was exhausting, so much so that those who knew him would say that when the conflict officially ended Steak Knife was almost a broken man.

In what was probably the climax of the FRU's operations in the mid-1980s, some of its key players crossed paths.

Steak Knife, as part of his Republican existence, was represented, like many other IRA members, by a feisty Belfast lawyer named Patrick Finucane. While he was on the run, he used to call Finucane regularly, anxiously hoping to hear that the charges against him had been dropped and he could come home. As revealed by British phone taps, Finucane's main concern when talking to Steak Knife, who used to call from phone boxes in the Republic, was how long it would be before Steak Knife could return and fix the tiles in the lawyer's bathroom (as part of his regular job as a builder, he had decorated Finucane's house).

At the time, the FRU was also running another agent, Brian Nelson, who had manoeuvred to become chief of intelligence for the largest Loyalist terror group, the Ulster Defence Association (UDA). In his position, Nelson could save lives, helping the army tip off people – mostly Catholics – whom the UDA planned to assassinate. But it emerged later that Nelson also played a more sinister role, using his contacts with the FRU not only to pass on intelligence but also to gather it for the UDA and its attacks.

In 1989, Finucane, then aged thirty-nine, was murdered at home in front of his wife and three children, who hid under the dinner table. And it was not long before suspicion grew that Nelson had both known about the plan to kill him and helped to advance it. An agent working for the RUC Special Branch had also, it turned out, provided information about the threat to Finucane. This was much worse than McGartland's account, and, by going along with crimes he could not prevent, Nelson was allegedly instigating murder.

From Finucane's death sprang a series of official inquiries, including three by police chief constable Sir John (later Lord) Stevens – latterly commissioner of the Metropolitan Police – which, over the course of more than two decades, gradually uncovered a picture of collaboration between Protestant murder gangs and elements of the British security forces. The inquiries also made public the hitherto secret existence of the FRU.

The Finucane case illustrated the extreme dangers of running agents inside terror gangs. As the third Stevens Inquiry of 2003 concluded, 'informants and agents were allowed to operate without effective control and to participate in terrorist crimes'.[14] A Canadian judge, Peter Cory, who reviewed the Finucane case among others, said it was 'an indication that both the Security Service [MI5] and RUC SB [Special Branch] saw agent security as taking precedence over the need to warn a targeted individual that his life was at risk'.[15] And finally, in 2011, an investigation by a leading British criminal barrister, Sir Desmond de Silva, QC, into the Finucane case blamed 'agents of the state' but stopped short of accusing the British government of planning Finucane's death. He found 'there was a wilful and abject failure by successive governments to provide the clear policy and legal framework necessary for agent-handling operations to take place effectively within the law'. The prime minister, David Cameron, recognized the gravity of the case and apologized for 'the shocking levels of State collusion' that de Silva detailed.[16]

Another of the FRU's top sources in the 1980s had the code name Melodius. His real name was Frank Hegarty and he lived on the Bogside, the Catholic enclave in Londonderry. Like Steak Knife, he was recruited by the FRU after they learned he was a man slighted. He had been sacked by Martin McGuinness as the local IRA quartermaster – essentially the man who looked after supplies of weapons and bombs. McGuinness, who was highly moralistic about sexual matters, had disapproved when Hegarty left his wife for his mistress.

With coaching from the FRU, Hegarty began to regain the IRA's confidence and, after a while, he resumed his former role. It was from this position that, in January 1986, he alerted the British to a large shipment of arms that had arrived from Colonel Gaddafi's Libya and was stored in three separate hides in the Irish Republic.

The shipment was so large, it was impossible to use the army's usual tactic of tracking the guns through several hands before their seizure. There were too many guns to keep track of and the risk was high that some would be lost. Instead, Hegarty was removed for his safety out of Northern Ireland and resettled in Sittingbourne, Kent. Unfortunately, he left most of his family behind and he could not resist calling them repeatedly.

According to one FRU insider, an MI5 phone tap picked up a record of Martin McGuinness, then a senior IRA commander, urging him to come home. 'It became a famous tape. "Come back, you will be safe," he said.' This was echoed by the firebrand Protestant leader the Reverend Ian Paisley, who said that McGuinness had visited Hegarty's mother. 'He assured the mother, Rose, that if Frank came home, he could sort the matter out and all would be well,' Paisley told the House of Commons. It was 'a firm assurance for a mother's heart torn about her son. She persuaded her boy to come home. A rendezvous was arranged by Mr. McGuinness.'[17]

On 25 May, a few days after Hegarty had slipped back into Northern Ireland, his body was found dumped by the roadside. His eyes were taped and he had been shot several times. Two days later the *Irish News* reported, 'Most people who knew of his disappearance were baffled by his decision to return home to Derry three weeks ago, despite knowing that the IRA suspected that he had been involved in the Sligo and Roscommon arms find.'[18]

McGuinness has always denied any role in the killing. In fact by then, he has said, he had left the IRA. He once told the *Irish Times* it was incorrect that he had told anyone it was safe for Hegarty to return:

'That is not true, and the Hegarty family know that. I could articulate . . . exactly what happened, but if I did that it would be very hurtful and indeed very damaging to the Hegarty family,' he said. He claimed one member of the family knew what had happened, 'and I am not going to put that person in a predicament'. Speaking generally about his past, Mr McGuinness said people in Northern Ireland were not 'obsessed by any of this'. He added: 'The reality is that the past is a very, very dark place for everybody.'[19]

In 1993, ITV's *Cook Report* investigated the Hegarty murder as part of a wider look at McGuinness's past. After the broadcast they got a phone call from a Freddie Scappaticci, the man later identified as Steak Knife. In a conversation recorded by the journalists, and not published until years later, Scappaticci said that McGuinness had both lured Hegarty home and been 'the instrument of him being taken away and shot'. He went on, 'He is ruthless. I can say this unequivocally. He has the final say on an informer, whether that person lives or dies . . . Hegarty was an affront. He [McGuinness] took it very personally . . . There is something quite wrong with his head . . . He would be praying in chapel one minute, go outside and think nothing about ordering a shooting.'

The reporter asked how he knew so much.

'Well, I was at the heart of things for a long time, right?'

Scappaticci said he had served in the Northern Command, like McGuinness.[20] He also said 'a friend of mine' was supposed to interrogate Hegarty, but McGuinness and two others had interrogated him instead and then McGuinness had ordered him shot dead.

If Scappaticci really was Steak Knife and really was an FRU agent, then the 'friend' who nearly interrogated Hegarty, his fellow FRU agent, was perhaps Scappaticci himself. It is easy to see why the incident might have affected him so deeply.

After he was named in the press as Steak Knife, Scappaticci was asked about the *Cook Report* tapes. He said he had not realized he was being recorded. 'In relation to the contents, you have to understand that when I spoke to the journalists, I had been out of the movement for about three years. I felt disillusioned and it's fair to say that I left on bad terms. A lot of what I said was untrue . . .'[21]

By the 1990s MI5 had taken over the handling of Steak Knife from the FRU. It was obvious that his handlers had not approved his approach to ITV. At the request of MI5, who told the *Cook Report* that Scappaticci was a valuable informer, the tape was never broadcast and lay buried for ten years, until the Steak Knife story emerged elsewhere.

While British operations in Northern Ireland may prove the value of human intelligence and provide a model for how spies can be recruited against terrorists, those wishing to apply the lessons elsewhere should realize, first, how spying almost always worked in combination with some form of technical intelligence and, second, how spying was a sword whose blade came to be blunted over time.

Some of the technical methods used to support spying have been mentioned already. Together with tips from agents, the British were forewarned about numerous ambushes and bombs, and, with advance knowledge, were able to defuse bombs and arrest perpetrators. But technical methods also played a major role in suppressing attacks for which the spies had given no warning: for example, the invention of electronic jamming devices played a significant part in reducing remote-controlled bombs.

Spying's impact became blunted because spying was a victim of its own success. 'It was like a soup of spies. So many agencies, so many agents. They were tripping over each other constantly,' said one ex-FRU member.

Giving evidence in Parliament, Lord Stevens described how things had got out of hand: 'When you talk about intelligence, of the 210 people we [the inquiry team] arrested, only three were not agents. Some of them were agents for all of those ... particular organizations [the RUC, MI5 and the army], fighting against each other, doing things and making a large sum of money, which was all against the public interest and creating mayhem in Northern Ireland.'[22]

Many people used contacts with the British security services to their own advantage. In the case of men like Nelson, it was to collude in crime. But there were also positive purposes. The secret contact between the IRA leadership and SIS provided a channel that was ultimately used to hasten the peace process. But this was not spying. The IRA members involved – and the go-between, a businessman – were intelligence contacts, but they were not 'agents' – those who betrayed any secrets.

There were many blurred relationships. Liam Clarke, a veteran journalist in Northern Ireland, explained how the term 'agent' came to mean different things:

Martin McGartland, who infiltrated the IRA in west Belfast, was an agent in the purest sense. He joined the IRA at the request of his handlers and did exactly what he was told; it involved no switch of loyalties.

Several members of the IRA's internal security team, like Steak Knife, were double-agents. They were trusted by the IRA to frustrate Crown forces, but were 'doubled' by the intelligence services to spy on the IRA, instead.

After that, it gets more complicated. It is clear now that many of those who passed information to the authorities believed they were in charge of the relationship and didn't tell all they knew. Many 'worked their passage' with the police, passing on this and that in return for favours, to settle grudges or to save their life. They may not have thought of themselves as agents at all, especially the loyalists.[23]

A conflict, particularly a long-drawn-out civil war, is like an ecosystem: nothing can be seen in isolation and nothing is of itself decisive. Spying can help to suppress one group, but over time the group targeted by intelligence, whether consciously or subconsciously, evolves defence mechanisms. (For example, by a form of Darwinian 'natural selection', the weakest and easily targeted PIRA members would tend to die or be arrested, while the most security-conscious and secretive PIRA operatives would tend to survive and rise in the organization.) Steak Knife – and even Brian Nelson – probably on balance saved many dozens of innocent lives, even if, as some argue, they also cost the lives of others. I am aware that there were other significant agents in Northern Ireland – people of equal importance to Steak Knife whose existence may never be revealed. They too saved lives. But their success also gradually modified the enemy's behaviour. Even with superb intelligence penetration at the highest level, the tight cell-based structure the IRA could develop meant that the detail of most attacks was not known in advance. And, as Clarke says, whether it was the money-motivated street source or the sophisticated leader seeking political options, few spies were pure agents delivering a simple one-way flow of intelligence.

I was discussing Margaret Thatcher's campaign of ambushing the IRA with a former FRU officer. It was called, rather misleadingly, a 'shoot to kill' policy – misleading because soldiers usually shoot to kill. It was a euphemism for what was alleged to be an assassination programme.

I suggested that, viewed thirty years later, in a world in which terrorist leaders were routinely killed by robotic drones, the startling thing was that there really had been no 'shoot to kill'. Few senior leaders of the IRA were targeted at all.

'But you know why,' he said.

'Rule of law. It would have been illegal,' I replied.

'Yes. There's that. But something else too. You know it already.'

'Our penetration of the leadership?'

'You can't imagine it, how far it went.' Having implied that the level of penetration gave the leadership protection, he added, 'But then the question was always: who was working for whom, which way round it was?'

We talked about names; some of them surprised me.

'If we were so successful, why did the war go on so long?' I asked.

'Like I said,' the old agent-runner retorted, and perhaps he was just in a particularly dark mood, 'I cannot be entirely sure. The question was: who was working for whom?'

Spying then, even for those privy to its secrets, does not lend itself to a clear and unambiguous picture. There are many variables and those involved harbour many doubts. But, for all that, not everything is grey and uncertain. Looking through the mists of spying, it is possible to discern something of the shape of the thing.

While we have seen elsewhere that veteran intelligence officers have real doubts about what good spying achieves, Ulster showed that, against the threat of terrorism, spying is not only possible but vital. There were compromises and dangers, and they needed careful thought; some things were handled incorrectly, even criminally, but ultimately the overall effort had impact.

If it had not been for British intelligence and traitors among Irish Republicans, British rule in Ulster would have come to an earlier end, overwhelmed by the sheer ruthlessness and professionalism of what the Provisional IRA became. The underlying problems were political; spying did not solve anything. But it did suppress the revolt.

From the war in Ireland, we learned the kinds of lessons about spying often unlearned in much of the Cold War spy game. It was a master class in targeted recruitment and engineered betrayal. Success here was one of the reasons that, after the debacle of Philby's betrayal, British intelligence re-earned its reputation for high-quality HUMINT.

From Ireland, we also learned that money can buy spies. Some in Ulster swore by it. In fact, there are recruiters who insist everyone has a price. 'It is amazing what people will do for cash,' said one ex-RUC operative. But we should also remember that handling the best of spies, using them in a meaningful way, almost always involves much more delicate things, including the art of friendship, which has to be patiently exploited. Throughout Steak Knife's career, his intelligence was brought to the attention of politicians at the top of the UK government. The key lesson for politicians was not to interfere. Any attempt to hasten his rise through IRA ranks or make him spy more aggressively could have been fatal.

★

As the Berlin Wall came down, ending the Cold War, and as peace came to Ulster, the lessons learned from spying against the Soviets and non-state groups like the IRA needed to be applied and adapted to a whole new set of threats and enemies.

As James Woolsey, in his confirmation hearing for the post of CIA director in 1993, warned, 'We have slain a large dragon, but we now live in a jungle filled with a bewildering variety of poisonous snakes. And in many ways, the dragon was easier to keep track of.'[24]

In this new jungle, new spies needed to be recruited and old tactics adapted. But the lessons of the past remained as relevant as ever, even if they were sometimes ignored.

PART TWO

New Spies (1989–2008)

Chapter 4
Thunderbolt

'The Cold War is over: the most dangerous threat to a nation's security
comes from organized crime. What matters is using
intelligence to crack the criminal at source'

– Raymond Kendall, secretary-general of Interpol, June 1996[1]

On 4 October 1955, in the Troodos Mountains in Cyprus, a young man
crouched, limbs aching, on a treetop branch of a thick-limbed Turkish
pine. He had been there two hours, his face covered with a mask. He was
watching a path that led to a bungalow nestled up in the hills. Just before
6 p.m., he heard the cough and stutter of an ageing Land Rover. It wound
up the zigzags to the hilltop. The boy reached for his rifle as the car
crunched in the gravel.

In the driver's seat was Stanley Hollowday, the 52-year-old chief engineer of an open-cast asbestos mine on the terraces of the opposite hill.
Sitting next to him was his wife, Zanina. They had married twenty-seven
years earlier in the local village, Amiantos.

Hollowday had forgotten to buy the newspaper that day and the couple
had driven down to collect one. Stepping out of the car, Zanina recalled,
they 'walked to the edge of our garden to admire just a few minutes of the
glorious sunset, in front of us a sky aflame and its reflection gilding below
us in the valleys and hills. So beautiful and so still!'[2]

Then she heard the outburst of the 'horrid noise of gunfire, its echo
surrounding us from all sides'. It was impossible to pinpoint where it came
from. Their Alsatian dog, Ranny, was crouched at Zanina's feet. She called
out, 'Let us go in, Stan, we seem to have trouble again in the village.'

But Stan did not reply. Zanina called again and stretched out her arm to
him. There was a bush between them and she was surprised not to see his
head and shoulders. She heard him whisper, 'I can't Yana. I have been hit.'

She saw him on the ground, two feet away. There was no blood. He said, 'Phone, call the ambulance and police, open my collar and tie.'[3]

The youngster in the tree who pulled the trigger was a Greek Cypriot called Andrew (or Andreas) Antoniades. These were the early days of civil war between the British rulers of Cyprus and the rebel group called EOKA. The rebels believed that Hollowday was an undercover 'chief of intelligence' who was helping to get their members arrested.[4] According to the *Cyprus Mail*, he was the first civilian British victim of an EOKA attack.

At different times, the young Antoniades was a petty criminal, a terrorist, a man who shot at British soldiers and planted bombs. He also became a nightclub host, a gambler, a fixer of sports matches and a gangster. He was shot on a number of occasions, including in the head, and survived. He also became a spy. The one-time hit man who fired at Stanley Hollowday would go on to work undercover for decades as a secret agent for Her Majesty.

Antoniades came to exemplify the New Spy – the sort of person who became a top priority once the secret services turned their attentions away from their old Cold War adversaries and governments woke up to the dangers of a more open world where money, people and therefore crime could move more freely.

Although Antoniades worked briefly for the CIA, he was a very different spy from those the agency had employed to collect military and political information. He would spy on organized crime, and his case reveals both what can be achieved by using one gangster to catch another and also the pitfalls involved when the world of espionage comes up against the chaotic, violent and unfamiliar criminal mind. Finally, it also provides some clues as to the wider role that spies in the criminal world might play in reporting on those who have come to be seen as the biggest modern threat: terrorist groups.

To some in the British state, Antoniades was one of the best spies they ever had in the criminal underworld. To others, he was a simple rogue who hoodwinked them all and became one of the country's top drug importers.

From the beginning in Cyprus, he had an angry nickname: Keravnos, which means Black Lightning or Thunderbolt. When I met him, he was eighty-three years old and still as angry as ever. 'I will kill them all,' he said of his enemies.

*

Snitch, snout, tout, informer, grass, sneak, stool pigeon, double-crosser, canary, nark, rat, squealer, turncoat, weasel: criminals use many words to describe those who betray them. The British police came to prefer civil service jargon. In their world, a spy was called a covert human intelligence source or CHIS.

Law enforcement – whether police or national agencies such as the customs or National Crime Agency – has always had its own sorts of spies. As the saying goes, there is no honour among thieves, and as criminal organizations struggle to control a larger share of territory and illicit earnings, tipping off the cops has always been part of the game. But those called informers by the police were usually a different breed of people from those defined as secret agents or spies by secret services.

Some of the difference was in the language. Policemen and spymasters used different terms. In 'spy-speak', an informer was often a mere tipster, someone who sold titbits of information, as opposed to an agent, whose activities were more closely directed. A former senior French counter-intelligence officer put it like this: 'In our work an agent is at a much higher level than an informant. An informant gives you local information and points out targets. Then you can send in an agent and he'll make contacts and work his way up.' But in other secret services, the terms were not so tightly defined. One former head of CIA covert operations said that 'source', 'informer' and 'agent' were used interchangeably. Some were just more reliable and more under control than others.

A bigger difference was that while the police in most countries both needed and had the legal authority to pay active criminals to be their sources, most secret services were barred or, as a matter of good practice, simply shunned contact with criminals. Working with criminals was seen as too risky because they were deemed unreliable and likely to reveal secrets. Such work could bring the agencies into disrepute or, when their agents got into trouble, draw them into revealing their hand in a courtroom. As part of its covert attempts to overthrow Cuban leader Fidel Castro, the CIA made contact with several members of the US Mafia. This revelation dogged the agency for years, illustrating the cost of such relationships. In all, then, police informers were usually a different breed from the people recruited by secret services as agents.

As the twenty-first century approached, however, some of these distinctions were challenged as the lines between policeman and intelligence officer started to be blurred. One impetus was the growing political power of gangsters. Several leaders of organized crime had reached such power-ful and influential positions in their countries that it became of strategic value to infiltrate their circles. One example is Russia, where in the 1990s barely disguised mobsters became billionaires and began to wield huge influence in the Kremlin.

But the biggest driver of this blurring of the lines came in domestic pol-itics with a push to use intelligence tactics to reduce crime on the streets of America and Europe. It was a two-pronged assault: the secret services were redirected towards crime fighting, and law enforcement tried to emulate them.

The collapse of the Iron Curtain and international agreements to liber-alize trade helped to free up the movement of people and goods across borders and, as a by-product, also let well-organized criminals like drug smugglers roam freely and establish allies or branches of their gangs in other countries. And drug addiction – fuelled by this illegal international drugs trade – was commonly held to be behind most burglaries and rob-beries in the US and Britain. These patterns led influential people in law enforcement to argue that effective action against crime in local commu-nities meant taking the battle to the ringleaders of the trade. Raymond Kendall, secretary-general of the international police agency Interpol, urged 'using intelligence to crack the criminal at source'.

Kendall and others argued that the tried-and-tested methods of solving crimes were failing to catch the most serious offenders, particularly those who operated across borders, as well as gangsters at the top of large crim-inal empires who let their henchmen do their dirty work. The solution was to use more aggressive methods: proactively targeting criminals by tapping their telephones, bugging their cars and homes, putting them under surveillance, recruiting spies within their gangs and networks, and introducing undercover operatives to collect evidence and mount sting operations.

Law enforcement called these tactics 'intelligence-led policing' and both police and customs units created new departments devoted to intelligence collection and covert operations. But such theories were also sweet music to agencies like SIS, MI5 and the CIA: assisting the police or customs by taking on an anti-criminal caseload was a way of staying in business in the absence of the Soviet threat. When talking to the press and lobbying politicians, intelligence officers floated the theory that spying on gangland might be at the heart of a new form of espionage.

Getting involved in crime fighting meant, for example, MI5 sharing some of the technology they had developed against the Russians: helping to install covert bugs to listen in on a drug dealer's conversations, electronic surveillance to watch his every move or computer analysis to map out his network of contacts. It meant SIS (which established an 'organized crime operations group') offering techniques of 'disruption', covert actions like emptying a criminal's foreign bank account or liaising with foreign agencies to raid drug factories.

The new role for SIS required a change in the law, which took place in 1994. Its role was now defined as being not only to protect national security and the economy but also to act 'in support of the prevention or detection of serious crime'.[5] Within two years, other legislation was amended to give MI5 the same tasks.

There were some fundamental cultural clashes that took years to resolve. Intelligence officers, for instance, had little experience of the process of bringing their targets to justice in a courtroom. 'They couldn't really get their heads round it. I had to explain our world, working towards evidence and court cases,' said one former customs officer. As for MI5, 'They were terrified of courts. They didn't altogether understand why you had to finish up before a judge.'

In the years ahead, MI5 surveillance officers became accustomed to appearing in court to give evidence. But a more delicate problem for the new crime fighters was how or if to deploy secret agents in the criminal underworld. While it was obvious that a spy inside an organized crime group could be invaluable, recruiting or deploying such agents meant dealing with thorny questions that secret services had rarely had to think about before, such as how a court would react to the presence of a government-employed agent inside a gang. Would they have to disclose the presence of that agent to lawyers defending a criminal? Or would the agent be considered a provocateur that had instigated the crime? These questions were just as challenging for the police and customs, as they too began to make more use of human intelligence. The increased use of intelligence methods in law enforcement came at a time when, in Western legal systems, judges in criminal cases were requiring prosecutors to disclose more details of any undercover work used during an investigation to lawyers for a criminal defendant. This would require careful handling.

In the past, secret services like SIS and the CIA had shied away from recruiting criminals. They were dangerous, unreliable and their mindset was just too different. As they pitched to get involved in crime fighting, intelligence officers tried to think laterally. They suggested hiring people on the edge of gangs who might be more reliable and who could avoid participating in the crimes, such as the girlfriends of gangsters, or their accountants, or shopkeepers who sold them mobile phones. Another option for police and law enforcement was to expand their army of professional undercover operatives – policemen or customs officers who lived under an assumed identity, organized sting operations and could then testify against criminals in court. Peripheral agents and undercover operatives were tried out, but, as when confronting any serious adversary, sometimes only a real insider, a trusted member of the gang who was privy to secrets, would really do as an agent. As both intelligence agencies and law enforcement sought to expand their ways of gathering human intelligence, they needed to ask whether it was possible to handle spies among criminals when the danger was the operation could backfire, particularly in a courtroom. But while working with criminals might be unpalatable for most intelligence officers, they had to work with the intelligence targets they were given by governments. As non-state groups, whether crime gangs or terrorists, began to be designated the new threat and the new main target, would men like Keravnos turn out to be the spies they needed?

To rely on such men was to enter a violent and chaotic world.

Andrew Antoniades might be unknown in the wider world, but under his nickname Keravnos in his native Cyprus he is both legendary and unforgiven by many. The only thing that seems to divide some old comrades is whether or not he had always planned to betray them. Some even wonder if, should he return, it is not too late to kill him in revenge.

Antoniades was born in 1932 in Foini (also spelled Phini), a village about fifteen miles north-west of Limassol, one of six children. His father died when he was five years old and he left school early to become an apprentice tailor. By all accounts, he was the classic tearaway, often in trouble with the police. His greatest love was motorbikes. One day he was arrested by police after climbing down the chimney to burgle a house. One of the police officers asked him to fix his bike, but after he had done so Antoniades jumped on it and roared off, crashing through the gate. The policeman said he sped away 'like black lightning' – which is how he earned the name Keravnos.

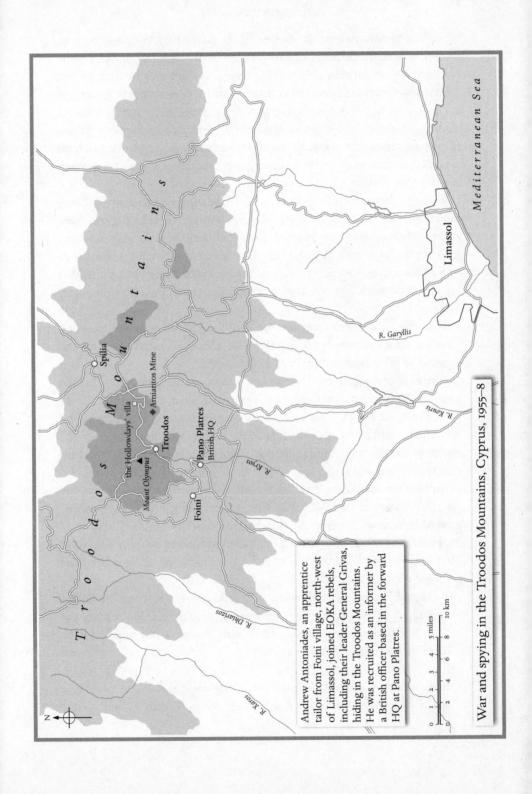

Mediterranean Sea

Limassol

T r o o d o s *M o u n t a i n s*

Spilia

Amiantos Mine

the Hollowdays' villa

◆ Troodos

▲ Mount Olympus

Pano Platres
British HQ

Foini

R. Garyllis

R. Kouris

R. Kryos

R. Dhiarizos

R. Xeros

N

Andrew Antoniades, an apprentice
tailor from Foini village, north-west
of Limassol, joined EOKA rebels,
including their leader General Grivas,
hiding in the Troodos Mountains.
He was recruited as an informer by
a British officer based in the forward
HQ at Pano Platres.

0   1   2   3   4   5 miles

0   2   4   6   8   10 km

War and spying in the Troodos Mountains, Cyprus, 1955–8

He was twenty-two when the war broke out in 1955. Fighting the British Army was the Ethnikí Orgánosis Kipriakoú Agónos (EOKA) – the National Organization of Cypriot Struggle. Its aim was to eject British colonial forces and to unite the country with Greece. A total of 371 British soldiers died, but over the course of four years EOKA – led by General Georgios Grivas – proved equally ruthless when killing Cypriots. While EOKA recorded that 108 of its members had died, it also claimed to have executed some ninety 'traitors' among over 200 Greek Cypriots who perished in the violence.

Joining a secret society such as EOKA was supposed to involve a long initiation, but Antoniades simply forced his way in. He and his friend Alexandros Michaelides, code-named Koungas, headed into the hills and started planting Greek flags high in the trees near the Amiantos mine. It was a provocation certain to draw the attention of British troops. EOKA fighters, who were hiding nearby, were afraid it exposed them to discovery and capture.

'The choice was to co-opt him or to kill him,' said Renos Kyriakides, then the area commander for EOKA. He chose to co-opt the pair, and they swore allegiance to the rebels before a priest.

The first thing Antoniades was ordered to do as a fledgling EOKA member, he recalled, was to plant a bomb in Akrotiri, a town with a large British base. 'Then they sent me to shoot somebody, a Greek man who was supposed to be an informant, and I did it.' He also joined a raid on the explosive store at the Amiantos mine. Then he volunteered for the mission to kill Hollowday.

Antoniades said he received orders directly from General Grivas. He was to go with his pal Koungas. He remembered Hollowday's whitewashed bungalow as being surrounded by a fence, with a dog and noisy ducks running about inside. The plan was to get there early and lie in wait. They hoped to shoot him when he returned at dusk, meaning it would be getting dark as they escaped.

Remarkably, Zanina Hollowday already knew much about the young Antoniades who was on his way to try to kill her husband. In the diary she kept of her time in Cyprus, she wrote how that very day she had been warned he was in the neighbourhood:

In the morning our good gardener told me the feared guerrilla 'black lightning' [Keravnos] was once more in Amiantos. He worked on his own, used arms, terrified the villagers, stole, set fire to houses, and gloried in his evil deeds . . . Nobody dared to spy on him. It was said it was he who killed our policeman. Only recently was he discharged from prison . . . He was barely twenty-two, slim, small in build, and very agile. We did not like having him in our neighbourhood.[6]

The EOKA duo crept up behind the compound about 4 p.m. Antoniades recalled he had a Swedish sub-machine gun. 'Hollowday stopped the car and he came out. He was a big man. I could see him from here. Next I shot him. Maybe six bullets.' Hollowday fell. Antoniades dropped down from the tree and fled.

Barely three months later the British employed Antoniades. It happened in the classic way that spies in rebel groups are recruited, while he was under arrest. After a series of what the British called 'sweeping operations' through the Troodos Mountains, many EOKA fighters had joined up with their leader, General Grivas, in a hideout above the village of Spilia. When the British attacked Spilia on 12 December, some remained and fought, while most of the group split. Many returned to hideouts near their own villages. Antoniades returned to Foini, but, after staging a lone attack on a British patrol, he was captured again.

He was now in the hands of what he remembered as a Scottish regiment of the British Army, whose crude interrogation methods were freshly honed from fighting Mau Mau rebels in Kenya. 'They break my teeth. You know these Scottish. They beat me up for two days.' He said it was not the beating that made him change his allegiance, but a friendship he struck up in the cells with a young Englishman. Lionel Savery was a 27-year-old army captain who was already a veteran of another insurgency in Malaya. He had been posted as a district intelligence officer to Pano Platres, about two miles from Foini. The pair forged an immediate and lifelong bond.

Antoniades was allowed to escape, jumping into a van that came to collect the prison dustbins – 'They arranged it for me,' he said – and, back in EOKA, he set to work as an informer. Years later, when I interviewed him, Antoniades was still coy about how far he had gone in helping the British. Wary of being labelled a traitor, he suggested that he had been working for both sides, keeping his British handlers happy but inflicting no harm on EOKA. 'I was stuck in the middle,' he said. (To some Cypriots, that would merely make him a double traitor.)

During this time, he and Savery grew closer. The defining moment came in 1957, when they went out on a patrol to hunt EOKA and were ambushed. One Englishman was shot dead and Savery, who was on a hit list drawn up by Grivas, took several bullets in his leg. Antoniades and another man dragged him to safety. It was about the best decision he made in his life. 'After that we became very close. I had saved his life and because of that he saved mine.' Savery himself was awarded a Military Cross for the incident.[7]

Antoniades, now openly working with the British, became one of EOKA's prime targets. They tried to kill him three times, including in two roadside ambushes. One would-be assassin found him in a café in the village square. 'I felt someone touch me in the back . . . then, bang, he shot me in the head. He dropped the gun and I saw him run. I recognized him – he was my second cousin.' Antoniades later showed me the scars on the back of his neck. The bullet just missed an artery and came out through his mouth. 'It was a million to one.'

It was clear that Antoniades needed to be extracted, so Savery arranged for him to obtain a British passport and a plane ticket to London. He was waving goodbye to his life as an informer against terrorists and beginning a new one as a renowned criminal. But it was not the end of his spying.

Antoniades arrived in England on 29 November 1958. The army had rented a house for him in Wembley, but even before he arrived he got into a fight in the West End. And so it continued. Within a year he was in court at the Old Bailey, accused and then convicted of organizing a drive-by shooting that wounded a Greek café owner in Camden, north London, with a volley from a sub-machine gun. At his trial, Captain Savery gave evidence to defend his former agent's character and explain the dangerous work he had done previously. *The Times* reported that Savery 'agreed that Cypriots who were loyal British subjects might well have been described as traitors by other Cypriots in Britain'.[8]

This was just the beginning of more than two decades of life as a gangster, punctuated by spells in prison and efforts by Savery, who remained in touch, to keep him out. At different times, Antoniades ran two casinos in London, was involved in multiple shootings and stabbings, and fought street battles with, among others, infamous gangland rivals Charlie and Reggie Kray. He tried to fix horse races, staged a diamond robbery in Antwerp, staged another robbery in Greece (where he also foiled an assassination attempt) and smuggled cigarettes to Italy and Spain, where he was arrested and jailed again.

Antoniades's reputation as Keravnos always both dogged and elevated him. Cypriots in London at first spread the word that he was a grass. When challenged, he would respond with violence. 'When you know two or three fat bastards are wandering around Soho saying, "Andrew is an informant, Andrew is this and that", then – fuck off – then I had to put them right, these people. I had to fight.' He talked with ease of glassing someone with an ashtray, stabbing another with a knife that broke inside the man's arm, beating up someone 'very badly'. Always making money; always losing it.

There were many, many criminal adventures. Things came to a head in the early 1980s in Spain, with Antoniades in jail once more and his old friend Savery again giving evidence in court about his good character. 'We were close friends. He knows I love him and he loves me,' recalled Antoniades. When Savery was out in Spain, they got chatting and a new idea took shape. It so happened that among his different criminal escapades, Antoniades had never been involved in drug trafficking; meeting heroin addicts in hospital had turned him against it, he claimed. Now Savery devised a plan using Antoniades's criminal reputation as a front for an undercover role fighting the drugs trade, and in particular the Turkish-Kurdish gangs then taking over the supply of heroin into Britain.

It was the start of Antoniades's second career as a spy. 'I said if I come to London I can kill these fucking Turkish. I know them and they listen to me.' There was one problem: he had too many enemies back in England. But, he said, Savery told him he could be protected. 'If you help us, somebody will help you.' He brought out to Spain a senior officer from customs who made the arrangements.

The game began the day he returned to London. He was sitting in a restaurant in Streatham, south London, with a customs officer. As he remembered it, someone recognized him.

'Welcome, Keravnos. How are you?'

'Good.'

'I've some people here from Liverpool. They want to do some business.'

The people were drug dealers, who told them of a Pakistani who wanted to sell fifty kilos of heroin.

'I said if it's good, we accept,' recalled Antoniades.

The very next day he was led to the Pakistani's house and found the drugs, which were then all seized by customs.

From then on, and for the next twenty years, he was registered as an official informant, initially under the code name Mario. 'I did a couple of hundred jobs for customs. I did it because I hate heroin.' He was also paid a lot of money.

His method of working was to make people believe that he was a ready buyer for their drugs. He played on his reputation as the untouchable and on his years spent in the underworld. Who would believe he was playing for the other side?

A Pakistani barrister once approached him via a friend and said, 'I've got some heroin arriving. Can you sell it?'

Antoniades replied, 'No problem. That's my business.'

The heroin was due to arrive at Heathrow Airport in two days. Antoniades went to the airport on the appointed day with the barrister and they waited in a nearby hotel. The barrister told him that his friend – a steward on an incoming Pakistan Airlines flight – would call them when he got through immigration and customs controls with the drugs 'and we will collect it'.

Meanwhile, Antoniades had passed on the flight number and the name of the steward to Nick Baker, a senior customs officer who had become his handler. Antoniades recalled that Baker had taken thirty or forty customs officers and surrounded the plane. They searched the PIA plane and found no heroin or anything illegal. The steward himself was also questioned and searched, but had to be released. After a few hours of this fruitless search, Baker phoned and said, 'Andrew, we look stupid.' But Antoniades replied, 'It's not possible. The man is with me.'

He spoke to the barrister and asked him to call his friend, the steward, and find out the reason for the hold-up. 'He rang and the man said, "I already am in the hotel in room 346."'

No one ever explained how the heroin had made it through the customs net – one possibility was that it had been smuggled in catering trollies. But it had now reached the hotel and the steward said to come and collect it. Antoniades went to the toilet in the hotel room and, from there, called Baker on his mobile phone to tell him it was in room 346.

Customs officers rushed over and raided the room and found a Pakistani – and the heroin. Meanwhile, the barrister had told Antoniades,

'Let's go and get it.' But when they got to the hotel door they looked through and saw a young Pakistani man in handcuffs. Antoniades explained, 'We said, "Oh, my God, let's run away." So we left. He didn't suspect me because I'm good at acting.'

There were numerous other cases. Antoniades reeled them off, even though his memory played tricks with some of the details: two tonnes of hashish seized in Canada via a tip-off to the US Drug Enforcement Agency; fifty kilos of heroin found in Streatham; more in Brixton; a big haul in Maida Vale; twenty kilos in a BMW at Dover; the time when he was sent by customs to pretend to buy drugs in Germany; and an operation in Liverpool when many kilos of heroin were concealed inside steel tubes. It was an impressive list and one that some of his former handlers in customs confirmed in outline, even if, because of their enduring duty to protect a source, they refused to discuss which exact cases he was involved with.

But there was another view of this work, a suggestion that he was cheating and dealing in drugs, among other things, himself. Just as a spy among terrorists might be tempted to get involved in operations to maintain his credibility and survive, so a spy among criminals might want to keep his hand in crime. But, whether a spy worked among terrorists or ordinary criminals, no spy handler had a licence to turn a blind eye to such conduct.

I had first heard the names Antoniades and Keravnos from the police. In the late 1990s, when I was writing about crime for the *Sunday Times*, certain policemen said they were convinced that he and some of the biggest drug dealers in Britain were getting extraordinary protection from Her Majesty's Customs & Excise.[9] They felt informants such as Antoniades were using their connections with law enforcement to cover their back, earn cash or eliminate the opposition, even as they continued their own life of crime. It was well known that drug dealers often informed on their rivals. Years before, one of the country's top customs officers had told me, 'There is no major drug dealer who isn't an informant.' But suggesting that these informants thereby got protection was another matter and much more serious.

It was not necessarily an outlandish idea. In the US, it eventually became clear that James 'Whitey' Bulger, a gangster who for decades from 1975 had served as an FBI informer, had used his protected informant status – passing on information about rival gangs – to get away with at least eleven murders. More than twelve FBI agents were found to have broken the rules in handling him, a federal judge ruled.[10]

Detective Inspector John Collins, a streetwise policeman of thirty years, was one of the critics. He had become convinced that some informants were not only receiving protection but also being allowed to commit crimes, including murder. He led a twelve-man drugs squad in north London in the 1990s and in one year they seized more than 100 kilos of heroin. With the help of authorized wire taps, he listened to the private conversations of some of the capital's biggest gangsters. However, as his small unit tried to move against the major players, he felt hidden resistance.

Collins was an expert on the police use of human intelligence against the underworld. His skill was reading people generally and the criminal mind in particular. I used to credit him with having the sort of X-ray spectacles once advertised in comic books. Walk on the street with him and he would casually point out a criminal team that might be mingling among the crowds, selling drugs or pickpocketing. He saw what normal people did not see.

Perhaps it was his background. Before becoming a policeman, he had been a taxi driver in south London and had grown up knowing the local gangs. In those days, part of the job of a taxi driver was to deliver bungs (bags of cash) to policemen in pubs. Once a policeman himself, Collins never worked the streets south of the river in London. He was too well known.

In 1999, after twenty-six years on the street, Collins started working at the National Criminal Intelligence Service (NCIS), an agency founded in 1992 to bring together the different crime-fighting agencies. It was located just across the railway track from the headquarters of SIS at Vauxhall Bridge. Collins was part of a special unit that gathered intelligence on heroin trafficking.

As the fight against top-level criminals became more organized in the 1990s, police and customs had created a shared computer system that NCIS hosted. When someone became a target for investigation by one unit, he was 'flagged' in that system so as to prevent another unit from pursuing the same target and spoiling the investigation. If a Mr Big was under long-term customs surveillance, for instance, with the objective of tracing his suppliers, it could wreck years of work if a police unit charged clumsily in and arrested him for a smaller offence.

With access now to more restricted information flows, Collins noticed that gangsters like Antoniades were being flagged for years in the computer as under active investigation by customs, but no criminal charges were ever brought against them. Collins would not comment on the specific intelligence files, but speaking in general he recalled it was apparent that some people labelled as major dealers were 'not worked on' by any investigating team. He said, 'You could draw the file out and see very quickly the guy was an informant. If the current intelligence is that the guy is a drug dealer in north London and [the file] didn't show me that they were being worked on, then it became obvious it was a false flag.'

Surely such false flags were a legitimate device to protect an informant?

'You won't get informants unless you protect them,' he agreed. But Antoniades and two others were the top 'three criminals who were running the drugs trade and had ownership of 80 per cent of the drugs trade in the UK at the time. If you protect those people to get information about the guys who are dealing with a kilo, it really doesn't make the system work.'

I had approached Collins for a comment after having been shown reports filed by NCIS that labelled Antoniades as a major dealer. One said he was 'suspected of being involved in organizing large shipments of heroin being imported into the UK by various methods'. Another said, 'This target arranges the importation and subsequent delivery of heroin across NE London.'

Interviewed after his retirement, Antoniades's former handler, Nick Baker, said the reports were false. They had been placed there on the computer – with the knowledge of Collins's boss at NCIS – as a smokescreen to protect an informer. As Antoniades himself said, 'Sometimes they put in the computer I am a dangerous drug dealer because they know some people are going to check.' Baker said that Collins was well-meaning but, for reasons of security, did not have access to the full picture. However, according to Baker, Collins's superiors at NCIS were fully informed that Antoniades was in fact not a drug dealer but a covert agent.

Collins, who still had his ear to the ground in north London, is convinced the reports were genuine and that Antoniades was a serious criminal. 'Intelligence suggested that he was trading big drugs. His favourite trick was to sell someone the heroin and then arrange for his heavies to go and steal the heroin off the guy he had sold it to. He had moved down to the south coast and the suggestion was that he was using boats to bring drugs in. We came up with the top ten criminals in the UK that were dealing in drugs whom no one had tried to arrest and Antoniades appeared on our list. It was quite obvious that he was a major player.'[11]

Collins saw all this as corruption. There was too much emphasis on targets for the numbers of tonnes of drugs seized each year. Informers were being used to organize big seizures, but the system was allowing the villains responsible to escape justice.

In 2001 Antoniades travelled to South Africa, where he was arrested on an old Greek warrant for drug trafficking. He talked his way out of it, but in June he was arrested again on the same Interpol warrant, this time in Germany. British customs officers were now forced to reveal their hand to protect their agent. On 31 July the Foreign Office sent a telegram to the British Embassy in Berlin. It ordered staff to 'press the case for Mr Antoniades' release immediately' with state and federal justice ministers. The man still flagged in national police computers as 'suspected of being involved in organizing large shipments of heroin' was being protected by the British government.

I was leaked the document:

CONFIDENTIAL
FM FCO TO IMMEDIATE BERLIN
TELNO 156 OF 311619Z JULY 01
AND TO IMMEDIATE FRANKFURT, ATHENS
INFO IMMEDIATE CUSTOMS AND EXCISE, ACTOR, WHIRL
INFO ROUTINE HOME OFFICE, NICOSIA, NCIS

YOUR TELNO 334

SUBJECT: ANTONIADES
Summary
Agree suggested lobbying action in your telno 334. Customs and Excise ready to fly in to support. Main line of argument – need to protect informants.

Detail
We agree that the Consul-General should meet the State Secretary to press the case for Mr Antoniades' release immediately.

The telegram – sent at the behest of customs – told diplomats in Germany to make the case that:

A public trial in Greece would reveal Mr Antoniades' long career as an informant for Customs and Excise (1987 to date) and put his life at risk from criminal elements . . . Most importantly, Mr Antoniades continues to be a vital informant. His continued extradition would prevent one current anti-drugs operation from proceeding. [. . .] Were Mr Antoniades sent to Greece to face trial, it would make recruitment of informants very difficult, and ultimately harm our collective efforts to stem the drugs trade.

The telegram mentioned a document prepared by Savery, Antoniades's old handler, about his 'earlier career', but said this should be kept in reserve. If necessary the document could be handed over, with a warning 'that a public trial might reveal this historical background thereby opening the possibility of an attempt on his life. So we would prefer to keep the Savery document in reserve.'

The message was signed in capitals – like all Foreign Office telegrams – with the Foreign Secretary's last name: 'STRAW'.

It was followed by a statement to the court from Nick Baker that testified that Antoniades, particularly between 1989 and 1992, had given 'extremely valuable intelligence in relation to heroin trafficking and was responsible for a number of high value seizures including the biggest ever seizure at the time'. That was a reference to a tip from Antoniades that led to the 1991 arrest of a Thai intelligence officer at Heathrow with forty-nine kilos of heroin.[12]

When he heard of the lobbying to free Antoniades, Collins was livid. 'I got information that senior customs officers were travelling to Germany to secure his release,' he said. 'I was shocked. I could not believe it. He was one of the top ten drug dealers in the UK . . . He had been on the periphery of lots of murders.' A meeting was called with customs at which, Collins recalled, the police were told that Antoniades 'had been the best informant customs ever had and what he had given the UK far exceeded the damage he had done'. Collins thought this was 'absolute rubbish'.

In Germany, the pressure worked and the court released Antoniades. But the intervention seemed premature. Under British rules, if informants wanted to avoid prosecution they needed strict approval in advance for committing a crime that was necessary to maintain their cover. Without such approval they had no protection from either prosecution or trial, and rightly so. They had no general licence to commit crime. If an informant was arrested and charged with breaking the law, unless their actions had been approved already, the informant's help to the authorities could only be taken as mitigation after his conviction: a judge could then secretly use this background as grounds for a more lenient sentence.[13] In the US, the FBI used a similar but more transparent system that gave informants a basis for committing minor crimes with approval from the Department of Justice. But the key point in both countries was that the crimes had already been approved. To run spies is to enter a grey zone, particularly when dealing with the criminal world. Compromises have to be made and interests weighed up. But a decision to sanction one crime to prevent another should not be made by the officers or even the agency that handles a particular agent; such waivers should be requested by a senior elected official or politician and signed off by someone independent, ideally a judge, who should also first make sure that he has all the evidence, approaching other agencies as necessary to ascertain how clean the agent really is.

By the early 2000s, Her Majesty's Customs – a British national institution established in 1203 by King John and pre-dating Parliament – was in turmoil. It had always had its oddities. At the old headquarters on the Thames, the investigative branch, which was known for its camaraderie and high jinks, was housed in a big hall known as the Long Room. According to several former officers, bottles of whisky were sometimes stashed in the drawers and they occasionally used to play a game called the 'Long Room steeple chase' which involved highly trained officers leaping from desk to desk without touching the floor.

However, the real issue was not oddities or jollities, but how customs handled its informers in the underworld. In particular, a series of convictions for smuggling and duty evasion were overturned because customs or its lawyers had concealed the fact that some of their star witnesses in court were also secretly employed as agents. There had also been a series of more straightforward blunders in agent handling. For years, customs had allowed some shipments of drugs to be brought from Pakistan into Britain by informers. These were so-called 'controlled deliveries', used to catch buyers in the act of handing over cash for the drugs. But in one disastrous case the drugs vanished on to the streets, making customs a supplier of heroin to criminals.

It was not that customs had a particular problem but rather that there was a sort of perfect storm brewing: just as intelligence activities were coming in for much higher scrutiny by the courts and the public, there was this push to deploy more covert agents in the risky criminal world. As part of their efforts to establish a new role after the Cold War, intelligence agencies had put themselves into the public domain. But, in both Europe and the US, this openness also triggered an unprecedented scrutiny of intelligence activities. The more experimental business of placing spies inside organized crime could not always bear such scrutiny. The final indignity for British customs was a corruption inquiry, ironically named Operation Virtue, launched by Thames Valley Police, one strand of which involved Antoniades and the men who handled his case.

By the early 2000s, Antoniades's value as an informant had diminished. The London crime scene had come to suspect who Antoniades was working for: when drug dealers were arrested, their defence lawyers demanded to know from prosecutors if he was involved in the case. Even if they were caught red-handed with drugs, they would claim that Antoniades had put them up to things.

In July 2002 there was a more serious incident. Chris Yakovidis, a businessman who had been arrested over an alleged £1.4 million VAT fraud, swore in a statement that he had paid a fee of over £250,000 to Antoniades to get himself cleared of the charges. He said Antoniades had promised to get it done using his contacts in customs. When the charges were not dropped, he decided to finger Antoniades.

The police suspected more than just fraud by Antoniades; they were concerned about serious corruption within customs. That summer Operation Virtue officers swooped in dawn raids, arresting both Nick Baker and Lionel Savery, Antoniades's long-term handlers. Baker, who had risen to become chief of customs' covert operations, was suspended from duty for several months, though he was later cleared of all suspicions, as were Savery and other customs officers. Antoniades, however, had been out of the country at the time and a police warrant was issued for his arrest. Until it was dropped, he declared he had no intention of returning.

Though the customs officers were cleared, their institution was dying. The main investigative branch of customs was wound up and folded into a new outfit, the Serious and Organized Crime Agency (SOCA), in which former or detached intelligence officers were placed in many leading roles. It was thought, perhaps, that those who had been supposedly trained in handling agents could do a better job of spying on criminals than police or customs had managed so far.

Baker, who retired soon after, had obviously been harmed by the police investigation, yet he remained sanguine. 'In this business, we level hard accusations against people. You have to expect people to throw accusations back, however baseless they may be,' he said.

Through it all, he remained loyal to his agent, Antoniades. I asked him if customs had really been so sure that Antoniades was not gaming the system and working both as a criminal and an informer. He replied that all kinds of checks were in place to stop that.

'We did use him to provide information, to identify targets,' Baker said, but after getting information on a drug dealer, for example, many other methods were used to double-check the tip. Other sources said extensive use was made of phone taps. Customs had more 'lines', as phone intercepts were called, than any other agency. Baker insisted that nothing they received from Antoniades was relied upon without verification; it was merely raw material that was checked and rechecked. As far as he was concerned, Antoniades had performed a vital service for British customs, achieving more than almost any other agent of theirs.

As for Antoniades, he always denied the accusations made by police that he remained criminally active. But, he revealed, he did play the system. He said that customs at first distrusted him and followed his every move, deploying people to track him and bugging his calls. 'Do you think they left me alone?' Later, though, things changed. 'In the end, they trust me fully. They let me do what I want.'

He had a network of people who supplied him with information (his 'sub-sources' in intelligence speak). He said that customs knew he 'made people believe' that if they gave him information he would not only pay them but, if they asked for help, he would give it. He tipped off some drug couriers to avoid arrest. Conversely, he said that he also issued threats, telling dealers, 'I know what you do. Give me some information or you are going to see problems.'

Over the years, he admitted that three people who had worked for him were killed by other criminals: 'Not because they were informants but because they were stupid.' His reputation also kept many of his other informers alive: 'They mentioned my name and said if you bother me I am going to call my friend Keravnos. When they mention my name people shut up, you understand?'

So, I asked, was he running a form of protection?

'Listen, my friend,' he said, 'people know me. They know I've been shot ten times and been in prison three times and still I'm here. They know this man is something.'

On Friday 11 February 2011 I got an email out of the blue. I was sitting in a hotel in Afghanistan. It was from Antoniades's stepson, Fahim.

> Dear Stephen
>
> A few years back you wrote about my father, Andreas Antoniades. He is now 80 and ready to talk about his past activities. If you are interested please get in touch.
>
> Many thanks, Fahim Antoniades

The message referred to an article I had written on Antoniades for the *Sunday Times*. Over lunch at a Mayfair restaurant, Fahim and his mother, Hafiza, Antoniades's wife, filled me in on their story. They revealed that Antoniades was in Tunisia, where he had gone to try to establish another casino. He could not return to London because there was still an arrest warrant from Thames Valley Police, from the team that had been investigating allegations of corruption at customs. Could I fly out and see him?

When I got to Tunisia, where the dictator, President Zine el Abidine Ben Ali, had just been toppled, it was clear that Antoniades was trapped. So many things seemed to be closing in on him. He was angry that after all these years he had no money and no pension. He couldn't come to Britain and no one in Britain would try to cut a deal with the police to negotiate his return. It all made him furious.

I began to research Antoniades's history as an informer, going back to his time with EOKA. In Cyprus, I met some of his old comrades – both those who despised him as a traitor and those who defended him. I also discovered the fate of Holloway, who, contrary to what Antoniades had thought all those years, had not died in the attack, but instead had been crippled by a bullet that pierced his spinal cord. He spent the rest of his days in a wheelchair, returning home to Lincolnshire and then dying in Portugal in 1967.[14] His wife, who died a few years later, left behind a beautiful account of their life among the pine and almond trees of Cyprus, which the couple's daughter-in-law kindly shared with me. I never met Lionel Savery. I left a couple of messages on his answer machine but then I heard, in April 2012, that he had died. A tribute in the *Daily Telegraph* testified to his 'dangerous life as an intelligence officer in Malaya and Cyprus'. After leaving the military, he had become a 'labour relations adviser' in the magazine industry. That sounded rather like the cover story of a spy to me. His wife, Marisa, also had connections to British intelligence, according to friends.

From Antoniades there were yet more tales of adventure. After his release in Germany, he started another secret venture: this time for the CIA. Hafiza was an Afghan and after the fall of the Taliban, using her contacts, he went into business helping the CIA to buy back weapons from the former anti-Soviet mujahideen warlords they had once supplied. The operation went well until, while he was away in Dubai, his British security guard, an ex-soldier, shot dead two Afghans in an unexplained struggle at a hotel. It was the end of another scheme – and a blow to Hafiza's hopes of returning to live in her country.

I had often wondered how much to believe Antoniades, even though I came to like him a great deal. I could verify his work as an informer: I had seen the documents and spoken to his handlers. But should I believe his protestations, despite what policemen such as Collins said, that he did not continue, on the side, to be a major criminal? As a writer, I always wanted to reach a conclusion, to come to some certainty about where the truth lay. But with him, just when I thought I had got the story straight, a little detail changed and somehow that provoked new doubts. But, from another angle, his ability to keep you guessing also indicated why he was so good, why he was such a survivor. When I asked him once what it took to be an informer, he suggested that the trick was fooling people. 'You have to be smart,' he said. An informer stayed alive only by using his wits to maintain an act. 'Because I have been an informant for twenty years and everybody thinks I was a drug dealer. Even now the police think I played a double game.' He had survived so long as an informer by deceiving people; he had the ability to talk his way out of any situation. But knowing he had the skill to betray others so well always left me with the nagging worry that I was being cheated too.

Back in England, Nick Baker still took phone calls from Antoniades and was there to help his former agent, or at least to do what he could from retirement. He always remained a believer. But that was his professional obligation, just as it was Savery's. 'It's like a marriage,' said Baker. 'When you recruit someone like this you are with them all your life, good and bad.'

As for most of the secret services, they moved on from such work. The priority of fighting crime kept them occupied for a few years, but only until something else appeared. By the late 1990s it was already becoming clear to some that a more pressing problem than drug dealing was on the horizon: they would be called upon to combat a terrifying new threat, an ultra-brutal form of terrorist who considered ordinary Westerners as justifiable targets, and aimed to instigate attacks wherever hundreds of civilians would be killed. But even as secret services turned their attentions to this threat, the deployment of spies in the criminal world did not end, and nor did the recruitment of criminals or ex-criminals as spies.

Despite some mistakes in the way his case had been handled, Antoniades had proved that agents could be used for successful operations against major criminals and drug gangs. But for secret services engaged in more sensitive spying work such as combating Islamist terror, he had some character traits that were less than ideal – or even positively dangerous. Antoniades had always been a flamboyant, larger than life person, with a strong sense of his own importance as a known figure in his community. This meant he could never blend into the shadows or ignore a slight; he was never going to be a subtle spy. Moreover, he was both incredibly generous and addicted to gambling, which meant that every penny he earned would be either given or frittered away. He would never retire gracefully and, all in all, was a security risk.

On the other hand, Antoniades's versatility, resourcefulness and willingness to work against any enemy were incredibly valuable qualities. As we shall see, agents with his kind of raw courage, combined with a tough background, proved to be among those able to be a 'man on the rock', an agent at the heart of a radical terror group.

Just as the Taliban, in their search for cash, had been willing to deal with Antoniades, almost any radical Islamist terror group – however pure and spiritual or political its motives – found people with criminal contacts immensely useful. Any serious campaign of violence required weapons and explosives, and help with illicit identity documents, cash and travel tickets. Frequently, the group also looked to a ready source of illicit income. All of these might draw the terrorists close to someone like Antoniades who knew this world, even if they had no motives in common. And, for the intelligence agency, Antoniades may have been chaotic but his principal motives – money, excitement and loyalty to his handlers – were much easier to deal with than those of a religious extremist.

Ex-criminals might make risky spies and were hardly agents of choice, but they would prove their value as New Spies.

It is so often the fate of secret agents that, long after they have completed all useful work, they never accept retirement and never accept that they have been well compensated. Worst of all are the agents once protected by defunct agencies whose legacy has few defenders.

Antoniades, despite it all, remains proud. But he is angry too. 'You believe one thing. I am eighty years of age. And I passed so many difficulties. The only people who beat me up are the British when they arrested me. No gangster punched me or gave me black eye. Strong people came to see me and left with broken noses or cut eyes. I had to fight every day in London but I wasn't touched.'

How much had he done for Britain and how much had Britain done for him?

'I was with them thirty years. Now they throw me into the street. No pension. No money. I am just like a dog. I helped the Americans too in Afghanistan. Now like a dog. They chew the lemon and then spit it out.'

Chapter 5
Jihad

'The reason we didn't prevent 9/11 is simple: neither the CIA nor
its intelligence allies, Western or Muslim, had a spy or an
informant inside al-Qaeda's command structure'

– Michael Scheuer, former head of the Osama bin Laden unit, CIA[1]

It was close to the last time to do some shopping before the start of the
holy month of Ramadan; the streets of Algiers were full of people stock-
ing up on supplies. At around 3.20 p.m. on 30 January 1995 terror struck,
transforming the busy thoroughfare into a scene of bloody twisted carn-
age. A car packed with more than 220 pounds of explosives, driven by
what the security forces called a 'volunteer of death', was detonated in
front of a bank and close to police headquarters. Forty-two people were
killed.

The horrific brutality of the attack caused consternation. It was blamed
on a group known as the Armed Islamic Group (GIA), the breakaway
military wing of Algeria's Islamic Salvation Front, a movement that had
been banned after almost winning a national election.

Algeria's ruler, President Liamine Zeroual, reiterated his intention to
hold presidential elections that year despite the violence and opposition
from all main political parties, including the now-outlawed fundamentalist movement. He vowed to 'fight terrorism until it is eradicated'. In
Washington, the White House issued a statement from President Clinton
condemning the 'senseless terror' that 'cannot be excused or justified'.

Across the border in neighbouring Morocco, one man knew a secret
that, if disclosed, could have made all that rhetoric seem hollow. While
employed as an agent for the French secret service, the Direction Générale de la Sécurité Extérieure (DGSE), he had, just days before, driven a
carload of explosives and weapons from Belgium, through France and

Spain, to North Africa. He was a member of a GIA cell in Brussels and the weapons were for the GIA in Algeria. He had not imagined the purpose of the shipment, but he seemed to have supplied the very explosives used in the Algiers bomb. 'It was obvious for me it was mine,' he said later of the explosion. He had done the smuggling 'to convince them that I am one of them, to spy more deeply on them. I am risking my life there.'[2]

I will refer to this Moroccan as Omar Nasiri, a pseudonym he later chose. His employer, the DGSE, had once planted and detonated a bomb on the Greenpeace ship *Rainbow Warrior* in a harbour in New Zealand, killing a photographer. The agency had a ruthless reputation – which was why Nasiri chose to work for it.

Nasiri, whose job for the GIA was to buy and traffic arms from criminals, had contacted the French several months earlier. Like many potential agents, he had believed the fiction about spying and overestimated the importance of what he knew. He had hoped to pass on his secrets in return for a huge reward, for protection and a new identity. But the French valued his position above his knowledge. They asked him to stay in the group and find out more.

As he began to spy, he faced the classic dilemma of all spies active inside a gang of murderers. In both the old and new worlds of espionage, such issues were always present, but now they would become even more significant. The GIA was not a political group or government agency plotting only mild evil; these men were the authors of massacres. The danger for an agent was not so much how to get inside such a group but how to stay in it. Could or should innocent lives be lost to save other lives? Officially, among Western secret services, the answer was always a firm no. But was that really the way things worked? Did they evade the dilemma by keeping their agents at arm's length? This was the same question the British had faced in Northern Ireland, but, given the Islamists' callousness about taking innocent lives, the problem was more acute.

Intelligence agencies have come up with plenty of tactics for spying on people who plot to kill without having their agents commit murder. Spymasters try to recruit, say, a terrorist's girlfriend or driver, not a fellow gunslinger. But someone like Nasiri, close to the inner circle of a terror cell, was always a tantalizing prospect.

Nasiri's story is not typical. Intelligence services normally run a mile from someone as self-willed and unpredictable as he was. 'If you have to deal with a difficult agent, it is with fear and trepidation and with a gun in your pocket,' as one former senior CIA officer said. Nasiri, I discovered, was a case study in conflicted loyalties. Given how far he ventured into the world of jihadism, and his candour about his own mentality, it did illustrate the special challenges of penetrating the modern Islamist terror group, of finding someone able to go deep inside and possibly disappear for months who you could also trust to come back and not kill you. Sometimes the 'man on the rock' was the man you did not want.

Secret agents themselves can sometimes live in denial – a psychological concept meaning that they refuse to confront or even acknowledge something difficult or painful. Among agents, the difficulty is their conflicted role within the group they have penetrated: on the one hand, trying to support the group in order to avoid being exposed and stay alive, and on the other, trying secretly to defeat the group. Nasiri's way of dealing with this dilemma at the time of the Algiers bomb was to brush it aside. He had both a thick skin and other priorities. Recalling the event years later, he said, 'I was mainly concerned with not getting caught – and getting hold of hash.'³ Of the bombing, he said he felt no guilt. He had needed to establish his cover story. He had also said before, 'I have no conception of damage. I have no conception of killing. I have no conception of responsibility.'⁴ But this was a sensitive subject to recall. As the years passed, he would give different answers about that bomb, some of them contradictory.

On Christmas Eve 1994, while Nasiri was still in Belgium and a few weeks before the Algiers bomb blast, a plane was hijacked at Marseilles airport. Special forces stormed the plane in a gun battle. Again, Nasiri had wondered if the weapons involved had come from him. 'I saw the bullet going off from the Kalashnikov and I thought this is my bullet, the one I buy,' he said.⁵

This incident, he claimed, had affected him deeply. The Brussels gang had sat around and gloated as they listened to a tape of the fighting inside the plane. The hijackers had wanted to blow it up over Paris in a giant fireball – with materials that Nasiri feared he had supplied. As he wrote:

Everything on the tape was horrible. It was the first time I truly felt how close I was to all this horror. I know I could have thought about it earlier, but I'd chosen not to. I bought the guns for Yasin [a friend and member of the GIA cell] because it was exciting; because I needed the money . . . Everything was different now. The people on the plane were real to me . . . The GIA had tried to kill them all. It was horrifying to me, and when I heard the tape, I knew I was connected to it. I hadn't pulled the trigger, but maybe I had supplied the guns and the bullets. I was a killer, just like them.[6]

But, he explained later, it was important to realize he was not against killing. He was not bothered in the least by attacks on the repressive Algerian government or Western forces like the French that interfered. But he did object to the GIA's tactics of killing other Muslims: 'They were killing other Muslims inside Algeria and that's the biggest reason I went to the French Consulate. I was ready to die to stop them because I felt myself part of the killing.'[7]

On a cold, grey day in May 2013, I was sitting on a bench outside Cologne's cathedral by the Rhine, waiting to meet Nasiri. It was a public holiday, the feast of the Blessed Sacrament, Corpus Christi. High above, deep-throated bells were tolling in the soot-stained Gothic spires – the second tallest in the world. A crowd thronged the cobbled square to watch a long procession of worshippers that paraded through the cathedral's thick wooden doors and sang hymns. It felt like a scene from a *Godfather* movie, before the massacre.

I saw him strolling up to me. It was nearly twenty years since he had become a spy and Nasiri was now about fifty years old, with a slightly squeaky voice. He had supposedly retired long ago from his intelligence work. As he said, 'I am still without a job.' He did have some employment, but he obviously could not stop thinking about the world of radicalism that had been his life. He was keen to explain to me the mentality of the militants. He still followed it all; he was still absorbed by the Islamist mindset.

He talked about the ongoing civil war in Syria and Jabhat al-Nusra, an Islamist faction that was loyal to al-Qaeda and had just been designated a terrorist group. He presciently thought the Islamists would soon predominate among the rebels. 'Does it shock you to know that I would go and fight with them tomorrow if I had the chance?' he asked.

I had wanted to meet Nasiri because he came closer than anyone that I have heard about to being that 'man on the rock' the former senior CIA operative had spoken of – the spy who could have sat next to Osama bin Laden and known his thoughts and plans. He had written a book, *Inside the Global Jihad*, about his time spying inside the training camps that had come to be associated with al-Qaeda. He had met some of its key figures – even before the organization had begun to call itself al-Qaeda. Nasiri was another of the New Spies – the breed of agent hired post-Cold War to be pitted against the new enemies that had emerged in the 1990s, such as the modern Islamist terror group. Though it had been years since he had worked as a spy, he still had the habits of someone who had worked with intelligence agencies. He referred to them, as insiders did, as the 'services'. He insisted on walking and talking, constantly moving from place to place as if still trying to dodge surveillance. He insisted that I did not publish the name that his handler from the DGSE had used, even though it was certainly a pseudonym. He had made the man a promise, even if he now disliked him. 'If you make zigzags with your word, you have no chance to meet someone again.'

Among the secret services, Nasiri had always attracted mixed views. His work as an undercover arms dealer helped the French and Belgian authorities to capture an Algerian terror cell active in Brussels. Later, after a trip to the mountains of the Hindu Kush, he had helped reveal what was happening in secret military training camps in Afghanistan. He then moved to London and reported for both the French and Britain's MI5 on the radicals who were sheltering there. But though Nasiri appeared to be a cool operator, he clashed repeatedly with French and British spymasters.

Finally, he would part company with the secret services, after a breakdown of trust. He was a free thinker. He constantly resisted control. His obstinate behaviour underscored another of spying's dilemmas, because while such a self-willed agent presented a risk for the agencies, equally his resolve helped to push him further and explained why – even when subject to hostile suspicions – he could hold his ground and worm his way deep into the terror gangs. A case officer would always need to assess the value of someone such as Nasiri against the risk he posed of, say, making their operations public. Really, said insiders, no two cases were ever alike.

He was obviously hard work. As we talked, strolling round down by the Rhine and through the rambling streets of the old town, he described his meetings with the British secret services. They had been pressing him on whether he was being truthful about something.

'You want to talk to me about the truth?' he remembered asking an MI5 officer, 'Daniel', on one such occasion. 'And you want to pretend that you are not lying to me even now? You are from a lying profession that tells lies constantly. You lie even to your wife. Can you go into the street and say who you are? Of course not. So why talk to me about the truth?'

The British officer, he said, had just shrugged his shoulders in frustration. That was how MI5 remembered him: as a bit of a handful.

Fighting terrorism was hardly something new for secret intelligence agencies. For the New Spies it just became a more important pursuit. In different countries, secret services have a history of suppressing terror cells (and in some places sponsoring them as a covert instrument of state power). As they reinvented themselves after the Cold War, and tried to protect their budgets, agencies across the West diverted more effort and resources into collecting secret intelligence on and disrupting terrorist groups. This new work was often in support of the police: for example, as intelligence agencies assisted with recruiting street-level informers and targeting suspects with surveillance, raids and arrests. But it could also mean taking covert measures to try to disrupt the terrorists' plans and run secret agents inside their groups.

Although countries like Britain and France had had years of counter-terror experience, they like others were slow to adapt to the new threat.

On the British mainland, intelligence work against the IRA had been led by Scotland Yard's Special Branch. MI5 took charge only in 1992, after the end of communism. MI5 had already established a counterterrorism branch in 1984 and it had had some success: for example, interdicting arms shipments from Libya to the Provisional IRA. But with its background as a counterintelligence and vetting agency, MI5 had far less experience than SIS or even the British Army in running live agents, and still less running them inside a violent terror gang. It was used to playing a game as different as chess is to poker. Until after the Cold War, MI5 had been little more than a 'collating agency', according to one former SIS officer. 'They never used to run agents. It was only to meet some secretary from the Communist Party of Great Britain in the park.' He added, 'We [SIS] got all the bright guys. They couldn't get anyone from the fast stream. But now it's different.'

Apart from general inexperience, by the early 1990s MI5 had been making a successful transition from a mainly anti-subversive agency to the lead anti-terrorist organization. But the intense focus on Northern Ireland made it slow to appreciate the new Islamist threat. As the MI5 official historian, Professor Christopher Andrew, noted:

> For most of the 1990s the Service believed that the main terrorist threat to Britain, apart from the Provisional IRA, came from Middle Eastern state-sponsored terrorism, and particularly from operations by the Iranian Ministry of Intelligence and Security (MOIS), whose chief targets included the British writer Salman Rushdie. While continuing to warn of the threat from MOIS, the Service told police Special Branches in December 1995 that: 'Suggestions in the press of a world-wide Islamic extremist network poised to launch terrorist attacks against the West are greatly exaggerated.'[8]

That statement was issued by MI5 just as Nasiri was completing his training in Afghanistan and would soon come to work for the agency in London. It took a public declaration by Osama bin Laden in 1998 for MI5 and most others to start paying attention to al-Qaeda.

In contrast to Britain and France, the US did not have an empire to lose and had little experience of domestic terrorism. But with the formation of the CIA, its clandestine service – the Department of the Third World – had gained long experience of working semi-secretly with different foreign governments that clung to power in the face of communist-led rebellions that sometimes used terror tactics.

Jack Devine, a former acting head of the CIA's clandestine service, worked in Latin America in the 1970s. 'It was hot full of revolutionaries. The difference was that terrorists then were more discriminating. They were going for government officials.' Devine said he grew up as an officer in the field and emphasized that he 'only had a vision into the country I was in'. He said recruiting agents among terrorists had gone in cycles. 'We were universally successful. All of these groups were penetrated and we had sources in every group.' But it came and went. 'For a while we would have a good source and then he would get shot or no longer have access.'

According to Devine, the key to recruitment was access. To find targets, you might work with a local police force, which could bring potential sources into a police station. Against more rural movements, the liaison might be with the military. 'Sometimes the only way you were going to get inside these groups was to head up the hill with a gun. Maybe you could capture some and let some [recruited agent] escape – let them work their way back inside the group.'[9]

In the 1980s, under President Reagan, the US and the CIA became increasingly embroiled in combating terror groups in the Middle East after a series of attacks that targeted Americans. Going on the offensive, the CIA went after groups like the pro-Palestinian Abu Nidal Organization and, less successfully, Iranian-sponsored organizations like Hezbollah in Lebanon that were engaged in hostage taking. In 1986, the CIA formed a counterterrorism centre led by a colourful clandestine service officer named Duane 'Dewey' Clarridge. Later indicted and then pardoned over his role in the arms-for-hostages Iran-Contra scandal, Clarridge believed in action. His legacy was the CIA focus on using disruptive measures (like snatch operations) to fight terrorism.

In continental Europe, Germany had been confronted with the Baader-Meinhof terrorist campaign and Italy with the Red Brigades in the 1970s, but at the end of the Cold War it was France that was best prepared among all Western countries to combat Islamist terrorism.

During the collapse of its empire, France had, like Britain, faced lengthy terror campaigns. The Algerian war of independence had spilled over into mainland France. And the French had thereafter also faced bombs and shootings from separatist groups on its Celtic fringes, particularly on the island of Corsica and among the Basques (in the region straddling the mountainous border with Spain). Because of its involvement in North Africa, and Algeria in particular, a total of five million people of Arab origin lived in the country; France came to be, unenviably, both a safe haven for Algerian dissidents and a target for them because it backed the Algerian government. Because of this, France took early notice of the threat posed by a new wave of Islamist militants at whose nucleus were fighters who had returned from fighting as part of the mujahideen against the Soviet army in Afghanistan in the 1980s. French agencies began to think about tactics to put spies among them. In 1995, while Nasiri was in Afghanistan, the GIA struck the Paris metro, killing eight and seriously wounding nearly 200 people.[10]

Louis Caprioli is a former assistant director of the Direction de la Surveillance du Territoire (DST), a branch of the French National Police, which was France's domestic intelligence service. He explained that, like MI5, his agency had been founded to undertake counterintelligence, which was conducted at a relatively relaxed pace. By contrast in counterterrorism, 'You have to always be ready to immediately neutralize a network and you work in a world of prevention; you are always working in urgency.' Dealing with the KGB had also been far more focused, concentrating on a handful of people, whereas tracking a terrorist group might involve hundreds of people who were suspected of being involved.

'When we worked on the services like the KGB, we were dealing with organizations that had a structure,' he said. At first, terror groups also had a hierarchy, mirroring the states like Libya and Syria that sponsored them. The Palestinian terror groups such as the Popular Front for the Liberation of Palestine (PFLP) or Fatah, which had carried out the aircraft hijackings of the 1970s, were also highly structured. By the time the Islamists came along the French might have been used to terrorism, 'but we were no longer facing such a hierarchical organization'. This required new tactics.

Running spies, Caprioli taught, had always been hard; it was now harder still. 'The agent is the best thing in the world, but he is also the most dangerous person in the world to the handler. He's the man who can betray you at any moment. So if you lose your critical approach, you can have a ten-month relationship and one day, for whatever reason, the agent turns and you go to a meet thinking that he's a friend and you're dead.'

The French also saw how a legal framework needed to be put in place to allow the police to act on the intelligence that was gathered from secret sources. Caprioli described an operation back in 1983 when the DST had recruited a 'well-placed source' inside an Armenian terror group. 'We had them under physical surveillance, everything. We were working on eighty people. It was enormous.' But, despite the operation, they did not prevent an attack. At 2.07 p.m. on 15 July 1983 a bomb went off at the Turkish Airlines office at Paris's Orly Airport. Eight were killed and fifty injured. They knew who was responsible and when they raided the suspects' homes they found forty kilos of explosives, rifles and grenades, together with plans for more attacks. 'But it was a failure,' said Caprioli. They had not prevented the loss of life.

Over the course of 1995 and 1996, the French law was changed to permit preventive detention of terror suspects and convictions for 'association' with lawbreakers.[11] These measures were repressive, but they seemed to work. From July to October 1995, there were eight bombings or thwarted bombings in Paris, killing eight and injuring around 200 people. In 1996, there was just one bombing that killed four people. Attacks by the GIA and the Basque and Corsican separatists dwindled, just as preventive arrests escalated.

★

Omar Nasiri's journey into this world of violence and repression began with his brother's discovery of religion and his own feelings of alienation. He was born in Morocco but had lived in Belgium between the ages of five and fifteen. When his mother brought the family back to their homeland, his Arabic was poor and he came to feel a stranger. Then, while Nasiri was in his late teens, his brother, who had remained in Belgium, discovered radical Islam and encouraged Nasiri to follow him.

Like many youngsters, Nasiri had been influenced by the Afghan War, in which it appeared that Islamic fighters in flimsy sandals had brought down the Soviet Union. Among radicals like his brother, it was an inspiration for resistance against all oppressors. They had brought down a superpower – the opportunities for toppling other regimes seemed limitless. While the 1979 Iranian Revolution led by Ayatollah Khomeini had radicalized the Shia branch of Islam, it was the 1980s Afghan War that had a similar impact on the much larger Sunni branch of Islam, in particular because of a decision by the US's conservative Sunni ally, Saudi Arabia, to exhort and fund young Sunni Muslims from across the world to join the fighting.

'The war in Afghanistan brought me back to feeling as a Muslim and a Moroccan,' said Nasiri.[12] But probably more significant for him than religion or politics was the fact that joining his brother and his group in Belgium felt like an escape route out of Morocco. He learned to pray just like his brother and in 1993 he was invited to join him in Brussels.

Once in Belgium, Nasiri slipped into his brother's social network and got involved in distributing issues of the GIA's magazine, *Al-Ansar*. More importantly, he showed a knack for developing contacts in Belgium's criminal underworld, from where he learned how to buy and transport weapons and shift them to the militants. He had little conscience. 'Do you want me to say I was crying every night? I didn't even think about it,' he would tell the BBC.[13]

He became a spy because he was greedy, he said. One day he stole some money from the group. His comrades worked out that he was the thief and his brother let Nasiri know they would kill him if he did not return the money. It was a situation that would become a pattern: a young man at a crossroads of criminality and Islamic militancy who turns out to be an effective spy for a modern secret service.

Short on options, Nasiri figured the knowledge he had of the GIA's activities could be worth something. With that in mind, he sought out the DGSE by walking into the French Consulate in Brussels. He knew the DGSE was ruthless and he knew it was hunting down the GIA. As soon as he walked through the doors, he felt different. 'It was a very difficult moment. I felt my body tremble. My heart was beating faster and faster, but my brain was saying you have no other choice. This is the way to do it and this is the only thing to do. I knew from that moment when I went in, my life would change forever.'[14]

Put in touch with an intelligence officer whom he refers to as 'Gilles', Nasiri was told his knowledge of the group was of only limited worth; his real value would come from staying inside it and feeding live information to the French. Gilles told him, 'I can protect your family . . . but I can't give you everything you want. You haven't given us enough yet. If you want all these things you'll have to do more for us.'[15]

According to Nasiri:

[Gilles] had the temperament of a dictator: he always wanted to be in control. He wanted to tell me what to do, what to tell the members of the GIA cell . . . He was constantly pushing me to get into their 'inner circle' and telling me how to do it. But I had the power. I had the information he needed – and I didn't like him ordering me around. I told him so, again and again, and I knew he was frustrated.[16]

Without proper control over him, the French were in dangerous waters. Nasiri was involved in the trafficking of weapons and the French would have wanted to track his every step to prevent potential catastrophe. But he constantly resisted their authority. Nasiri said he was encouraged by the French to become more immersed in the group. This culminated in his drive from Belgium to Morocco – through France and Spain – in a car packed with explosives, weapons and money. The car kept overheating because it was so weighed down: 'every piece of the structure of the car didn't work . . . even the electric window did not work'.[17] The Semtex explosives he was transporting were later taken on to Algeria, he was told. Based on the timing, it seemed impossible they were not used in the police station attack.

As the British had found in Northern Ireland, a secret agent inside a terror group faced a standard dilemma: how far to go. 'Of course, that's why handling agents is so difficult,' said Caprioli. 'When an agent is in the core of an organization and one day they are told to go kill someone, what do we do?' He said in France the aim was to 'withdraw the source as soon as you've identified all the members of the network. So one of our principles is to avoid letting the agent go too far, because if he goes too far he is part of the attack.'

Hank Crumpton, a former head of operations of the CIA counterterrorism centre, wrote in his memoirs that the first problem encountered in recruiting agent-terrorists was the physical danger to a CIA case officer when approaching someone and asking them to spy. This is known in intelligence jargon as the 'pitch'. 'It was different from pitching a foreign diplomat, military officer, or trade official.' It was much riskier. 'A foreign diplomat could report the pitch, perhaps resulting in a diplomatic flap. A terrorist could respond in other ways, such as tossing a grenade at the case officer – which had recently happened. Our officer barely escaped down a stairwell as the grenade exploded behind him.'[18]

Then there was, as Crumpton wrote, 'the dilemma of employing those who may have murdered people or supported those who did'. There had to be some limits on whom they recruited. 'We did not recruit, support, and encourage any asset to murder innocent people – even if such action advanced their access and influence within a terrorist group. That was flat wrong. But where did we draw the line?'[19] The answer, he said, was to consult lawyers at the Department of Justice. He did not elaborate on what they advised.

Few with knowledge of such counterterrorist operations would argue that an entirely clean and harm-free approach to running spies among terrorists could possibly work. There was always an inescapable judgement call: was it worth being complicit in a lesser crime for the sake of preventing a bigger one? Everyone involved agreed there was a line to draw – but they differed on where to draw it and who should draw it. And rules needed to be flexible, Caprioli suggested: 'The situation itself dictates how you handle it. The reality on the ground is more than theory. You can have theories and principles, but when you're dealing with reality that's what dictates your behaviour.' Nevertheless, principles were important. 'You have to have principles to say, "OK, time to stop."'

In March 1995, the French and Belgians decided it was time to arrest members of Nasiri's cell in Brussels. He objected. He thought it was too early, and he feared that he would be double-crossed by the DGSE and arrested and prosecuted too. While he took its money, he never trusted the French agency; and his actions then showed why they were also right to not trust him. In his anger, Nasiri said, he confessed to fellow members of the cell that he had been spying for the French. 'I did tip them off. I gave them twenty-four hours' warning' ahead of the arrests, he admitted – a fact he had never told the DGSE. The gang had a day to dispose of evidence, though it meant one of them was caught with a gun in his car on a Brussels street as he tried to move it.

The DGSE did not know about – or at least did not mention – his betrayal. So after the arrests the relationship resumed. But with the Belgian cell dismantled and suspicion directed at him, Nasiri and the French concluded that his cover was blown as an agent in Europe. He could no longer work safely. Oddly, the confession Nasiri said he made to his GIA comrades (and there must be some doubt about his account here) had either not been believed or, for whatever reason, not been widely circulated. But in militant circles there were still questions about why he was the only cell member to avoid arrest. Meanwhile, the French were content to pay him off and 'would have been happy if I just disappeared'. But Nasiri wanted more. 'I hadn't even started,' he said. In the months that followed, he was to journey even deeper into the dark network of jihadism.

Both Gilles and Nasiri knew of the whispers in militant circles about people who were disappearing. They were said to be going for training in special camps in Afghanistan. After the Soviet defeat, Afghanistan had passed into the control of different mujahideen fighters-turned-warlords. Some of the many Arabs who had joined the mujahideen (the so-called 'Afghan Arabs') had also stayed behind. They were regrouping and setting up camps in districts close to the Pakistan border where they had operated during the war. It was rumoured they were training fresh recruits to continue their jihad on new fronts – whether Bosnia, Kashmir, Algeria, Egypt or Chechnya. What was missing was first-hand information from the camps themselves. No outsider had penetrated the set-up.

Nasiri and his French case officer discussed how it might be possible to get inside the Afghan camps. In his impetuous way, Nasiri suggested flying straight out to Pakistan, but the French thought that too brazen, he recalled. They felt he should head for Turkey and find a radical circle there that would direct him onwards with the right introductions. Nasiri tried that, but after weeks of fruitless travelling and a scare when he crashed his car the French finally accepted Nasiri's plan.

In the spring of 1995, he took a flight to Karachi with $15,000 in his pocket from the French.[20] What followed was a combination of luck and guile. On the plane, he met an observant Muslim who gave him directions to the headquarters in Lahore of the conservative-minded Islamic evangelical movement Tablighi Jamaat. They welcomed young Muslims from across the world, including Nasiri. But he found they had a philosophy of peace, not of violent jihad. Nasiri was disappointed. He wasn't looking for peace-mongers.

What he hadn't realized was that Tablighi Jamaat was also infiltrated by radicals. When Nasiri decided to leave, disillusioned by their peaceful preaching, a spotter who had been present at Tablighi Jamaat stopped him and passed on the introductions he needed to go further into the militant network. He was heading for the border city of Peshawar, at the start of the Khyber Pass to Afghanistan. Nasiri said he met a man called Abu Zubaydah there, a militant whom the US government later named as one of the top leaders of al-Qaeda. Abu Zubaydah was the gatekeeper to the Arab mujahideen camps, the man to decide who would be accepted for jihad training. Some called Abu Zubaydah a sort of 'travel agent' for al-Qaeda. 'He was a master counterfeiter. He made identity documents,' said Nasiri, 'and he was a master of knowing how to get people from A to B without getting caught.'[21] After 9/11, he was interrogated and waterboarded in CIA secret prisons known as black sites. Thinking about his encounters with the man, Nasiri wondered if Abu Zubaydah was mildly autistic. (He was brilliant at many things, but never put in charge of any planning.) Abu Zubaydah sent Nasiri across the border to the movement's most important camp, Khalden. Another person who would later be named by the US as an infamous terrorist leader, Ibn al-Sheikh al-Libi, was in charge. He was a genial but commanding figure. 'He was a tall man, very, very shy. When he gave you his hand to salute you, you wouldn't feel his hand, it was so soft, so warm, so incredibly paternal, and when he spoke with you, you would see this smile spread over his face.'[22] Captured in November 2001, al-Libi would be interrogated later by both the CIA and the Egyptian secret police. He was finally transferred by extraordinary rendition to Gaddafi's Libya, where he died in prison. While Nasiri was at al-Libi's camp, he heard that funds were coming from another mysterious 'Sheikh'. This was Osama bin Laden, who was then still in Sudan.[23]

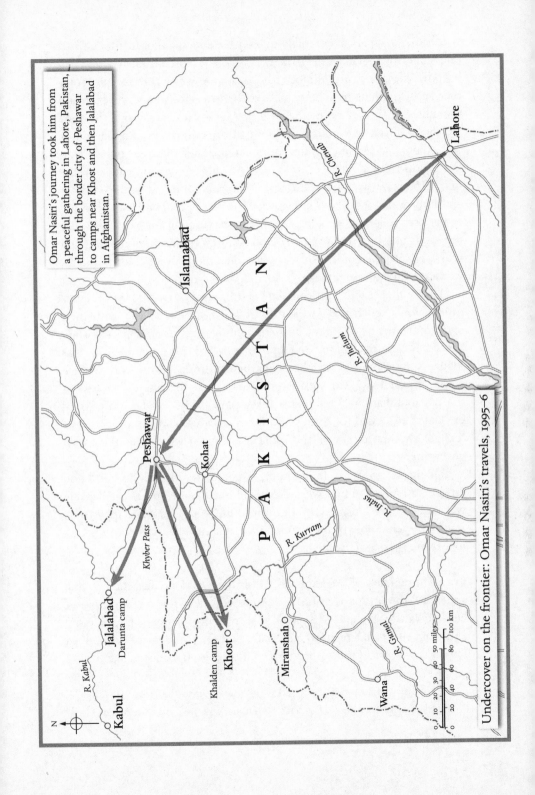

Omar Nasiri's journey took him from a peaceful gathering in Lahore, Pakistan, through the border city of Peshawar to camps near Khost and then Jalalabad in Afghanistan.

Undercover on the frontier: Omar Nasiri's travels, 1995–6

It had all happened incredibly quickly. Less than a month after he had said goodbye to Gilles in Turkey, Nasiri was ensconced in what had become 'jihad central'. Al-Libi's Khalden camp was where recruits combined basic training in military skills with instruction in both religion and the ethics of jihad. And it was here that almost every famous al-Qaeda recruit had been or would go. In 1993, at the same camp, Ramzi Yousef and others had plotted the first bomb attack later that year on Manhattan's World Trade Center. Mohamed Atta, the Egyptian leader of the 9/11 hijackers, was taught here too.[24] Nasiri was present in the summer and autumn of 1995. The training was about 30 per cent with weapons and 70 per cent religious ideology. The weapons training felt like a gift: 'For me it was like a present for a boy who had expected something for many years and then he got it.'[25] It was also much more about classic guerrilla warfare than terrorist attacks.

Despite their significant role for what became al-Qaeda, these camps catered for a much wider coalition of jihadi groups at war with their own governments, whether Chechens fighting the Russian army, Pakistan-backed Kashmiris fighting the Indian army or Algerians. Al-Libi was regularly asked, said Nasiri, about a particular group in some country. 'He would stop and say, "No, we are not here to make the difference between this one and that one. Our enemy is the same: Saddam [Hussein of Iraq] or [Hafez al-] Assad [of Syria]." So Ibn Sheikh's job was to train people to fight the first target of the [radical Islamists] which was their own government.'[26]

Talking to prisoners in Bagram, Afghanistan, before his rendition onwards to Libya, al-Libi was asked, 'Ibn Sheikh, are you al-Qaeda?' He was said to have replied, 'No, I'm not.' But he said he was happy to be arrested as a member of the group. 'I'm proud my enemy, the Americans, names me as part of al-Qaeda.'[27]

In the mountains of Afghanistan, Nasiri began to be absorbed by the appeal of the jihadis. 'As the weeks passed,' he wrote in his book, 'it became harder for me to separate myself from my brothers. It took more and more effort each night to remember that I was not one of them. That I was a spy.'[28] Nasiri rationalized his confusion in Afghanistan like this:

My two missions, spy and mujahid were now one and the same. I had lost myself totally in my role. But that's what any spy must do to succeed. No one can lead a double life for long and expect to get away with it. I had to immerse myself completely ... Was I a good spy because I could lose myself so completely in my role as mujahid? Or was I a good mujahid who just happened to be a spy?[29]

Nasiri's account raised the question of whether his susceptibility to militant propaganda (some might say gullibility) had been an important safety net. His own true beliefs, it appeared, were in flux. But should his account of the camps and elsewhere be taken at face value? In general, much of what he said was credible, revealing deep knowledge of the nature of the camps and the people involved across militant circles. Security sources in different agencies have also confirmed aspects of his account, including his later work in Britain and France. Michael Scheuer, former head of the CIA's bin Laden unit, said that Nasiri's tale 'tracks very well with the information we had in classified holdings during the late 90s and since then'.[30] But parts of his account, described in his book *Inside the Global Jihad*, did not ring true and seemed like the words of a ghostwriter chosen for an American audience.

Based on my own meeting with him, it struck me that the French would have always taken care to maintain a distance between themselves and Nasiri. While they would have been eager to encourage his adventures and listen to their outcome, he might have had more of a semi-detached relationship with French intelligence than he made out. They subsidized his activities and extensively debriefed him, but they clearly had substantial doubts about his qualities as a secret agent and his loyalty. For instance, if the French had really wanted him to spy inside the Afghan camps, they would have given him some training first.

I challenged Nasiri about whether in fact he really had been living the kind of dual spy-jihadi existence in Afghanistan that his book implied. Instead, I suggested, maybe he had become at ease with the philosophy of jihad and stopped even thinking of himself as a spy?

'It's true,' he admitted, 'I was genuine.'

Nasiri said that the book had been a 'negotiation' with publishers in which he had had to 'close my eyes' to some of what was written. He struggled most to get the book to reflect his own radical perspective: namely, that while the GIA was wrong to attack civilians, the bomb attack on the Egyptian Embassy in Islamabad, for example, which took place while he was in the camps, was justifiable. Attacks on the Russians in

Chechnya were praiseworthy. He admitted that his real goal in going to the camps – which the French had unwittingly assisted – was to be sent on a mission to Chechnya. 'I really did want to go and kill Russians. Not civilians but the soldiers, the ones killing Muslims,' he said. Only when Ibn al-Sheikh al-Libi insisted that he go back to Europe did the other side of his mission, to spy for the French, kick back in. In other words, although he returned and delivered his report, if circumstances had been different he might never have gone back.

When I met Nasiri, it seemed obvious that, in an almost schizophrenic way, he thoroughly accepted both the dogma of jihad and having worked with some of its enemies. In the camps, he had gone a long way down the militant path. He even volunteered to defuse an improvised bomb that had failed to explode. His group was asked, 'Who wants to become a *shaheed* [martyr]?' Only Nasiri raised his hand and walked off to dismantle the device. That kind of devotion gave him the credibility a penetration agent needed to survive. But, he said, he did it 'because I believe in Islam'. It meant he had little to hide. 'I was genuine. I was not lying. I was not fabricating. And you know why? This is the best way to get anywhere you want in life because they can even cut off your hand or nose and you will still just say the truth.'

There is a lesson here about spycraft. A successful spymaster is said to have an ability to get inside an enemy's mind. But if you draw close to that dividing line between friend and foe and begin to think like your opponent, you risk slipping over. This goes some way to explain why intelligence agencies themselves present such an 'insider threat'. From Kim Philby to Edward Snowden, the biggest betrayals were from agencies established to prevent betrayal that made so much of their role in defence of the nation.

As Nasiri put it, trying to recruit spies inside Islamist organizations required a wholehearted approach. Cheap tactics, such as offering them money, were bound to fail. 'Because those people in the camps, those people in the groups, they always know who is really attracted to this life they lead.' The only effective way to penetrate groups like al-Qaeda, he said, was to 'build up a Muslim guy, really Muslim guy, 100 per cent Muslim guy and send him back to spy on the Muslims'. But, he claimed, there was a 99 per cent chance it would backfire and the agent would come back and kill. 'When he will come back, if he comes back, he will blow you up.' Nasiri laughed as he said it, although he insisted he was not joking.

Although he may have become hardened over the years, it was obvious from meeting him that he must always have been incredibly headstrong. At Khalden he was one of the few who questioned the orders of the camp's 'sheikh', al-Libi. Such poise may have protected him from exposure and suspicion. But, he admitted, he was equally uncompromising with his unfortunate handlers in Western intelligence. They tried in vain to control him and he regarded them as consistently dishonest.

In the winter of late 1995/early 1996 Nasiri moved on, via Peshawar again, to a second, more specialized camp. This was Darunta, on the road from the Khyber Pass to Kabul, near the eastern Afghan city of Jalalabad. The camp was under the control of an Afghan mujahideen group, Hesbi-Islami, but a portion was reserved for training militants under the authority of al-Libi. This was more like a terrorist camp than Khalden had been. Rather than use supplied military hardware, trainees were taught how to make and then detonate explosives themselves. At this time, the camp leadership was deciding what to do with Nasiri. He was still hoping to go to Chechnya, but al-Libi told him his mission was to return to Europe and establish himself there.[31] It was not important exactly where, but he was to set up his own cell and then identify targets that the 'brothers' could use for future assaults.

Nasiri returned to Europe in May 1996, just as Osama bin Laden took a chartered jet from Sudan to Afghanistan to lead the jihadi movement.

By the time of the 9/11 attacks, agents like Nasiri who had infiltrated al-Qaeda were still a rarity. The lack of effort by Western intelligence agencies was due not only to the dangers and difficulties but also to the cuts made in intelligence budgets since the end of the Cold War, as well as what became known as the 'wash' of disreputable sources (for example, those with records of human rights abuses). Former officers of both the CIA and SIS rightly said that human intelligence efforts were then at a low point. The British had cut their budget for human intelligence operations nearly as much as the Americans had done, as several former SIS officers confirmed.

But the main reason why there was so little effort to get spies among the extreme Sunni Islamists was the failure of most in the West to grasp the scale of the threat posed. Until agencies realized the true measure of the danger, hard-to-control agents like Nasiri were rarely going to be seen as worth the trouble. The French, whose citizens had been murdered in numerous terrorist attacks in Paris during the 1990s, had a better grasp of the risk. And they were highly critical of the British, for instance, for being almost wilfully blind to the operational role of extremists living in their midst and actively plotting terrorism. Officials at MI5 would later acknowledge that failure.

When he returned from Afghanistan, Nasiri made contact with the French again. He felt vindicated. 'I was on top of the world. No one had believed in me; no one thought I had anything to offer. The DGSE had been ready to throw me in jail and wash their hands of me. Then they tried to pay me off to disappear. But now here I was, just back from the Afghan training camps with vast stores of information. They wouldn't try and get rid of me this time. Now they needed me.'[32]

The DGSE responded, he recalled, with a mixture of joy that he was alive, disbelief about what he had done and, most of all, uncertainty about what to do with him next. They did debrief him extensively, in a hotel in Istanbul, but they hardly seemed interested in the level of detail he could provide about the location and layout of the camps, the training programmes and the personalities who were coming and going. While much of his account cannot be independently verified, his description of the camps did accord with what other intelligence operatives and visitors there would later indicate.

Nasiri ended up in London, where the GIA had regrouped and where the French decided he should be run jointly with the British. But he did not get on with his MI5 handler, 'Daniel', whom he disliked in almost all respects. 'I disliked the way he threw his briefcase, I disliked the way he spoke, I disliked the way he told me he'd be "handling" me as if I were a circus animal.'[33]

Like him or not, Nasiri presented MI5 with another dilemma. Al-Libi had sent Nasiri back in part to fund-raise, meaning he was expected to wire money to the camp. At first the French and British baulked at giving him cash that would essentially fund terror training, but on three occasions, he said, they agreed.

Nasiri began hearing about a preacher based at a mosque at the Four Feathers Youth Centre near Baker Street in London. He was known as Abu Qatada, a Palestinian-Jordanian whose real name was Omar Mahmoud Othman and who was later labelled, with justification, bin

Laden's ambassador in Europe. He was one of the key clerics who gave vital scholarly endorsement to bin Laden's actions. Nasiri identified him as the most compelling threat in the city. He also says he passed on messages between Abu Qatada in London and Abu Zubaydah and al-Libi in Pakistan.

At the time, though, British intelligence had little ability to identify real operational extremists like Abu Qatada, according to Nasiri. They were more interested in far less credible preachers like the Finsbury Park mosque's Abu Hamza (an Egyptian whose real name was Mustafa Kamel Mustafa). Despite his previous training in Afghanistan, Abu Hamza was then little more than a rabble-rousing fraud. He had little or no active connection to the hard-core jihadi network. Nasiri knew someone who had trained with him and had learned that – contrary to what Abu Hamza claimed in his speeches – he had lost his arm not in combat but in an accident while making explosives. In the years that followed Abu Hamza's influence grew in London among young radicals. He was extradited in 2012 to the United States on terrorism charges and was found guilty in 2014.

Nasiri never discovered why MI5 told him to drop his focus on Abu Qatada. (At the time of writing, and after a legal battle stretching over many years, Abu Qatada had just been deported from the UK back to Jordan, where he was acquitted on the initial charges, but indicted on new ones.) Meanwhile, Nasiri's French contacts, whom he also saw in London, were still focused on finding the camps where Algerians trained and had little interest in the wider threat from Islamists. There was a basic lack of trust based on the belief that Nasiri was still uncertain as to where his loyalties lay. 'I think they were afraid of me and what I would do. They were following me everywhere.' A divorce seemed inevitable.

After his relationship with MI5 broke down, it was made clear to Nasiri that he should leave the country, particularly after he proved uncooperative following al-Qaeda's 1998 embassy attacks. That day, fed up with surveillance, he took the battery out of his mobile phone and left it in his flat. 'I let them go and they don't know where I was any more. They was crazy, they had to call my future wife to tell her, "Please, please where is he?" They called her and said, "Where is he?" and I was just in London.'

After a spell back in North Africa, Nasiri agreed to move on to assist German intelligence in combating Islamists on their soil. But he lost patience with the Germans too. He never got the new identity and the protection he had hoped for. 'I feel I risked my life for nothing. For absolutely nothing,' he said.[34]

In the years after Nasiri's spying missions, the 'Afghan Arabs' became more prominent and the name they had adopted, al-Qaeda, became known to the world. Al-Qaeda-linked groups attacked US interests in Yemen, Somalia, Kenya and Tanzania. There were further attacks, and attempted attacks, in the US and Jordan at the time of the millennium celebrations.

Only a small group of people, inside or outside the secret services, fully understood the threat that al-Qaeda posed. And the CIA, working with anti-Taliban factions, did make some attempts to kick-start a programme to infiltrate the jihadists. Still, when the strike came on 11 September 2001, the US and Britain had not a single spy inside al-Qaeda. It was a critical weakness.

As the official US inquiry into 9/11 confirmed, there had been a 'lack of reliable and knowledgeable human sources' inside al-Qaeda. 'Prior to September 11, 2001, the Intelligence Community did not effectively develop and use human sources to penetrate the al-Qa'ida inner circle.'[35] Michael Scheuer – one of those at the CIA who had rung alarm bells – asserted, 'The reason we didn't prevent 9/11 is simple: neither CIA nor its intelligence allies, Western or Muslim, had a spy or an informant inside al-Qaeda's command structure.'

Watching coverage of the attacks at home in Germany, Nasiri felt physically sick. He wondered whether, if people had listened to him and the authorities had kept a closer eye on those who had gone for training in the Afghan camps, they might have been prevented. 'I tried to get them to understand the reason that all those boys go to Afghanistan and train and be ready to die for a cause – not for their mother or son but because of the humiliation of Islam and Muslims.'[36]

Nasiri had his weaknesses as an agent and seemed at times perilously uncertain of his own loyalties. As he warned, someone able to think like a radical and live among them for months might easily be drawn into their ranks. But these questions of loyalty are always present in the spy business, particularly with long-term infiltrations. What emerges from his story is not that finding a way into such groups was too difficult but rather that there was little serious attempt to try. This came from a failure to listen, a basic lack of interest or concern at that time by the secret services (and by the policymakers who directed them) about a movement that was forming far beyond their borders. Even if, no doubt, another more compliant and level-headed person would have made a better agent, Nasiri showed that the Afghan camps could be infiltrated.

There would be great challenges ahead and new tradecraft and new specialists would be required if the Western agencies were to succeed. 'We're still kind of stuck in the Cold War approach to this,' said Scheuer in a newspaper interview a dozen years after Nasiri's venture. 'This is a much more difficult target than the Soviets were. These people are true believers. They're living according to their beliefs, not in the lap of luxury.'[37] In other words, bribery would not motivate them to spy. But none of these differences were insurmountable; they were instead a reason to adapt.

But while the Belgians, French and British worried about attacks at home, they took little interest in the international movement that was coalescing. As Nasiri explained, the Soviet war had inspired the 'myth of the mujahideen' and this, combined with the seething anger of the Arab street and new extremist ideas, brought together a coalition of radicals that would pose a terrible threat. Within Western security agencies, almost no one cared about what had become of far-off Afghanistan; few people were worried about the alienation of youngsters in the Middle East or were even troubling to learn Arabic any longer; and fewer still bothered to study the potent religious ideas that were swirling around. Small wonder that the intelligence services had little to show when disaster struck.[38] Nasiri may not have had all the mental qualities or the loyalty necessary to make a good spy and to convince the West to take the Sunni radicals seriously, but his story illustrated both that you needed spies in remote places and that it was possible to get them there. It was a chicken and egg problem: unless you had someone in the camp to appreciate what was happening and the threats posed, you were unlikely to be able to persuade somebody to send a spy there. This is why good spying works in tandem with good analysis, because someone needs the wisdom to decide where to look.

Successful spying, then, is driven by tradecraft, resources and the quality of recruits, and also by the direction set. It requires such a concentration of effort that unless something is made a real priority results are unlikely. That was the case with al-Qaeda before the attacks of 9/11.

But there is also the reverse problem. When a subject gets too great a priority and governments want to see success too quickly, the consequences can be equally disastrous. Without great care and professionalism, there is an incentive to exaggerate, even to fabricate, and the spy game can fall into disrepute. This is what happened in the run-up to the Iraq War of 2003, which showed the very personal, human way that spying can turn into lying.

Chapter 6
Caveat Emptor

'They tried too hard. They wanted to make a difference, to change policy, change the world. That is always a mistake'

– retired senior officer, SIS

An intelligence expert was reading from a book about a secret agent with the code name Curveball. The agent had become famous for telling the world that Iraq's late dictator, Saddam Hussein, had mobile laboratories to make biological weapons (or germ weapons as they are popularly known). The book was labelled non-fiction. It had won many awards. But it began with a statement by the author that he was using a false name for Curveball and that, despite writing 280 pages about him, they had never met.

As the expert – someone who had intimately scrutinized the agent's case – leafed through the pages he started to scribble furious notes in the margin. He was getting angry. The opening pages were a fantasy, he said. They were about Curveball's 1999 arrival in Germany and how he was recruited by the country's secret intelligence service, the Bundesnachrichtendienst (BND).

He selected a passage from the book: '*Staring out the window, Ahmed Hassan Mohamed could see little of his new home. In the spring or summer arriving passengers at Munich's Franz Josef Strauss International Airport normally glimpse . . .*'

This made the expert angry. 'He never went there! He arrived overland from France.'

'*Ahmed's plane flew from North Africa . . .*'

'It was France!'

The expert listened as I read aloud a long description that continued for three pages: *[his] bags betrayed new riches . . . the man brought back stuffed dates and preserved lemons, kif candy and almond cookies . . . Airport workers in neon yellow slickers scurried near the plane . . . Utility vehicles painted cautionary orange . . . The long line moved slowly but the traveller [Curveball] was patient . . .'*

'The first two and a half pages completely made up! I suppose they need to do this to sell books.'

'The border officer pressed a button on his desk, and another man . . . escorted the traveller across the hall to a small office with a desk.'

'No.'

He talked to the passport officers. *'I am from Baghdad, northeast Baghdad. I live with my mother and father.'*

'His father was dead.'

'I attended the University of Baghdad . . .'

'No. It was the Technical University.'

'Yes, I am married.'

'Divorced.'

'Clutching the slips of paper and his bag, he walked purposefully through the huge airport to reach the bus stand outside.'

'No. He never went to the airport.'

The account I was reading was from the best-selling book by an American journalist, Bob Drogin. It was the story of a monstrous lie, told by the agent known as Curveball, that was so large he was blamed for helping start the 2003 Iraq War, which led to the deaths of thousands of people. Drogin's 2007 book, *Curveball*, was subtitled *Spies, Lies, and the Con Man Who Caused a War*. A quote on the cover was provided by thriller-writer Frederick Forsyth, who referred to events as 'the biggest fiasco in the history of secret intelligence'. Joschka Fischer, the German foreign minister at the time of the war, took a similar view: 'It was Curveball. That's it. The war was based on lies.'[1] Of all the evidence compiled about Saddam Hussein, the accusations about germ weapons had been the most compelling and most fleshed out. Curveball had provided that evidence. An official inquiry into the US intelligence failure on Iraq's weapons of mass destruction (known as the WMD Commission) had called him the 'pivotal' source on bio-weapons. The inquiry concluded, 'Virtually all of the Intelligence Community's information on Iraq's alleged mobile biological weapons facilities was supplied by a source, codenamed "Curveball," who was a fabricator.'[2]

But how did those fabrications come into being and get endorsed by the world's leading intelligence agencies? And what did this process reveal about the profession of spying and the worth of spymasters and HUMINT in the modern age? When conservative-minded US president George W. Bush and liberal-spirited UK prime minister Tony Blair joined forces to launch the Iraq invasion, despite many protests, they were acting in the spirit of the age, giving form to a public desire to intervene ahead of trouble, to prevent massacres and human rights abuses and surprise attacks such as those of 11 September 2001. However, such an approach to foreign intervention required highly accurate, reliable intelligence. A close look at the Curveball case shows that, even when the lives of thousands depend upon it, spying can turn to lying without much of a conscious effort, or even any malice. It also offers clues about how to avoid such disasters in the future.

Drogin had written the book about Curveball before he knew much about the true identity and personal circumstances of this agent. In the way of many journalists, he filled in blanks. 'Like any author,' he wrote, 'I flesh out the written record and the memories of participants to bring life to the page.'[3] But in doing so Drogin had inadvertently mirrored the life of the worst kind of secret agent – someone who filled in the gaps in what he knew with second-hand accounts to 'bring life' to his reports.

As the expert read on, he identified more than forty errors before he got bored. Many were trivial, but some touched on the heart of this story: how the lie had been conceived, born, shaped and matured. Drogin's erroneous information, he said, included details of the key man who debriefed Curveball:

> *The case officer stood straight-backed and tall . . . already in his late 50s he had spied for Germany across Africa in the 1980s . . . He was most fluent in the pitiless vernacular of spying: he used dishonest means – theft, lies, blackmail, and worse – to get at the truth. Even at the BND, most people knew Ahmed's [Curveball's] chief case officer only by his cover-name, Schumann . . . Schumann's special skill was persuading informants to talk.*

All false, he said. Schumann did not exist. There was no such case officer. Everyone had known who handled Curveball and it was no one like that.

'*Schumann was lost. What did it all mean? He was neither an engineer nor a microbiologist.*'

'In fact his debriefer, "Dr Peter" [not his real name], was a trained scientist, [with] a PhD.'

'. . . *broken English* . . .'

'No, Curveball spoke English. His university courses were in English.'

'. . . *they ran concealed tape recorders and video cameras* . . .'

'The BND had no secret recordings and no transcripts.'

To criticize Bob Drogin for his mistakes was to miss the point. Without his original scoop, published in the *Los Angeles Times*, which had alerted the world to the con, we might never have heard of Curveball at all. What mattered was not so much the literary techniques he used to tell his story, but more – as Drogin himself suggested in an interview – that the full truth about events in intelligence rarely emerges at the first telling. I asked Drogin if, in an account of intelligence failures, there was 'an irony in the literary approach where you fill in the blanks'. He said he did not see it that way. 'I never, ever expected that my book would be the last word: unthinkable.' He pointed to the example of Agent Zigzag, the British wartime double agent whose story took seventy-five years to emerge. There were errors too, he said, in the best-seller *Black Hawk Down* by Mark Bowden, which missed bin Laden's role in training the men who shot down the helicopter, he said.

When he was researching the book, the civil war in Iraq was at its worst and no spy had yet confessed to their role in the US invasion that started the conflict. 'I was trying to unravel a story that involved a congenital liar. It involved intelligence agencies that lie as a part of their mission, politicians that had no reason to be honest about what happened, and documents that, even if I got access to them, would be wrong.'

Drogin agreed that his account's biggest gap was the 'criminal' way Curveball was handled by German intelligence. Because where his imaginative sections had misled was in conjuring the idea of a con man that had defeated the efforts of sharp interrogators led by a handler '*fluent in the pitiless vernacular of spying*'. And it is at that ground level, not in some Washington intrigue, where the lie was born.

It has long been a widely held view that the Iraq intelligence failure was the result of a plot in Washington and London to embellish the case for a war that President Bush and Prime Minister Blair were determined to fight regardless. In this view, the overall case that Saddam Hussein had been hiding weapons of mass destruction was a fabrication, woven together by systematically exaggerating the accounts of agents like Curveball. 'It wasn't intelligence, it was propaganda,' said Karen Kwiatkowski, a retired lieutenant-colonel who, at the time of the Iraq War, was a Pentagon analyst. 'They'd take a little bit of intelligence, cherry-pick it, make it sound much more exciting, usually by taking it out of context, often by juxtaposition of two pieces of information that don't belong together.'[4] In the US, this plot to cow the intelligence establishment was said to have been directed by Vice-President Dick Cheney, whom *The Economist* had already labelled – before he took office – 'the power behind the throne'.[5] Britain's famously cautious spymasters were, in turn, said to have been bullied into submission by Blair's own Cardinal Richelieu, his press secretary, Alastair Campbell. BBC journalist Andrew Gilligan quoted inside sources who claimed that the intelligence dossier about weapons of mass destruction made public by Britain had been 'sexed-up'. A headline in a newspaper article by Gilligan read: 'I asked my intelligence source why Blair misled us all over Saddam's WMD. His response? One word . . . CAMPBELL.'[6] (In their defence, both Cheney and Campbell denied distorting any facts, but defended their right and duty, as senior officials, to pose challenging questions to intelligence agencies and hold them to account, when appropriate.)

The extent of intelligence manipulation became plain, said critics, in the infamous 'Downing Street memo', marked 'UK Eyes Only', which was written on 23 July 2002 by Tony Blair's private secretary, Matthew Rycroft. It was a record of a meeting chaired by Blair and in it Rycroft wrote, 'This record is extremely sensitive. No further copies should be made. It should be shown only to those with a genuine need to know its contents.' He then went on to quote 'C', as Sir Richard Dearlove, the head of SIS, was known: 'C reported on his recent talks in Washington. There was a perceptible shift in attitude. Military action was now seen as inevitable. Bush wanted to remove Saddam, through military action, justified by the conjunction of terrorism and WMD. But the intelligence and facts were being fixed around the policy.'

Dearlove later corrected Rycroft's minutes at the time of the memo's circulation. He asked Rycroft to remove the phrase about fixing intelligence. But to many Dearlove had – wittingly or not – confirmed the broader picture. By rallying convenient facts and half-truths, the senior leadership of the American intelligence apparatus had become stooges for Cheney and his boss, Bush, sacrificing their integrity to persuade a gullible public to accept the war they were determined to launch, regardless.

The official WMD Commission reached a softer, though also damning, conclusion. It alleged that the secret services were reckless with the truth. For instance, on biological weapons, the US Defense Intelligence Agency (DIA), which had given Curveball his code name and handled his intelligence, had 'abdicated responsibility' to vet a crucial source, they said. The CIA's analysts, meanwhile, had emphasized what Curveball reported over and above other intelligence because the tales he told 'were consistent with what they already believed'. Intelligence chiefs were also faulted for failing 'to tell policymakers about Curveball's flaws in the weeks before war'.[7]

As first recounted by Drogin, the CIA's senior leadership were so complicit in the false narrative that they ignored specific warnings that Curveball was a fake, including the concerns raised by Tyler Drumheller, the CIA operations chief for Europe, whose job it was to liaise with German intelligence. Drumheller recalled that on the night before Colin Powell gave his UN speech, he warned CIA director George Tenet by telephone that the Germans had misgivings about their own source. (Tenet denied receiving such a warning.) Drumheller mentioned a lunch in Washington with the BND chief, who told him that Curveball was probably mad, a warning he said that he circulated to CIA directors. He had also passed on to Tenet a warning letter about Curveball from August Hanning, then chief of the BND. In a contradictory account, Tenet said he never saw the letter and only found out two years after the war – 'too late to do a damn thing about it' – that Germany had had doubts about his source.[8]

Those critics who cite the Downing Street memo or Drumheller's evidence are implying that intelligence chiefs on both sides of the Atlantic played politics and deliberately pushed intelligence they knew was based on shaky foundations – if not downright false. It had all been a conspiracy against the public. But were things that simple? It is true that intelligence was presented to the world without essential qualification. As the official British report on Iraq intelligence said, the 'caveats on the intelligence were dropped'.[9] Both the politicians and the spy chiefs resorted to exaggeration and redaction, ignoring doubts. This misinformation helped cause a war. Yet to judge this as a deliberate plot to mislead is to commit the same error that Blair and Bush made, which was to ignore the full picture and erase the caveats. Critics of the secret service leadership were trying to see a very grey world in black and white. (And there were sensible people inside the CIA who disagreed with Drumheller's version of events; some had honestly believed in Curveball and other parts of the intelligence case.)

The really disturbing thing was not the spinning of evidence or the imagined conspiracy, but rather that the intelligence itself was wrong. And moreover, while in Britain and America there were some dissidents inside the intelligence services, most insiders believed that wrong intelligence (just as there are leading critics of the Iraq War inside the CIA who reject Drumheller's account and defend Tenet's honesty, if not his judgement). Lies had found their way into the system and been swallowed whole. And that made the very machinery of spying smell rotten. In SIS, staff felt it as keenly as the discovery of Philby's betrayal, recalled Gordon Corera, BBC security correspondent. 'One by one [SIS's] prized sources were melting away like mirages in the desert heat,' he wrote, and panic consumed Vauxhall Cross.[10]

To find out what lay behind this debacle, it is worth going back to that key source, the human agent in Germany, and witnessing the birth of the lie. Let's try to tell his story again.

Rafid Ahmed Alwan, an Iraqi of the Janabi tribe, was born in 1967 in the capital city, Baghdad. In 1999, he left his country for unknown reasons; some have suggested that he had been accused of petty fraud. He travelled to Jordan, Egypt, Morocco and then France. Just after Christmas, he drove across the German border and headed towards Nuremberg in Bavaria. His destination was in the city suburbs, the Zirndorf processing camp for those who wished to claim political asylum in Germany. He considered the barracks an unpleasant sort of place, a form of house arrest, but Zirndorf was a compulsory first stop.

The word among the inmates at the camp was that, to speed up asylum applications, it was worth visiting a German intelligence office behind the refugee centre. Here, it was said, they sifted the applications for people who might know useful things. This was the Zirndorf branch of the Central Office for Questioning, a subdivision of the BND.[11] In early 2000, Alwan walked in to tell his story. He outlined his background: he had studied chemical engineering at Baghdad Technical University; during military service he was posted to Saddam Hussein's weapons research programme, the Military Industrialization Commission; then he had worked at the Chemical Engineering and Design Centre (CEDC) in Baghdad on equipment to process seeds and biological agents.

When this information was passed on, the BND found Alwan's background tantalizing. It was of particular interest to a team of weapons experts at the spy agency's pre-unification headquarters in Pullach, five miles south of central Munich. Given his potential value, Alwan was whisked out of Zirndorf and into his own flat, and was then subjected to months of interrogation by a specialist analyst, Dr Peter. The officer completed over a hundred debriefing reports, more than ninety-five of which made their way to the United States.[12] None were written after 2001.

Alwan would later tell the *Guardian* that he already had a plan in mind by then. He wanted to use these meetings to undermine the Iraqi regime; he decided to fool the world. 'I had a problem with the Saddam regime,' he said. 'I wanted to get rid of him and now I had this chance.'[13] And what a tale he spun. He told interrogators that he had worked at the CEDC until 1998 and that, while there, he had seen a plan to make mobile laboratories that could make germ weapons like anthrax and smallpox. He said he had witnessed an accident there in which many died, with the victims having to be buried in lead coffins.

In truth, Alwan could not have witnessed any of it as he had been sacked from the CEDC four years earlier. Nevertheless, this same false story was repeated three years later, on 5 February 2003, in a speech by the hapless US secretary of state, Colin Powell, to the UN. By then it had been months since Curveball's last interrogation. When Powell spoke, Alwan – aka Curveball – was taking casual jobs, washing dishes in a Chinese restaurant and frying hamburgers at Burger King.

With German foreign minister Fischer in the chair, Powell offered the Security Council what he called a glimpse inside the US intelligence file on Iraq. 'We have first-hand descriptions of biological weapons factories on wheels and on rails,' he claimed, going on:

> The trucks and train cars are easily moved and are designed to evade detection by inspectors. In a matter of months, they can produce a quantity of biological poison equal to the entire amount that Iraq claimed to have produced in the years prior to the Gulf War . . .

The source was an eye witness, an Iraqi chemical engineer who supervised one of these facilities. He actually was present during biological agent production runs. He was also at the site when an accident occurred in 1998. Twelve technicians died from exposure to biological agents.

He reported that when UNSCOM [the UN inspection mission for Iraq from 1991 to 1999] was in the country and inspecting, the biological weapons agent production always began on Thursdays at midnight because Iraq thought UNSCOM would not inspect on the Muslim Holy Day, Thursday night through Friday. He added that this was important because the units could not be broken down in the middle of a production run, which had to be completed by Friday evening before the inspectors might arrive again.

This defector is currently hiding in another country with the certain knowledge that Saddam Hussein will kill him if he finds him.[14]

This was all from Germany, from just one source: Curveball. As the defector would confess eight years later, it was a total lie; he made it up. 'I had the chance to fabricate something to topple the regime,' he said in 2011. 'I and my sons are proud of that, and we are proud that we were the reason to give Iraq the margin of democracy.'[15] (It was not clear what he meant exactly by 'the margin'.)

He said the same to the BBC. When a reporter put it to him, 'The fact is we went to war in Iraq on a lie and that lie was your lie,' Curveball replied, 'Yes,' with a smirk.[16]

But the account still feels too naive, like another fabrication. If we check the details again, Alwan arrived in December 1999, when Saddam Hussein was at the height of his powers. There were no drumbeats for war just yet. Alwan might have wanted to exaggerate his story to get a German passport, or even just a residence permit. But was he really clever enough to have come up with such a grandiose plan to overthrow the regime and confident enough to invent an account that could withstand scrutiny? He had a record as a petty criminal, but he had never been a political opponent of the regime.

And can we be sure that all of what he said was entirely wrong? Had he really made it all up? It is too easy to swing from one extreme to another. Reducing the story to spy-as-fabricator is just as lazy as blaming politician-as-fabricator.

★

I wanted to explore these contradictions with the man himself, Rafid Alwan. In the decade after the Iraq War, he had been exposed, tracked down and, after first denying that he had told any lies, had finally 'confessed' to his fabrications.

As I asked around for his contact details, fellow journalists told me that he had been paid handsomely for his various interviews. He had a reputation for being difficult. And indeed, when I finally got to see him, in the autumn of 2013, he once again had something to sell, this time memoirs of his life as a spy. He was looking for a ghostwriter or co-author.

We met, amid the warning bells of the street trams, in the southern German city of Karlsruhe, where he had been resettled by the BND. A stocky figure in blue jeans, he had a round face, a twinkling smile and a warm handshake. We walked to a nearby coffee shop.

I had been waiting around for the meeting for a few hours. He had not returned my calls. But while I explored the area, he had already been to my hotel to look for me and managed to have a row with an unhelpful hotel receptionist. 'She was racist,' he said.

Alwan knew about my previous book on the CIA. I gave him a signed copy of the German edition. Now he wanted to know whether I would be interested in helping him tell his story. He already had a draft in Arabic that he wanted me to read and plenty of supporting documents I could see at his lawyer's office. They revealed a lot about the way the BND operated, including the false companies they had set up and how they had cheated him, he said.

I asked Alwan what it was he wanted from his book. Speaking in good English, he said he wanted to correct the record, to challenge the lies written about him. It seemed a little ironic. Alwan said he never lied in order to support an asylum claim. 'I had received asylum before I started talking. I can prove it.' He said that, contrary to reports, he and his family had a long history of working against Saddam Hussein (he mentioned one of the opposition parties). He had a motive to help bring about Saddam's toppling. When I asked him more about this, he said it would have to wait. He did not want to give me anything for my book: he was afraid of losing his best lines.

I had come a long way for this meeting, but it was a huge anticlimax and did not last long. The reason he was late, he said, was that his daughter had suddenly been taken ill and was in hospital. He had to rush off to see her in intensive care. We agreed to meet the next day.

★

Captain Francis Cromie, thirty-six, was killed at the British Embassy in wartime Petrograd on 31 August 1918 by revolutionary militia amid Bolshevik claims of a coup plot by British intelligence.

Sidney Reilly – the so-called 'ace of spies' – was posted by Britain's Secret Intelligence Service (SIS) to Russia, where he unsuccessfully plotted to overthrow the Bolsheviks.

Soviet agent Kim Philby joined SIS in August 1940 and came to be chief of anti-Soviet operations. His treachery remains a low point in the agency's history. (Photo: Getty Images.)

Milton Bearden (*centre*), pictured with Afghan rebels fighting the Soviet army. He ran CIA operations from Pakistan against the Soviet army in Afghanistan. He later became the CIA's chief of global anti-Soviet operations. *Above right*: Bearden today. (Photos: courtesy of Milton Bearden.)

Freddie Scappaticci, the Belfast-born son of an Italian immigrant, was identified by press reports as Steak Knife, Britain's best agent in the Provisional IRA. He denies the claim. (Photo: courtesy of Kelvin Boyes.)

Andrew (or Andreas) Antoniades became an informer for British intelligence for more than four decades after joining EOKA rebels in Cyprus.

Stanley Hollowday, a British engineer, pictured on his wedding day with his wife, Zanina. Antoniades was ordered to shoot him.

Antoniades pictured in Tunisia in 2012 while wanted for questioning by British police. His work for British customs was now over. (Photo: Stephen Grey.)

After returning to the UK, Antoniades was jailed for a drive-by shooting at the Beirut Café in Camden, north London. (Photo: court files.)

Sir Richard Dearlove was the chief of the Secret Intelligence Service. He defends his role in preparing an intelligence case for invading Iraq.

US Secretary of State Colin Powell makes the case for invasion at the United Nations. He based parts of his speech on intelligence from Curveball.

Rafid Ahmed Alwan, an Iraqi, was exposed as the agent known as Curveball – the man who provided key intelligence on biological weapons used to justify the 2003 invasion of Iraq. (Photo: Gustavo Alabiso.)

Above: Zabet Amanullah out election campaigning before he was killed in a US air strike. He was said by US intelligence to have a secret life as a Taliban commander.
Right: a copy of Amanullah's passport.

Amanullah was well known to many Westerners. Former UN official Michael Semple (*above*) was friends with him; he had his phone number stored on his phone – the same number that US intelligence tracked to kill him. Semple proved Amanullah was no double-agent.

Asim (*above left*), a Pakistani agent for French intelligence, infiltrated the Tariq bin Ziyad mosque in Barcelona, Spain (*above right*). He testified that he discovered a plot to bomb the city's metro (*below*) and led to the jailing of eleven alleged terrorists. (Photos: Stephen Grey.)

Danish convert Morten Storm became an agent for Danish intelligence, the CIA and MI5. He helped the CIA track and assassinate Yemeni-American preacher Anwar Awlaki in 2011, in both Britain and in Yemen.

LOSIVE HAZARD) IED EXPLOSION RPT (PBIED) OGA : 8
KIA 8 CF WIA 1 CIV KIA 1 UE KIA

The military log that recorded the attack at Camp Chapman. OGA was the military term for the CIA. (Source: Wikileaks.)

)-12-30 06:14:00

T: 2-377 (TF STEEL)
PE: SUICIDE BOMBER
HO: PRT KHOWST
HERE: FOB CHAPMAN
PORT: @ 1218Z FOB CHAPMAN REPORTS IDF WITH A MASS CASU...

- UNK
- IDF
- WC WB 88704 88668
T- 1640I
R-
MC

123
TO

12
SA

13
13

1
6

1 X KIA (LN)
8 X WIA (US)

...ATION

...BER, REPORTING MASS ...
...F

...RGENT WU CHAPMA...

...ALERNO WITH CA...

...KIA (US) 1 X K...
...TO CHAPMAN

...TO INVESTIG...

...X WIA DIED WH...

The two faces of Humam al-Balawi: as a Palestinian doctor (*left*) and as militant extremist Abu Dujanah al-Khorasani (*right*), preparing for an attack against the CIA. (Photo: Jihadi video.)

Former SIS officer Alastair Crooke specialized in secret peacemaking with violent groups. (Photo: conflicts forum.)

Hamas leader Sheikh Ahmed Yassin opened a dialogue with Crooke before Yassin was killed by the Israelis. (Photo: Reuters – Mohammad Salem.)

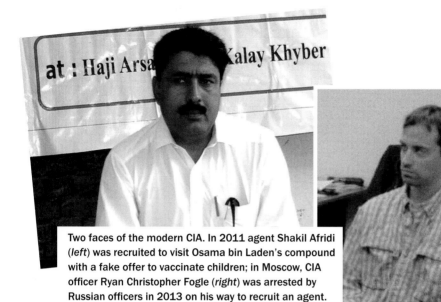

Two faces of the modern CIA. In 2011 agent Shakil Afridi (*left*) was recruited to visit Osama bin Laden's compound with a fake offer to vaccinate children; in Moscow, CIA officer Ryan Christopher Fogle (*right*) was arrested by Russian officers in 2013 on his way to recruit an agent. (Photos: Getty Images and Russia Handout.)

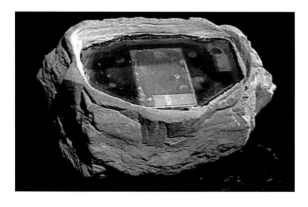

Fogle was caught with a toolkit for spying that included wigs, sunglasses, a compass, a Bic lighter, a Moscow atlas, $100,000 in euros and a metal shield for credit cards.

In 2006 Britain's SIS was accused by the Russians of using this fake rock to hide electronic equipment for communicating with its agents in Moscow.

We all know that spies make up stories. But not all fabricated evidence is completely false. Just because we know Curveball told some lies, it does not follow that he made up everything. Moreover, not all lies or even exaggerations are deliberate; it is possible that he believed everything he said. Falsehoods like that are particularly hard to spot.

There were plenty of con men along the road to war. In Italy, a forger concocted 'proof' that Saddam had tried to buy uranium from Niger; the evidence was a series of letters originating in the Nigerian Embassy in Rome. Although they were identified as forgeries by the French intelligence services and others, they still made their way into George Bush's State of the Union address in 2002. But the Curveball story was more complex than a straight forgery. If it was true that people could behave honestly but still, through their actions, manage to create a fabrication, the implications were very disturbing for the spy game.

A few weeks before my meeting with Alwan, I was in a café in Germany chatting with John Goetz, the reporter in Germany who has done more than anyone to uncover the truth of this case. After Curveball's real name was published by CBS News, it was Goetz who was the first to track him down. Their handshake on the doorstep was the moment that Alwan knew his cover was blown. Now Goetz and I were on our way to talk to some of those involved from German intelligence.

Over the years, Goetz had tracked down most of the key figures in the case. His working theory was that the fabrication was not so much created by Curveball but encouraged by the way he was handled. As a German saying puts it, 'A hammer is always looking for nails.' In his view, both Curveball and his handler, the BND officer and biologist Dr Peter, who was always looking for biological weapons, were to blame. We had been told, 'Dr Peter was for a long time the only person that Curveball had in his life.' Alwan himself would later underline that point. 'The central thing in my story is —' he said, using the BND scientist's real name.

Goetz says that even after the Iraq War many in German intelligence continued to believe Curveball's story: 'I spoke to everyone involved. They believed in him . . . Even two years after the war, even after they had scoured Iraq and found nothing, even then they still believed Curveball.' Goetz was told this in 2005 by the men who had worked the case.

He remembers sitting down with one expert at the BND and showing him all the Senate and Iraq Survey Group reports that indicated that what Curveball had said couldn't be true. But his source was dubious. At the BND, 'they always believed in him ... in a kind of stare-you-in-the-eye way'.

Goetz had talked for years about how it was that people ended up believing incredible things, despite all the contradictory facts before them. It was one of the things that made us despair about our profession of fact-finding. You could amass fact after fact, but people would not draw the obvious conclusions.

We talked about an interview with a former CIA station chief called Jim. He was discussing recruitment pitches taught at Camp Peary, the CIA training school in Virginia known as the Farm. Trainee spymasters were told to analyse the 'target' and then guess what motive could be exploited to persuade him to become an agent and betray his country or employer. 'That's all bullshit,' Jim had said. 'It never actually works like that. The key thing is to get the guy to betray something, to cross the line. He will work out his own justification.' A carefully nurtured recruitment was often based on an unspoken understanding. Human beings had incredible ways of inventing rational excuses for what they did or were going to do, he said.

Perhaps we were heading too far into Sigmund Freud and psychological territory. Jim's point was that fathoming motives, and discussing those motives with the target, could sometimes be not only counterproductive but also irrelevant to what people ended up doing. Persuasion came through habit as much as logic, and human beings were indeed incredibly suggestible.

Applying Jim's explanations of recruitment to the art of interrogation and analysis, it was obvious that the logic could be reversed and help to explain how an agent might, in effect, recruit his interrogator (or indirectly those analysts who read his statements). Just as a recruiter might slowly lead his potential agent towards a betrayal, so an agent might, little by little, establish confidence before planting the lie. Then, just as an agent might invent reasons to justify the act of betrayal, so a recruiter might invent logic to validate what the agent was saying, whether the agent's information really made sense or not. The recruiter could become an instrument for the lie, helping to paper over every inconsistency. All this could take place subconsciously. The more an interrogator developed empathy for his subject, the more chance there was he himself would, quite honestly, invent rationales to explain away what seemed awry about his subject's account.

Our working theory about Curveball and Dr Peter rested on the notion of suggestion, that Curveball had provided what Germany's intelligence service had made clear they needed. It was not deliberate coaching; just the psychology of the agency's relationship with him. One reason for thinking this was the amount of accurate information Curveball had provided. A problem with accepting the consensus view that Curveball's story was pure fabrication lay with how much Curveball had got right, about both Iraqi facilities and the production of bio-weapons. How could he have known all this detail? Drogin resolved that paradox by suggesting that Curveball gathered facts by hooking himself up to the Internet.

'That was a mistake,' said Goetz. His research showed that Alwan had no Internet connection back then.

Nevertheless, Curveball was getting his information from somewhere. One idea was that he was simply phoning ex-colleagues and friends in Iraq, in effect running what are called 'sub-sources'. Alwan himself would later say that he was able to make up his story using textbooks and documents supplied by Dr Peter. 'I did not have the Internet but I had a computer. I still have all the documents I used for writing my material,' he added.

But there was another potential source. What if the interrogator was sufficiently gullible and naive and insufficiently self-aware not to realize how many ideas and pieces of technical information he was passing to Curveball?

The surprising thing was that Alwan had seen Dr Peter before he left Iraq, when the German scientist had worked as a UN weapons inspector and visited Alwan's workplace. When Alwan was being interrogated, he recalled, 'it took me some time but I recognized him after a while. I realized he had come and seen us. It was in 1992 when I was working in the Military Industrialization Commission. When I saw him in Germany, he introduced himself as an asylum officer. He admitted later he had been a weapons inspector. I had said to him, "I know who you are."' He said Dr Peter showed him nothing but kindness, but 'he was not professional'. When I asked if he manipulated Dr Peter, Alwan just smiled.

Our car tyres scrunched into the gravel driveway of a suburban house. Goetz and I were coming to see a source in German intelligence who was deeply involved in the Curveball saga. What he, and several others directly involved, revealed was just how much it had really been a personal story between the agent and his handler. The details – largely unearthed by Goetz – have never been told before.

It was Dr Peter who spotted Curveball's interesting CV, with its mention of 'mobile bio-chemical labs', among the pile of asylum applications from Zirndorf. And it was he who conducted all the interviews. (Dr Peter himself declined to be interviewed, citing his professional obligation of secrecy.)

Dr Peter was not a trained agent handler, or even a case officer. He was a biologist. In theory, Curveball had a professional case officer – one of the agent runners from the BND's Abteilung I (Department I). They organized Curveball's accommodation, they ferried him to and from meetings, but none of them became close to Curveball. It was Dr Peter who handled the debriefing sessions and wrote up reports of them. The professionals had abdicated from their job.

Dr Peter's passionate interest was biological weapons, the source said. Apart from serving as an international inspector in Iraq, he had monitored Iraq's interest in germ warfare since the 1980s. According to the source, before Dr Peter had discovered Curveball, 'he already suspected that Saddam was still working on biological weapons – particularly smallpox'. Then along came Curveball and appeared to confirm these suspicions.

'Curveball was always about smallpox,' Dr Peter used to tell people. 'This guy has real information and he is not clever enough to make it up himself.' Dr Peter would always complain that when Curveball's intelligence was summarized for the public, the smallpox part was excised. Colin Powell's speech referred – without mentioning the source – only to Saddam having the 'wherewithal to develop smallpox'. But if Saddam was actually developing smallpox (the Variola virus) it was disturbing – a far more dangerous threat to humanity than his anthrax programme, for instance. Smallpox had been globally eradicated in 1980; what remained of the virus was being held in just two labs in the world: the United States Centers for Disease Control in Atlanta and the State Research Institute for Viral Preparations in Moscow. Dr Peter, however, had come to believe that Saddam Hussein might also have stocks.

Dr Peter appeared to be impressed, said our source, that while Alwan seemed to have real technical knowledge and a good memory (mentioning, for example, the exact temperature at which germ agents were held and giving precise descriptions of locations), he never seemed to exaggerate his knowledge (for example, by saying exactly what was being made where). 'Curveball used to talk about Agent A, Agent B and so on and describe how they were handled. But he never said this one was anthrax or smallpox or whatever.'

In his conversations with colleagues, Dr Peter had recounted how Alwan often got things wrong the first time. But then, when reinterrogated, he would come up with the right detail. Dr Peter rationalized this error by assuming that, as a refugee still in the precarious stage of seeking asylum, Alwan had his own motives for not wanting to be fully truthful first time round. By his logic, the movement to a true version was evidence of a successful interrogation, not of fabrication. Using the same set of facts, Dr Peter was gifted with the ability to draw completely different conclusions from other people, according to colleagues. It was either genius or delusion.

It was Dr Peter's determination to investigate Curveball's intelligence on smallpox that led him to arrange the only encounter that took place between an American officer and Curveball prior to the Iraq War. Dr Peter had noticed that Curveball had the distinctive scarring on his upper arm that usually signalled someone had been inoculated against smallpox. Curveball said he had been vaccinated when he joined the germ warfare programme. Smallpox antibodies last only ten years after vaccination, so by looking for them in Alwan's blood Dr Peter hoped to determine if this vaccine dated from childhood (which would be usual) or was more recent and evidence of adult involvement in a bio-weapons programme. To conduct the test, Dr Peter wanted American expertise – not only to study the blood but also to take the sample. 'He wanted no one to be able to challenge the conclusions when they came,' said a person closely involved.

In May 2000, a CIA doctor named 'Les', who was attached to the DIA, was duly summoned from Washington. The Germans had told the US that Curveball hated Americans, so Les was under strict instructions not to breathe a word. If, by his accent, he revealed his nationality, the BND had warned, then Curveball would refuse to cooperate.[17] So he kept quiet. Later, on the eve of Colin Powell's 2003 speech, Les wrote an email begging them to question Curveball's evidence. He claimed that when they met, Curveball had acted in a particularly odd way; Les felt Curveball must have been drinking alcohol the previous night and had 'a terrible hangover' the morning of the meeting. According to a colleague, Les believed that Curveball 'might be an alcoholic and that bothered him a lot'.[18] (In fact, the 'hangover' story was a misapprehension. That day Alwan had a broken rib and was in considerable pain. This might have explained his grumpy mood better. He wasn't perhaps the best Muslim in the world, but he did not drink or eat pork.)

Les also concluded that Curveball's handler, Dr Peter, was far too close to him. As he recounted in his email later, 'this is an opinion of mine and I really have nothing else to base it on, but it was obvious to me that his case officer, for lack of better words, had fallen in love with his asset and the asset could do no wrong. I mean, the story was 100 percent correct as far as [redacted words] was concerned.'[19]

The way the Germans treated the subsequent blood test results showed that they believed Curveball. When Alwan's blood was analysed in Germany, Britain and the US, only the American lab showed faint traces of antibodies. For everyone but the Germans, the results were inconclusive. But Dr Peter made clear he regarded them as confirmation that Curveball had been immunized in adulthood against smallpox – and thus had been part of an illicit germ warfare programme.

In May 2001, Dr Peter convened a special conference in Germany to consider Curveball's evidence and the bio-weapons threat. Officers from German, US, British and Israeli intelligence were present. And the conclusion of that conference led to an expensive purchase by Germany of large stocks of smallpox vaccines. 'In Germany, that was [Dr Peter's] lasting impact,' said a German official.

'It demonstrates that Dr Peter and everyone else who counted at the BND had swallowed what Curveball was saying,' said Goetz. 'And the interesting thing is they – even later – kept believing.'

As the interrogations continued, some glaring problems arose with what Curveball said. Though he claimed not to know many specifics, Curveball had described in great detail a warehouse in Djerf al-Nadaf, just south of Baghdad, where mobile trucks would come to be replenished. He said the trucks had equipment on board to ferment and dry out the germ spores. The existence of this drying capacity, thought the BND experts, meant its only purpose was military. The place Curveball described was known to Western intelligence and to UN inspectors (most of whom were intelligence officers on secondment). It belonged to the CEDC where Curveball had worked. But they knew it was a small, cramped building surrounded by walls. Curveball needed to explain how the trucks could move in and out. Asked about this, he said the trucks exited by a hinged wall at the corner of the warehouse.

The trouble was the hinged wall did not exist. And nor could the large trucks even move in the yard. This became clear from photographs taken in 2001 by American satellites that revealed there was an additional wall in the way. Curveball was told of the images. But he appeared unfazed and clung to his account. Again, the rationalizations kicked in. Dr Peter and US analysts just concluded that the structure seen on the satellites must be temporary or part of a ruse.

When the UN weapons inspectors returned in 2002, one of the first things they did was check out what they had heard in Colin Powell's speech. They travelled to Djerf al-Nadaf and confirmed that the wall was not temporary at all. And the corner of the warehouse was not hinged or movable in any way.

The next flaw in Curveball's account was exposed by British intelligence. One of his stories was that a son of his former boss at the CEDC, Dr Basil Latif, had been sent to the UK in 1995 to procure parts for the weapons programme. Britain naturally wanted to know more, and they were able to exploit the fact that Curveball had said he ultimately wanted to settle in Britain. An SIS officer called 'G—' was sent to masquerade as an immigration officer. To maintain cover, G— could ask what Curveball knew about the UK only. So it was not a thorough debrief. Nevertheless, G— left the interview less than convinced. According to German colleagues, G— told them, 'He is telling a lie, adding to the story. There is something about it that doesn't add up.'

By the time of 9/11 and the subsequent push for war, Dr Peter had left the BND. He had been passed over for promotion and did not want to move with his unit to the new BND headquarters in Berlin. But as interest in Curveball revived he was pulled out of retirement to join a special mission with British secret intelligence. SIS had discovered that Curveball's ex-boss Latif was now living in Oman.

The interrogation of Latif was conducted by the same SIS officer, G—, and by Dr Peter. But it was incomplete. To avoid giving away who their source was, the pair could not ask any specific questions about Alwan. So the two interrogators failed, for example, to get from Latif that Alwan had been fired from the CEDC in 1995. If they had asked him and clarified this point, they could have alerted the UK and Germany before the war that Curveball's claims to have witnessed up-to-date germ weapons production and the accident in 1998 were fanciful. This is an example of how the secrecy involved in source protection can prove very costly.

Nevertheless, what Latif did tell G— and Dr Peter made the story about Latif's son seem doubtful. As Latif said after the war, 'I don't know what he [Alwan] said. But in 1995 my son was sixteen years old and in that year he came to the UK to do his GCSEs and he's still here. How could he be involved in these things? I heard [Curveball] mentioned several things about my family, my son. But he's clearly not that clever. If people lie they should fabricate it well! My son was sixteen in 1995.'[20]

It was after this trip that SIS penned a report in April 2002 that summarized their conclusions about Curveball and rather neatly hedged their bets. The classified cable to the CIA said that SIS was 'inclined to believe that a significant part of [Curveball's] reporting is true' in the light of his detailed technical descriptions. But also they were 'not convinced that Curveball is a wholly reliable source' and said that 'elements of [Curveball's] behaviour strike us as typical of individuals we would normally assess as fabricators'. Despite all this, the CIA noted that SIS 'continued officially to back Curveball's reporting throughout this period'.[21]

Whatever the doubts that emerged, Dr Peter kept faith with Curveball, even if, as a professional, he emphasized that he was a single source that needed confirmation. One way he and colleagues rationalized growing contradictions was by developing a theory that some of Curveball's intelligence might be hearsay from a 'sub-source'. They knew he was speaking to people in Baghdad by telephone. Dr Peter asked the BND to tap Curveball's phone. He was told they lacked both the resources and the legal authority. The way some in the BND came to see it, if Curveball's information was second-hand but still accurate, did it really matter?

It was not just the Germans who found a way to rationalize their doubts. As the WMD Commission exposed, while analysts at the hugely resourced US agencies had been hired to be sceptical, they instead viewed intelligence like movies, constantly suspending disbelief. One CIA analyst had remarked, 'Mobile BW [biological weapon] information comes from [several] sources, one of whom is credible and the other is of undetermined reliability. We have raised our collection posture in a bid to locate these production units, but years of fruitless searches by UNSCOM indicate they are well hidden.'[22] The WMD Commission report notes caustically, 'The analysts appear never to have considered the idea that the searches were fruitless because the weapons were not there.'[23]

Eventually, after every corner of Iraq had been searched and nothing found, and after even Curveball admitted he had lied, Dr Peter finally accepted that Alwan's story was a fabrication, according to friends. But, they added, the retired BND scientist continued to puzzle over where the information had come from. He apparently sensed a darker conspiracy. 'My feeling is that he was being fed by someone else,' he told an ex-colleague. Curveball had had so much detail on so many places, but so little on others. 'Only two countries in the world have the capability of it,' he would say – and by that he meant Israel and the United States. No one had the heart to suggest to Dr Peter that the man who had really been feeding Curveball all his lies – perhaps unconsciously and without malice – was Dr Peter himself.

As it turned out, Curveball was not a spy who single-handedly took the world to war, but his story did illustrate how even honest men could construct lies. It also showed that good human intelligence needed to start with a healthy and professional relationship between an agent and his handler, and for the ultimate consumers of intelligence to verify that it was being gathered in a professional way.

At a higher level, Curveball's story also exposed the arrogance of a tick-box approach that qualified intelligence as sufficient to justify political action simply because several sources appeared to suggest the same thing. Brian Jones, a senior intelligence analyst on Britain's Defence Intelligence Staff, was one of the few who had challenged the intelligence case before the war. But, when asked why SIS had set aside its own concern that Curveball was a 'possible fabricator', he said that most intelligence officers in Britain and the US had always been 'uneasy' about the story of mobile weapons laboratories. But that had changed when suddenly new sources appeared to corroborate the story, as well as new pressure to publish evidence.

'There was always plenty of caution around about "Curveball" on both sides of the Atlantic until certain critical documents were required,' Jones said, meaning that pressure to produce public documents had encouraged the intelligence chiefs to throw caution to the wind. 'The bottom line on what went wrong is that forceful political leadership in both the UK and US left no doubt about what they believed the assessment on Iraq should say.'[24] The intelligence agencies were in transition, 'still adapting to an alien and nonsensical culture of satisfying the customer to stay in business', and it was this effort that had killed their better judgement.

One of the sources that appeared to back up Curveball's account was run by SIS and code-named Red River. According to the WMD Commission, this source 'provided a single report that Iraq had mobile fermentation units mounted on trucks and railway cars'. He was mentioned when Colin Powell spoke of how a source 'in a position to know' had reported that Iraq had mobile production systems mounted on trucks and railway cars.[25]

A secret annexe to the WMD Commission report accused SIS of misleading the CIA on Red River. Though supposedly 'in a position to know', the agencies had dealt with this source second-hand: it was someone whom SIS officers had not directly met or vetted. According to the Commission, classified material discussed the 'CIA's discovery (after the war) that the fourth source, whose reporting the Director of Central Intelligence [Tenet] stated corroborated Curveball's reporting, was not the direct source of the reporting sourced to him on Biological Weapons'.[26]

That criticism is disputed by some of those involved at SIS. At the time, said one officer, Dearlove and Tenet were constantly in touch. They had a special one-to-one 'cipher phone' to maintain a direct, personal channel. According to a senior SIS figure:

Red River was indeed a sub-source, but it is out of the question that our reservations were not shared with the CIA . . . He was a valid sub-source who, because of the sensitive position he was in, fled Iraq in the build-up to the war and settled in another Arab country. His intelligence about biological weapons has not been discredited, nor the source's whose sub-source he was.[27]

As other highly experienced officers argued, the point was not that Red River was a useless source, it was just that, like other Iraq sources, his evidence had been overplayed. This was a lesson in how the word of secret agents, even in combination, could rarely be presented as proof. HUMINT by its nature, as the modern spy agency should have known from decades of experience, was rarely conclusive. 'The best readers of human intelligence are artists not scientists. HUMINT is about texture. And so we did not expect our reports to lead to some great reversal of policy,' said a senior British spymaster.

Little by little, the unravelling of the intelligence case for war in Iraq had shown how, despite all the technical means of intelligence collection at the West's disposal, so much still depended on the fragile nature of human intelligence, and it had been found wanting. Those few good spies that Britain and America had in place in Iraq did not offer the clear indication of a threat from Saddam Hussein that the political leadership wanted.

As some former American and British officers argued, the real problem proved not to be the shortage of agents inside Iraq but a shortage of professional intelligence officers who would dare, to use the old Quaker adage, to 'speak truth unto power'.

Dearlove, said one ex-colleague, had extraordinary self-confidence and was the 'classic bullshitter extraordinaire', but, according to another former SIS officer, his weakness was that he was a 'failure on the sofa' in Downing Street. 'He was just too eager to please. He had no experience of really upsetting people.' A retired SIS officer, speaking to the official Chilcot Inquiry into the Iraq War, described 'wishful thinking' from the service's leaders that 'promised the crock of gold at the end of the rainbow'.[28] Elsewhere, a former senior SIS figure said the main point was that the agency's then leadership had 'tried too hard. They wanted to make a difference, to change policy, change the world. That is always a mistake.'

Dearlove rejected the personal accusations. 'I'm well aware of the criticisms of me, that I had too close a relationship with the Prime Minister and all this. This is complete rubbish,' he told the Chilcot Inquiry. His subordinates could not be relied on to judge that relationship. 'If you are looking up from underneath, you have no idea what the job of Chief is like, particularly when the world is in crisis.' He then added:

I challenge anyone to show me any single document that that was some-how improper. I mean, [Stewart] Menzies [the wartime chief of SIS] had a close relationship with [Winston] Churchill during World War 2. During any crisis, the head of intelligence, particularly when a crisis is so angular and difficult, is going to have to deal frequently with ministers. I wasn't sipping Chardonnay in the evenings with Tony Blair, or nipping off to have breakfast with him in Chequers. I was going to meetings, as the head of SIS, to discuss SIS business in relation to the development of national security policy.[29]

But there were dissidents in SIS who accused its senior leadership of not only overselling intelligence about the Iraq case externally, but of drag-ooning case officers and sources internally to follow a 'party line'. One former British intelligence insider claimed that case officers were sent back again and again to revisit their agents and ask them once more to dig up information on WMD. 'Eventually their sources might come up and say, "Well, if he had WMD, it might be kept here" [mentioning some location in Iraq], and then that was dressed up as real intelligence.' The former officer added, 'There were people sent home, dismissed outright, for refusing to play along.'

Given how much secrecy surrounds SIS, it is hard to assess such claims. One former senior spymaster, no friend of Dearlove, said it was an exaggerated picture. But, he added, 'there was real concern by some of those who actually dealt with the sources about the way their intelligence was being hawked about, being exaggerated'. An officer told Chilcot the problem was too much interference in cases by leadership. 'You cut out expertise, and perhaps you also disable that element of challenge which is, I think, a very important part of operational life in the Service.'[30]

In short, there had been insiders who thought that while Saddam might have had WMD there was not sufficient intelligence to make that case. These critics, few in number, were drowned out. But, as the Curveball case showed, the rot went deeper. Too many were thoroughly convinced of the argument and most of their actions can be explained by zeal. It was a case of self-deception. And it underlined how, despite their hubris, the modern spymasters, living cloistered like monks in the seclusion of their Top Secret world, could be desperately vulnerable to group-think.

One veteran said, 'SIS was painfully arrogant before Iraq. It's a dangerous game because when you strut around like that, then no one was going to care when you go down. We had the sh*t ripped out of us.'

Few at SIS felt proud of this episode. The role played in their own building by Dearlove and his successor, John Scarlett, who had chaired the Joint Intelligence Committee in the pre-war period, was a source of painful division, even if Scarlett would later win back the trust of many with a self-effacing approach.

In the US and Britain, Tenet, Dearlove and other professional intelligence chiefs would forever be forced to live with having signed off on an unprofessional intelligence assessment. Its biggest flaw was not to have been wrong, but rather to have lost sight of the caveats: to have portrayed judgements as clear-cut when the business is, in reality, always grey. But even now it would be just as naive to assume that the failure to find WMD proves that there never were any, as it was naive pre-war to be so certain that they were there. Before the war, there was a whisper of warning, a disquieting note that those in power decided to tune out. After the war, the pendulum of opinion has swung right over, to the point that loose ends, such as indications that Saddam might have actually had some WMD, were brushed aside. The official inquiries, as one former senior SIS officer said, 'found no room for intelligence that remained unexplained'. What, he asked, about:

- Signal intelligence about Iraqi military's large-scale purchase of atropine (the antidote to nerve gas)?
- A significant line of reporting on the trickle production (in laboratories not industrially) of VX (nerve agent) and its limited weaponization in field artillery rockets?
- Intelligence from the Ukrainian Intelligence Service about the Russians helping to move compromising material out of Iraq into Syria before the inspections got under way?
- Satellite 'overhead' images covering the passage of vehicles over the border (Iraq to Syria)?

These questions could be seen as clutching at straws. But that misses the point. The spying game is never over. However difficult, gathering good intelligence needs people to listen to the tunes played in a minor key – and to never, ever stop challenging the received wisdom, whatever it is.

As we were having coffee, Curveball said that he had been offered plastic surgery by the BND and a new home and identity in Italy. But he had refused. 'I want to stay Rafid Alwan. That's who I am,' he said. He also said the Americans asked, as recently as 2008, for help with information about Syria. He promised me there were many more explosive revelations to come from his story. He hoped to make some money. It is possible, of course, that he will do just that. But few will believe him.

PART THREE

The Flock of Birds (2008–13)

Chapter 7
Cover Blown

'All over the world, people in terrorist groups are living like normal people'

– French secret agent, code-named F1

On Wednesday 16 January 2008, a Pakistani man with a well-trimmed black beard stepped off the train and on to one of the neon-lit underground platforms of the Estación de Francia, the second busiest mainline station in Barcelona.[1] Asim had travelled all night from Paris. He was tired and sweaty – and he was nervous, for good reason. He was on a dangerous, secret mission. But after travelling for nearly twelve hours across Europe he had escaped attention. Spain and France were both inside the common borders of the European Union's Schengen scheme. So no one had checked his passport or identity card at the frontier in the Pyrenees.

He took the escalator up into the wide and crowded concourse. The people around were diverse – businessmen, manual workers, hawkers and tramps, brightly dressed, chattering tourists, and plenty too from India and Pakistan. He blended in. Glancing around the crowd, he looked for a fellow Muslim.

'As-salaam aleikum. Peace be with you. Can you tell me the way to Tariq bin Ziyad mosque?' he asked a passer-by.

Asim noticed that there were policemen everywhere. In two months' time, Spain was holding a general election and the atmosphere was febrile. 'Everyone was expecting another attack,' recalled Antonio Baquero, a security correspondent with the regional paper. Three days before the last elections, four years earlier, Islamists had planted bombs on commuter trains in Madrid, killing 191 people and injuring over 1,500. Some claimed that the handling of that attack had cost the ruling conservative party (Partido Popular) the election. (Initially the government wrongly blamed Basque separatists for planting the bombs.) This time round, security forces were taking no chances and were watching out for a repeat incident.

After receiving directions, Asim walked down the street to the nearest metro. Looking around, he wondered if he stood out. His destination was the working-class Raval district, on the edge of the rabbit warren of medieval streets known as the Ramblas. This was one of Barcelona's main tourist attractions, but the Raval was a little poorer, bleaker. He jumped on the metro, then changed once, taking the L3 line to Liceu station. Along the platform was a McDonald's advertisement and pictures of half-naked girls promoting a travel company. At the far end there were electronic barriers and, beyond the stone steps, the Ramblas. Later in the day the wide boulevard would be filled with tourists and strolling families, all wandering down the famous central pavement shaded by tall plane trees, with its newspaper kiosks, café and stands of parked scooters. A sign in the window advertised a 30-euro massage.

The way to the Raval was down a one-way side street, Carrer de l'Hospital, with a pavement that became gradually narrower. The five-storey apartment buildings on each side appeared to lean inwards, the balconies jutting out. The T-shirt shops and youth hostels gave way to drab-looking mobile phone stores and halal butchers. After passing the forbidding fortress-like walls of the medieval Catalonia Hospital, now a school and art gallery, he reached the unmarked back door to the mosque at number 91, just before a Pakistani bakery and a Sikh temple.

This entrance was locked, so he was sent down a narrow echoing alleyway sliced between the apartment buildings, laundry flapping from the balconies above. Turning right into a new road, he felt the atmosphere suddenly become more edgy. He could see young men with mobile phones making whispered drug deals; fake blonde prostitutes were leaning against the walls. Then he saw the sign: the Mezquita Tariq bin Ziyad.

It was the biggest mosque in Barcelona. Hidden behind the shabby entrance were six floors of prayer rooms. But even this was not enough space. Up to 1,000 people gathered here for midday prayers on a Friday, sometimes spilling into the streets. The mosque's name had symbolic resonance. Bin Ziyad was an eighth-century governor of Tangiers who became a general, defeated the Visigoths and conquered Spain for Islam. (Gibraltar is named after him too: a corruption of Jabal Tariq, the mountain of Tariq.)

Asim had arrived too early. The front entrance of the mosque was closed too. He found a nearby kebab restaurant and waited. But he returned at noon and joined the worshippers. Afterwards, he introduced himself to some of the religious leaders. He addressed them as 'Maulana', the honorific title given to Muslim clerics by South Asians. 'At the time,' he remembered, 'I talked to them like a normal person. I didn't know they were part of the organization.'[2]

The people who ran the mosque and all those he met were ostensibly devotees of the Muslim proselytizing group called Tablighi Jamaat. This was the same conservative global movement that had welcomed Nasiri in Pakistan – and disgusted him with its moderate views. But among its millions of followers violent militants were not unknown. Tablighi Jamaat is proscribed in five countries even though the organization denies any links with violence.[3] Later, a prosecuting judge in Barcelona, Ismael Moreno, would accuse it of promoting 'indiscriminate' violence for political ends.[4] But this was an unusual viewpoint.

As Asim would recall, the group he met in Barcelona was under the authority of al-Qaeda itself; its orders came directly from one of al-Qaeda's sworn allies, the Pakistani Taliban (known as the TTP). Asim claimed that his instructions came from Baitullah Mehsud, the TTP commander.

Asim would claim he had been working secretly for the TTP around Europe for two years.[5] Mehsud had personally given him the code name Ahmed. Ostensibly, Asim lived the normal life of an illegal immigrant in Paris, working 'in the black' – in other words, without being officially registered – for a French electricity company. But, he said later, 'all over the world, people in terrorist groups are living like normal people'. During his holidays and at weekends he had travelled around France, Belgium, the Netherlands and Italy, delivering cash to militant cells. He also claimed to have taken several breaks from work to go on training missions in Waziristan, the most lawless part of the Pakistan frontier region, and on into Afghanistan itself. Sometimes he was away for months on end. 'I was a member of al-Qaeda,' he declared later in court.[6]

He had come to Barcelona on fresh orders from his immediate commanders in Paris. 'They told me maybe I would stay in Barcelona or maybe I would go to another country to take part in an explosion.' He had not been briefed on his role in the attack. His Paris contacts said that all would be explained by the leader of the radical group based at the mosque, who used the code name Ashraf.

As Asim waited after the noon prayers, Maulana Ahmed Maroof, a 38-year-old imam, came downstairs. Asim was obviously looking tense, so Maroof told him to relax and speak freely. He explained that he was the Ashraf that Asim was looking for and that the small group of eight now gathering in the corridor were to be trusted. Most of them were recent immigrants to Spain.

The following account is based on later testimony given by Asim. His version of events is disputed by the others involved, but a Spanish court held that he was telling the truth.

According to Asim, that afternoon Maroof outlined some details of an audacious plan to blow up Barcelona's underground railway. He was speaking in a mixture of Punjabi and Urdu.

'Why are we going to attack the metro?' asked Asim.

'Because if we attack the metro, the emergency services cannot get there. One person will wear a rucksack, another one will detonate the bomb from a distance . . . If the first [attack] does not work, we will mount a second and a third in Spain.'[7]

Asim was still waiting to hear what his role would be in the attack. Later that day, he joined the group as they left together. 'It's too dangerous to sleep in the mosque,' Maroof told him. They went to an apartment half a mile away, the home of a Maulana Shahid Iqbal.[8] The latter's expertise, it was becoming clear to Asim, was in bomb-making and not holy scripture. Asim spent the night there.

From a hidden lookout post in a building opposite, a surveillance team – officers of the National Intelligence Centre – was watching. They snapped pictures of Asim and the others entering the apartment block.

The next day, Thursday 17 January, Asim and the bomb-maker, Maulana Shahid, returned to the main mosque. Asim was introduced to two fellow Pakistanis, Mohamed Shoaib and Mehmood Khalid. The former had arrived from Germany the previous November; the latter from Stockholm the previous October. The terrorist cell was now complete. Its commander, Maroof, gave them more details of the plan. There would be two waves of attacks.

'After the first bomb blast, there will be demands from al-Qaeda, and Baitullah Mehsud will announce them,' said Maroof.

About 5 p.m. that day, Maulana Shahid asked Asim if he wanted to call his wife.[9]

'I can't. It's forbidden.'

Shahid handed him a mobile. 'Here, call her. Maulana Maroof has given you permission to speak with your wife.'

Using a prepaid phone card that Shahid gave him, Asim rang his wife. After the call, the men went for a walk and Shahid broke the news.[10]

'That was the last talk with your family. You won't see them again.'

Asim was destined to be a suicide bomber. When he agreed to come to Barcelona, it had never occurred to him that this would happen – nor had he thought that the attack would be so soon.

'Why did you not tell me before?' he asked.

'You might have been too emotional on the phone.'

Asim was now thinking quietly to himself that he had to do something to stop this.

Around 10 p.m., the Spanish surveillance team watched Maulana Qadeer Malik, one of the other leaders of the group, leave the apartment with a black bag that he dropped in a street bin, which they later searched.[11] It contained a cable cutter, a screwdriver, a box cutter, nine pairs of latex gloves, one pair of rubber gloves, eight empty firework carton cylinders and four pieces of plastic also belonging to the fireworks, an empty metal box for shot pellets, an empty shot pellet tin, two bundles of batteries, three devices described by police as 'mechanical timers', eight electric plugs, pieces of fifteen-centimetre cable and a mobile phone top-up card.[12]

The next day was Friday, the day of prayer. At the big mosque, Asim stayed with the group; it was hard to break away. But just after 4 p.m., he said he had to use the toilet. He then checked that the other wooden booths of the men's toilet were empty. At last he had a few moments alone. Reaching into his pocket, he pulled out his own mobile phone and switched it on. Using the same prepaid calling card that Shahid had forgotten to take back, he dialled a number in Paris.

Asim spoke quickly. 'I am here in Barcelona. I am in the Tariq bin Zayid mosque. Tomorrow morning in Barcelona, something bad will happen, some terrorism.'

He listened to the reply and then continued: 'I am living with the group and can't stop it . . . If there is anything you can do, please stop it.'

Asim switched off his phone. He had been speaking to a man, he explained during the trial, he knew to be an undercover police officer.

'I have one friend in France,' he told a court later. 'He is French. Sometimes he sits there in the bar near my house. I know he works for the police, but I don't know which department.'[13]

The officer was in fact a member of the French secret service (it is not clear if he was working then for one of the service's two domestic branches or its foreign branch, the DGSE[14]). The French officer had been in contact with Asim for nearly two years. Whether Asim knew who the officer really was, was already being run as an agent and had travelled to Spain with French knowledge were matters of later debate. In court, Asim denied it. He said, 'In all Europe, I just know one policeman as my friend. I just took a chance to call this man.' But regardless of when he was actually recruited, his phone call back to France was the culmination of French efforts. Here was a mole inside al-Qaeda who was delivering news of a live plot. A modern spymaster could ask for no more.

People like Asim were indeed rare, but it was even rarer for the existence of such an infiltration to be made public almost immediately. Within a few hours of Asim's phone call, most members of the group were inside a jail cell and Spain's Guardia Civil would be persuading Asim to give a statement as a special 'protected witness'. Within a fortnight, the revelation of a French spy in the Barcelona terror plot would be front-page news in Spain, thanks to a news agency that reported on 2 February that the 'French secret service' had urgently warned of a 'terrorist plot' in Barcelona and sent an agent to the city.[15]

Henceforth, Asim would be known to the public as the anonymous agent F1. (Although he was known by his real identity to the accused in Barcelona, and his name was given to the court and later published in certain places, it is prohibited to publish his full name under Spanish law.)

The case caused a row between France and Spain. France wanted to know why Asim's cover was blown so easily. Was it necessary for security forces to storm in so urgently after the phone call to thwart the operation? Whatever the rights and wrongs, the case would underline the difficulty of acting on a spy's information without revealing his existence and so ending his operational life.

When the alleged plotters were later brought to court, the case also showed the clash between secret methods and criminal justice. The police case depended on what Asim described, but he was a flawed witness. There was too much he could not say in open court. His story of a conscience-stricken phone call to his police friend was unconvincing and seemed like a lie to avoid having to disclose that he had been an agent all along. If he confessed to being a long-term agent, he might have betrayed other ongoing or previous operations. But concealing it had another consequence: namely, restricting the other alleged plotters' legal defence. If he was a self-confessed agent, defence lawyers could have demanded information about what the authorities knew in advance and made the case that the defendants had been set up.

Asim detailed later what Maulana Shahid explained about the plot. Shahid told him that Baitullah Mehsud himself had made the decision to upgrade Asim's job from bomb-maker to suicide bomber. This was supposed to be an honour. There would be four martyrs. Asim and Mohamed Imran Cheema, the first pair, were to attack the metro. The second pair were to be Mehmood Khalid and Mohamed Shoaib, though it was not clear whether they would target the metro, or trains or buses.

Shahid had brought a white plastic bag. He took it up to the mosque's library with Asim and Maroof. Behind some books they found a black bag. Both bags contained some grey powder.

Shahid took some powder, rubbed it on his fingers and explained to Maroof, 'The quality is not so good. If something bad happens, I am responsible.'

'Don't worry. I think this powder is OK. Even if it's bad, we can go and get the new and best one.'

Maroof told the group they should take the powder and some computers to another mosque. First, everyone gathered in the courtyard, where they said a special prayer to bless their forthcoming sacrifice. Emotions ran high and Maroof prayed, 'Please, God, accept our sacrifice. We are giving away our lives.'

Maroof, by Asim's account, ordered everyone – a group of twelve – to move out of the Tariq bin Ziyad mosque and head for the Tablighi Jamaat movement's other mosque, near Barcelona's Jaume I metro station. It was known as the Mezquita an-Nour (the mosque of light). It had a second floor where visiting Tablighi Jamaat preachers could cook and eat. Each of the group carried a rucksack and they were told to move in pairs. 'All the people together is too dangerous,' said Maroof.

The new mosque was small. According to Asim, Maroof told the suicide bombers to go upstairs and sleep while the cell leaders, the *maulanas*, stayed below. He said they were going to do some work on their computers, but Asim believed their real intention was to begin assembling the bombs. When the bombs were ready they would launch the attack.

'When we slept that night, I didn't know if it was going to be the next day, the morning or evening. Only Maulana Maroof knows. They were going to start bomb-making and we don't know what time it will be ready and we have to go into the metro.'

At ten minutes to midnight, members of Spain's elite Unidad Especial de Intervención (Special Intervention Unit) raided the mosque and arrested fourteen men, two of whom were later released without charge. When an officer tried to arrest one of the Pakistanis in the group, Abdul Hafeez Ahmed, whom the police considered the lead bomb-maker, he resisted strongly and was said to have told the arresting officer, 'In my country, I have killed many policemen like you.'[16]

As news of the arrests broke, it was greeted with both excitement and alarm in Spain. 'A great al-Qaeda terrorist attack aborted', reported *El Periódico de Catalunya*.[17] Judge Baltasar Garzón, then Spain's most celebrated anti-terrorism magistrate, said that those arrested were 'ready to go into action as terrorists in Spain'. The plot had come as a surprise, but it confirmed that jihadis from Pakistan were the biggest emerging threat in Europe. According to Garzón, 'Pakistan is an ideological and training hotbed for jihadists, and they are being exported here.' In the US, the plot was taken seriously too. Mike McConnell, then director of US National Intelligence, told a congressional committee, 'We had twenty terrorists show up in Spain that had been trained in Pakistan that were going to be suicide bombers, fanning out over Europe.'[18]

The French were not happy, however. The Associated Press news agency reported that counterterrorism teams in France had expressed 'astonishment' about the way Spanish authorities had handled the case. The French 'were furious that the use of their agent appeared in Spanish media, and that authorities had decided to make him a "protected witness"'.[19] While that protected status kept F1's name secret for now, the revelation of such a witness had telegraphed to the members of an alleged terrorist group both the existence of an agent and, without too much thought, his identity. Until then, it was suggested, the plotters had thought F1 was one of them. 'Spain's handling of the French informant has enraged officials at France's intelligence agencies and eroded trust between the countries,' the *New York Times* reported, quoting French and other European officials. 'The informant's value as a source was destroyed when he was made a prosecution witness and the contents of his statements were leaked to the news media.'[20]

It is often hard to decide when to act on intelligence, and even harder if the intelligence warns of a deadly plot. Acting too early may expose the informant or pre-empt the collection of sufficient evidence to convict the criminals. But acting too late could mean that people die. As the Spanish prosecutor González Mota explained, 'Suicide attacks don't allow for a lot of margin to make a decision. Acting after an attack would be a tragedy.'[21] Particularly in democracies, where political leaders fear being held accountable, the security services will allow few active plots they discover to continue for long if there is any risk of people being killed as a consequence. 'In counterterrorism, intelligence is subordinate to action,' said a former SIS officer. The murderous intent of terror groups means any plan to use an agent for long-term intelligence collection is regularly pushed aside.

But were the Barcelona plotters – if that is what they were – so close to striking? Interior Minister Alfredo Pérez Rubalcaba admitted to 'doubts' about how close the cell had been to executing their attack.[22] Was the cover of a very rare and precious spy blown for nothing?

A British intelligence official described a trip he had made to Israel at some time in the 2000s. The chief of Mossad had told the official he was getting complaints: 'Life as a spy is getting so boring. We all have to live like Muslims!' A whole new generation of Mossad officers were doing all they could to walk, talk and think like their enemy. Not only was the routine of constant prayer, study of the Koran and abstinence from both alcohol and casual sex something of a drawback, but a number of experienced spymasters questioned if such efforts would achieve much.

Ever since the attacks of September 2001, political leaders across the Western world had been handing over cheques for billions to their spy agencies and they were now pestering the spy chiefs, wanting to know if they had anyone inside al-Qaeda. As the senior CIA operative had said, both insiders and outsiders wondered if a 'man on the rock' next to bin Laden might have prevented 9/11. But was it even possible now to recruit such a spy or was it too late?

In London in 2008, the former chief of SIS Sir Richard Dearlove argued at a Whitehall think-tank meeting that the recruitment of spies was becoming harder because the 'war on terror' had changed the very nature of the spy game. For instance, in times gone by, the starting point of getting a spy inside any organization was to obtain a list of its members. 'We used to prize internal telephone directories. They were a key to understanding an organization's structure,' he said.

As former intelligence officers explained to me, while the rudimentary step for an agent of getting a phone directory may have been an apparently trivial act of spying, it took the agent over an invisible line of betrayal; it was a small compromise from which it was hard to turn back. And, as Dearlove pointed out, the phone directory was of intrinsic interest. It allowed a spy agency to map the hierarchy of its adversary. But what was the equivalent of al-Qaeda's telephone directory? The absurdity of the question, Dearlove said, was a measure of how the intelligence world had been shaken up.

At the time of the 9/11 attacks, al-Qaeda was headed by a shura, a council with a defined membership that, for example, approved or rejected proposals for major terrorist attacks. Below this ruling shura was a series of subcommittees that organized media activities, finance, military planning, etc.

But as Western agencies got al-Qaeda in their sights, it was as if the organization began to vanish. The so-called Global War on Terror had disrupted al-Qaeda, replacing a centralized terror group with an alliance splintered into interconnected but independent parts. That made al-Qaeda harder than ever to penetrate.

Even before 9/11, al-Qaeda operated franchises. Methods, rules and objectives were mostly public, and satellite groups could make their own choice of targets and time to attack. Islamic terrorists were like a 'flock of birds' that was 'coming together and dispersing apparently spontaneously', with a collapsed hierarchy and no permanent relationships, Dearlove explained to the think tank. Within a modern terror group, individuals were expendable. That meant an agent inside had only a very short time in which to gather useful information. There was no clear hierarchy to ascend and penetrate. And, as happened with F1, a recruit might even be expected to volunteer for a suicide mission.

This transient structure called into question whether serious penetration of the movement was either possible or indeed useful. It meant that intelligence might be good for just a few days, or even hours. That was because not only did people and plots change constantly but also, since there was little requirement to consult others, the precise details of any attack or plot might not be decided, let alone communicated to anyone else, until the very final stages.

Spy agencies were used to thinking long-term, a legacy of the Cold War. If it took five years to develop a good agent in the KGB, for example, it might take another five years to steer that same mole into a position in the KGB where he might access important secrets. Likewise in Northern Ireland, an IRA recruit working for the British could take years to become a trusted member of an active service unit. And throughout this period the organization would be testing the recruit's loyalty. This made penetration difficult but also highly rewarding. Once his loyalty had been proved and he had been steered into a useful position, he could acquire knowledge about people, strategy and plans that might be relevant for years ahead.

Getting a source in that kind of position was much rarer now. According to Dearlove, human intelligence was fast becoming a dying art; the type of spying practised and refined for centuries simply did not work any longer. Human intelligence was 'being undermined because of the difficulty of recruitment of sources'. Instead, he said, we should learn to live with widespread electronic surveillance. 'In this new environment, what you need is access to data flows', such as Internet chat rooms, emails, telephones, the banking system, emigration and immigration records, travel bookings – all of which need to be analysed with sophisticated computer capability.

He was implying that if it was impossible to penetrate a terror group and find out who was really a threat, then the whole of society might have to be monitored intensively in such a way that suspicious patterns of behaviour could be identified early. We might have to accept a much greater invasion of our privacy.

This was an intriguing analysis. But while he had given a good explanation of why old-style spying was not effective against these new targets, he did not explain why spying could not be done differently. Instead, it was a description of a failure to adapt.

The transient structure of militant Islam certainly demanded a nimbler and more flexible form of spying that was far removed from the painstaking efforts of former times. After 9/11, British secret services tried very hard to get their eyes and ears inside the mosques. MI5 and local police forces all started to recruit informers to sit through sermons and warn about any group of extremists that was beginning to form inside a mosque, or in some more informal place of worship. But, as the spy chief had predicted, the success mostly came not from spying but from the use of the standard counterintelligence techniques: surveillance and interception of communications.

That was not the whole story, though. Little by little, the secret services were teaching themselves to operate in a new, more efficient way, as well as learning the vulnerabilities of the jihadi cells and how to penetrate them. If they could not get to the top or run an agent inside for extended periods, at least they could place the agent far enough inside to gather some useful information.

One chink in the jihadi armour was al-Qaeda's constant requirement for recruits. Another was its willingness to use recent converts to the religion. In 2008, one British security source told a newspaper that there might be 'up to 1,500 converts to the fundamentalist cause across Britain'. At one level this was a headache for the security services because, 'obviously, these people blend in and do not raise any flags'. But at another, it demonstrated that complete outsiders, whether black or white, could quickly insert themselves into militant circles. Among examples of such operationalized converts (spyspeak for people who turned their new-found belief in jihad into action) was the so-called Shoe Bomber, Richard Reid, who in 2001 tried to blow up a transatlantic jet. In another case in 2006, a white, 20-year-old ex-grammar school boy from High Wycombe, Buckinghamshire, was arrested and, although later cleared by a jury of the charges, was accused by prosecutors of being prepared to take part in blowing up jets with liquid explosives. He had only been a Muslim for four months at the time of the arrest. There was something credible about new converts in militant circles. 'New religious recruits always tend to be more zealous than those who have grown up with that specific religion,' Robert Leiken, director of the Immigration and National Security Programme, told the *Scotsman*.

According to Lord Alex Carlile, a British lawyer who became the government's independent reviewer of anti-terrorism legislation, Islamic radicals were targeting converts in prison: ex-criminals were to prove a plentiful source of recruits both to join the jihad and to work as agents.[23]

One of those who showed that jihadism could be penetrated was just such a jail-house convert. He was a larger-than-life Danish ex-convict and biker called Morten Storm who had turned to Islam in the late 1990s as a way from escaping from a life of constant fighting, drug taking and drunkenness. Though he found religion, Storm had not abandoned his love of action. He was drawn into more and more radical circles. Known as

'Murad Storm', he came to meet militants living in Great Britain, went to study Arabic and Islam in Yemen (he was there in September 2001) and yearned to fight with Islamic radicals who were taking over Somalia. When his son was born in 2001, he named him Osama, after bin Laden. But, for all his involvement in militant circles, there was something holding him back. Perhaps it was, as he says, 'I was not fully submitted to the acceptance that you can kill unarmed civilians.' When a projected trip to Yemen was cancelled, he became so frustrated that he began to question the tenets of the whole religion he had followed for nearly a decade. 'All my dreams about jihad were ruined. I was like, "that can't happen, why?" I was so hurt and really, really upset . . . It made me sit up all night.' As he thought more about it, his faith in radical Islam evaporated and he became excited by a new prospect – the idea of spying against it.

At some time in 2006, Storm first contacted the Danish intelligence service (PET), but due to connections he had built in radical circles in Britain, he was also asked to assist with Britain's MI5 and with SIS too. Storm's account of his work as an agent cannot be verified independently, but he did collect a vast amount of evidence to document his espionage – including emails, videos and a tape-recorded meeting with the CIA, of which more later.

What Storm did demonstrate was how an agent among jihadis could be run for quite a lengthy period, as long as he did not involve himself too deeply with any one group. Clever handling also showed that his work could be used to spot potential troublemakers and plots-in-the-making without involving him in any prosecution cases.

In Denmark, Storm noticed that a radical named Hammad Khurshid had shaved off his beard, so he tipped off PET that this could be in preparation for an attack. The authorities used hidden cameras to photograph Khurshid and another extremist experimenting with explosives. They were arrested in September 2007 and sentenced to twelve and seven years respectively. Storm was kept away from the courtroom.

Likewise in Britain, in a Somali mosque in Birmingham, Storm got to know a man called Omar, a Syrian whose real name was Hassan Tabbakh, who told Storm he was planning to make bombs. Police raided his home in December 2007 and found bomb-making chemicals and instructions. It was enough to send Tabbakh to jail for seven years, again without the need for Storm to give evidence.[24]

The crucial difference between Storm and Asim was that it had been necessary to put Asim in the witness box. The full story of what happened in Barcelona has yet to be publicly revealed, and key questions also remain about how Asim was recruited and indeed of his credibility. Subsequent research by Spanish journalists has revealed more about his background, including his earlier life, like Storm, on the edges of criminality. The journalists discovered that Asim was still wanted in Pakistan as an alleged 'people smuggler': he was accused of having for years run a racket selling false identity papers to help people get into European countries and also of defrauding people by taking money in return for false promises to make arrangements for them to be smuggled into Europe. Former associates speculated that he became a spy for French intelligence as a way of escaping the criminal charges back home.

None of these details were mentioned when Asim told his story in the Barcelona court, but they did not necessarily undermine it. In protecting spies, details were often withheld from open court. And the threat of legal compromise was a classic recruitment ploy used by some intelligence services, even if not everyone approved. 'These kinds of methods of blackmail can backfire terribly,' said one former SIS officer. But according to a well-informed Spanish source, Asim had been a walk-in to French intelligence, not someone actively targeted. 'He had come to them about two years before.' The source did not know his motives.

When the Guardia Civil stormed the Barcelona mosques Asim was arrested, but he was then transferred for special treatment. He would claim he never knew if his tip-off was the cause of the arrests. Giving evidence in court at the trial of the Barcelona plotters, he questioned if the Guardia Civil already had the gang under surveillance. The court was never told whether they had in fact been watching the gang.

Asim, who joined a Spanish witness protection programme, provided a few clues about how he came to be in touch with the French authorities. Much of his story was barely credible. He told the court he had met his French 'civilian police' friend in a local bar. 'I met the friend two and a half years before because every time I was coming into the bar, he was there. We were sitting every day and came to know each other. We were like bar or coffee shop friends.' Although the pair exchanged phone numbers, Asim denied knowing the French policeman was working for a secret service. He also said he hadn't told the policeman about his terrorist links.

When he went for training on the Afghanistan border, he gave the French-man different reasons. Once he said he was going to visit his sick mother. Another time it was to help in the aftermath of the earthquake. 'I made many excuses to go back to Pakistan.'

Asim insisted his spying for the police began and ended with that one phone call. But he also admitted that he knew the policeman was not in the bar casually but was there to pick up information. 'I came to know he was working for the police – [it was clear] they wanted to get information. I never said he was with the *secret* police.'

Evidence emerged in 2011, however, that Asim had lied to the court and that he had been a long-term secret agent, not just a last-minute informer. This came in a little-noticed cable from the US Embassy in Madrid, published on the Wikileaks website and marked 'Secret' and 'NOFORN' – meaning it wasn't to be shown to any foreign country. It was headed: 'SPAIN: PROSECUTOR DISAVOWS AL-QAIDA TIES TO BARCELONA SUBWAY PLOT' and read:

> 1. (S//NF) Contrary to self-incriminating court testimony by the govern-ment's star witness in the recently concluded trial regarding the plot to attack the Barcelona metro system, National Court Prosecutor Vicente Gonzalez Mota on January 13 privately confirmed to POLOFF [a US Embassy political officer] that there were no Al-Qaida ties to the radical Islamist cell and that the witness was in fact a third-country undercover agent, as the defence had alleged.

The secret cable said Mota revealed this at a US–Spain working group on terrorism and organized crime. He had explained that Spanish law 'allows for security services officials to remain undercover', concealing – in other words, lying about – their true identity and affiliation 'while testifying in court'. Pre-vious embassy reports, said the cable, had pointed out F1's 'sworn testimony' that he was a 'former member of the cell who turned on his colleagues and notified authorities of the plot' and 'that he has been a member of Al-Qaida since 2005', forming part of their finance network. In contradiction to what Asim said in open court, the cable stated that 'the judges were aware that the witness was an undercover agent rather than an al-Qaida member'.[25]

If the cable was true and Asim had lied, then in their quest to protect the source, the authorities may have also denied the alleged plotters a reasonable defence. Without being informed of Asim's background, it was hard for them to challenge the reliability of his account. And little convincing evidence was presented besides his testimony. 'There are real doubts about his case,' Antonio Baquero, the Spanish journalist, said. 'I'm not sure anyone did the job well here.' As the defence had pointed out in the trial, the police had found no explosives – just a few bits of wire and batteries and powder taken from fireworks. The most suspicious items were eight grams of nitrocellulose with particles of potassium perchlorate (also called 'flash powder') from the fireworks, the timers and 783 pellets from an air gun. (However murderous the potential intention, it hardly seemed a recipe for a serious attack.) The Spanish police believed that the real cache of explosives was never found, but they also distrusted Asim. Despite his emphatic testimony about plans for an imminent attack, prosecutors themselves admitted the bomb-makers must have been some way away from completing their work.

During the trial, Roshan Jamal Khan, an Indian businessman who was arrested and later convicted as a member of the cell, insisted that he had come to Spain to source supplies of olive oil to export to Bombay. While he was a member of Tablighi Jamaat and worshipped at the mosque, he said he hardly knew the others who were arrested and knew nothing of a bomb plot. Tablighi Jamaat was a peaceful group, he insisted. 'It was very funny. We were going to spread love with people. Nobody expected suicide, making explosions of killing people.'[26]

Khan said that he had lived all his life in India and had never heard of the Pakistan Taliban leader Baitullah Mehsud. His family in Bombay later claimed, 'It was only on the basis of a fantasy of a wannabe James Bond that it was surmised that a terror attack was imminent on the Barcelona metro. Thus, the police supposedly got into the act to foil it.'[27]

Two men had been arrested in the raids but were released without charge; they insisted on the innocence of the others. Rafqat Ali, a 27-year-old construction worker, 'accused police of beating him and holding him in a darkened cell for hours', according to a news agency. Sheikh Saeed Akhtar, aged fifty-two, who worked in a shop, said, 'We are not terrorists. None of us are. We are just immigrants from Pakistan who work and go to the mosque.' Akhtar said the police discovered electric cables and batteries at the mosque 'because they are doing building work there. We have no interest in these Taliban.'[28]

In December 2009, all eleven alleged plotters were found guilty of membership of a terrorist group and two (Shahid Iqbal and Qadeer Malik) were found guilty of possession of explosives. Shahid and Qadeer were sentenced to fourteen and a half years in jail, Maroof Ahmed Mirza to ten and a half years and the rest to eight years and six months. No one was even charged with plotting a terror attack or attempted murder. On appeal to the Supreme Court, the explosives charges were quashed and the sentence reduced to eight years for Maroof and to six for the others, as, according to the court, the plot was 'at such an embryonic stage'.[29]

Some details of Asim's story, then, remain conflicting and mysterious. But whether a long-term or short-term agent, whether inside al-Qaeda or with a lower-level group of would-be jihadi militants, he was living proof that – however hard it was – spies could be placed inside a terror group and among people with access to the training camps of Pakistan and secret terror cells of Europe. Such agents were worth their weight in platinum and their intelligence needed to be used with great discretion. Blowing the cover of that spy for a plot allegedly based on a few scoops of firework dust had been a costly mistake. Wherever Asim had been recruited, whatever the merits of the prosecution case in Barcelona, he had the potential to go much deeper into militant circles. Putting him in the witness box was a highly unusual use of an agent, since, to preserve the integrity of intelligence methods, he could never tell an honest story. That was why, experienced operatives would argue, it was better to use a human source only as the starting point for evidence collection, someone who could suggest whose phones to tap or which rooms to bug. In this way, a case could be built without the agent needing to be compromised. It was also a means of verifying the agent's account and assessing if his reports were exaggerated. But running the agent longer and building up a case could not be done on the authority of an intelligence agency or a prosecutor alone. It needed backing from political leadership with the courage to let the operation run despite the obvious risks that, if there were mistakes, a group of terrorists could slip out of surveillance. In Spain, just before an election, that courage was lacking.

Running a spy like Asim inside an active cell of militants required not only audacity but also wise judgement – the skill both to assess when the cell was in danger of becoming operational and to determine, as the CIA was soon forced to do, if an agent inside al-Qaeda could really be trusted.

Chapter 8
Allah Has Plans

'They plan, and Allah plans. And Allah is the best of planners'

– Koran, 8:30[1]

On 20 January 2009, the newly elected Barack Obama stood before the Capitol to be sworn in as the forty-fourth president of the United States. Nearly two million people had gathered that freezing morning in Washington, DC, for one of the most widely viewed events in history. His campaign slogan had been 'Yes we can'. After years of painful and divisive wars, and a recent domestic economic slump, Obama embodied an infectious, hopeful spirit that, just for a moment, transcended the familiar grudge-match wrestle of American political factions.

His speech was uplifting. Borrowing the phrase from President Abraham Lincoln's promise in his 1863 Gettysburg Address during the Civil War, Obama looked to a 'new birth of freedom'. Earlier generations, said Obama, had faced down fascism and communism 'not just with missiles and tanks'. They had persevered with their values: 'They understood that our power alone cannot protect us, nor does it entitle us to do as we please. Instead, they knew that our power grows through its prudent use. Our security emanates from the justness of our cause, the force of our example, the tempering qualities of humility and restraint.'

Obama said the country was at war, but the war was coming to an end. 'We'll begin to responsibly leave Iraq to its people and forge a hard-earned peace in Afghanistan.' He had promised to reverse many policies of his predecessor, President Bush. He had promised to close the camp at Guantanamo Bay, Cuba. He had promised an end to the CIA's programme of rendition, torture and secret detention. Here, at the Capitol, he promised to bring the troops back home.[2]

But the war was far from over.

Six thousand miles away, a 31-year-old man was a prisoner of the war. As Obama spoke, he was being questioned for a second day. Humam al-Balawi, a doctor employed in a Palestinian refugee camp, was in a secret police cell. He was in Jordan, a close ally and oil-less dependant of the United States. His prison was a hilltop fort that overlooked Wadi Assur, the Valley of Orchards, in Amman, the capital city. It served as headquarters of the General Intelligence Department (GID). The doctor was getting a dose of reality.

Since America had invaded Jordan's neighbour, Iraq, five years earlier, Humam had been waging battle against what he regarded as the devil's own forces, the US and Israel. True, his war had been conducted mostly from his comfortable bedroom in a leafy part of Amman. But his words, which lionized the jihadi fighters of Iraq and Afghanistan and urged every young Muslim to join the cause, provided inspiration to others and so had impact. Thanks to the speed with which information spreads on the Internet, his online nom-de-guerre had become known from Washington to Riyadh. He called himself Abu Dujanah al-Khorasani. 'Abu Dujanah' was a heroic battlefield companion of the Prophet Muhammad and 'Al-Khorasani' means someone from Khorasan, an ancient name for eastern Persia, including the area of modern Afghanistan. The legend of a 'Greater Khorasan' and its prophecies formed part of al-Qaeda propaganda. Militants were looking to a moment predicted by the Prophet when a new Islamic army, carrying black banners, would assemble in Khorasan and be triumphant. Although the hadiths – accounts of the personal sayings of the Prophet, as distinct from the Koran – were not unchallenged by scholars, some recalled the Prophet saying: 'If you see the black flags coming from Khorasan, join that army, even if you have to crawl over ice, for this is the army of the Caliph, the Mahdi and no one can stop that army until it reaches Jerusalem.'[3] It was inspirational.

Humam's arrest was timed, perhaps not accidentally, at a significant moment in his life. He had come to feel that he had reached a crossroads and he must make some decisions. He might be full of clever words, but was he really man enough to do what he so vehemently preached? A few days before his arrest, he had published an article online that explained his mental anguish. It was headlined: 'When Will My Words Drink from My Blood?'

> I feel as though my words have become vain and expired, and are dying between the hands of their writer, I feel as though I have become old and aged; people pass by me and whisper: an old man whose offspring have died. For every day that I spend sitting back steals some of my age and health and determination, thus broadening the gap between what I dream of and what I am actually.

The time had come for action. 'For my words will die if I do not save them with my blood. And my feelings will die if I do not ignite them with my death . . . for I fear that I die on my bed as the cattle die, and By Allah I don't bear that.'[4]

Humam had a loving Turkish wife, Defne, and two young children, Leyla, aged seven, and Lina, aged five. But he asked his article's readers how he would explain to martyrs on the Day of Judgement why he had shunned the path of sacrifice taken by others to remain at home 'dining with my wife and children in a peaceful house'. The spark for his outrage and sense of disempowerment had been television pictures of Israeli women observing an air raid on Palestinian-ruled Gaza. He recalled later the impact of these events on him:

> I can't forget the scene I saw on al-Jazeera channel, in which the daughters of Zion were watching Gaza as it was being bombed by F-16 fighter jets. They were using binoculars and watching the Muslims get killed, and it was as if they were just observing some natural phenomenon, or as if they were watching a theatrical film or something similar.[5]

Humam's online call-to-arms was posted on the same date, 27 December 2008, as the Israeli tanks rolled into Gaza. The article did not go unnoticed by the Jordanian authorities. And so, at 11.30 p.m., six hours after sunset on a hazy moonless night, at the end of the day before Obama's inaugural speech, GID vans pulled up outside the elegant house of Humam's father, where Humam lived with his wife. 'There are police outside,' she told him. They arrested him with a warrant for 'possession of prohibited materials' and seized his computers. There was no time to erase his computer disk drives. It was going to be hard for him to explain away his blogging hobby to the secret police.

It was reported later that Humam cracked quickly, that he began to see the error of his ways and soon started to give up the identity of some of the militants that he knew. And if he wanted excitement, the GID was offering it. He was given the chance to be an informer, a spy of sorts. 'So this step began with this proposal,' he recounted later. 'They proposed that I go to Waziristan and Afghanistan to spy on Muslims.'[6]

The GID had not, in truth, begun quite so boldly. In the first few days, in line with standard spy-recruitment methodology, the agency tried to start Humam on the path of compromise, getting him to divulge a few names and details – to cross the line into betrayal. They also made threats. If Humam did not help, then his family would be in trouble. He was no longer Abu Dujanah, the invisible soldier of Allah. He was now the very ordinary Humam al-Balawi of Urwa Bin Al-Ward Street, the son of Khalil and husband of Defne. He was a marked man. Whatever he did from now on would be scrutinized by the state.

So, after just three days inside a jail, Humam agreed to betray his brothers. His handcuffs were removed and he was driven away from the hilltop. The GID dropped him home in a pickup truck and he stepped out a new man: Agent Panzer.

Or was he just playing along? He would say later that it had all been a ruse, that the idea he could have changed his mind so quickly was laughable.

So they think that if a man is offered money, it is possible for him to abandon his creed. How amazing! [Proposing such things] to a man whose last article just a short while ago was called 'When Will My Words Drink from My Blood?'; a man who burns with desire for martyrdom . . . How can you have the gall to say to him, 'Go and spy on the Mujahedeen'?! You'll never find such idiocy except in Jordanian Intelligence.[7]

In reality, no one would know what decision he had reached at this point. Most likely, he had not made up his mind what to do yet. The Jordanians realized that he was still a work-in-progress.

As Humam al-Balawi was aware, thousands of miles east from his home, in what he called the 'land of Jihad', a new type of war was under way.

The battle zone was in the wild mountains of the north-west frontier of Pakistan and the war was characterized by the near-constant threat of attack from the sky.

For years now, with the secret acquiescence of Pakistani security forces, the CIA had been flying unmanned drones over the territory. As a covert military operation, conducted without any declaration of war, this fell to the CIA to organize, rather than the US Air Force. Some of these propeller-driven Predators even took off from and landed inside Pakistan, at a remote Pakistani Air Force base. The Pakistanis had also created an air corridor, known as 'the boulevard', for unrestricted transit of US war-planes across the country.[8] The Predators stayed aloft for hours on end, maintaining watch on the mountains of the Afghan border. Then, from time to time, they unleashed a Hellfire missile, killing a militant and, quite often, killing bystanders too. An updated version of the Predator could drop bombs as well as missiles.

Since July 2008, this drone war has intensified. The CIA was getting more accurate and striking more often. President Bush had authorized the CIA to strike before warning Pakistan. The new approach breached Pakistani sovereignty but was justified by intelligence that showed some members of Pakistan's combined foreign and domestic spy agency, known as Inter Service Intelligence (ISI), were actively assisting the militants. These ISI officers were helping them cross the border to attack US troops in Afghanistan. There was also evidence that the Pakistan Taliban were plotting or encouraging attacks abroad, including in the United States. This gave the US legal grounds for widening the drone attacks, against not only al-Qaeda but also the Pakistani Taliban, now they were formally judged to be a threat to the US. If anyone was a genuine danger, then by US law a president could attack them pre-emptively without even declaring war. Bush ordered a cross-border raid by Special Forces against a training camp.

When Obama took office, there was a brief pause, but the new president quickly established that he was, if anything, keener on drone attacks than Bush had been. He might have opposed torture, waterboarding and renditions, but did not object to what was in effect an assassination programme. This was apparent from the statistics. From 2004 to 2007, there were only ten publicly observed drone strikes in Pakistan. According to estimates by the New America Foundation, a Washington think tank, the attacks killed somewhere between ninety-five and 107 civilians and between forty-three and seventy-six militants. In 2008, there had been six strikes by July. Then, after Bush's decision to escalate, another thirty strikes by the end of the year. These killed an estimated 157 to 265 militants and twenty-three to twenty-eight civilians. In 2009, there were two strikes in early January, followed by a pause until Obama was inaugurated. Then, in February 2009, one of the top commanders of the Taliban in the north-west frontier, Baitullah Mehsud, announced the launch of the Shura Ittihad ul-Mujahideen, a united council of fighters with three common enemies: the Pakistani state, the United States and the Afghan government. Mehsud was the leader allegedly behind the Barcelona plot. He was also blamed for the assassination in December 2007 of the Pakistani politician Benazir Bhutto. Mehsud's pact was intended to end squabbles among militants. It was also a gift to the US, because it provided a clear legal basis for attacking his network. By the end of the year there had been a total of fifty-two strikes into Pakistan. The death toll: 241 to 508 militants and sixty-six to eighty civilians.[9]

While Mehsud was busy making alliances, in Jordan officers from the GIA were discussing with their CIA liaison contacts a plan to send the new informant, Agent Panzer, to Pakistan. The idea was that Humam would continue his life as a secret jihadi operative while also reporting to the GID – in other words, become a double agent.

This was not going to be an easy task. Experienced spymasters knew that to successfully run a 'double' in place was one of the hardest things an intelligence officer could do. Betrayal is a double-edged sword. As the KGB had found when running Kim Philby, it was hard to work out who was really playing whom. Once the fear of betrayal took hold – as it had when James Angleton ruled as CIA counterintelligence chief from 1954 to 1975 – operations could become paralysed and pointless. As the CIA advised its staff in 1963, 'The double agent operation is one of the most demanding and complex counterintelligence activities in which an intelligence service can engage. Directing even one double agent is a time-consuming and tricky undertaking that should be attempted only by a service having both competence and sophistication.'[10]

To handle such operations, the CIA had in place a series of procedures, not least of which was the supervision of a double-agent case by the agency's counterintelligence staff. Such rules had been drawn up in 1963, when the CIA faced its most serious and professional adversary, the KGB. As they confronted al-Qaeda and all its affiliates, the CIA had dropped its guard. They failed to appreciate the counterintelligence threat that al-Qaeda posed.

The Sunni radical movement that morphed, among other incarnations, into al-Qaeda had, as a whole, a prolonged experience of contact with intelligence services. Among the junior ranks of militant Islam – the fresh recruits destined to wear the suicide vests, for example – though plenty were paranoid about spies in their midst, most were ignorant about spycraft. Many were 'clean skins', meaning there was no intelligence on file about them, and so had little first-hand knowledge of the intelligence services. The senior veterans were different; their lifetime's struggle had been defined by their stand against different agencies of state security, with whom they had often come into direct contact. Much of what passes for jihadi philosophy had been conceived in the torture chambers and dungeons of the Middle East secret police. (One of the most influential thinkers of political Islam, Sayyid Qutb, wrote his 1964 jihadist manifesto, *Ma'alim fi-l-Tariq* (Milestones), while in the custody of Egyptian State Security and incarcerated in Al Aqrab, the feared Scorpion prison in Cairo.) The violent tactics of the Salafists, those like Qutb and, later, members of al-Qaeda who looked back to the early life of the Prophet Muhammad as inspiration for their politics, developed from these experiences. Secret terrorist cells developed as weapons of resistance to this secret state power in societies where open political opposition was prohibited. And the relationship with the spymaster was not just repressive. At different times, militant groups were actively supported by or at least tolerated by the state. Because of the violent nature of these groups, contact with the state needed to remain secret and was therefore invariably handled by intelligence operatives.

The very top of al-Qaeda had extensive experience of such a relationship. Contrary to the conspiracy theory, Osama bin Laden, its leader, was never funded or supported by the CIA. But, as a financier of Arab fighters in the war against the Soviets in Afghanistan, bin Laden for a long time had dealings with the Saudi GIP. As Steve Coll, his family's biographer, recorded, 'Prince Turki [the former GIP chief] and other Saudi intelligence officials said years later that bin Laden was never a professional Saudi intelligence agent. Still, while the exact character and timeline of his dealings [with GIP] remain uncertain, it seems clear that bin Laden did have a substantial relationship with Saudi intelligence.'[11] According to Coll, some in the CIA later concluded that 'bin Laden operated as a semi-official liaison' between the Saudi GIP, international Islamist religious networks and 'the leading Saudi-backed Afghan commanders'.[12]

In other words, although secret services might find it hard to penetrate Islamist networks, it was not because they had ever lacked contact or access to them. Before they headed for the mountains, these radical groups had emerged from a wider struggle that, from its inception, had been alternately monitored and encouraged, inspired and repressed, by the secret services. The story of the West versus al-Qaeda is one of an almost continuous confrontation with secret agencies. This did not occur only in the Middle East. A normal American or European citizen might never come across MI5 or the FBI. But a militant Islamist could come across them when he was stopped at the borders, or called into the embassy for a 'few questions', or received an early-morning knock on the door. Those who fought on the front line often got to meet their enemy.

But if they had some experience of the spymasters, did the militants have much skill at running spies themselves? Few really knew for sure. Volunteers for al-Qaeda were certainly expected to behave a little like spies, at least when they operated in the West. When they took their *bayat* (oath) they were sworn into a secret society and the terrorist shared the secret agent's need to be covert. While preparing for an attack, a jihadi needed to blend in with normal society, or at least manage well enough to avoid attention. As Ibn al-Sheikh al-Libi had explained to Nasiri in Afghanistan, they might also have to collect information like spies:

> We must fight the Zionists efficiently . . . We need brothers who can live among them, who can watch them, surveil them. We need blueprints and photos of their clubs, their synagogues, their banks, their consulates . . . We can't just send anyone to do this job . . . We need a brother who can resist all temptation, and remain pure in himself while he lives amongst the kafir. We need someone with unlimited resources of patience and determination.[13]

Apart from the need for operational security, al-Qaeda demonstrated early on its awareness of the need for good counterintelligence. As far back as the late 1990s the widely circulated 'Jihad Manual' warned about the spies favoured by the US. One section read:

Types of Agents Preferred by the American Intelligence Agency [CIA]:

1. Foreign officials who are disenchanted with their country's policies and are looking towards the U.S. for guidance and direction.
2. The ideologist (who is in his country but against his government) is considered a valuable catch and a good candidate for American Intelligence Agency [CIA].
3. Officials who have a lavish lifestyle and cannot keep up using their regular wages, or those who have weaknesses for women, other men, or alcoholic beverages. The agent who can be bought using the aforementioned means is an easy target, but the agent who considers what he does a noble cause is difficult to recruit by enemy intelligence.
4. For that purpose, students and soldiers in Third World countries are considered valuable targets. Soldiers are the dominating and controlling elements of those countries.[14]

Al-Qaeda's targets for recruiting their own spies were listed in the same document as:

1. smugglers;
2. those seeking political asylum;
3. adventurers;
4. workers at coffee shops, restaurants, and hotels;
5. people in need;
6. employees at borders, airports, and seaports.

But it warned: 'Recruiting agents is the most dangerous task that an enlisted brother can perform. Because of this dangerous task, the brother may be killed or imprisoned. Thus, the recruitment task must be performed by special types of members.'[15]

A more authoritative al-Qaeda study on intelligence techniques was written in October 2006 by someone described by counterterrorism researchers at the US Military Academy, West Point, as al-Qaeda's spymaster.[16] In his 152-page pamphlet, 'The Myth of Delusion', Muhammad Khalil al-Hakaymah demonstrated avid reading of publicly available material about weaknesses in US human intelligence. He explained why both the FBI and the CIA had trouble finding reliable agents: the agencies' shortages of Arabic translators and operatives, how older intelligence professionals had been driven out by younger, more ideological officers, and how overdependence on the polygraph (a lie-detecting machine) as well as excessive security measures had hindered recruitment.

Al-Hakaymah failed to predict the coming drone war. He warned that the greatest intelligence threat to al-Qaeda was penetration by spies rather than by technology. He wanted al-Qaeda to ready its defences. According to him, in the old days Western spies came disguised as 'businessmen, journalists or clergy' but the New Spies, after all the lessons learned from 9/11, would 'closely and literally imitate the operating system of the Islamic Jihadist groups'. It was a new Great Game (my words), with 'young officers seeking adventure and risk to their lives, wearing Islamic costumes and practicing the rite of the Muslims if necessary to protect their cover by melting into Arab and Islamic societies'.[17]

Three years after al-Hakaymah wrote his article, there was no sign that any such penetration by Western agents had really materialized. The CIA was not getting even close. Bin Laden and his deputy Ayman al-Zawahiri eluded capture and a sanctuary remained for Islamists in the mountains of Pakistan, in most of Somalia and parts of Yemen. Nevertheless, al-Qaeda was starting to lose momentum. Not only had key operational leaders like Khalid Sheikh Mohamed (the suspected architect of 9/11) been captured and imprisoned, the organization was showing its political ineptness. It haemorrhaged popular support due to what many fellow radical Muslims saw as its relentless focus on 'martyrdom operations' (suicide attacks), in which other Muslims, particularly in Iraq and Pakistan, were the usual victims.

Al-Hakaymah recognized what was occurring and that al-Qaeda's greatest danger was itself. In another article, 'Towards a New Strategy in Resisting the Occupier', he encouraged listening to public opinion and criticized mass casualty attacks that killed Muslim civilians.

However, not all jihadi thinkers were dismayed by the bloodshed. Activists like Humam revelled in it. One of his idols was fellow Jordanian Abu Musab al-Zarqawi, the human butcher who led al-Qaeda in Iraq on a murderous wave of hostage-taking, videoed beheadings and indiscriminate car bombs. In 2005, al-Zarqawi's supporters had mounted a triple suicide attack on luxury hotels in Amman that left sixty dead. A year later he too was dead, killed in a targeted strike by US forces.

Just before Humam was arrested, he had dreamed of al-Zarqawi frequently. In these dreams he would see al-Zarqawi in his house. Humam asked him, 'Aren't you dead?' and al-Zarqawi replied, 'I was killed, but I am as you see me, alive.' As Humam remembered it, 'His face was like a full moon, and he was busy, as if he was getting ready for an operation. I wished I could take him to a secure place, and take him out in my car, and I also wished that we could be bombed so we could be killed together.'[18]

The al-Qaeda propagandist al-Hakaymah was dead now too. In 2008, he had travelled back from a sanctuary in Iran to join his brothers on the front line in north-west Pakistan. The US was offering a million dollars as a bounty for his death or capture, but in November 2008 he was killed in a drone strike in northern Waziristan. Technology was catching up.

Two months after his arrest in Jordan, Humam caught a plane to Pakistan and began his real-life spy mission. He had told his family (all except his younger brother) that he was travelling to Turkey to take some exams. Over the course of his eight-hour journey, flying via Dubai, he could reflect back on a hectic last few weeks.

When he had returned from interrogation, he seemed to his family a quiet, broken man. 'Did they beat you?' his father asked. 'No,' Humam replied. 'They humiliated me.'[19]

At night, Humam began cautiously slipping out to meet with someone he knew as Abu Zeid, his new GID handler. Abu Zeid's real name was Sharif Ali bin Zeid al-Aoun. He was no ordinary intelligence officer but a member of the Hashemite royal family, the rulers of Jordan. A former intern with US Senator John Kerry and an alumnus of Boston University, bin Zeid was a highly Westernized fluent English speaker. He had also become friends with a CIA officer recently stationed in Amman, Darren LaBonte, who had previously served as an Army Ranger and later with the FBI. The two had both married that year and their wives, Fida and Racheal, socialized together. To the CIA, bin Zeid seemed like one of Jordan's best. They constantly sought him out for advice and as a trusted liaison with the GID. But was he the right man to handle Humam?

To the slim, ascetic and conservative Palestinian, the intelligence officer must have looked like a polar opposite. Bin Zeid was rather overweight and affluent, driving round in an expensive 4x4. During the days after Humam's release, bin Zeid took him to smart restaurants to chat. The bills totalled over $70 per visit – an extravagance in Amman. He took

Humam to the glitzy Safeway superstore and bought him up to $400 worth of groceries for his family. Was he being tempted by this taste of the life-style that could be his if he cooperated? Or was Humam just swallowing his feelings of repulsion?

During their chats, bin Zeid outlined the benefits of being a spy. If Humam went to the 'land of jihad' and helped to capture or kill a top al-Qaeda target, his reward would be huge. 'They tried to entice me with money and offered me amounts reaching into the millions of dollars according to the man being targeted, particularly the leaders of Qaida al-Jihad in the Land of Khorasan . . . these weren't mere empty promises.'[20]

Although it is hard to know what he really felt, Humam would speak dismissively later about his GID handler, claiming, 'The intelligence officer was an idiot.' Bin Zeid was proposing a mission to the very place that Humam had been longing to go to, albeit for different reasons. 'The amazing thing which I could hardly believe is that I had been trying to mobilize to Jihad in Allah's path but had been unsuccessful. Then this idiotic man comes along and proposes that I go to the fields of Jihad. All praise is due to Allah . . . it was a dream come true!'[21]

So, on a March day, Humam walked down the steps of the plane in the frontier city of Peshawar. He was entering what had become one of the world's greatest hotspots for intrigue and espionage. As an Arab, he would have been conspicuous. The local secret police were on the lookout for foreigners who were arriving in large numbers to train for and partake in 'jihad'. Everything these Arab fighters did spelled trouble for Pakistan. (While, in the CIA's view, the ISI gave concrete support to the Afghan Taliban, foreign fighters linked to al-Qaeda were mortal enemies of the Pakistan state.) But as a trained medical doctor, Humam had a good cover story, with a convincing account of what he was doing in these parts. The Jordanian GID had provided him with money, paid for his ticket and helped him to forge the documents he needed for his Pakistani visa.[22]

Humam probably crossed town, like most people did, in a three-wheeled motorized rickshaw. His destination was the crowded Kabuli market, where buses set off for the tribal areas along the border. These were supposed to be closed to foreigners like him, but he caught a bus to Kohat, a gateway town to the tribal areas, then went onwards into North Waziristan, the principal sanctuary of the Taliban and al-Qaeda. And then he disappeared. Had he been arrested? Or killed? Or was he too

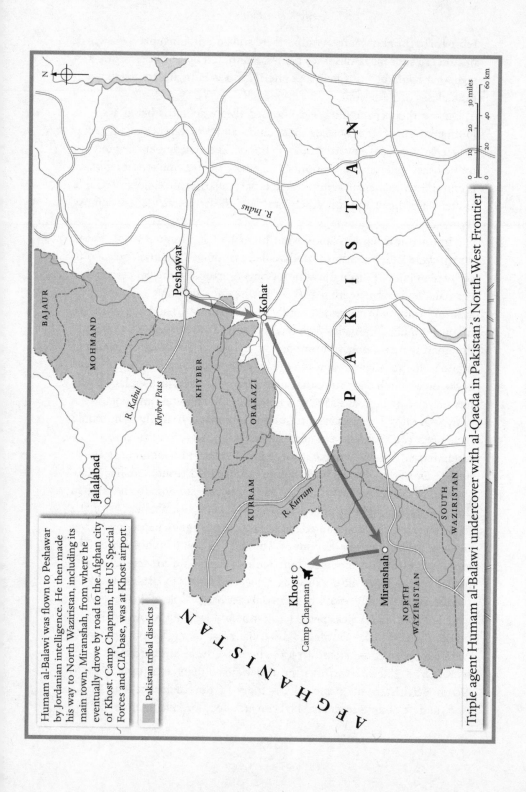

Humam al-Balawi was flown to Peshawar by Jordanian intelligence. He then made his way to North Waziristan, including its main town, Miranshah, from where he eventually drove by road to the Afghan city of Khost. Camp Chapman, the US Special Forces and CIA base, was at Khost airport.

Pakistan tribal districts

Triple agent Humam al-Balawi undercover with al-Qaeda in Pakistan's North-West Frontier scared to perform his mission? From March until August, his handler, Ali bin Zeid, and Darren LaBonte of the CIA, could only wonder. He would not have been the first agent sent into the frontier region to vanish without a trace.

At that time, a stranger like Humam who arrived in the tribal zone was in mortal danger. The locals were consumed by spy fever. Night and day, the American drones were criss-crossing the sky, hunting for new targets among the militants. The planes were said to hunt in packs, monitoring a potential target from multiple angles and remaining on station overhead. Such total surveillance was known by the US military as the 'Unblinking Eye'.[23] Drones were usually invisible, blending into the grey skies. But people on the ground could sometimes catch a glimpse of the planes when cloud cover forced them to fly lower than usual, and more often they could hear the hum of the propellers. The sound could be terrifying, particularly for those who got mixed up with militants.

None of the locals understood how the drones found their targets. They appeared to be highly accurate. Contrary to what US officials sometimes said, they did kill plenty of innocents. By and large, these were people who were standing close to a missile's intended target. The more accurate the drones became, the more desperate the hunt for spies. The CIA offered big rewards for the scalps of top militants, whose henchmen in turn started rounding up suspected informers, torturing them to extract 'confessions' and then executing them in public as a warning (and sometimes recording it all on gruesome videos). They were hunting too for little electronic homing beacons, which were believed to be tossed over the walls of militant compounds by informers and supposedly guided the drones to their targets.

How had the CIA improved its targeting? With reportedly up to 200 officers deployed to Pakistan, was it the result of running spies in the region? According to one person involved, the CIA had some agents but there was little that US intelligence could do in the tribal areas without running into the ISI. Much of what passed for 'human intelligence' was just small, imprecise snatches of information passed on by the ISI. Some informants did come forward to offer specific information. But, as they operated in such remote areas, it was hard to confirm what they reported with a second pair of eyes. By contrast, the technical methods used by the CIA were getting better and better. Mobile phones could be intercepted and tracked. The militants knew this but, for some fatalistic reason, still continued to use them. Vehicles and compounds could be watched from above. But what really counted was the US presence over the border in Afghanistan. Because so many militants in that country were also operating in Pakistan, when they were captured they could provide detailed knowledge about the tribal areas. It had taken a very long time, but gradually the CIA had assembled a voluminous database of who was who and what normal life looked like on the frontier (mirroring the laborious work once done in Empire days by British political agents and recorded in huge bound volumes). It had reached the point that the CIA knew almost all the key compounds where the militants lived.

The war was also becoming even more ruthless, as when, in April, the CIA killed a militant early one day and then in the afternoon hit those who were gathered at his funeral. The targets had been top followers of Baitullah Mehsud. Late in August, the US finally got Mehsud. He was on the roof of a building with his wife when a missile struck. As an example of their precision, CIA sources would later claim that they had made such a careful choice of munitions that they hit the roof and killed Mehsud and his wife without collapsing the building.[24]

As suddenly as he had vanished, Humam then reappeared. Some said he had been living with Baitullah Mehsud until the commander's death, acting as his personal doctor. No one really knew where he had been. But what Ali bin Zeid saw in his email inbox one morning sent a shiver through him. Attached to a message was a video clip showing that Humam was not just alive but that he had stayed true to his mission and had managed to penetrate the inner circle of al-Qaeda. On the clip was a figure close to Osama bin Laden named Atiyah Adb al-Rahman, a Libyan and fellow veteran of the 2001 Battle of Tora Bora, when the al-Qaeda leader had escaped encirclement by US Special Forces and their local allies. According to intelligence sources interviewed by Joby Warrick, a *Washington Post* journalist who wrote a book about the case, al-Rahman could be seen next to Humam.

Agent or traitor, Humam was no longer just a dangle, a long-shot play at getting someone inside al-Qaeda. Without doubt he had now entered the game as a real player. The news woke up the GID with a jolt. It woke up the CIA too. Bin Zeid and his buddy LaBonte had a live one, a fish on their line.

'The bait fell in the right spot,' Humam recalled, 'and they went head over heels with excitement.'[25] Humam would come to say his initial disappearance had all been a ruse. 'The fact is, after consulting with the Mujahedeen, I cut off ties for four months in order for Jordanian intelligence to stew in its own juices thinking that this guy had abandoned it, so that if he came back to them and told them that conditions were difficult, they would buy his story quickly. And that's what happened.'[26]

In September 2009, Humam gave an interview to al-Qaeda's *Vanguards of Khorasan* online magazine. He was introduced as 'Brother Abu Dujanah al-Khorasani' and described as a 'Well-Known Blogger in Jihadi Forums, and a Newcomer to the Land of Khorasan'.[27] Ironically, what he told the magazine was pleasing to both sides of the spy game: his handlers in Jordan would observe him maintaining his cover story; his global jihadi readers would receive inspiration. Asked about his background, Humam lied: 'Your young brother comes from the northern Arabian Peninsula [Saudi Arabia], may Allah release it from its state of imprisonment.' He then added truthfully, 'I am a little over 30 years old. I'm married and I have two young daughters, praise be to Allah. Allow me to give this much information.' As always, Humam spoke lyrically about jihad:

> A person once said, 'there is love that kills.' I only see the truth of this in my love for jihad, as this love will either kill you with regret if you should choose to stay away from jihad, or else you will die as a martyr for the cause of Allah if you choose to go to jihad – and it is up to every human to choose between these two fates.

Humam said he felt 'newly born' living in the mountains. He was 'happy like an innocent child playing with a friend'. But fighters with him had good friends who had already been martyred.

> I have learned from them that silence is clearer than speech. This is a group, half of whom are in Paradise and the other half is still on earth waiting. I wonder why do they not cry in front of me when they mention their martyred brothers? If I should mention the name of a martyr before them; of those known to them, you would find the tears frozen in their eyes like a drizzle on a flower.[28]

Humam started emailing regular reports to Jordan. He kept it brief and usually vague, but gave details of the effects of drone attacks in the frontier territory. He even suggested a specific target for another air strike. He said later it was all a trick: 'I gave them some erroneous, made-up coordinates of targets to make them drool even more, along with some worthless or incorrect information. For example, if the Mujahideen had some work to do somewhere, I would tell them that it was in another place, thereby providing cover for the Mujahideen.'[29]

If by then he really had been turned so that he was working for al-Qaeda and had betrayed the GID, Humam was using what amounted to classic counterintelligence ploys: namely, giving away what he said were snatches of seemingly important 'accurate information which we thought the enemy probably already had knowledge of'.[30] His trick recalled the CIA's guidance on Soviet techniques: 'To create or enhance confidence in an important double agent they are willing to sacrifice through him information of sufficient value to mislead the reacting service into accepting his bona fides.'[31]

In October, Humam offered some momentous news. He had a new patient, none other than the deputy leader of al-Qaeda, Ayman al-Zawahiri. To prove it, he provided the GIA with some specific medical details that had never been made public before. All of a sudden, Humam's status was ratcheted up several notches – from being a Jordanian who was maybe of some importance, he rapidly became possibly the best agent on the ground. The CIA wanted to take over the case. Like Curveball, he was becoming a top source handled by another agency. And if the CIA were to have direct control they would need to meet him.

At this stage, even before the meeting had taken place, the White House was informed. It was a measure of just how rare and important this situation was, and further indication that the CIA was still searching for their 'man on the rock'. 'In the eight years since the start of the war against al-Qaeda, no one had ever gotten so close,' said Warrick.[32]

Leon Panetta, the CIA director, told President Obama, 'There are indications that he might have access to Zawahiri . . . If we can meet with him and give him the right technology, we have a chance to go after Zawahiri.'[33]

The Jordanians were proud. 'You've lifted our heads!' wrote bin Zeid to Humam. 'You've lifted our heads in front of the Americans.'[34]

★

In its 1963 guidance, the CIA spelled out a warning about inheriting a double agent case from an ally:

> Sometimes a double agent operation is turned over by a liaison service . . . When such a transfer is to be made, the inheriting service ought to delve into the true origins of the case and acquire as much information as possible about its earlier history . . . For predictive purposes the most important clue embedded in the origins of an operation is the agent's original or primary affiliation, whether it was formed voluntarily or not, the length of its duration, and its intensity.[35]

The guidance said double agents fell into three categories: first, the 'Walk-in or Talk-in'; second, the 'Agent Detected and Doubled'; and third, the 'Provocation Agent'. Humam fell into the second category. 'A service discovering an adversary agent may offer him employment as a double. His agreement, obtained under open or implied duress, is unlikely, however, to be accompanied by a genuine switch of loyalties,' it stated. Such an agent ran the risk of his duplicity being discovered and at that point he would be 're-doubled' (also known as becoming a triple agent).

In early December 2009, Ali bin Zeid and Darren LaBonte left for what they hoped would be a short trip to the Afghan border to meet their star agent. Due to the difficulties involved and the importance of the operation, the Jordanians had now agreed to let the Americans take charge.

The destination was Camp Chapman, a CIA and US Special Forces' base by the city airport of Khost, eastern Afghanistan. Khost was a perfect place for spy work. It lay opposite the Taliban's sanctuaries in the Pakistani frontier 'agencies' of North and South Waziristan. Agents could be dispatched easily over the border because local Pashtuns needed no passport and also because of the physical geography: although Khost was in Afghanistan, the big mountain crossings lay to the west, on the road to Kabul; the passes into Pakistan were relatively low-level and easy to cross. Khost was also a key place where frontier people came to shop and trade. This gave anyone in Waziristan a believable excuse to pay a visit. The currency used in Khost market was the Pakistani rupee and not the afghani.

Camp Chapman itself was, by late 2009, at the centre of a huge spying operation overlooking the border. No fewer than five different sub-bases nearby were controlled by the CIA, which the military referred to as the

OGA (Other Government Agency).[36] Inside the bases was an array of listening gear to intercept any kind of electronic message that militants across the border might generate. The bases were also there to prevent or monitor the militants crossing. For that, the CIA had raised its own private army, the Khost Protection Force (KPF), one of a number of militias across the country which it dubbed Counterterrorism Pursuit Teams (CPTs). According to media reports, the CPTs not only guarded the border but also sent operatives across it on raids.[37] That was an exaggeration, according to two officers of the KPF I interviewed, but given their contacts with tribes that spanned the border, the KPF was certainly a tremendous source of gossip and low-level intelligence.

Camp Chapman was technically a CIA 'sub-station', subordinate to the main Kabul 'station'. The person in charge of all CIA activities in the area since around April that year was called Jennifer Matthews, a former analyst with the CIA's bin Laden unit (which was known as Alec Station). She was someone skilled in the main mission here: targeting the enemy. Matthews had been credited with tracking down and capturing Abu Zubaydah, the al-Qaeda logistics chief that Nasiri had met. Since then she had worked extensively on the wider al-Qaeda manhunt and been posted to London as chief of counterterrorism liaison with Britain's MI5. What she lacked, however, as LaBonte and bin Zeid would discover, was experience in arranging or conducting a meeting with a secret agent. She had all the skills required for the job, except this most critical one. She was not a spymaster.

As the meeting with Humam was being planned, the pressure rose. This might be the only chance in years for the CIA to kill al-Qaeda's Number Two. According to Warrick, the agent, now code-named Wolf, had first proposed a meeting in Miranshah, the main town of North Waziristan, but the 'Taliban stronghold' didn't please the Jordanian intelligence officer. Humam was told that meeting in Miranshah was too dangerous and he was asked to find an excuse instead to slip across the border to Khost. Perhaps he could say he was going to buy medical supplies for Zawahiri? Normally a CIA meeting with an agent would involve one or at most two handlers, the location would be discreet, perhaps just the back seat of a moving car, and the meeting would not last long. But the CIA had much to accomplish with Humam. They needed to work out what he knew and if he could be trusted. They also needed to train and equip him with the latest technology. That was why Matthews wanted Humam brought on to the base and had a larger than usual team assembled to meet him.

Darren LaBonte did not like the plan at all. As an ex-soldier, it went against all his training. But it was approved by headquarters.

Thomas Pickering, the former US ambassador who jointly led a review into the Khost attack, said, 'We don't know if Darren ever articulated his concerns in a cohesive way.' But Pickering also said that circumstantial evidence suggested that Matthews did not heed warnings from her security advisers not to greet Humam with too many people – a breach of long-standing tradecraft.[38]

There were other warnings: in early December a Jordanian intelligence officer had warned a CIA officer in Amman of his concerns about Humam being a double agent. The officer discounted the warning and didn't pass it on to headquarters or the team.[39]

In the last days before the meeting, Humam claimed, while communicating with bin Zeid, that he was scared to go. He said he was afraid of being spotted by Taliban spies. The CIA base was well known; even the guards at the gate could be working for the Taliban. Bin Zeid promised Humam that he could be rushed straight past them so that no one would see him. He would be brought directly to the CIA and his handlers. Straight to his enemies.

It was Humam's thirty-second birthday on 25 December. As Warrick relates, Matthews had told colleagues that 'he must be made to feel welcome' since he was going to be asked to do something phenomenally dangerous. She ordered a birthday cake to be made for him. In the weeks that followed, the CIA would be asked why it took such incredible risks on the case, bearing in mind Humam was a complete unknown. The CIA explained that it was precisely because it had realized the fact – that was why its officers needed to meet him so badly.

On the night before he died, Humam was trying to appear confident, so confident that he recorded hours of video statements and wrote thousands of words. He explained what he had planned, how he would do it, and he described all the events of the last year. Propaganda or not, most of his account has turned out to be true.

In his statements, Humam said the original plan had called for luring bin Zeid to Peshawar, where he would be captured or killed:

> The initial objective was the arrest or killing of [bin] Zeid in Peshawar. The
> date had been set, and an operation had been planned to arrest him; but

were he to offer any resistance whatsoever, he was to have been killed. However, due to security conditions, we decided that such an operation might be too dangerous at this particular time.

The Jordanians were still keen to hold a meeting, though, and bin Zeid 'was able to convince an entire CIA team responsible for spy drones to come . . . We planned for something but got a bigger gift, a gift from Allah.'[40]

The change of plan provided Humam with, he said, 'valuable prey'. It also meant this was no longer a kidnap plan. He was going to have to die. In one video he tried to speak in English. He sounded almost delirious: 'Inshallah, we will get you, CIA team. Inshallah, we will bring you down. Don't think that just by pressing a button and killing Mujahideen, you are safe. Inshallah, we'll come to you in an unexpected way. Look, this is for you. It's not a watch, it's a detonator, to kill as many as I can, inshallah.'[41]

Was it bravado? Did he really want to carry out this mission? And had he really planned all along to betray bin Zeid? Had the CIA officers been the victims of a 'dangle' – a trap laid from the start, into which the Jordanians and LaBonte had fallen? Or was it the case, as some speculated, that seeing the casualties of drone strikes had changed Humam's mind?

At about 4.30 p.m., a dust cloud could be seen swirling behind a car that was approaching Camp Chapman at speed, helter-skeltering down the track beside Khost airport. Normally, this would be a danger signal. The barriers were there to slow down such vehicles. But today, one after another, the barriers were raised and the car never stopped. The guards were even told to avert their eyes as the vehicle sped by.

Humam's car was being driven by Arghawan, a 30-year-old Afghan trusted by the CIA. He had picked him up at the border. No one else was in the car and Arghawan knew nothing of Humam's plans. As they approached the camp, Humam could see something he had never expected. He was getting a VIP's welcome. Beyond the perimeter of the base a knot of people were waiting in line. Most were in khaki cargo pants, the uniform of the modern-day adventurer. He could make out his handler, bin Zeid, and maybe ten others. About fifty yards short stood two men with rifles slung over their shoulders: CIA security guards.

The car pulled up with a screech of brakes next to the security guards. Matthews's plan required them to search Humam gently. One edged forward to open the door. Humam took a look at him and recoiled. He shuffled across to the other side of the vehicle and let himself out, for some reason carrying a crutch. As he had promised, Humam was now murmuring to himself, reciting the articles of Islamic faith: '*La Ilaha illallah Muhammadur Rasulullah* [There is no God but Allah, and Muhammad is his Messenger].' According to a hadith, the Holy Prophet had said, 'The one who utters La Ilaha illallah as his last words before death will enter Paradise.'[42]

There were shouts now and guns were raised. Something was obviously wrong. Humam pressed the detonator. As he explained in the testaments he left behind, the attack was 'revenge for the killing of Abu Mus'ab al-Zarqawi and the killing of many of our brothers by the spy drones in Waziristan'. He also said, 'So this is a new era for the Mujahideen, Allah willing, in which the Mujahideen will use intelligence-based tactics and methods which rival or even exceed those of the security apparatuses of the strongest of states, like Jordan and America, with the permission of Allah, Lord of the worlds. So this was the fundamental reason.'[43]

The procedures followed by the CIA that day made no sense. For years, in covering the wars in Iraq and Afghanistan, I had passed through dozens of these US military installations, gone through innumerable searches and seen all the blast barriers built to protect those inside. It seemed incredible, unbelievable, that someone should be allowed in without even the simplest of searches. It also seemed to reflect a basic misunderstanding of Arab culture. Yes, to search someone's body might imply disrespect. But this was war and Humam was now on an American base with no means of turning back. A simple respectful search could have been carried out by one man, perhaps just bin Zeid, who could have met the vehicle at a distance, checked Humam with a cursory rub-down (even disguised as a hug, common between men in the Middle East) and only then allowed him to walk through and meet the others. It reflected not just a failure of spycraft but also a complete absence of common sense. Combined with the birthday cake idea, it illustrated an almost crass naivety.

It had not seemed so crazy at the time to Jennifer Matthews, despite the concerns of some. After all, when had the CIA ever had an exploding agent before? Never.

Back home in the US, Matthews's husband, Gary Anderson, was left to raise their three children. At the time of the attack they were aged six, nine and twelve. He became incensed at the blame attached to his late wife. When he spoke publicly, he told the *Washington Post*, 'The suicide bomber was a bad guy, but at the time, nobody could clearly see it. I think the agency prepared my wife to be a chief of the Khost base, but not in terms of preparing for this asset. This guy wasn't vetted.'[44] What galled him most was the lack of preparation, together with the optimism: 'When you look at the history of this guy, he was flipped in a matter of days, which is ridiculous. Why wasn't he checked in transit to the base?' He had heard that LaBonte raised concerns about Humam. 'Why couldn't he convince Jennifer that they shouldn't let this guy on the base without being searched? This stuff should have gone back to headquarters and someone should have made a call.'[45]

The attack had killed seven US citizens: Jennifer Matthews, aged forty-five, CIA base chief; Elizabeth Hanson, aged thirty, CIA targeter; Harold Brown, aged thirty-seven, CIA officer, Afghanistan; Darren LaBonte, aged thirty-five, CIA officer, Amman station; Scott Roberson, aged thirty-nine, CIA base security officer; Jeremy Wise, aged thirty-five, and Dane Paresi, aged forty-six, security guards from Xe Services (formerly known as Blackwater[46]). The others killed were Sharif Ali bin Zeid (Jordanian GID) and the Afghan driver, Arghawan.

A poem appeared on the Internet soon after, written by one Asadullah Alshishani and entitled 'Our James Bond'. It was dedicated to the 'shaheed [martyr] Abu Dujanah al-Khorasani' with the hope that God would accept him and 'bless him with palaces and the Hoor Al Ayn [the women of Paradise] in a garden where the flowers never wilt. Amen'.

> Our James Bond, who is he?
> He is Abu Dujanah!
> His motto: Let me die or live free!
>
> Our James Bond, what is he like?
> A roaring lion, a stinging bee,
> Not a cowardly kike.

Allah Has Plans

Our James Bond, what did he seek?
Not power or money,
But justice for the weak.

Our James Bond, what drove his ambition?
It was love for Allah and a longing for Jannah [Paradise: lit. the garden]
That motivated his mission.[47]

Chapter 9
Faith in the Machine

'As far as Washington was concerned, if the big eye in the
sky didn't see it, it didn't happen'

– Bob Baer, former CIA officer[1]

Early in the morning on 2 September 2010, four cars sped down the road
in Takhar Province, Afghanistan, throwing up clouds of dust behind
them. Inside the third car, a white Toyota Corolla, a little man was talking
excitedly on his mobile phone. Friends called him Murcha, or the Ant.
They said he never stopped talking. He had come that day because of
national parliamentary elections, but after living away for many years it
was also a kind of homecoming. 'That day was like a celebration,' said a
local schoolteacher, Ihsannullah, who was in the last vehicle. 'We were
campaigning for the elections. We were making friends, inviting them
along with us.'

In the village of Kaiwan, a mile or so away, they were expecting the
Ant. Two other cars had gone ahead to gather up a crowd. Flowers were
being threaded on to strings. Banners were being put up across the road.
They were hoping to welcome back a hero.

The little convoy had made its way up the switchback bends of the
dusty mountain road, had crossed a high plateau and was now descending
into Rustaq District, heading for another snake-like gully that would take
them down to the village. 'We had no idea they were all about to die,' said
Ihsannullah.

It was about 8.15 a.m. Afghan time or 3.45 a.m. Zulu time, as the American military referred to GMT. Far away, the convoy was being watched on
giant TV screens screwed to an unvarnished pine wall. Already, a set of
cross hairs was trained on one of the vehicles. An operator sipped coffee
from a Styrofoam cup, waiting for the moment.

So far this had all the appearance of a normal scene in the long-running war in Afghanistan. But something was going particularly wrong that day and the events leading up to it would illustrate a key weakness of modern espionage, in particular when decisions are taken on the basis of technical intelligence alone, and in the absence of good human intelligence. This story also provided an insight into how intelligence and technology were evolving in modern warfare abroad, in a powerful combination that would be emulated by business and domestic law enforcement. As we have seen, human spies can be terribly frail and unreliable, but without any element of understanding and verification through human intelligence, and without basic common sense, terrible errors are bound to follow.

It was time. The order came. The lead pilot of a pair of F-16s lifted the guarded switch cover and armed a GBU12 laser-guided bomb. He fired the laser and, watching intently through his targeting pod camera, he released the weapon and counted down to impact.

At the sprawling ex-Soviet airbase of Bagram, 150 miles south, an officer within a unit code-named Task Force 535 was in charge of the kill mission. He was watching events unfold from inside a super-secret building and – relayed by satellite – he could see the same bomb's eye view as it hurtled to the ground. He was in a 'fusion centre', where all branches of the US secret intelligence machine came together with the military. They believed they were fighting the war with new tactics: a lethal combination of information and force that had been invented during the occupation of Iraq. 'What we do has been nine years in the making,' said one senior US officer intimately involved, describing this new kind of warfare as a 'magnificent story'. But sometimes the system failed and the wrong people were killed.

In the moments after a blast, everything is silent. Shock numbs pain and you go temporarily deaf. A fog of smoke and dust obscures everything. Then, all of a sudden, you can see again, and then a bit later you can hear again, and feel again.

On the road into Kaiwan, the white Corolla lay upside down by the road. Its four occupants were crawling out, staggering on to their feet. The other three cars stopped and people started looking for cover. In this first strike, no one died.

In the military, the people who desperately run for cover out of damaged buildings or blown-up cars are known as 'squirters'.[2] On the screens at Bagram, little figures could be seen moving by the vehicles. The pilots were told to engage again.

The F-16s dropped another bomb. This time it struck the Corolla dead centre. The second strike killed seven people, including a young student and his brother, a teacher. 'The vehicle was burning,' remembered Ihsannullah. 'The flames were three metres high . . . the ground was covered with body parts and blood.'[3] The Ant was injured but still alive.

At that moment, two Apache helicopters – until then hovering unseen on the horizon – swept into attack. While one circled and kept watch, the other came raking down the line of the convoy, blasting the survivors with its cannon. At that point the Ant and one other fell dead. Another person was mortally wounded. It was a cruel business, but unless you mopped up the stragglers, said soldiers, there was a chance you would miss the main target.

Local police had arrived at the scene soon after the attack. Someone recorded a video. One person could be heard shouting, 'Get them out of here. Come on, people! Lift him, lift him. Get him off the ground!' Another shouted, 'They hit an election convoy! These poor people.'[4]

News of the strike quickly reached local journalists and Afghan officials. The governor of Takhar Province, Abdul Jabbar Taqwa, told a local radio station that foreign forces had bombed the entourage of a candidate in the parliamentary elections and that ten election workers had been killed. 'Without any coordination, without informing provisional authorities, they attacked, on their own, civilian people who were in a campaign convoy,' he said.[5]

The official headquarters of foreign troops in Afghanistan was then a base in central Kabul run by American-led NATO. The phones began ringing there in the press office as journalists asked for comment. Staff worried that they were handling yet another incident of civilian casualties. US officers called their contacts over at the secretive Task Force 535, which also operated independently of NATO. What should be stated publicly? The response was silence. A statement was being prepared.

In the hours that followed the strike, signallers from the US military's Electronic Warfare branch were, as usual, eavesdropping on the Taliban's network of radios and mobile phones. Eventually they passed word to the Task Force. The Taliban were talking to contacts and warning that a senior commander had been killed. 'Mohamed Amin is dead,' had said one militant. The US officer who commanded the mission could now inform his men: Mission Accomplished. And NATO was now permitted to issue a statement announcing that 'coalition forces' had conducted a 'precision air strike' on a senior member of the Islamic Movement of Uzbekistan (IMU), a militant group operating in the north of the country that the US believed to be linked to both al-Qaeda and the Taliban. This leader was also 'assessed to be deputy shadow governor for Takhar Province', a reference to the Taliban's network of parallel leaders that mirrored those officially appointed by the Afghan government. The statement continued: 'Intelligence tracked the insurgents traveling in a sedan on a series of remote roads in Rustaq District . . . initial reflections indicate eight to 12 insurgents were killed or injured in the strike, including a Taliban commander. Multiple passengers of the vehicle were positively identified carrying weapons.'[6]

In Takhar Province, NATO's version of events was immediately challenged. The most prominent among the dead was someone who, as far as every local person was concerned, could hardly be a Taliban or IMU leader. The man nicknamed the Ant was a 45-year-old public figure named Zabet Amanullah, whose history was well known. In the past, he had been in the Taliban movement. But after the attacks of 9/11, he had surrendered and been allowed to move to Pakistan. In 2008 he had returned and had been living openly in Kabul since then. Now that his nephew Abdul Wahid Khorassani was standing for election in Takhar, Amanullah had made his first trip back to the province for years to campaign for him. The Taliban had urged an election boycott and their members adamantly did not stand for or support candidates in the election. So it did not seem likely that Amanullah was a Taliban leader.

That evening, US Secretary of Defense Robert Gates happened to be in Afghanistan and he held a press conference with the country's president, Hamid Karzai. When that day's attack was mentioned, the president spoke bitterly. 'Pro-democracy people should be distinguished from those who fight against democracy,' he said. Gates responded, 'This is the first I have heard that civilians have been killed and we will look into that.'[7] But, ten days later, NATO issued a new statement reiterating that the right target had been struck, even though civilian casualties 'could not be ruled out'.[8] NATO also confirmed media reports that the target's name was 'Muhammad Amin'. This caused new confusion. Was this some kind of code name for Zabet Amanullah? Either Amin was another man among those in the convoy who died in the air strike or, if the US was to be believed, the Ant was a Taliban leader with two identities – in effect a double agent.

As was often the case, NATO's comments on the Takhar air strike emphasized the difference between how Afghans viewed their country and how it looked to foreign eyes. Even Afghan officials who dealt with NATO and welcomed its presence in the country often concluded that, for all its high-tech wizardry, America's spy machinery was rotten. Every day there were more raids and more strikes against the enemy. Sometimes, for propaganda reasons, it had suited President Karzai and others to criticize American air strikes, even when the Afghan government privately knew that the victims were probably Taliban fighters. But at other times, when it was obvious to them that the US was using bad intelligence to kill the wrong people, they were furious. The death of Amanullah epitomized those errors.

Intelligence about the enemy's plans and disposition and about the zone of combat has always been essential to soldiers. But it took on an even greater importance in the war against the Taliban. This had begun in 2001, when the US invaded Afghanistan and toppled the Taliban's regime. By the mid-2000s, the Taliban had regrouped. By the time of the Takhar strike nearly 100,000 American military personnel were deployed to the country, along with 40,000 other NATO-led foreign troops (including 9,000 Britons). This was more than the Soviet Army had there in the 1980s.[9] By the end of 2010, over 2,200 troops in the US-led coalition had been killed.

The conflict in Afghanistan was what the military call an unconventional, or asymmetric, war: Afghan government and coalition forces in uniform were fighting a Taliban that acted as irregular rebels, dressing as non-combatants, living secretly among the population, adopting guerrilla tactics of surprise ambushes and avoiding conventional battle. In military-speak, this was a classic insurgency. And although, historically, rebels tended to win such conflicts, the only known way of defeating them was by making use of super-precise intelligence. A successful counter-insurgency strategy was based as much on trying to separate and protect the population from the insurgents as it was on fighting them. For this to happen, intelligence was needed on who should be protected (friendly or neutral people) and who should be targeted (the enemy). This was hard because to foreign eyes they all looked alike and often lived together.

Intelligence for NATO's campaign came from the military's own intelligence specialists – whether from intelligence officers working in frontline battalions or specialized military cadres, like the Defense Intelligence Agency (DIA) or the National Security Agency (NSA). They were assisted by deployments from the civilian secret services, primarily the CIA or SIS. These agencies handled particularly sensitive sources or specifically political agents, as well as dealing with Afghan spy agencies and conducting their own covert operations.

As the violence intensified, both diplomats and secret service operatives based in Kabul faced increasing threats to their lives and, bound by strict health and safety rules, they were often restricted from going out and making their own contacts. What intelligence they did get from spies was mostly second-hand, the product of their liaising with and mentoring of local security forces. These included, as previously described, the various semi-private paramilitary groups the CIA ran directly, as well as Afghanistan's own security service, the National Directorate of Security (NDS). 'Even if we had people who had learned to speak like locals, we would never have looked like them,' said one British intelligence officer. 'There was a limit to what we could have done ourselves.' The NDS had many faults (it sometimes tortured its prisoners, for instance), 'but it had a network of sources nationwide. We could never have competed with that.'

The trouble with having few spies of their own was that Western agencies were always vulnerable to being used to settle local feuds. It was common, for instance, for Afghans to relay tip-offs from someone in one clan that someone in another was linked to the Taliban or al-Qaeda. Many of Amanullah's friends wondered if the Americans had been fed information by a particular local politician who, historically, had been a major rival of Amanullah's family.

Intelligence agencies were also aware of an inbuilt Afghan suspicion of foreigners or outsiders. Before British and other NATO troops began deploying in large numbers in southern Afghanistan in 2006, and got drawn into heavy fighting, SIS operatives had reconnoitred the area with Britain's elite Special Air Service (SAS). The mission reported that at the time no insurgency existed but, given the population's hatred of armed foreigners, there would be one if the army engaged.

This specific warning was ignored, and so was the implication that basic intelligence about the instincts and allegiances of ordinary people in the countryside was at least as important as specific intelligence about who was a Taliban fighter or leader and where he was hiding (whether that was obtained using a spy or a radio intercept).

One NATO intelligence chief, then Major General Michael Flynn, had revisited this weakness in early 2010 when he wrote that intelligence officers had focused so much effort on insurgent groups that 'the vast intelligence apparatus is unable to answer fundamental questions about the environment in which US and allied forces operate and the people they seek to persuade'. US intelligence officers and analysts were 'ignorant of local economics and landowners, hazy about who the powerbrokers are and how they might be influenced, incurious about the correlations between various development projects and the levels of cooperation among villagers, and disengaged from people in the best position to find answers'.[10]

The gap Flynn had identified was human intelligence, but it was not the sort of high-level secret intelligence that could come only from a top spy. Rather, it was the sort of cultural understanding that ordinary dialogue with local people might have brought about.

Military officers sometimes complained that their partners in the civilian intelligence agencies had become too ill-equipped and too bureaucratic to operate in a war zone. One former Western commander described offering an SIS officer a trip on a helicopter the next day to meet locals in a recently captured town. 'Sorry, I'm not sure I can get the business case through London by then,' the intelligence officer told him. This response seemed to sum up multiple problems.

But as I witnessed while covering the war as a journalist and spending many days with frontline troops and commanders, over the years of Afghan engagement, intelligence gradually improved; the British and American armies devoted huge efforts to becoming more sensitive to the local human environment. But it was never enough and the improvements were from a very low base. For example, barely three dozen people in the entire British Army in the mid-2000s could speak fluent Pashto, the language of southern Afghanistan. They may have tried, but the military was not equipped to gather the intelligence it needed. And the realization of their deficiencies here came too late. While some intelligence officers would write off this kind of missing intelligence as 'low-level atmospherics' beyond their responsibilities, its absence was one of the reasons why the military campaign went wrong. The US and NATO had frequently blundered into one valley or another in cooperation with deeply unpopular warlords or corrupt government officials who were linked to a particular tribe. That had only antagonized other tribes and strengthened the Taliban's hand.

While this wider picture about the terrain of battle was, at least at first, far too neglected, US intelligence agencies worked hard on helping their military develop its aggressive and innovative manhunt for top enemy commanders: people like, as the military believed, Amanullah. The object of what was called the 'kill/capture campaign' was to pummel the enemy by assassinating or capturing its leadership. The targets were to be identified and located by both spies and other human sources, as well as with data from video surveillance and the interception and tracking of phones and radios. As described above, all relevant information was combined in the 'fusion centre', which was designed to make different agencies work together effectively. First assembled at Balad airbase, north of Baghdad, the centres used makeshift buildings laid out as spokes around a central hub. At Balad, some began to call it the Death Star, and the name stuck as the same operation was moved to Afghanistan. The system had been pioneered in Iraq by a US Special Forces general, Stanley McChrystal. He had then been commander of the secretive Joint Special Operation Command (JSOC), which directed the activities of America's elite Special Forces, the Navy Seals and Delta Force, supported by the Ranger Battalion and working also with Britain's SAS and its Special Boat Service (SBS). McChrystal's idea was to pull together almost every conceivable intelligence tool available to the US and focus on cracking a single objective. Its most successful implementation was in finding, locating and then killing the bloodthirsty al-Qaeda leader in Iraq, Abu Musab al-Zarqawi. Task Force 535 was just the latest cover name for JSOC's forward headquarters and operations in Afghanistan.

Everything about the Death Star approach was based on intelligence, but it also depended on speed. One key person involved said, 'With targeted killings you either defeat or you shape the enemy . . . If you get the tempo high enough then it's difficult for them to come up for air. It's like hitting a boxer with body blows; it's not a knockout but you stop them from breathing; you're keeping them off-balance.'[11]

This was war by raiding, and the tempo was maintained, not so much by kill operations like the one against Amanullah in Takhar, but by Special Forces ground raids at night to kill or capture prisoners. If the target surrendered, he would be taken back for interrogation and, even if he did not, his home would be searched for every type of material. Intelligence pulled together on one night could be used to launch another raid on the next. The soldiers looked not only for bigger items like laptops but also for 'pocket litter'. This meant phones, SIM cards, notebooks, scraps of paper, anything that gave clues about the target's network – who he was connected to. The McChrystal approach was all about tracing connections, using every available piece of information to move rapidly from one target to another. According to someone involved, 'We have had decades of manhunting. We hunt individuals, but what's changed is we have started to target entire networks.'

The biggest source of HUMINT for the manhunt was prisoners. With the help of interpreters, JSOC got night-and-day access to question the enemy in jail cells close to their headquarters. The US asserted the right to run its own military prisons and only hand over prisoners to the Afghan authorities after their thorough debriefing. One visitor to the Death Star described hearing a live audio feed from an interrogation room being piped to his work station. 'It was like listening in to the enemy's mind. It was incredible,' he said.

The final major source of information – the key to what happened in Takhar – was technical intelligence: the constant interception and, as important, tracking of mobile phones and VHF radios, as well as visual surveillance of buildings, vehicles and gatherings of people by means of spy satellites, surveillance planes, helicopters and what had become a huge fleet of drones, each of which had several cameras.

But there were flaws. One of the biggest was that, in order to persuade the special agencies to gather together and share all they knew, the headquarters had to be kept very secure and secret, and could only use the most elite of security-cleared soldiers and the minimum of outsiders.

As he was discussing it, one US military officer involved in the Amanullah case tellingly made constant reference to the world 'outside'. The war had divided people into insiders and outsiders who lived in parallel. Insiders like this officer lived within the 'bubble' of bases fortified by razor wire. When they did venture out it was usually to some other 'secure location' or, if not, in a posse of men armed to the teeth. Ordinary human interaction became impossible. They were cut off from real people.

While this elite had access to tremendous technical tools with which to observe the world, all the secrecy and isolation stymied their ability to check and understand what they picked up. It was hard to look at a problem as a whole or understand the significance of certain elements. In intelligence-speak, nuggets of information tended to get lost in vast 'silos'. Because everything was kept secret from the wider world, some basic false assumptions – obviously wrong to any man in the street – would never be challenged. And all this scientific espionage was also bewitching. Cool gadgets and smart techniques inspired awe and a confidence that was comparable to religious zeal. It defied good sense.

And there was a further big problem: the absence of good spies. Some reliable secret agents among the Taliban could have made all the difference. But the tempo of JSOC operations made that difficult. Certainly, prisoners held at Bagram could be recruited, but the complex task of running such agents among insurgents in the field was a different matter and not to be tackled lightly. Yet in the absence of high-level secret information from human sources, it could be hard to challenge compelling, if misleading, intelligence from technical sources. Common sense dictated that Amanullah was innocent. But if his voice had been captured by secret interception and the words he spoke seemed suspicious, the Death Star would have needed a reliable source very close to his circle to exonerate him by explaining that what he said was innocent. Technical intelligence, unencumbered by coverage from human sources, could be dangerously persuasive. To find the truth, intrusive surveillance almost requires its mirror image: intrusive spying.

Obscure and remote as it was, the assassination of Zabet Amanullah in September 2010 caused a shock. He was widely known back in the Afghan capital, Kabul, including by some influential and well-connected people. It was their anger about his killing that motivated their efforts to discover how he was targeted. Their investigation has provided a unique window into the twenty-first-century intelligence machine.

One person who knew Amanullah well was an Irishman named Michael Semple. He was one of those rare people who, by virtue of his work, straddled the worlds of the secret and of the ordinary, which in turn gave him some unique insights. He had come to the region twenty years earlier. Working for the UN and then the EU, he had gradually become involved in trying to foster political reconciliation in Afghanistan. As he made contact with every kind of political, military and religious group, he came to know the men of violence. In 2008, President Karzai had expelled him from the country for allegedly unauthorized contacts with the Taliban, but Semple carried on the same work from Pakistan, where most of the Taliban leadership lived. As an interlocutor, he also frequently crossed paths with Western military and secret intelligence.[12]

What Semple noticed was just how often those in the secret services convinced themselves of false notions. And just such wrong-headed thinking had led to Amanullah's killing. Semple had known the man for years and would not accept that he had been a secret Taliban commander. Even years before, when the Taliban ruled the country, Semple remembered that Amanullah had helped research the regime's human rights abuses. And then, after the US invaded and the Taliban was toppled, the pair stayed in touch. Semple remembered introducing him to a delegation of British Members of Parliament in Peshawar one week in 2003.

Since 2008, he said, Amanullah had lived peacefully in Kabul and 'nobody would have considered him a Taliban looking at him there'. If Amanullah had still been with the Taliban, he would not have been involved in the election campaign in Takhar, said Semple. It had meant 'travelling village to village very publicly and giving speeches. Everybody saw that. So much of Zabet Amanullah's life was in the public domain. And it had nothing whatsoever to do with insurgency.'

Another of those who knew Amanullah was a former BBC foreign correspondent, Kate Clark, who had lived in Kabul under the Taliban and stayed on after. She left journalism to join an academic group called the Afghan Analysts Network, but she had not lost her detective instincts. She first met Amanullah two years before his death, in circumstances that convinced her he could not be an active fighter. He had described being tortured by Pakistan's ISI for refusing to join the Taliban. Even if the US had been right and he had a secret role with the insurgency, why, she wondered, had they simply not arrested him at his Kabul home? She knew he had settled in Kabul, had bought a pharmacy and was studying English and computer science. After his death, she collected paperwork that proved it. The implication from US intelligence was that Amanullah was leading a dual life, that he was some sort of Taliban secret double agent. But then another explanation gradually dawned on her: US intelligence was not even aware of his home and life in the Afghan capital.

Investigating doggedly, Clark used field research to establish that Amanullah was the only person of importance in the convoy, the target of the strike, and that he was definitely the person that NATO referred to as the IMU/Taliban leader 'Mohamed Amin'. Using her contacts, she then pressed NATO commanders in Kabul for an explanation and finally established direct contact with some officers from JSOC (aka Task Force 535) who ran the operation.

The version of events that can now be revealed is based on what Clark published as a result of her inquiries, on what Semple uncovered and also on further interviews I conducted with some US persons intimately involved (all on condition of anonymity). In addition, much detail is disclosed in an account of the killing, based on insider sources, which was written by a private intelligence operation run in Afghanistan and Pakistan by Duane 'Dewey' Clarridge, a legendary and controversial former head of counterterrorism at the CIA.[13] All of them provide a unique picture of how elite military units make use of intelligence – and the consequence of ignoring the 'human factor'.

The intelligence story that led to the assassination of Amanullah started in January 2010, when American soldiers took prisoner a man in his twenties named Abdul Rahman, from Takhar Province. Interrogated at Bagram airbase, he named an uncle of his, Mohamed Amin, as a Taliban commander in Takhar. 'Rahman boasted of having an uncle, Mohammad Amin, who was important in the Taliban and IMU,' recounted Clarridge, and that 'if spoken to nicely, Rahman could deliver them all for a peace process'.[14] Rahman gave his interrogators some mobile numbers for Amin and his contacts.

US intelligence started to track and intercept the phone numbers provided by Rahman, as well as the telephones that they in turn called. One of them, +93 77 5431938, was tracked from Kabul to Takhar Province, and US intelligence came to believe that this was the phone of 'Mohamed Amin'. Semple knew this number as Amanullah's number. He still had it stored in the address book of his mobile phone years later.

According to a later report by Clark:

The intelligence operation which ultimately led to the 2 September 2010 attack started, according to the Special Forces unit, with information [that] came from a detainee in US custody. This allowed them ultimately to identify a relative of the detainee as the shadow deputy governor of Takhar, one Muhammad Amin, and to map a Taliban and IMU-related cluster through the monitoring of cell phones. The intelligence analysts came to believe that the SIM card of one of the numbers that Muhammad Amin had been calling in Kabul was passed on to him.[15]

An American involved in the operation said that intercepted phone calls from Amanullah's phone had confirmed that it was used by an active commander who was ordering attacks. There was also talk on the phone of a plan to bribe a judge. The intercepts started in Takhar in March 2010, as well as in Kunduz, Kabul and Pakistan. At one point, he said, Amin had 'self-identified' as Zabet Amanullah (presumably intelligence speak for Amanullah saying his name out loud). The US believed Amin was using 'Amanullah' as an undercover alias. Clark was also told there was a 'voice fingerprint' that confirmed that the two men, Amin and Amanullah, were one and the same.

According to Clarridge, once it was decided that Amanullah's phone was being carried by a Taliban commander, his fate was sealed. When he travelled up from Kabul to Takhar for the election, JSOC picked up the trail of his phone by technical means, and they planned their strike without the slightest knowledge of real events on the ground, including that he would be travelling with election workers. 'They're tracking the phone and they hear that the guy is going to be in the convoy. It wasn't the guy they were after; it was his *phone*. And that to me says everything about the problem with signals intelligence.' They should have been checking the information with 'guys on the ground', Clarridge said, but they did not.[16]

Errors frequently occur in war and, cruel as it may be, in conflict no army is able to ensure that no innocent is ever targeted or hurt. Perhaps the death of Amanullah was simply a mistake – the sort of thing that always happens in the chaos of war. Soldiers talk of Snafu: situation normal all fucked up. But they accept it, because they know the victor is not error-free but just someone who makes fewer important errors than his opponent.

What gave this case resonance, pointing to a more systematic failure in intelligence, was not the fact of the mistake but the vehemence with which those involved defended their actions, as well as the bitter irony of targeting a convoy of people taking part in a democratic election that the US was in the country to promote. It seemed that, despite all their sincerity of purpose, they had lost the ability to see beyond their security bubble and to think like normal people.

Senior US officials involved remained adamant. According to one:

We are very, very confident that Mohamed Amin the individual who was targeted in that strike was an insurgent leader, a member of shadow government in Takhar, and actively involved in insurgent activities. We are very confident that the name Zabet Amanullah was an alias for the individual we know as Mohamed Amin. The individual we targeted used the alias Zabet Amanullah.

That confidence went all the way up to the commander of US and NATO troops in Afghanistan at the time, David Petraeus. Going on to direct the CIA, Petraeus had made his reputation in the Iraq campaign by telling soldiers to get it right – to stop harming the people they had come to save. But, when I asked him about Takhar and what made him think that Amanullah was the right target, his eyes turned steely. Petraeus responded, 'Well, we didn't think, in this case, with respect, we knew. We had days and days of what's called "The Unblinking Eye", confirmed by other forms of intelligence that informed us that there is no question about who this individual was.'

But how was it that the man who was killed was living openly in Kabul and Afghan government officials said he was innocent? What had convinced him? 'Very precise intelligence that tells us exactly what he was doing when he was in Kabul, and exactly what he was doing up there. So again, there is not a question about this one, with respect.'[17]

The truth, as all outsiders who investigated found, was different. It showed that US intelligence was not only questionable but – with respect – completely wrong. It revealed the Ant, Zabet Amanullah, as the Taliban double agent who wasn't.

When Rahman was arrested, he really did have an uncle who was a member of the Taliban and the deputy shadow governor of Takhar. (The Taliban appointed 'shadow' administrators for each province in Afghanistan.) His name was Mohamed Aalem. He was forty-nine and the son of a well-known commander who had been killed in the jihad against the Soviets. Aalem, like most rebels, had adopted a nom de guerre in the war against NATO. His alias was 'Mohamed Amin'. In short, he was the man the Americans had been looking for. All of his biography, including the names of his family and the fact that he had a home near Peshawar in Pakistan, matched the biography that US officials provided of their target.[18]

Amanullah and Aalem (aka Mohamed Amin) were chalk and cheese.

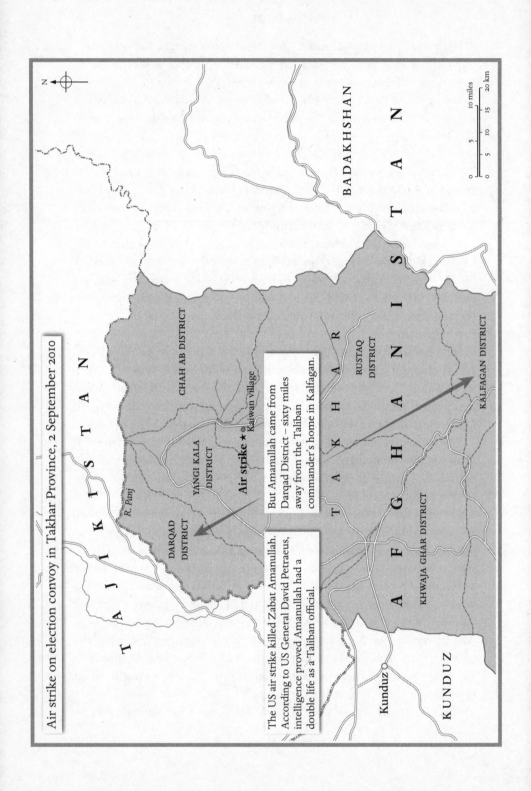

Air strike on election convoy in Takhar Province, 2 September 2010

The US air strike killed Zabat Amanullah. According to US General David Petraeus, intelligence proved Amanullah had a double life as a Taliban official.

But Amanullah came from Darqad District – sixty miles away from the Taliban commander's home in Kalfagan.

Air strike ★

Kaiwan village

TAJIKISTAN

BADAKHSHAN

CHAH AB DISTRICT

DARQAD DISTRICT

YANGI KALA DISTRICT

RUSTAQ DISTRICT

KALFAGAN DISTRICT

KHWAJA GHAR DISTRICT

T A K H A R

A F G H A N I S T A N

R. Panj

Kunduz

KUNDUZ

N

0   5   10 miles
0   5   10   15   20 km

They were different people. Both were ethnic Uzbeks from Takhar Province, but while Amanullah came from Darqad District, Aalem came from sixty miles away in Kalfagan. The former had been living with his wife in Kabul, while the other still lived with his wife near Peshawar. One local elder in Kalfagan, Haji Khair Mohamed, confirmed that he knew Aalem and his nephew well. The nephew was in prison, he said, adding unprompted that Aalem was the Taliban's 'deputy governor for Takhar province'.[19] None of this fitted any profile of Amanullah. And, despite what the US thought, Amanullah was not an alias. He was a famous man, a local hero. But these details were far too trivial for the mighty beast of US intelligence to know about.

Looking back, those who inquired into Amanullah's death concluded that he and Amin had been conflated accidentally. Perhaps some contact between the real Mohamed Amin and Zabet Amanullah was confused by eavesdroppers, so that Amin was imagined to be making the call, not receiving it. There was no doubt the Americans had recorded conversations involving someone who was a Taliban commander plotting an attack, but without access to their secret records, no one could be sure who exactly they were listening to on which phone at the time.

A few months after Amanullah was killed, I travelled round northern Afghanistan for a couple of days with the regional police chief, General Mohamed Daud. He was not a friend of the Taliban, but at the same time he knew them personally. Our days together were punctuated by taunting mobile phone calls back and forth between Daud and his enemy. Without context, without an understanding of the nuances of this man's relationship with the Taliban, someone who was tracing the Taliban commander's contacts could have mistakenly taken Daud to be a friend. In fact, he was killed by the Taliban soon after I last saw him, by a suicide bomber in Takhar, of all places.[20]

Without access to secret records of the Amanullah case, no one can be entirely sure where the errors crept in. Michael Semple was convinced, though, that 'one way or another some kind of blunder was made here. It's a classic case of somebody, who has legitimate reason for being in contact with someone designated as a terrorist, getting treated as "the terrorist".'[21]

In March 2011, Semple left his home on a farm outside Islamabad and made the familiar drive to the frontier city of Peshawar. With him were two trusted friends who witnessed what happened next. He was greeted in a hotel room by a middle-aged man with a black turban. The man showed him his Pakistani refugee ID card. It read 'Mohamed Amin'. This was his alias, but he also had other papers that confirmed his true identity – Mohamed Aalem. Talking to Semple, he said he was aware of the NATO strike on 2 September. He was not surprised to be targeted. 'This is war!' he said. But, just like Mark Twain, he noted that reports of his death had been greatly exaggerated.

Aalem said he had been promoted since the attack and was no longer the deputy governor. He also said that the Taliban had studied the incident and concluded that perhaps it had been a mistake by NATO signals intelligence. More importantly, Aalem added, a local informant with a grudge had simply told NATO that he and Amanullah were the same person and had then given them Amanullah's phone number. 'This is not an isolated case,' he said.

Semple liked Aalem. He struck him as a 'classic example' of someone the US had been targeting with the kill/capture campaign. 'It's a tragedy that all we can do is kill such people, because he is a good Afghan.'

In May 2011, back in England, my phone rang. It was a call from Afghanistan, from someone who had been involved in the operation to kill Amanullah. I had to give JSOC full credit. On three occasions, I had been granted top-level access to ask questions about this with US officials. People involved in JSOC were smart, highly aware of the complexities of the Afghan environment, where the enemy would be eating, drinking tea and sleeping with the same population that the US was there to protect.

The official now calling appeared candid about some of the US intelligence gaps. He admitted, 'We never disputed it was an election convoy. We just didn't know it [at the time],' he said. When asked about how the air strike was carried out, he also agreed that innocents might have died. 'I accept a possibility that some of the people killed in the convoy were not combatants. Vehicles were each filled with armed men.'

But even now, after hearing what Semple had discovered, there was no trace of doubt that they had killed the right person. The incident had been reviewed again and again. An analyst who had checked and rechecked reported back, 'There is absolutely no doubt in my mind that Mohamed Amin is one and the same person as the person who is known as Zabet Amanullah.' What about the man in Pakistan who was alive and said he was Mohamed Amin, then? The official replied, 'Whoever this is in Pakistan, he is welcome to come and talk to us! We are dealing with an enemy that can create personae with ease. They can travel at will back and forth across the border with false papers.'

The American on the phone was perfectly reasonable and aware of all the contradictions, but clearly had total faith in the intelligence machine: 'I realize that I am predisposed to believe the intelligence we had. But we really have looked to see if it's possible we blew this. There is no indication at all we can find we blew this.'

As in so many intelligence stories, it was impossible to be definitive here. JSOC never revealed all its sources. It is possible they also had some kind of human intelligence, an agent who gave them information that convinced them they had the right person. US sources certainly insisted that they had some 'human intelligence'. But they were clearly missing a good spy, someone inside the network they were targeting who could have cut through all the confusion and told them who Mohamed Amin was, what his role was and where to find him. It cannot be proved that Zabet Amanullah was living a completely blameless life. Whatever the recollection of his friends, proving a negative like innocence is logically impossible. What can be proved, however, is that Zabet Amanullah and Mohamed Amin were two different people. Despite the assurances of highly placed figures in the US military, including the commander of all US and NATO forces in the war, and regardless of the outcome of internal scrutiny, the intelligence machine had been shown to be flawed.

Amanullah's assassination did not demonstrate that the methods used by the military in modern warfare – as exemplified by JSOC's campaign – were wrong. They regularly found and captured or killed the targets they intended. The principle of focusing everything on to a single target and the methods of network analysis based on tracking and analysing phone records, combined with prisoner interrogations, were generally solid. In the months ahead, they would lead US intelligence to the highest of targets. But these modern technical-based methods did not always work; it was easy to be confused by the data and make too many wrong assumptions.

As the campaign matured, officers in Special Forces who led the hard edge of the war in Afghanistan, as well as soldiers in regular battalions on the ground, all became wiser to their game and the nuances of the local environment. They were increasingly aware of tribal rivalries and how biased local informants could be. But often that made HUMINT look even less appealing.

As the real world 'outside' began to seem ever more complex, it was ever more tempting to fall back on the certainties that non-human sources seemed to provide. When the CIA or SIS gave tips to the military, such as which village a Taliban group was hiding in, those involved recount how 'before dropping the bomb' the military very wisely verified this human intelligence by technical means, such as seeing if the Taliban's mobile phones were in that village. But the reverse was not always true: there was not always solid human reporting to back a technical find. The new machines of warfare – the combination of technology and all-encompassing surveillance – were so intoxicating they appeared to blind many of their users, including well-meaning and highly intelligent people, to their limitations.

The problem was not the failure of particular technologies or methods. The glitches that caused Amanullah's misidentification may have been fixed the day after he was killed. The issue was over-confidence in the idea of technology itself: the infectious belief that somehow science and computation could overcome the insuperable problem of operating in a baffling and dangerous foreign environment.

The absence of sufficient HUMINT in a military campaign that depended on excellent intelligence had manifested itself in the wider battle to win over and protect the population, a campaign in which NATO had constantly made alliances with the wrong people. The same intelligence gap was also apparent in the narrow tactical campaign when, despite great efforts to avoid it, too often the wrong people were killed. In both cases the military were simply failing to work out who the real enemy was.

If there was too much faith in machines, what was the alternative in modern warfare? Was the need for more spies providing concrete secret intelligence – a 'man on the rock' in each Taliban lair – or simply for more engagement that, addressing a wider intelligence failure, provided deeper context?

Both, in fact, were lacking. But of the two, the bigger gap was in strategic understanding, of the enemy and the wider population. Using spies to get more Taliban secrets to kill or capture more of the Taliban leadership was not going to solve the problem. Although fuelled by outside intervention, the Afghan War was a rebellion, which is to say a political and military conflict. However much the military might batter the rebels, they should have been asking whether the causes of the rebellion were being addressed and, valley by valley, whether the intervention of foreign troops was genuinely acting as a force for good. Answering these questions required an acute political awareness that went far beyond ordinary espionage.

Nevertheless, in practice there was a blurred line between the work of secret intelligence sources and the gathering of ordinary contacts and common-sense information. It is a truism (and amusing to observe in the field) that professional spymasters tend to dress up rather ordinary contacts as their 'agents'. And since the enemy, the Taliban, lived among the people and were of the people, plenty of ordinary people knew specific secret information, such as the make-up of a Taliban group and where they were hiding. Moreover, the reverse was also true. Since very few Afghans were really prepared to be 'recruited' as loyal agents for a foreign intelligence service, the best of agents might frustratingly provide little concrete intelligence, but only be useful in providing a broad overview of the conflict. In the circumstances, some argued that the best way of collecting intelligence on the enemy was to be open and do something as simple as picking up the phone to them, or joining them somewhere neutral for a cup of tea.

Such efforts were more like discreet diplomacy than espionage. But in Afghanistan, and in any dangerous or difficult place where contacts with hostile groups were politically sensitive, such engagements were becoming an essential part of the work of a modern spymaster.

Chapter 10
The Peacemaker Spy

'The successful Field Officers will be generally found to have three
important characteristics. They will be personalities in their
own right. They will have humanity and a capacity for
friendship and they will have a sense of humour'

– Nicholas Elliott, former SIS officer, and colleague and friend of Kim Philby[1]

Inside a bright yellow taxi one summer's day in 2002, a 53-year-old man,
dressed in jeans and a T-shirt, gazed out of the window from the back seat
as his driver weaved his way through the narrow streets of a town in Palestine. The route was circuitous.

The driver put on the radio. There was plenty in the news. Every day,
young men from these parts were crossing to Israel strapped with explosives and blowing themselves up. The Israeli Defence Force (IDF) was
striking back – entering Palestinian villages and towns, arresting suspected
militants and bulldozing their homes. Yasser Arafat, the veteran leader of
the Palestinians, was trapped inside his compound in Ramallah, surrounded by Israeli troops.

The passenger was a spy of sorts: one of Her Majesty's intelligence officers. But he did not behave as you might expect such a man to do. Despite
the danger, he did not carry a gun or even a phone. He was not wearing
body armour. He was not gifted in any local language. His mission was
neither to steal secrets nor to stage-manage a betrayal.

The taxi pulled up at the bustling gates of a refugee camp and the man
got out. The place was called Balata, just outside Nablus. He looked
around and spotted a small boy who walked up and asked, 'Meester Alees-
tair?' The man nodded and the boy set off, beckoning him to follow.

Heading through a maze of buildings, they walked down a street,
through a building and out the back entrance into an alley, then across to

another building. It would be hard to remember later. And that was the point.

Finally, they arrived in a squat and half-lit apartment. The man was ushered forward into a small room and the boy disappeared. Inside were waiting a small knot of men, mostly in their forties, dressed in jeans and neat shirts. Each of them was a representative of a different faction engaged in armed struggle.

'So,' said one of the militants, 'where do we start?'

For the SIS officer sitting opposite, Alastair Warren Crooke, the story could be said to have begun long ago. His life in the secret service had been spent talking to men of violence. It had taken him to his birthplace, Ireland, as well as South Africa, Namibia, Colombia, Pakistan and Afghanistan. Finally, in 2000, he had come to Israel and Palestine. He had undertaken a one-person programme of talks with Palestinian militants, at a time when such contacts were officially denied.

Crooke would later be sacked by SIS. When he carried on talking to militants unofficially, he was described by some as having 'gone native', the old colonial jibe used against someone who had developed too close an affinity for the indigenous people. He would become persona non grata with Britain's Foreign Office. Right-wing establishment commentators would portray him as 'odious' and worse. One described him as a 'Beirut-based public relations firm for the Islamic Republic' with 'sympathies with the rocketeers and human shield-warriors of Gaza'.[2] Even some of his friends considered that he had begun to get too close to, and defend too often, the men of violence with whom he was liaising.

For all the noise and the manner of his departure, Crooke's career remained a window into an enduring but rarely talked about tradition of intelligence work: the secret channel for peace. His personal story, one of spying without betrayal, should not be aggrandized. Others had also done such work, notably in 2003 when an SIS team headed by Sir Mark Allen, a devoted falconer and student of Bedouin ways, led successful negotiations, also involving Stephen Kappes of the CIA, that helped bring reconciliation with Colonel Muammar Gaddafi and ended Libya's attempt to acquire nuclear technology. Further back, in the 1970s, the CIA engaged in extensive dialogue with Palestinian terror groups. But because much of Crooke's career has been made public it is easier to tell without restriction. As we explore what modern spying looks and should look like, his story sheds light on the fine line between espionage and discreet diplomacy, and whether getting secret intelligence on a threatening group is as important as simply understanding them. In most cases of such secret contact, the details and identities of the officers involved have never been made known. And even in Crooke's case, there were strict limits on what he could reveal about his past activities. But, thanks to his very public 'outing' as a spy in the Israeli press, the veil could be lifted a little.[3]

If ever a Briton had been born for a life of adventure in foreign lands, it was Alastair Crooke. 'I had never really lived in England,' he said. 'I had mostly lived overseas in many places and was brought up in a very mixed atmosphere.' That was his rather mild and grossly understated way of putting it.

The Crookes' roots were diverse. Alastair was a descendant of one Sir Thomas Crooke, who came from England to the town of Baltimore, County Cork, in 1606 and established a base to trade with pirates. Despite the town's subsequent sacking by such pirates in 1631, the family lived nearby for another eight generations. It was in Ireland, in 1949, that Alastair was born.

His family was also Australian. His great-grandfather William Crooke, a doctor, had sailed from Ireland in 1841, aged twenty-six, as a free settler to the penal colony of Tasmania (then Van Diemen's Land) with his brother, a teacher. Both later moved to Melbourne. Alastair's father, Frederick Montague Warren Crooke, was born in 1896 in Sydney. He left a city public school, Newington College, to volunteer for the Australian Expeditionary Force during the First World War. He fought with them in the bloody Gallipoli beachhead in Turkey and in the trenches of the western front.[4]

But he was also an Englishman. His father, who used his middle name 'Warren', recorded his nationality as 'English' on his travel documents. That was even before he had left the Australian forces and enlisted with the Gurkha regiment in India. Though dispirited by the agonies of the trenches, the young Warren saw hope of an old-style, more decent type of conflict in the Empire's service. He explained his transfer as a 'career choice' to become a professional soldier. 'Should like it also, as it is rather an interesting kind of warefare [sic] out there, mere play compared to the slaughter in France.'[5] As a career officer in the Indian Army, Frederick participated in the last of Britain's three Afghan Wars. In the Second World War, as an acting lieutenant-colonel, he commanded a British brigade.

The family then put down African roots. After Crooke's father retired, he bought a tobacco farm in the former colony Rhodesia (modern Zimbabwe). Crooke spent his childhood there, before being dispatched to the experimental Aiglon College in Switzerland, run by a teacher named John C. Corlette.

Aiglon was a school for adventurers. It valued self-reliance above all else in a regime particularly aimed at the troublesome sons of the pampered rich; many were from broken homes. The boys matured through physical challenges, like a hard climb, said Crooke: 'When they have a little ledge, a couple of inches, to walk along and it is icy and the weather is raining and they have to walk along it without ropes and they know they may slip and there is a 1,000-foot fall and Mummy and Daddy can do absolutely nothing to help them, it has a profound effect in suddenly maturing people.'

Vladimir Putin, the former KGB officer turned Russian president, recalled being told once by his former service, 'We don't take people who come to us on their own initiative.'[6] In the 1970s, the British secret service was like that too. No job advertisements were posted. Recruitment was by invitation.

Crooke will never quite confirm he was a member of SIS, even though it is public knowledge and even if he is prepared to comment, as an interested observer, on the nature of intelligence work and on his deployments abroad. He is still minded that the Official Secrets Act applies. But, based on several interviews with people who knew and worked with him, it is possible to piece together his career.

SIS first approached Crooke while he was at St Andrews, Scotland's oldest university. He studied politics and economics there from 1968 to 1972. Initially, he turned them down. He had become interested in economic theory, but, after graduating, a brief spell as a junior banker in the City of London convinced him of the moneyman's narrow perspective. He changed direction and, approached again by SIS, this time he said yes.

The intelligence profession appealed not only for the adventure but also for the nonconformity. This was never supposed to be a sought-after or esteemed job, he felt, looking back. Its mission was to deliver uncomfortable messages to government even if 'you get no thanks and rewards for coming along with the bad news'. But there was something noble about the job. Crooke believed there should be a constant interplay between intelligence analysis and recruiting sources. It was a form of detective work. 'Intelligence is when you read the papers or hear something and suddenly the hairs on the back of your neck prick up and you say, "That doesn't fit." ' The profession was 'iconoclastic'. Its aim was to pick up on an anomaly and use 'dogged determination' to solve the mystery that lay beneath 'and see if it brings down the whole structure of thinking'.

SIS basic training, whatever it was (he would not disclose the information), clearly did not last too long. To Crooke's mind, the art of intelligence was in any case something you either had or didn't have. 'It was always evident from the recruitment that good intelligence work is something like art, it is about nuance.'

By 1975, Crooke had been posted back to the country of his birth, Ireland. Officially, the 26-year-old British officer was a junior diplomat handling relations with the press. These were heady days. In February that year, a ceasefire was called by the IRA in Ulster. But peace did not last and the violence spread south into the Irish Republic. In July 1976, the new British ambassador to Ireland, Christopher Ewart-Biggs, was blown up by a landmine. The IRA claimed that he had been sent to Dublin 'to coordinate British intelligence activities'.[7]

Even as the IRA resumed its violence, SIS was exploring ways to speak to its leaders. SIS usually dealt only with conflicts outside British territory. This included Ireland, but not the province of Northern Ireland, which was the terrain of the rival domestic Security Service (MI5). But when the Troubles had begun in 1968, MI5 was judged too inexperienced to run agents inside terrorist groups, so SIS initially took the leading role in both the south and north.

In 1973, an independent-minded SIS officer named Michael Oatley, newly arrived in Northern Ireland, opened an indirect channel to the terrorists. Following the events of Bloody Sunday a year before, the British government had banned any contact by its representatives with the IRA. But against orders and initially without anyone's knowledge, Oatley (and others who have not been named publicly) pushed at the door that would eventually lead to peace in Northern Ireland. The IRA knew him by the code name Mountain Climber.

The novice secret servant Crooke was also busy, using his Irish blood to good effect. He made contact with the more left-wing and less sectarian Official IRA: 'For strange reasons I was taken up and became very close

to one of the main leaders.' The Officials had split from the more violent Provisional wing of the IRA (PIRA) back in 1969. Gradually the
Officials – or 'stickies' – were persuaded down the path of constitutional
politics, even if many fighters defected to PIRA. But in the mid-1970s, the
transition was not complete.

'I used to go to Galway to their dinner parties and used to sit at the dinner table, and this wasn't some sort of nice, civil society middle of the
road.' He also went to Drogheda, on the east coast between Dublin and
Belfast, which was dangerous territory in those years for British Embassy
staff. 'The last few people staying there had been kneecapped and thrown
out.' The official IRA was based around trade unions. He would go to
their meetings and afterwards they would 'take great pleasure in saying
Sean here has just done this or that. He is the Active Service Unit [com-
mander] in Belfast and he is just out of the Maze [prison]. And you would
spend hours discussing Irish history with them. Thank God I had done my
background.'

All the while, the two sides were simultaneously shooting at and dis-
creetly talking with each other. This twin track was replicated in Crooke's
own family. His brother Ian, seven years older, was in the British Army,
fighting in Northern Ireland with the elite 22 SAS. He later commanded
the regiment's reserve unit, 23 SAS, and was famed for his role as operations officer in the 1980 assault on the Iranian Embassy in London.

In public, the British government insisted it would treat the IRA as
criminals, never as a rebel army. IRA prisoners were accused and tried as
felons, never designated prisoners of war. The government claimed that it
would not be moved by threats; they would engage in dialogue only if the
terrorists first laid down their arms. But that approach was always 'fantasy', said Crooke. The idea that 'you don't start the process [of talking]
until there is an agreement to give up weapons or stop violence' was seriously flawed and no one really believed it. After all, the Americans had sat
down with their Vietnamese enemy in Paris even as the killing continued
on the battlefield.

But, to use Winston Churchill's vocabulary, keeping 'war-war' and
'jaw-jaw' going in parallel was never easy. One track was bound 'to explode
into the other track at some time', according to Crooke. If an enemy realized that a secret intelligence officer had made contact simply as a means
of gathering information to kill him, then trust would evaporate and

things could become dangerous. 'The main thing is how you build a track that can isolate itself and can, if you like, cover over the wounds inflicted on the military side.'

A profile of Crooke in the *Financial Times* would later describe the point of SIS's talks with the IRA as trying to find moderates 'whom they then hoped to "separate" from the extremists'.[8] The same was later said of SIS and CIA efforts to talk to Taliban rebels during the war in Afghanistan after 2001. Britain said the object was to find the 'reconcilables' and persuade them to either abandon their struggle or change sides completely.

But if one's aim was to suborn moderates, then contact with the enemy was both hostile and disingenuous. The approach was aimed not at seeking dialogue but rather at provoking discord. What Crooke did not say, but others emphasized, was that the use of such tactics by SIS and the CIA exposed the fault line between the intelligence officer's day job of making war on an enemy, by attempting to recruit a traitor among them or find other points of weakness, and his role as honest broker, maintaining a peaceable dialogue with that enemy.

Crooke said that in any case it was 'complete nonsense' to think hunting reconcilables helped to end conflict. Why? Because, in his view, a violent organization's liberal or moderate wing was never likely to deliver peace: 'Every attempt at finding the middle ground is pretty well doomed to failure.' For him, it was a fiction to think 'that if you speak to "moderates like us" they will somehow be empowered to find a way to bring about a solution'.

Crooke parted company with liberals here. He was sceptical of all the amateur theatrics of peacemaking, all the well-meaning but misguided attempts (by churches or voluntary groups, for instance) to unite 'people of goodwill'. In truth, peace came when you dealt with and convinced the tough guys – the ones with guns and bombs – that it was in their best interests. 'The people who bring about a solution in nearly every case I have seen, in nearly all conflicts, have been the people who command the allegiance of the military [wing].' That was why in Northern Ireland the centrist Republicans of the Social Democratic and Labour Party (SDLP) were eventually eviscerated. It was Martin McGuinness and Gerry Adams – key figures in both the IRA military command and its political wing, Sinn Féin – who finally delivered the lasting ceasefire and the peace agreement.

Secret 'peacemaking' in modern civil wars could achieve wonders only if the time was right. In the early days of a conflict, when embittered youngsters were typically filled with a killing rage, no amount of talking was going to assuage them. Crooke used to say that 'fighters have to grow old' before they tire of killing. It was a lesson still unlearned by the US after 9/11, when their kill/capture campaign of assassination in Afghanistan and Pakistan served to constantly rejuvenate the Taliban leadership.

After leaving Ireland in 1979, Crooke's next foray was to apartheid South Africa. Exactly what he did there remains a mystery, but it did involve dealing with SWAPO, the Soviet-backed liberation movement in what is now Namibia but was then known as South West Africa and under South African rule. One of his tasks was to press UN demands that SWAPO should disarm.

Crooke alleged there was a sharp politicization of both SIS and Britain's diplomatic service during these years: 'This was part of the Mrs Thatcher revolution: the job of the ambassador [became] to sell British goods and pass out the message of British policy. Not to start sending contrary messages back.' He felt the rot had started – far beyond the events in southern Africa – with a trend towards neo-liberal political thinking that had taken root in Chicago in the 1970s and which influenced conservative thinkers across the West. According to this viewpoint, said Crooke, democracy could only survive if citizens were mobilized against tyranny, and that required portraying the world in monotone, populated with good guys and bad guys.

He noticed this in South Africa, where British diplomats clashed with Thatcher, whose strident support for the apartheid government required all its opponents to be demonized. 'Ambassadors were warning about the consequences in Africa of this policy.' They would send back well-argued cables to London and 'a telegram came back from the PUS [Permanent Under-Secretary] saying: stop doing this'. This was the policy and the diplomats were supposed to go out there and do as they had been told. 'Here are the speaking points. Follow the speaking points.'

Even if Crooke disliked Thatcher's rhetoric, he still served her cause, most notably in Afghanistan. Ever since the Soviet invasion of 1979, President Ronald Reagan, Thatcher's great friend, had been ramping up covert assistance to the Islamic groups that were fighting the Soviets and the communist Afghan government (it had actually begun before the invasion). In 1985, Crooke was dispatched under diplomatic cover to Islamabad, Pakistan, to help with the war effort as deputy chief of the SIS station. The war was largely being run with the Pakistani government and its military dictator, General Muhammad Zia-ul-Haq. All money and weapons for the rebels had to go through the Pakistani intelligence service, the ISI.

Milton Bearden, then the CIA station chief in Islamabad, remembered Crooke as 'a natural on the frontier' and as 'a British agent straight out of the Great Game'.[9] In those days, Crooke's role involved not just talking with militants, but also supplying them with lethal hardware. While Bearden and other CIA officers were banned from crossing the border into Afghanistan, Crooke used to disappear across for days on end. He would then arrive back in Islamabad late at night and hurry over to Bearden's residence to show off his latest piece of captured hardware, Bearden remembered.

Some of the 'comrades'[10] with whom the British and Americans were fighting were hard-line Islamists, among them the Sunni Arab fighters of Osama bin Laden's group, which came to be called al-Qaeda. (Crooke would never say if bin Laden was among those he met. Contrary to rumour, as Bearden pointed out, no Western service gave any aid to bin Laden – as a rich Saudi, he hardly needed it – but he was an ally at the time.) As the war drew to an end, Crooke said he began to warn about the threat these militants would pose in future. But as one senator in Washington told him, 'The very people you warned us against, they sure kick communist ass!' And that was the problem. 'We looked aside,' said Crooke. But the cost of ignoring the Sunni Islamists became plain on 11 September.

Entirely the wrong lessons were also drawn from the defeat of the Soviet Union in Afghanistan, he said. The impact of US-funded mujahideen was exaggerated, and while such propaganda helped justify the billions the CIA had spent, it also established the founding myth for al-Qaeda and the Taliban: namely, how a band of sandal-clad jihadists could defeat a superpower. By Crooke's account, it was the old story of discordant human intelligence brushed aside. Two years before the Berlin Wall fell, Crooke was already seeing the Soviet Union collapse before him. He was witnessing the implosion of its undefeated army in Afghanistan. But, he said, no one wanted to hear: 'Both institutionally and most importantly psychologically [we were] totally unprepared for the collapse of the Soviet Union.' There was a strange fighting season when the Soviet Army refused to emerge from its barracks. 'I remember very well because I was in Afghanistan and talking to people: Uzbeks coming down from Tashkent and other places. I knew there were all sorts of things happening in these Soviet republics, like assassinations of off-duty Russian soldiers. Whenever I would raise this, it was just dismissed out of hand. They would say: "Of course these things are not happening. We would know about those things."'

It was this Soviet implosion that decisively altered the conflict from a point where the mujahideen were demoralized and almost defeated to one where the Russians were looking to withdraw, said Crooke. At the time and later, America ascribed this reversal to the CIA's covert actions and, in particular, the delivery of shoulder-launched Stinger missiles. The truth was, said Crooke, that after being transported by donkeys over mountain passes the Stingers were not effective. 'They had a very low success rate. The figures given by the Americans were just fanciful.' Others involved disagreed strongly and insisted to me that the Stingers had had a noticeable effect on the behaviour of Soviet helicopter pilots. But a study of Politburo records by Alan Kuperman, a political scientist at the Massachusetts Institute of Technology, discovered that the Soviets were preparing to leave Afghanistan before the Stingers became effective. The weapon 'was not utilized in Afghanistan until September 1986, a mere two months before the Politburo's decision to adopt a withdrawal deadline. At the key November 1986 Politburo meeting, no mention was made of the Stinger nor any other U.S. escalation'.[11] Bearden called the claim 'utterly specious'. Jack Devine, who headed the Afghan task force, said Kuperman's arguments 'turned history upside down'.

As the Soviet Union began to dissolve, everyone wanted to celebrate and reap the spoils of victory rather than hear about the next threat. Crooke said that he went to see the US ambassador in Islamabad after the Soviets had withdrawn from Afghanistan.

As Crooke recalled events, the ambassador slammed his fist down on his desk and shouted, 'Got them!'

'There's going to be a civil war!' Crooke replied.

'No, no, it will be over in thirty minutes. Najibullah [the Soviet-backed Afghan president] won't survive thirty minutes.'

They had a bitter argument. But, said Crooke, then the debate was closed. And more widely, in Western intelligence agencies no one was permitted to collect information about Afghanistan. 'If you had it you were not allowed to disseminate it. You had to tear it up and throw it in the waste bin.'

This was the madness of the post-Cold War 1990s, when the spy agencies were reinventing themselves. It was a time, he said, when they were determined to – using modern business-speak – 'put the customer first'. They were ruled by 'requirements', the formal list of intelligence priorities drawn up, in the UK and US, for example, in Whitehall and the US National Security Council, and signed off by politicians. It was not simply that warnings of future dangers were ignored, but that an uncommissioned warning – providing intelligence not covered by a specific requirement – was actually forbidden. The intelligence would be shredded. This was how bureaucratic the secret services had become, Crooke felt.

In later years, he alleged, the British secret service went further than the Foreign Office in becoming a means to 'deliver outcomes for the politicians'. By the 1990s, ahead of both 9/11 and the Iraq intelligence debacle, it had ceased to be that iconoclastic bearer of bad news that had inspired him. Faced with either budget cuts or extinction, the service made itself useful as another way of delivering political objectives and 'adding value to government policies' by underpinning an official 'narrative' of the globe as it was seen by the politicians. In contrast to SIS, regular Foreign Office diplomats, whose position was more secure, came to be seen as almost rebellious. The diplomats were, if anything, 'like good lawyers in the background, reminding us all of the problematic things that may come up'.

One of the UK 'requirements' in the 1990s was to assist the fight against trafficking of illegal drugs, as well as combating one of its by-products in South America: hostage taking. Crooke was sent to Brazil between 1991 and 1993, and from there to Colombia. He was cast again in the role of honest broker, talking to militants, though this time in their guise as kidnappers of Westerners. But there were lessons here for other conflicts too. Even when the gangs' demands were 'ridiculous' and quite impossible to meet, it was still important to facilitate dialogue: 'Because if you don't open up communications, you spend the next year negotiating about how to negotiate. And that's been the history.'

Opening talks did not mean negotiation. The priority was to increase understanding by making expectations on both sides a little more realistic. That was the lesson Crooke took to his next assignment: Palestine.

The Nobel Peace Prize has a chequered history. Its award can be a sign of imminent war. But in Palestine it did at least signal a respite that went on for six years. In 1994, the prize was shared between the ageing Palestinian leader, Yasser Arafat, and Israeli statesmen Yitzhak Rabin and Shimon Peres. The Oslo Accords, signed a year earlier, had brought the Palestine Liberation Organization (PLO) out of exile. They returned from Tunisia to Gaza and the West Bank as the ruling faction of an interim Palestinian self-government. The Accords were a victory for secret peacemaking and public compromise. They were also a victory for the street fighters. The peace agreement marked the end of the First Intifada, which had been waged since 1987, largely by stone-throwing youngsters.

In 2000, however, large-scale violence returned. Anger had been bubbling up for some time, the result of a failure to solve some intractable issues. (These included the continued expansion of Israeli settlements in occupied areas and an insistence by both sides that an undivided Jerusalem should be their capital.) For Palestinians, what became the Second Intifada was provoked by the visit of Israeli politician Ariel Sharon to the Temple Mount in Jerusalem, sacred to both Islam and Judaism. Sharon was already hated by Palestinians for ordering the Israeli invasion of Lebanon in 1982. He had been accused of allowing Israeli troops to be complicit in the massacres by Christian militia of the inhabitants of the Palestinian refugee camps of Sabra and Shatila in Beirut. The purpose of going to the Temple Mount was, he said, to demonstrate it was in 'our hands and will remain in our hands. It is the holiest site in Judaism and it is the right of every Jew to visit the Temple Mount.'[12]

Both sides had been preparing for violence. And it was a far bloodier intifada than the first. Once again young Palestinians threw stones at Israeli troops and were suppressed with lethal force. But their attacks on Israel were now becoming far more deadly as the Palestinians began to send across suicide bombers. These were trained and deployed not only by Arafat's Fatah movement – from its armed wing, Fatah Tanzim, and its offshoot the al-Aqsa Martyrs' Brigade – but also by Hamas, a resurgent Palestinian movement that had rejected the Oslo Accords and now appeared to be competing to produce the bloodiest attacks.

Into the fray stepped Alastair Crooke, delegated by SIS to join the staff of Javier Solana, the Spanish former secretary general of NATO who, in October 1999, was appointed the EU's first security chief. Crooke's task was to assist Solana on a fact-finding commission headed by former US Senate leader George Mitchell into the causes of the First Intifada. Mitchell reported in April 2001, but Crooke's mission had only just begun. Europe wanted to play a more assertive role in promoting Middle East peace and Crooke was asked to engage with all parties. Tony Blair was, at first, broadly supportive of his efforts. After the attacks of 9/11, Blair committed Bush to supporting a renewed Palestine–Israel dialogue as a quid pro quo for joining his 'War on Terror' coalition.

Against a background of terrible bloodshed, 2002 was not an auspicious year for peace. The violence came to a head with a Hamas attack on 27 March that killed thirty Jews celebrating Passover at the Park Hotel in Netanya, north of Tel Aviv. On 29 March, Israel responded with Operation Defensive Shield, launching troops into heavily populated towns that the Oslo Accords had ceded to Palestinian control and encircling and imprisoning Arafat in his headquarters. On 2 April, the Israelis laid siege to Jenin. When they eventually crushed opposition there – with the help of bulldozer tanks – many journalists alleged that there had been a massacre. The EU sent Crooke to investigate. He crossed over alone through Israeli lines. He saw how the town had been bulldozed by the Israeli soldiers. But he found no massacre. He was playing the role of the classic dispassionate eyewitness.

Also on 2 April, attention shifted to Bethlehem and the fourth-century Church of the Nativity in Manger Square, the legendary birthplace of Jesus. Some 200 Palestinians, both militant fighters and ordinary residents of the town, took sanctuary in the church at the start of what became a thirty-nine-day siege by Israeli forces.

The Israelis were after thirteen men in the church who were on their wanted list for their alleged role in organizing suicide attacks. According to one account, the men 'included nine from the al-Aqsa Martyrs' Brigade, some of them members of Bethlehem's Abbayat clan, blamed by the Israelis for a series of terrorist attacks over the last 20 months. Included too were three members of Hamas. The thirteenth was Abdullah Daoud, the Palestinian intelligence chief in Bethlehem.'[13]

In the protracted stand-off, while British and American diplomats talked to the Israeli leadership, Crooke dealt with the trapped Palestinians by slipping across the lines. The situation was understandably tense. Monks inside the church said food had run out. Gunmen in the church and Israeli troops outside exchanged shots. A Palestinian was shot dead in the church courtyard. 'At various times the Israelis would again stop firing and then I'd walk across that square to the Church of the Nativity – occasionally to take bodies out of it, and also to receive the list of who was in there.' To avoid being misidentified as a fighter by Israeli snipers, he would walk ten yards, stop, stand still, then walk on again. The process continued 'until I'd reached the appropriately termed Door of Humility, to pass through that'.

Crooke went back and forth until the siege was lifted with a deal. On 10 May the CIA took the thirteen wanted Palestinians away in a convoy of armoured cars. They fingerprinted them and then delivered them to an aircraft hangar from where Britain's Royal Air Force flew them to Cyprus and ultimately into exile.[14]

Over the summer, as the suicide attacks and the Israeli occupation of Palestinian towns continued, Crooke was trying to promote a ceasefire by talking to the two main groups fighting, Hamas and Fatah Tanzim. Since the Israelis were trying to assassinate a list of militants, Crooke needed to demonstrate to those he met that he was not collecting information on them but only offering dialogue. So, while the CIA might move about with bodyguards in armoured cars, he was the barefoot intelligence officer.

'I had no protection at all,' he said. Travelling to the refugee camps of Nablus and nearby Balata, he would go alone in Palestinian taxis. He would take no phone and even 'check my shoes to make sure the Israelis hadn't put anything in them'. A little boy would pick him up at the edge of a camp and guide him through the alleyways. He was 'completely vulnerable' and entirely under his host's power. He was relying on the old Middle Eastern tradition of hospitality: however duplicitous your host might be, he could not harm his guests.

One of the tricks was to show no fear. When passing through troubled neighbourhoods Crooke would wind down the window, smile and, if necessary, get out to greet people 'so they could see me completely'. Even though he spoke little Arabic, he took no interpreter: 'I never took anyone with me to meetings.' Unlike journalists, who often took guides and interpreters, he was convinced the militant groups 'would never trust those people'. He had been issued with a bulletproof vest but that stayed in the hotel cupboard.

Although it is said that he was a career spymaster, the most important factor was that he made it clear that he was not spying. He was talking to both sides, which meant things were complicated. He had to frame his questions carefully. 'I didn't ask people for their names, identities or any questions of a military nature.' What he was after was their thoughts and ideas. 'There was no intelligence aspect to it,' he insisted, although on this point he was misleading. What he meant was that he was not collecting secret intelligence. But what he was learning through this contact with the militants – about their character and intentions – was very useful and it was passed back to European governments.

He was trained in countersurveillance and did his best to avoid being followed. But he told the Palestinians to take their own precautions: 'You do what you have to do and I will conform with it. But I am not giving you any guarantees. I am happy to change my clothes and even take anything off.' Years later, two of the meetings he held were described in minutes supposedly kept by Fatah and seized by the Israelis when they invaded the Gaza Strip. They referred to encounters in June 2002 with Sheikh Ahmed Yassin, the religious leader of Hamas, in Gaza.[15]

According to the transcripts, Crooke had begun his meeting with Hamas by asserting, 'We are all currently entering a difficult time, not just in Palestine but in the entire region. The main problem is the Israeli occupation.' Such a statement called into question Crooke's good faith as a neutral interlocutor. But Crooke said the transcript was fantasy. The transcript quoted Yassin as saying that he was a man of peace. What nonsense, said Crooke. 'Yassin would actually boast to me: "I am a man of war."'

Crooke said Yassin had been impressive. 'He had a real twinkle in his eye. He was paraplegic. He had an earpiece because he couldn't hear. His hearing aid would give off high-pitched screams as you were talking to him and you couldn't know what he was hearing. But he was vitally alive as a person and tough as nails. He dominated. He just radiated this presence. He was a very powerful figure.' Yassin was killed in an Israeli bomb attack at a mosque in March 2004. The strike was not the result of an intelligence coup, said Crooke. Everyone in Gaza knew where he lived. 'He had never hid. He lived at home. He was paraplegic. If he went anywhere he had to use a special vehicle and be lifted into it.'

The true bit of the transcript was the debate over whether the talks should be made public. Hamas thought they should be: otherwise the details could be leaked in a distorted way by their opponents, as proved to be the case. But, at the time, Crooke had insisted the existence of their dialogue should be kept secret. Like it or not, talking to the enemy, to those willing to kill civilians, remained a taboo in much of the Western world – particularly after 9/11.

It was inevitable that someone, at some stage, should discover Crooke's secret service background. He was now a regular on the scene in Jerusalem. He tried to keep a low profile, eschewing the boutique American Colony Hotel beloved of journalists. But, by dealing with the numerous factions, his role was becoming public. It's not clear who leaked what, but in August 2002, in a profile in the Israeli newspaper *Ma'ariv*, for the first time in his career Crooke was outed as an operative of SIS, a rare event for a serving or even retired officer.

The result was a flurry of publicity, not all bad. Israeli newspapers poked some fun. Someone called him 'brave to the point of madness'. Another quoted an Israeli intelligence officer who said of him, 'Don't be fooled by his appearance. You don't want to meet him in a dark alley in the middle of the night. Ask the mujahideen in Afghanistan or the drug barons of Colombia.'

Initially, people stood by him, including – most importantly – Javier Solana and David Manning, Tony Blair's foreign policy and security adviser. But more problematic than his public outing was a policy shift under way in Britain. Blair had grown wary of talking to militants and now wanted a more aggressive approach, described as a 'counterinsurgency surge', said Crooke. 'Blair had secretly agreed with the Americans, and perhaps others, a change of policy which was to destroy Hamas, undermine its leadership.'

The hardening of Blair's views took place as he focused on making the case internationally for invading Iraq. Crooke was among a great many inside SIS and the Foreign Office who saw this 'invasion diplomacy' as the culmination of a politicization of the British foreign service. Crooke also saw it as a decisive rejection of compromise. As he recalled later:

> a senior British official had told me bluntly that my methods of building
> political solutions by building popular consent – holding 'town hall' meet-
> ings with all factions, working with Hamas, shuttling between Palestinians
> on the ground and President Arafat to ensure broad participation and con-
> tinued momentum – were passé. We were in a new era, and it required new

thinking: 'The road to Jerusalem now passes through Baghdad,' the official insisted.[16]

From the previous nuanced approach to the Arab–Israeli dispute, policy had hardened, subsumed into the language of counterterrorism. Hamas was now a 'virus' and the Palestinian conflict was just another to be solved by 'confronting extremists'.

The new thinking was underlined in an SIS paper, dated 1 March 2003 but only made public years later, which laid out a security strategy for the Palestinian Authority on how to repress groups like Hamas and the al-Aqsa Martyrs' Brigade that rejected the Oslo Accords.[17] Crooke knew nothing of the document and later summarized it as a plan 'to "degrade"' the capabilities of opponents to the Palestinian Authority, to disrupt their communications, intern their members, close their civil and charitable organizations, remove them from public bodies, and seize their assets'.[18] No one in the EU was told of it either: 'So Solana was working and continued to work with a policy of trying to include all of these groups at the same time as Mr Blair was undermining it.' It was a betrayal, Crooke felt in hindsight.

Other intelligence officers point out that, for basic security reasons, it would have made no sense at all to share any plans for attacking groups like Hamas with Crooke. As Crooke had himself argued, the peace channel needed to be sealed off from the military line for its own integrity.

The rift between Crooke and London was not about trust but about a disagreement on strategy. Since Britain was now in support of Israel's campaign to crush the militants by force, Crooke's chance of achieving a lasting cessation of violence was fading. When he had put together a ceasefire in August 2002, persuading both Hamas and Fatah to call off their attacks, it lasted only until Israeli jets dropped a one-tonne bomb and killed Sheikh Salah Shehadeh, the military head of Hamas, and also nine children and five other adults.[19] The suicide bombings resumed and so did Israeli retaliation. In the following months, Crooke tried again, repeatedly, to bring about a de-escalation of violence. Sometimes it worked for a few days, and it did save lives, but there was no sign of abatement. Now at odds with British policy, Crooke was summoned back to London. As the *Guardian* reported on 24 September 2003:

Yesterday, a British embassy spokesman in Tel Aviv said Mr Crooke would leave Jerusalem within days for 'personal security reasons . . . The deterioration in the security situation in the occupied territories made it impossible for him to do his job safely,' the spokesman said. The embassy acknowledged that Mr Crooke was leaving against his will but declined to discuss what his associates say were his growing differences with the Foreign Office . . .[20]

In the British tradition (as the *Guardian* put it), he was handed an honour from the Queen, a CMG ('Call Me God'), and then sacked. That was accomplished with a summons to SIS headquarters in Vauxhall. He was seen by a junior clerk before being sent home for good. Crooke would never discuss the incident, just as he would never confirm his service for SIS.

SIS itself has never commented on Crooke's enforced retirement. But when interviewed several former officers argued that, whatever the merits of his opinions, his fault was to be actively promoting his own policy. One said, 'He was highly intelligent but he had become an advocate.' That was no crime in itself, but he had pushed it too far and lobbied against British policy. Some also suspected that Crooke had gone along too readily with his outing as an SIS officer. 'He was doing God's work, and has done so ever since,' said another former colleague, 'but within a secret service you cannot do your own thing.' In evidence to Britain's Iraq war inquiry but speaking generally, Sir Richard Dearlove, then chief of the service, said that 'in SIS you cannot really afford dissenters. Dissent [redacted words] can cause phenomenal problems.'[21]

It was in 2013, almost a decade since Crooke had left the British secret service, that I took the thirty-minute hop by plane from Cyprus to visit him in the Lebanese capital, Beirut.

Kim Philby had come here when he first left SIS. Employed as a correspondent for the *Observer*, he had remained nearly seven years before defecting to the Soviet Union in January 1963. On my way to meet Crooke, I walked down the battered cornice to the marina, past the boarded up King George Hotel, where Philby used to get drunk on whisky every afternoon.

Crooke's haunt was the Albergo, a boutique hotel in a district controlled by the Lebanese Forces militia. Unlike Philby, his afternoon drink was non-alcoholic: a fresh mint and hot water, brewed in a silver teapot. Philby had come to escape his past. Crooke, though, was adamantly sticking to his path. Having become embroiled in Palestine and the Middle East, he refused to be retired. Far from betraying his cause, he was adamantly sticking to it.

After leaving SIS, he had founded a non-government group, the Conflicts Forum. It held meetings and created channels for dialogue between, on the one hand, influential Western thinkers and policymakers and, on the other, leaders of militant groups like Hamas and Hezbollah, even if they were designated as terrorists. He was not trying to start private negotiations, he argued, but rather to help build understanding and manage expectations on both sides.

I wrote a magazine article about one such gathering he organized in Lebanon headlined 'Mint Tea with the Terrorists'. It had a few trite lines that were later endlessly quoted back at Crooke. 'Invited to dinner with the participants in the Beirut talks, and sharing jokes with the Hamas men over tiger prawns, avocado, pasta and cherry tomatoes, I wondered privately how one would explain all this intimacy to the mother of a child killed by a suicide bomber.' I was surprised Crooke saw me again. But, as my article had hinted, in fostering contacts with militants, some commentators and ex-colleagues argued that he sometimes appeared to be crossing the fine line between encouraging the West to understand Hamas and being an advocate for them.

My interest in coming to Beirut this time, however, was less to discuss the merits of this public dialogue and more to do with the value of the kind of officially sanctioned dialogue he had once conducted for the British government and the EU. While it was hardly surprising that the secret services were used if a government wanted clandestine talks with a violent group, did this discreet diplomacy have anything to do with gathering intelligence? And what, I wanted to know, was its connection with spying?

Since the early twentieth century, spying has been almost a synonym for betrayal and, except in wartime or dire emergency, the secret services of powerful countries have rarely used their own intelligence officers as spies, preferring generally to hire agents. But the tradition that Crooke in Palestine and Mark Allen in Libya represented was an older form of spying, more akin to an explorer's journey, where the intelligence officer spoke directly to his enemy or potential enemy. Crooke argued that it was often more profitable to act in good faith and be open. Although he did not say it, in such an approach the spy was the intelligence officer, spying the land himself. But he was neither betraying anyone nor trying to recruit someone to betray someone else. In Crooke's words, the conflation of intelligence with betrayal was 'very problematic'.

As we talked over mint tea at the Albergo, Crooke ducked further elaboration about why it was problematic. He had no wish to debate espionage. Anyway, he insisted, the question of who was or was not a spy was overrated. How exactly a secret service collected intelligence was not so important. The bigger issue was what sort of intelligence they were after.

By his way of thinking, paraphrased, before 9/11 it would not have mattered whether the 'man on the rock' next to bin Laden was a spy or a sort of emissary. In the 1990s what had been lacking was any real interest in and attention to the movement from which bin Laden emerged. 'The thing is that no one made the effort. No one even tried to understand it.' Intelligence agencies had much to concern them. Not everyone could have been diverted to watching bin Laden and his ilk, but, said Crooke, the agencies did not 'even have a basic institutional capacity to have a feel and understanding of it. They had no real element, no one who took the trouble to meet any of these people and understand them.'

As we spoke in Beirut, civil war raged in nearby Syria and once again, he said, the trouble was not finding sources of information, but rather finding anyone really interested in the roots of the conflict, who dared 'in a risk-averse era' to be involved in human intelligence – whether through recruiting spies or the sort of dialogue-based engagement he favoured.

Meanwhile, he argued, too much store was set by technical spying, such as the interception of communications. 'Really, I can't say anything too specific. But the inability of people sitting mostly in London or Washington to understand a conversation involving someone like an Islamist is extraordinary.' Part of the error was cultural understanding, but it was also conceptual – the addiction to wire taps and physical evidence 'covered up the essential factor that intelligence, real intelligence that you get, is nearly always contradictory and episodic.' In other words, technical information provided false certainty and a sense of precision that human spies never could provide; but uncertainty was what filled real human life.

What of the question he avoided, the relationship between his secret dialogues and spying?

In practice, said other former intelligence officers, covert diplomacy was another part of secret service work and another form of HUMINT, but it was distinct from agent-running. 'It is not so complicated. When it is in the national interests, we get tasked with these kinds of contacts,' said one former SIS officer. It was not a panacea and was frequently impossible. There was also a world of difference, such intelligence officers said, between Oleg Gordievsky, a real spy who betrayed the KGB and would have been shot if his contacts with SIS had been discovered, and a Hamas official who met the CIA, albeit secretly, with his organization's approval. One of those differences was that the secret agent was there to provide information that was adverse to his group's cause. But a liaison contact would never deliberately betray the detail of some secret plot.

More contact with al-Qaeda in the 1990s may have exposed bin Laden's agenda and perhaps more of his organization's broad strategy and strength. This could have helped forge a counter-strategy to undermine its appeal. But it would not have provided the kind of tactical information required to have discovered the specific 9/11 plot.

There was sometimes a blur. As we have seen, some of the best spies were recruited through real friendships with their recruiters. A liaison relationship could, over time, be turned into a betrayal. Conversely, some people labelled as 'secret agents' by intelligence agencies were in effect a liaison with the enemy. This could be a way of testing the waters between two hostile powers. In Afghanistan, the former UN official Michael Semple, during his frequent discussions with senior Taliban leaders, heard them describe how agents that Western agencies often thought they had recruited within the Taliban were only talking after consulting widely within their own movement 'and even their command chain'. Although these were hardly the relationships likely to yield precious secrets, Semple argued, they were often opportunities missed. 'I believe people thought they were picking off individual traitors but actually their cooperation was far broader than they realized.' The Taliban had accepted various acts of probing. 'But they hoped they would get something out of it. They weren't being suborned.' Western agencies, he said, while prepared to recruit 'agents', had no political sanction for wider contacts with the Taliban. And, as the war dragged on, this left them short of understanding and with fewer options in the future. 'I don't think there has been a long-term investment to ensure that on the Western side there were people who maintained long-term relationships with people sitting in strategic places inside the Taliban.'

Call him an explorer spy or a secret diplomat, the type of intelligence officer that Crooke had exemplified, or that Semple implied was missing in Afghanistan, was a complement but not an alternative, then, to his siblings, the traitor spy and his case officer. It was different work, but equally important.

And whether it was the job of a secret servant or not, Crooke's career demonstrated the nature of the work that needed doing – a gap that was there to be filled between the collection of specific secret intelligence and a government's ordinary diplomacy. And it was needed more than ever as increasing numbers of threats that could not be dealt with in ordinary ways emerged. In most places, an ambassador or his aides simply could not go and meet the leaders of a militant group without causing great offence to the host government or appearing to lend that group support. But the group might have global significance and need to be understood and engaged with. It was not necessary to spy on every non-state group that emerged in the world in some top-secret operation. But a modern spymaster might expect to be called upon to deal with problems like this more and more frequently.

Much of the engagement that both Crooke and Semple described was concerned with acquiring broader understanding – strategic rather than specific detailed intelligence. But, though it was an important component of human intelligence, Crooke questioned if intelligence services were even interested in this. He argued that too often intelligence had become a narrow craft aimed at providing only that specific piece of secret information, such as the location of some designated target, that assisted the government with its narrow policy. Increasingly now a 'service provider', intelligence agencies were delivering on lists of what the 'customer' wanted: whether it was delivering a message, confirming a prejudice or eliminating another target. 'The pressure to perform produces error after error. People need statistics and want to tick the box about how many terrorists they have taken out.'

Crooke had been sacked, his ex-colleagues said, because he was too independent. It had been inevitable, some suggested. A secret service that promoted a different policy from its government was a rogue agency. And a secret servant who publicly lobbied for his own policy was a rogue officer. But while many disagreed with the stance Crooke was said to have taken, and also with some of his activities since his retirement, many shared his frustration at the narrow scope of contemporary human intelligence. What both Crooke and several other former insiders argued was that while political leaders should expect complete loyalty from their intelligence officers, they also needed ones who were free to think and challenge. The point of having spy agencies, and of human intelligence in general, was to have real people with deep insider knowledge of cultures and events abroad who could talk back, who could quietly correct a politician's misunderstanding of the world.

Crooke remained controversial in his former service. One former senior SIS officer said Crooke's view was skewed by his dismissal, but more importantly by improvements since the Iraq debacle. Another said that, before the fiasco over weapons of mass destruction, SIS had been both 'unbearably arrogant' and too willing to exaggerate intelligence to please its paymasters, but since then it had become far more modest and objective in its approach. As politicians stoked the fires of rebellion in Syria in 2011 and 2012, SIS briefed many policymakers – to precious little effect – that this unrest could lead to decades of civil war. Its capacity to challenge was not entirely missing.

As the huge investment by the CIA in drone wars illustrated, the US intelligence world still had a strong ethos that spying was less about understanding the world and more about hunting bad people. And with no wish to understand the new militants, to enter into their mindset, the enemy's logic could be 'dehumanized', as Crooke put it, and enemies could be picked off by assassination from the sky. The reasoning was, he said, that 'they are not really human. Why should we try to understand them?' But the consequence of such thinking was a groundless self-confidence. And despite their assertions that al-Qaeda had somehow been suppressed, America would discover that 'al-Qaeda' was just a name and that the same threat would be reborn in a different way, under a different name, and that its inspiration was 'actually spreading much more widely everywhere'.

Chapter 11
Vaccination

'It is well . . . for the man in the street to realize that there is no power
on earth that can protect him from being bombed. Whatever
people may tell him, the bomber will always get through'

– Stanley Baldwin, House of Commons, 10 November 1932[1]

In April 2011, Shakil Afridi, a medical doctor in his forties, knocked on the
big steel door of the compound. It was a peculiar place, about eight times
larger than other homes in the area, with surrounding walls between
twelve and eighteen feet high, and no phone or Internet connection.[2] It
stood out in Abbottabad, a highland military town north of Islamabad,
Pakistan. No one around knew who lived inside, but the doctor planned
to use a ruse to find out.

He was, as his name implied, an Afridi, the warrior tribe that controls
the Khyber and Kohat mountain passes into Afghanistan. In 1878, during
Britain's First Afghan War, a contingent of Afridi had blocked the Khyber
Pass to oppose Britain's Army of Retribution, which was returning to
reconquer Afghanistan after the massacre of the Kabul garrison. More
recently, Shakil Afridi's grandfather had fought with the British Army in
the First World War, winning a Victoria Cross for his bravery in the
trenches at Ypres.

Today this Afridi had a new guise, as a secret agent for the CIA. When
the door opened a crack, he announced that he was on a door-to-door
vaccination mission and wanted to vaccinate any children in the household against hepatitis B. He in fact intended to get a sample of their blood,
because the CIA hoped it was blood that would produce a DNA match
with the most wanted man on the planet.

The door was closed and Afridi was turned away empty-handed. But
although his mission was a failure that day, by knocking on the door he

had played his part in the dramatic finale of a decade of war. The CIA had never managed to get the secret agent it dreamed of, the 'man on the rock' next to bin Laden. Indeed, the al-Qaeda leader was no longer sitting on a rock. But instead the CIA had found a secret agent to bang on his metal front door.

This was the climax to the hunt that had begun after the fall of the Twin Towers. The shock, hurt and humiliation of the attacks of 11 September 2001 demanded a big and clever enemy. Consciously or unconsciously, all those who talked about security – whether journalist, politician or spymaster – had enlarged the persona of the bogeyman, Osama bin Laden, a name that had been known to only a few in the world just days before the attacks.

The military and the spies were given the task of hunting him. The public needed a storyline that could be strung out into a worthwhile quest. If he had died too early – for example, when they cornered him in the mountains of Tora Bora, Afghanistan, in December 2001 – the thirst for revenge might not have been quenched. When I asked a young American soldier in 2004 why he was in Iraq, he said, 'We've come to get bin Laden.' The thought of a manhunt helped that small-town boy understand why he was in the war.

But the public also needed him to be caught in the end. Few expected it to take quite so long. Hundreds of people were rounded up and shipped to Cuba, to Egypt and even to Syria. The style of interrogation ranged from the FBI's cold but professional questions to the use of harsh techniques like waterboarding in a secret Polish CIA jail or electric shocks delivered by the Mukhabarat in Egypt (used, for example, on the bin Laden lieutenant Ibn al-Sheikh al-Libi). The methods used were so controversial that, more than a decade after his capture in 2003, Khalid Sheikh Mohamed, the alleged principal ringleader of 9/11, has still not been put on trial. It would be too revealing, too embarrassing. And meanwhile, bin Laden was still out there, his gloomy face staring from the ranks of the Most Wanted gallery. As time went on, the hunt for him was putting all the new ways of gathering intelligence on trial.

Then, on the evening of 1 May 2011, a Sunday, President Obama announced that US forces had killed Osama bin Laden. Helicopters with Navy Seals on board had stolen over the border in the night from Afghanistan to Pakistan. They had killed him, thrown his body into a bag and dumped it into the Arabian Sea, after an appropriate prayer.

So how had they got him? Admiral William McRaven, chief of JSOC and commander of the operation, called the manhunt the best intelligence coup in a century. 'I think when the history is finally written [of] how the CIA determined that bin Laden was there, it will be one of the great intelligence operations in the history of intelligence organizations.'[3] Was it the result of a tip-off by a spy? Did they find him by bugging phone calls and deploying all the modern instruments of surveillance? Was it by putting together a puzzle of existing pieces? The answers were neither clear-cut nor convincing. But the aftermath of the assassination and the official accounts of it that were released did throw an extraordinary light on to what had become of spying.

Before Obama made the announcement, there had been Twitter messages that already guessed at the news. But, as he told his officials, 'No, no, there's no news until I say so. People can leak all they want. But it's not news until I say something.'[4] This had always been, after all, a war of narratives, a clash of storytellers. That was true until the end.

Within a couple of years, at least three best-selling books about bin Laden's killing were written. A blockbuster Hollywood film, *Zero Dark Thirty*, has been made on the subject, as well as numerous documentaries. Obama had to fight a presidential campaign in 2012: his advisers made sure the journalists were fed a good story that maintained his reputation and placated most of those involved.

Billions of dollars of taxpayers' money had been spent on hunting bin Laden. It was convenient to use his end to justify the cost. The explanation that served the purpose was to say that finding him was no flash of brilliance but rather teamwork: all made possible by that time and money. As the Dodo said in *Alice's Adventures in Wonderland*, 'Everybody has won, and all must have prizes.'

While the real story remained hidden, killing bin Laden became a victory for anything you chose it to be: for torture, for spycraft, for computer geekery, for soldiering, or for a woman's intuition.

Some said it involved a multi-billion-dollar computer system that sorted complex information and highlighted hidden connections. Plaudits were due to software made by a CIA-funded company called Palantir, which had produced the latest-generation application of the 'total information awareness' thinking, by which computers were programmed (thanks to multi-billion-dollar grants from the taxpayer) to grab and process huge amounts of 'unstructured data' (all kinds of information from multiple sources) and 'connect the dots' to find connections and meaning. In the case of Palantir, there was also a large dose of human intervention in their product – and exaggeration about its value. In his narrative of the raid, Mark Bowden wrote, 'Palantir developed a product that actually deserves the popular designation Killer App.'[5]

Much attention was paid to 'Jen', the key counterterrorism analyst (now called a 'targeter') among a team of mostly women. She was found weeping with relief at a military base in Afghanistan after the Seals returned there with bin Laden's body, it was reported.[6] Her character was re-created to star in the *Zero Dark Thirty* movie.

Getting bin Laden had definitely been an intelligence coup. But how much sophistication was involved? So much had been tried – including, arguably, the invasion of two countries, Iraq and Afghanistan. It looked in the end rather like what computer hackers call a 'brute force attack' – trying every combination on a locked safe until one of them succeeds. While with hindsight the detective work did look good, none of what has emerged about it was especially novel. The methods used look quite traditional.

Here is the story in a nutshell. After the attacks of 11 September, President George W. Bush told the CIA to catch bin Laden dead or alive, preferably dead. The message was passed on by Cofer Black, head of the CIA's counterterrorism centre, to the agency team that duly went where bin Laden was, Afghanistan:

> I don't want bin Laden and his thugs captured, I want them dead . . . They must be killed. I want to see photos of their heads on pikes. I want bin Laden's head shipped back in a box filled with dry ice. I want to be able to show bin Laden's head to the president. I promised him I would do that.[7]

The US duly toppled the Taliban who ruled that country. But, at the Battle of Tora Bora in December 2001, bin Laden slipped away.

After declaring a so-called War on Terror and rounding up an alliance of nations in support, the US military discovered it was not equipped to fight such a war – al-Qaeda did not have a standing army – so it engaged in largely symptomatic relief. Public anger translated into hunger for war was more than satiated by invading Afghanistan and Iraq, with subsequent attempts at 'nation-building' (putting back together the shattered pieces) and then quelling revolts. At the same time specialized military units, such as the guards and interrogators at Guantanamo Bay, could support (and also compete with) the CIA's hunt for the real enemy: those who had actually attacked the US.

After asking a great many people in a variety of ways the simple question, 'Where is bin Laden?' interrogators drew a blank. So the CIA fell back to the typical approach of any professional tracking a missing person, which was to watch out for sightings and to monitor the movement and communications of his inner circle, both his family and aides, including staying on the lookout for messengers. As long as he lived, bin Laden was likely to continue to assert his authority by releasing periodic media statements, typically on video or audio tape, as well as talking to his subordinates. That meant there had to be couriers.

How to identify members of his inner circle? The obvious place to look was in the records of all those 'debriefed' in the various prison camps. The CIA (and other agencies) had for a long time kept a list of known associates of bin Laden. When new interviews took place, analysts would ask interrogators to press for more details on these targets. So far so obvious.

According to briefings given by the CIA and the White House about the manhunt – quoted in books by the journalists Peter Bergen and Mark Bowden and confirmed by a report of the Senate Intelligence Committee[8] – the CIA was finally led to bin Laden by following the trail of a courier named Abu Ahmed al-Kuwaiti. This had not been a shift of approach. 'Couriers were tangential to all of the other information we were following, we had been focusing on the courier network for a long time, it was not new,' said Marty Martin, a former head of the bin Laden unit.[9] Bergen reported that a female CIA analyst had penned a memo in 2005 called 'Inroads', which came up with four 'pillars' of what should constitute the hunt for bin Laden in the absence of any concrete leads. These were: his courier network, his family members, his communications with other senior leaders and his outreach to the media.[10]

The CIA heard of al-Kuwaiti both from captured materials and from the testimony of captured prisoners, under questioning from foreign governments and the CIA. The prisoners included Khalid Sheikh Mohamed (captured in March 2003, who downplayed any involvement by al-Kuwaiti) and Hassan Ghul (an al-Qaeda courier who was arrested in 2004 and transferred to a CIA black site in Eastern Europe). According to Bergen, Ghul 'told interrogators that the Kuwaiti was bin Laden's courier and frequently travelled with [him]'.[11] These interrogations were the subject of a rather stupid and delusional public argument in the US after bin Laden's killing about whether the name of that courier had emerged from torture.

Those who, like Bowden, have consistently noted since 9/11, as a matter of dispassionate fact, that torture could be effective appeared to be at some pains to point out that torture had been part of getting hold of the courier's name. Bowden wrote, 'The Obama administration has claimed that torture played no role in tracking down bin Laden, but here, in the first two important steps down the trail, that claim crumbles.' He cited the documented torture used against two prisoners.[12]

But John McCain, the Republican senator who stood against Obama for president, insisted that, based on a detailed briefing from the CIA:

> The first mention of the name Abu Ahmed al-Kuwaiti, as well as a description of him as an important member of al-Qaida, came from a detainee held in another country. The United States did not conduct this detainee's interrogation, nor did we render him to that country for the purpose of interrogation. We did not learn Abu Ahmed's real name or alias as a result of waterboarding or any 'enhanced interrogation technique' used on a detainee in U.S. custody.[13]

McCain's conclusion was endorsed by the detailed Senate report on the CIA interrogation programme published in December 2014. It found most of the clues that identified al-Kuwaiti came from prisoners in foreign custody or prisoners who had yet to receive 'enhanced' CIA treatment,[14] as in the case of Ghul, who was arrested by Kurdish authorities. As the report stated: 'Seven of the 13 detainees that the CIA listed as having been subjected to the CIA's enhanced interrogation techniques provided information on Abu Ahmed al-Kuwaiti *prior* to being subjected to the CIA's enhanced interrogation techniques.' But the whole debate was really meaningless. Whether in foreign or CIA custody almost all prisoners had been mistreated.

There was no control sample of untortured high-value prisoners. More importantly – as the official versions make clear – no al-Qaeda prisoner in the CIA's hands gave up al-Kuwaiti's actual identity. As McCain had correctly stated, 'None of the three detainees who were waterboarded provided Abu Ahmed's real name, his whereabouts, or an accurate description of his role in al-Qaida.'[15] The name they did discuss was just a start.

Calling someone Abu Ahmed al-Kuwaiti translates literally as 'Ahmed's dad from Kuwait'. It was about as useful as saying that bin Laden knew a John in New York. It was a long way short of a traceable identity.

The difficult and brilliant part came next, with the discovery of Abu Ahmed's real name and phone number. At the time of writing, how that was accomplished is still a secret. The Senate report indicates, however, that the breakthrough may have occurred by rereading a five-year-old CIA report. A later memo dated 23 November 2007 and headed 'Probable Identification of Suspected Bin Laden Facilitator Abu Ahmed al-Kuwaiti', described how 'review of 2002 debriefings of a [foreign government] detainee who claimed to have travelled in 2000 from Kuwait to Afghanistan' with an 'Ahmed al-Kuwaiti' provided the breakthrough leading to the likely identification of Habib al-Rahman as Abu Ahmed.[16] The foreign government then helped to identify that he operated from the greater Peshawar area. A CIA summary said the name provided by the prisoner turned out to be the name of al-Kuwaiti's dead brother, but it was enough for the CIA to 'map out Abu Ahmed's entire family, including the true name of Abu Ahmed himself'.[17]

Having got the courier's real name, the agency also got his mobile phone number. With the help of the National Security Agency, they could start tracking him. Contrary to popular myth, the NSA cannot listen to or track everything on the globe simultaneously. First they need something to attract their attention, what police call a 'lead'. But once they have a starting point, with their network of ground stations and access to a constellation of signals intelligence satellites, they do have an incredible capacity to listen into and above all follow specific mobile phones. This was everyday intelligence business. It needed no flash of brilliance or special instructions to put the known numbers of one of bin Laden's inner circle on to a list of what the NSA called 'selectors', the priority watch list of phones to track.

At first, according to Bowden, Abu Ahmed's phone could not be traced. 'But in June of 2010, the United States was able to pinpoint the phone's location when it was in use, or even perhaps when not in use. This meant they could find the Kuwaiti, and watch him.'[18] Now it got interesting.

The phone had appeared in Pakistan, already the presumed location for bin Laden's hideout. Advanced technology helped here. Satellites, stealthy drones and surveillance planes could all have been used to spot Abu Ahmed's car. Agents were deployed to watch roads. His car was found to be a white Suzuki Jimny with a distinctive spare wheel cover on the back. It was tracked from Peshawar to a house surrounded by high walls in the city of Abbottabad, close to a Pakistan Army military base.

The hunt became conventional again. When any police force finds the lair of a villain, the choice is to raid it or watch it. The CIA still had no evidence that bin Laden lived here. More surveillance technology was deployed. The CIA sent operatives to establish a safe house in a nearby villa in order to watch the compound and its inhabitants. But owing to the compound's high walls, it was only surveillance from the sky (satellite or drone) that revealed the presence of the man of the household – a man who paced around and cast a tall shadow, soon to be nicknamed 'the pacer'.

The CIA now began to believe they had cornered their man. Analysts observed that he walked like the man their predecessors had seen in early 1999 through Predator cameras pacing around a desert compound in Afghanistan. He had later been positively identified as bin Laden, but, at the time, when the identity was still uncertain, President Clinton had refused to strike because of the real risk of killing innocent people.[19] His new identification in Pakistan was still a hunch. Every analyst knew that all the evidence might seem to stack up perfectly but could still be wrong. Deciding to launch the attack into Pakistan was a heck of a call for President Obama to make.

It was at this point that Shakil Afridi came into the frame. Afridis have a reputation for being independent and rarely open to being recruited, but Dr Afridi had a series of problems that made him susceptible. While working in the tribal areas, he had been accused of medical malpractice. He was kidnapped by a local strongman and had to pay a ransom to be released. Later he visited the US, where he may have come under scrutiny from US intelligence. Research by *GQ* magazine concluded that Afridi attended a training session by a British charity that was organizing vaccinations in Pakistan. One of the charity's directors introduced him to the CIA in Peshawar, it claimed. The charity denied this.

Human intelligence had already played some role in following the courier thus far. A Pakistani 'asset' had been the one who spotted his car in Peshawar and helped to follow him home to Abbottabad. Agents were involved in observing the compound and discovering that the courier and his family lied to other family and friends when telling them where they lived.[20] But the deployment of Afridi was the most significant use of human intelligence that emerged from the sanitized account of the bin

Laden operation. It was probably far from the whole story, but insiders insist that there was never an agent or well-placed ally who gathered anything so precise about bin Laden that they could have pointed to a map and said, 'Osama bin Laden lives there!'

When asked to explain how bin Laden was caught, analysts involved speak of putting together a jigsaw puzzle of thousands of pieces. Cindy Storer, a former CIA analyst, was quoted as saying, 'Pieces fall from the sky and add to the pile the analyst already has . . . There is no picture [to follow], no edge pieces. And not all of the pieces fit in the puzzle'. Nada Bakos, a former CIA targeting officer, wrote, 'I can't stress enough that it is a team effort. It's much more complicated than one hero catching the bad guys. It is multi-faceted and not focused on one individual and no one in the CIA has a crystal ball.'[21]

Even the jigsaw metaphor did not convey the amount of 'data points' involved in modern terrorism analysis, insiders claimed. So many people and factors were being pieced together at once that only a computer, backed by large teams of brainy humans, could make sense of the problem.

The plotting of links between people, places, telephones, bank accounts and so on was nothing terribly new. But what was new was the scale of information available and in need of processing with the aid of machines. A glut of data was transforming intelligence. And it rarely brought enlightenment. As the bin Laden operation showed, secret intelligence was going digital. It was adapting to the new technologies that society was using as well as adapting its own specific technologies. This digitization is still incomplete. It is a transformation that has taken, and will continue to take, many years and the outcome is still uncertain.

In the specialized world of secret agents, technology had always been both a help and a hindrance. The secret agent in the traditional James Bond films was armed before his mission by 'Q', his quartermaster, with a series of wondrous high-tech toys, from exploding lighters to rocket-firing Aston Martins. In the real world, agents and handlers in dangerous situations try to carry as few gadgets as possible: they are too incriminating. 'All those gadgets; that was just for Moscow hands,' said one senior former case officer in SIS. (Under constant KGB scrutiny, Western intelligence officers in the Soviet Union did have to use ingenious devices to communicate with their agents.)

In the twenty-first century, though, even the purists acknowledged that technology was beginning to play a much bigger role in spying, starting with the preparation process for a recruitment attempt. Technology could be used to map out potential targets, to identify sources and to research profiles of people who might be recruited. 'HUMINT informs and enables technical operations and vice versa,' wrote Hank Crumpton, the former deputy head of the CIA's Counterterrorism Center, after 9/11.[22] Human agents on the ground, for example, helped suggest targets for surveillance and for air strikes by Predator drones in Afghanistan. In turn, the data from Predators helped to verify the reports from spies.

Crumpton also described how bad human intelligence made technical operations fail. He once went to great lengths to place a bug in an intelligence target's apartment, only to have to remove it again after six months. The target had divulged nothing. It had been a bad choice. 'Never underestimate the human factor; it's the most important part of clandestine operations, more important than technology.'[23]

As had been the case with catching bin Laden, insiders said that the most important use of technology in fighting terrorism was in tracking, tracking and more tracking. It sometimes made an intelligence officer's task feel more like police work than spy work. Paul Pillar, who retired in 2005 after twenty-eight years as a CIA analyst, latterly as a national intelligence officer for the Near East, said in an interview that the 'basic process of taking information from human and technical sources and piecing it together' was very similar to what domestic law enforcement did. Trying to make sense of some criminal gang was 'very much part of the intelligence business. It was before 9/11 and it has been since then.'[24]

But whether used to track gangsters or terrorists, the science of surveillance became far more precise: borrowing the classic techniques of spy-catching from counterintelligence, adding the latest gadgetry of geolocation and bugging, and then turning them against the modern fanatic. 'The techniques of identifying suspects, covert surveillance and bugging were developed to counter the Soviet KGB and GRU,' said a former chief of GCHQ, Sir David Omand. These had been adapted, he said, and put to service against modern targets.[25]

Rather like JSOC had done in Iraq and Afghanistan, the civilian secret services began to adopt the technique of the 'fusion cell', where representatives of all the different secret agencies and of human and technical intelligence collection came together. In the US, this happened in the CIA's ever-expanding Counterterrorism Center; in the UK, such teams were put together for different operations, both inside MI5's headquarters on Millbank and over the river at SIS in Vauxhall. Even the listening agency, GCHQ, which traditionally kept aloof in its base in the West Country, sent its people to be fully integrated. Against the Soviets, where the counterintelligence risk was severe, the 'need to know principle' had been pre-eminent, but in this modern counterterror mission the (somewhat crass) slogan became 'Dare to Share!' Old hands at SIS found the change remarkable.

Modern global travel and communications had made the trail international. And that was why the secret services could be most effective. Planet Earth had no police force of its own; national and regional police forces struggled to get permission to operate in other countries, or get help from colleagues in other police forces. Foreign countries were often more willing to help if that assistance was kept secret. And if those countries would not help, then spy services had the option of jumping the fence and helping themselves to information.

As the West made counterterrorism the priority, a seemingly endless manhunt was launched that went far beyond the pursuit of people like Osama bin Laden who had already instigated murderous crimes of violence. Taking a lead from the French in the 1990s, secret services attempted to go after the crime in preparation, the conspiracy – what the 2002 movie *Minority Report* called 'pre-crime'. While network analysis might of itself have been nothing new, it was now to be used for a wider range of targets, and to try to anticipate future behaviour.

So while much modern counterterrorist work was, to my mind, essentially police activity, albeit frequently conducted in secret or across borders, the contribution of the intelligence officer to this increasingly joined-up fight, Omand argued, was his future-oriented mentality. 'Because the whole training of intelligence officers is forward-looking. It is predictive.' The need to look forward was changing both intelligence work and police work, fusing their operations.

The view that intelligence work meant prediction was not shared by all. One former senior SIS officer rejected the whole idea. 'It is a real fallacy, a widespread one, that we do prediction. Secret intelligence comes down to answering the question: "what's really happening?"' An agent or intercept could give an insight into what was happening off stage, what was being debated or planned, for example. But he could not say what would happen next. This distinction was important. In counterterrorism, while all agreed that good intelligence might identify an active terrorist plot-in-progress or specific plan of attack, there was real disagreement over the extent to which technology and more far-reaching surveillance could be used to peer even further into the future.

But whether or not intelligence was predictive, modern counterterrorism, as Omand rightly suggested, was definitely about looking towards the future. It required a logic of pre-emption. The pursuit and prosecution of criminals in the past would normally follow a crime being committed, he said. But in the era of the devastating suicide bomb, criminal punishment after the fact served as no deterrent to the martyr. So the requirement for the intelligence agencies and today's police, working together, he argued, was to identify the potential terrorists before they could organize and commit their criminal acts.

When deployed against Soviet spies or the IRA, surveillance techniques and the technology available were kept completely secret. But – even before the revelations of whistle-blowers like Edward Snowden in 2013 – the deployment of the intelligence services in the 1990s to assist in combating organized crime and then prosecuting terrorist plotters had allowed some of those secrets to slip out.

The techniques on display – as Dearlove had described – involved the broad surveillance of telephones, Internet and travel data, a focus on connections that appeared suspicious, the trawling of foreign communications (which could be conducted by the UK and US agencies without any special warrant) and then, when suspicions narrowed down, the application of more intrusive measures, like bugging cars and homes and listening to domestic phone calls.

What, then, was the role left for the human spy? At all levels, a human source might help focus inquiries or provide the basis for an interception warrant. But it was rare for agents to be central. That was partly because they were usually, for deliberate reasons, kept peripheral to any plot. As Omand said, 'All intelligence work involves managing moral hazard. For example, it will be hard to find informants within a terrorist gang who are not guilty of criminal offences and do not have blood on their hands. Thus there is always a risk of being accused of colluding with wrong-doing. It is hard enough with a narcotics gang, worse with a serious terrorist organization. The chances of infiltrating such networks with undercover officers are slight and recruiting those already inside the network is hard and dangerous for all involved.'[26]

On the other hand, much valuable information had been volunteered to the authorities by the communities in which the terrorists sought to hide or from which they had sprung. Ordinary people often wanted the chance 'to better themselves and not to be lumped in with the extremists in the eyes of the rest of society', according to Omand, who said they got 'much more of that kind of volunteered HUMINT than [information] from deep penetration agents'. Also, with much looser networks of terrorists and the 'increasing risk of lone wolves', there might 'not be a lot to penetrate by traditional HUMINT methods' – in other words, even a very good spy might get nowhere near discovering an active plot. It had, however, sometimes been possible 'to go up the food chain to the organizers and instigators of jihadist terrorism overseas, including by following their communications, contacts and movements'. That was the value of complementing human intelligence operations 'by having bulk access to global communications'.

The use of intensive surveillance techniques was evidenced by the operation that discovered the 2006 plot in London to detonate liquid explosives on transatlantic planes. Those involved – young Britons mostly of Pakistani origin – had already raised suspicions because of their association with Rashid Rauf, a British Pakistani living in Lahore who was identified as a militant leader. (This was where the NSA and Britain's GCHQ became effective, when they had a starting point from which they could plot onward connections. It was rare that they could simply spot some anomaly in the ether, something suspicious in a randomly intercepted email. The main reason they found bulk interception useful was that, with huge storage capacity, they could sift retrospectively through all the harvested information and find past calls and messages once targets were identified.)

The level of surveillance and the mapping of the plotters' links were ramped up to include monitoring of the content of phone calls and emails – under warrants signed by the British Home Secretary. As suspicions grew, MI5 planted bugging devices in the men's homes and cars. The final stage – the physical surveillance of targets and listening to the content of calls – was always the most time-consuming. That explained why the FBI or MI5 would never have the manpower to follow every single lead. Although digital voice processing was improving, recordings of suspects still needed to be listened to by a human being. Following a single person on foot, without attracting notice, could involve twenty or thirty people. That was why, as one director of MI5 would put it, 'Being on our radar does not necessarily mean being under our microscope.'[27]

Surveillance might be resource-intensive, but when directed against a small group – because of how society now embraced technology – a staggering volume of information became available. The fact that so many people carried a mobile camera-phone made everyone a potential spy. But the same camera-phone, and other personal technology, could be turned against a person and used to spy on them. The most valuable evidence-collectors were the suspects themselves.

Even among radical jihadists, who should have thought to be careful, it was surprising how many wanted to digitize their lives, to communicate online and record their innermost thoughts on their computers. Using different technical methods the NSA and GCHQ could frequently hack and copy such data.

Long before Snowden made so many of the tactics public, a member of the British Parliament's Intelligence and Security Committee disclosed: 'It is amazing how much these people are still chatting away to each other constantly, and how much we can pick up.' Such poor operational security reflected how these new recruits had been radicalized in the first place, through Internet propaganda and online forums. This was the dotcom generation of jihadis and they struggled to wean themselves off their digital fix.

For those who knew they were under surveillance, they might feel they were living in the dystopia foretold by George Orwell in his novel *Nineteen Eighty-Four*, where citizens 'live in a constant state of being monitored by the Party, through the use of advanced, invasive technology' and where hidden microphones and TVs with cameras inside could watch everyone ceaselessly. I once met an al-Qaeda suspect, an alleged financier, who felt so harried that he glanced in all directions constantly. As we sat in the café near St Paul's Cathedral, we could even spot an operative raising a camera to snap our little coffee rendezvous. But, unlike Orwell's description or, say, the Stasi in East Germany, where Orwell's vision was most closely realized, this surveillance was highly targeted. Unless a state chose the East German model and employed tens of thousands of operatives to monitor its own people, it was, if nothing else, impractical to watch everyone.

Nor was targeted surveillance as comprehensive and effective as implied, for example, by the 1998 film *Enemy of the State*, starring Will Smith as an embattled lawyer tracked everywhere by the NSA. Both electronic and physical surveillance had practical limits – and produced constant hiccups. In Britain, in July 2004, MI5 were tracking an al-Qaeda suspect, Dhiren Barot, who among other things wanted to blow up a tube train while it was under the Thames. But, though he was a prime target, MI5 embarrassingly lost track of Barot for five days in London. In 2006 he was sentenced to forty years in jail for his schemes.[28] In the US, the FBI trailed Najibullah Zazi all the way from Colorado to New York in 2009, but after he was stopped – on a pretext – by traffic cops on a bridge into the city, Zazi panicked. 'Even though [Zazi] is not the brightest bulb in the terrorist chandelier, the thinly-transparent ruse of a "random" checkpoint stop did not fool him,' his lawyer said later.[29] The result was that Zazi managed to lose his surveillance, and destroy or hide the explosive detonators and other materials he had for a bomb attack. Also in New York, the following year, a Pakistani-born US citizen, Faisal Shahzad, was quickly identified as the man who detonated a car bomb in Times Square, but he could not be located for three days. He was only found when he was sitting on board a Dubai-bound Emirates flight at Kennedy Airport in New York.

The main problem with all this spying by digital surveillance was overload. The secret services were hoovering up digital information about the world's population much faster than their analytic capability could develop. It was like the proverbial needle in a haystack. Intelligence agencies had multiplied the needles they were searching for but multiplied many times more the haystacks in which they were searching.

And counterterrorism was the victim of its own success. The more that agencies arrested, killed or just disrupted members of a terrorist network, the more they split the group into lone operatives. This atomized threat made both human and technical methods harder. Surveillance had no leads to start with and no human insider was present to warn about the operative.

It is frequently argued by the ill-informed that 'if only' a certain piece of data had been collected, then the attacks of 11 September and many others since would have been prevented. But the usual problem is different. Often the key piece of information has been collected but is, metaphorically speaking, shut in a drawer unread. The biggest problem, as ever, is to sift out the relevant from the irrelevant.

Surveillance can give only limited clues about future human behaviour for the same reason that human intelligence is difficult to re-create artificially. The human mind has almost limitless options. It is hard to predict with any confidence, despite past behaviour, what an individual is going to do in the future. This was why many in the secret intelligence world were so scornful of the idea their job was to predict anything. Regardless of the ethics, if security agencies try too hard to investigate 'pre-crime', it is easy to get overwhelmed with either false positives (someone who in fact has never even contemplated doing something bad) or unprovables (someone who might have contemplated doing something bad but would not actually do it). The reason the investigation of the London liquid bomb plot was successful was that Britain was prepared to risk the conspirators continuing their work until they had moved to the stage of very active preparation, signalling and providing proof of a clear intent to actually carry out the crimes they had talked of.

In the US, the bar for action and level of risk tolerance were far too low. The result was the endless trail of false leads, based on huge technical trawls, that made FBI work so tedious and boring after 9/11. 'We were always on the trail of ghosts,' as one former officer put it.

While many leads were false, the system got so overwhelmed that positive leads were being missed. On Christmas Day 2009, a 23-year-old Nigerian, Umar Farouk Abdulmutallab, tried to detonate explosives hidden in his underwear on a flight from Amsterdam to Detroit. It was later discovered that a month before the attack Abdulmutallab's father had gone to the US Embassy in Abuja to report that his son was mixing with extremists. A report had been filed by both consular officials and the CIA. It entered the American terrorism watch list (known as 'Tide'), but not with any kind of flag that would have required a special search of Abdulmutallab when he attempted to board the plane. (There were also eavesdropped emails or calls that were missed. By one account, intercepts in Yemen had mentioned 'an unnamed Nigerian was being groomed for an al-Qaeda mission, and other communications spoke of plans for a terrorist attack during Christmas'.)[30]

The knee-jerk response to cases like that of the 'underpants bomber', as he was called, was to collect and analyse yet more information. But that only guaranteed more information overload. As one technical expert warned, 'The more data you collect, the more you struggle to process, interpret, and move it. The bad news is that an avalanche can bury you alive.'[31] Intelligence collection was being overwhelmed by its own capabilities, but the same high-speed digitization capabilities that the NSA could so readily exploit were also the source of added real-world complexity, to some extent neutralizing the advantage gained. Digital financial transactions, for instance, meant money movements were easier to trace, but also that they were faster. The world itself was getting harder to read. As the director of NSA's signals intelligence, Maureen Baginski, had explained in 2001, 'You could literally stare for 25 years at the Soviet land mass and never have this kind of volume problem. They were slow, so it was okay if we were slow. Today, it's volume, it's velocity and it's variety.'[32]

One of the biggest weaknesses of the digital manhunt was that those most susceptible to being tracked digitally were the innocent. They had no special reason to encrypt their emails or adopt false identities or anonymize their use of the Internet. As the CIA discovered, when they worked through papers and files seized at his compound, Osama bin Laden had stayed completely off the telephone and Internet grid. He had sent couriers dozens of miles away to transmit his emails from random public computers. My research into the CIA's rendition programme showed that, at least in the early days after 2001, too often people had been wrongly labelled terrorist suspects because some overly simple link analysis had classed an innocent connection with a suspected militant as proof that that person was a militant too. An analysis of a terrorist's phone calls might show many calls to another number; he might have been calling his girlfriend, who had no knowledge of his crime. But the key call to a terrorist associate might actually be made via another phone – a payphone, for instance. This was the 'law of weak connection': the weakest link might actually be the most important.

When I asked veteran intelligence officers about the quality of technical intelligence – particularly intercepts – over the years since the Second World War, most suggested that it went in waves. Over several decades, the CIA were sent a copy of every telegram in and out of the United States. All overseas phone lines were at one point tapped. There were years when interception had huge coverage. Then people found other ways to communicate, different codes and encryption, and legal restrictions were enacted by Congress. Some even argue that the expansion of the digital world has left the ultimate customer, the political leader and the security agency, with broadly the same level of secret intelligence, only collected now at vastly greater expense. 'It's just impossible to keep up,' said one former CIA chief of clandestine operations, although he did not suggest not trying. But while that pessimism is justified when dealing with hard secret intelligence targets – those who try to conceal their secrets – the truth is that the modern citizen is easier to find and put under surveillance than ever before. What has also certainly changed, with advances in technology, is the ability of technical intelligence to work really well in hindsight – in reconstructing events and tracing known enemies. It remains, as always, much less good at looking forward and predicting new targets, new threats.

With all this tracking and technology, how have real spies fitted in?

In Britain, the intense study of travel plans and networks of suspected militants helped pinpoint targets for recruitment of agents. Of particular interest was anyone who had attended places where militants ran training camps (such as the Pakistani tribal areas or Somalia) or where there were active conflicts, such as in Syria. As Mike Sheehan, former counterterrorism coordinator at the NYPD, put it, 'Connectivity back to the camps is the key to being operationally effective.'[33]

According to some youngsters who were approached, and their lawyers, one method used by MI5 to recruit was to discover some violation of immigration laws in a suspect's family and then put pressure on the target to cooperate. MI5 has made use of new powers under the Terrorism Act 2000 to detain, question and search young British Muslims when they arrive back in the UK after a trip abroad. Although these individuals were not suspects, they said they were pressured to work as informants for MI5. Mohamed Nur, a 25-year-old community worker in Camden, north London, said he was visited by an MI5 officer and a policeman disguised as a postman. He told a newspaper, 'The MI5 agent said, "Mohamed, if you do not work for us we will tell any foreign country you try to travel to that you are a suspected terrorist." '[34] His claim could not be verified, but within certain Muslim communities many youngsters certainly felt harassed. It was also arguable that, if useful intelligence could be garnered by such methods, then some ill-feeling was a price worth paying.

Security officials in Western agencies typically denied using blackmail, claiming it would backfire, would produce unreliable information and would be unethical. But as one veteran CIA case officer put it, 'That's all bullshit. We do what we have to do.' He pointed out there was a distinction between a straight and unsubtle blackmail threat and a more nuanced exploitation of a weakness. A recruiter might, say, let the target realize he was aware of that target's weakness (for example, that he had entered the country illegally), without uttering any explicit threat to expose him. Or, even better, once such weakness had been identified, the recruiter could try to offer himself as a solution to that problem (for example, offer to legalize his status). But, while less brutal, this was still a form of blackmail, he argued.

One former British intelligence officer assessed the pressure like this: 'Faced with a huge indigestible mass of potential leads, coming mainly from technical sources, there is no time for the long-term patient cultivations of former times. So, yes, threats may be employed, and some of those doing the threatening will be incompetent, and, naturally, you will read of the approaches that failed and not of the ones that succeeded and, so far, keep us safe.' One recruitment attempt by MI5 deserved particular scrutiny. In May 2013, after the brutal daylight murder of a British soldier, Lee Rigby, outside the Royal Artillery Barracks in Woolwich, south London, it emerged that at least one of the two men involved, Michael Adebolajo, was well known to British intelligence. A friend of his told the BBC that when Adebolajo returned from a trip to Kenya, he was 'being harassed by MI5'. The friend, who was himself arrested after the interview, said, 'His wording was, "They are bugging me; they won't leave me alone" . . . He mentioned initially they wanted to ask him whether he knew certain individuals . . . But after him saying that he didn't know these individuals and so forth, what he said is they asked him whether he would be interested in working for them.'[35] Others confirmed he had complained previously about harassment.

Had pressure from British authorities contributed to Adebolajo's murderous nature? There was insufficient information made public to allow anyone to judge. But Adebolajo was a committed jihadist and mentally unstable long before any MI5 recruitment attempt. Both attackers were found guilty of Rigby's murder at trial in December 2013 and were later sentenced to life imprisonment.[36]

By getting agents in and among low-level operatives who came and went to training camps, there were some real successes in preventing attacks. With his operation in both Britain and Denmark, Morten Storm, the Danish ex-biker, showed the value of having agents in militant circles who could act as spotters, keeping an eye on those who either disappeared off for training or seemed to have a genuine desire to 'turn operational' and carry out an attack. Storm's own intuition in spotting such would-be terrorists demonstrated the value of the human touch.

Now also working for the CIA, Storm was sent back to Yemen, where he had studied Islam, and he befriended the now-notorious Yemeni-American preacher Anwar Awlaki, who had become both an influential online preacher of al-Qaeda propaganda and a leader within the movement's Yemen branch, al-Qaeda in the Arabian Peninsula (AQAP).

While running spies inside al-Qaeda is fraught with problems, Storm's case showed how lateral thinking could overcome some of the issues, with a modern blend of the human touch and technical wizardry. One weakness the CIA exploited was that, away from his life as a militant, Awlaki was a normal man with physical and emotional needs. Storm was able to establish contact with Awlaki, but avoid getting so close that he (or the agencies running him) was compromised, by acting as a trustworthy but not entirely convinced supporter who was willing to send him or bring him out supplies. As recorded in videos and emails, Storm (and indirectly the CIA) served as a matchmaker, finding Awlaki a new wife who arrived bearing a suitcase that was – very helpfully – fitted out with a tracking device.

When that bag went astray, the CIA sent Storm back again, passing on more tracking devices in various disguises. None of those appear to have worked, but Storm believes Awlaki was finally killed by a drone strike after he led the CIA to a courier used by the cleric, handing the courier a USB stick with an inbuilt tracking device.

Storm finally went public with the story of his spy operations after a disagreement with the CIA about whether he should receive the financial reward offered for Awlaki's death. He taped his final meeting with the agency with his iPhone. The CIA officer, 'Michael', explained that Storm's mission had been one among many attempts to get Awlaki, and it was another that succeeded. According to Storm, 'It's like being on the field at the World Cup, you're moving down the field and you're in the position to score, the other guy could have passed it to you but he didn't, he took the shot, he scores. And that's that. That's what happened.'[37]

But Storm also said that he came to understand why the CIA refused to acknowledge that he had led them to Awlaki: as he was a Danish asset, it would have meant that Danish intelligence had assisted with an assassination, something prohibited under Danish law. And this was a major problem with collaborations with the United States. Although Western spy agencies did have a common enemy, at the sharp end they took different approaches. SIS had previously made great efforts to persuade Storm to work for them while also trying to avoid any connection to targeted killings, which were prohibited under British law. But the CIA had offered Storm more money.

The other known successful recruitment of a spy inside AQAP was a British operation, run with the help of Saudi intelligence, that was able to thwart yet another attempt to blow up a passenger aircraft. According to intelligence officials, the plot was discovered by an agent run by Britain's MI5. Recruited in the UK, the agent, who was of Saudi origin, had been given a UK passport and sent to language school in Yemen to follow in the footprints of Umar Farouk Abdulmutallab, the Nigerian 'underpants bomber'. This new operative, a double agent, made it to the mountains of Shabwa, southern Yemen, where he penetrated the cell. He was finally sent on a mission with another underpants bomb, which he duly handed over to his handlers. The US then followed up with a series of drone strikes. This, for the agencies concerned, was nothing but good news. However, the British were furious when the existence of the agent emerged in a typical Washington farce. The Associated Press agency had learned of the agent from a source, later discovered to be an FBI contractor.[38] They were prevailed upon to delay publication. But when, on 7 May 2012, they disclosed that a bomb plot had been disrupted John Brennan, Obama's counterterrorism chief and a future CIA director, briefed several television pundits in advance that the plot had never really been a major threat because of 'inside control'. This was correctly interpreted to refer to an agent. Richard Clarke, a former White House official, then told ABC *Nightline*, 'The US government is saying it never came close because they had insider information, insider control, which implies that they had somebody on the inside who wasn't going to let it happen.'[39] All this led to an agent's existence becoming public. Presumably, the agent was quickly retired and is living under protection.

In contrast to operations in Yemen and Somalia, the protection given by the ISI in Pakistan to militants and tighter security in frontier regions near the country's border with Afghanistan meant there was less success in developing agent networks or running agents in the camps. The CIA tried to send as many operatives as possible into the country, and they also attached officers to the ISI base in Miranshah, North Waziristan, although they never left the base. This was not to say, however, that secret services got no agents into the camps. From time to time, they did, including some agents sent by the British through Peshawar.

Although US intelligence did get better at finding and striking in the tribal regions against senior leaders among the foreign militants – usually still labelled as al-Qaeda – they proved less successful at finding members of the Afghan Taliban who were hiding out. Nor could they find a US soldier, Private First Class Bowe Bergdahl, who was kidnapped in 2009 after wandering off his base and was held by the Haqqani faction of the Taliban, based in North Waziristan, Pakistan. (He was eventually released in a swap for Guantanamo Bay prisoners.)

According to one senior US intelligence official, the success of drone strikes had little to do with spies on the ground and much more to do with a combination of technical methods – mostly overhead surveillance and tracking phones – as well as secret operations led by JSOC to enlist the help of Taliban prisoners: 'The intelligence is almost entirely coming from us; we get almost nothing from the Pakistanis. Yes, some direct HUMINT, but really it's because we've been watching these places for years. When I say staring for years, I really mean *staring* for *years* now. We really know these places' (his emphasis).

He said that interrogation techniques had been refined since the days of crude and harsh interrogations after 9/11: 'We sit them down; it's all completely different than it used to be.' Apparently, 99 per cent of them would talk: 'It's like a survival experience. They're so happy they've emerged from this whole experience alive and now they're safe.'

Taliban who cooperated were given training and could be used to pinpoint precise compounds in Pakistan that militants used: 'They can describe who is in every room in that Haqqani madrasa or whatever.' Some even received training in surveillance technologies: 'We teach them. They get lessons in how to understand overhead imagery. They start with stuff that's irrelevant, just get taught the techniques. Then we show them things they should know about and they start saying, oh yeah, that's the place we used. They talk us through it all. It works.'

This rather amazing operation to recruit members of the Taliban to help target drone strikes, which to my knowledge has not been disclosed before, was part of an increasingly sophisticated machinery of war that was becoming intoxicating in its efficiency.[40]

Because Pakistan and Yemen were sovereign nations not at war with the United States, under American law it was the CIA that was officially in charge of the drone programme. But in practice the selection of targets and the operation of drones were a joint operation with the US Air Force and JSOC. Targets were typically approved by a joint committee of different intelligence agencies, both military and civilian. One JSOC officer who witnessed these decisions said, 'It was a joint thing and there was always a mixture of intelligence. I cannot recall any strike based on human intelligence alone; there was always a great deal of technical intelligence so you could know who it was in the compound.' He did add, however, that there was some leeway for striking based on thinner intelligence if it was a higher-value target.

The collaboration on drone assassinations – and the central role these began to take in counterterrorism policy – convinced many CIA veterans that they were witnessing an unhealthy militarization of the agency. 'This isn't espionage. You know, sitting there and looking through film, picking targets for Predators is something the military used to do,' said Robert Baer, a former senior CIA operative. 'The CIA runs human sources, National Security Agency do intercepts, the people who do overhead [photographic images] do that and the military run lethal weapons. This is something the CIA was dragged into after 9/11.' The work with Predators and killing people with them had come to completely absorb the agency, both its talent and resources.

Not only was the CIA becoming more militarized – diverted by drones as it had been by harsh interrogations – it was also getting tied up in dealing with the immediate, tactical threat: the latest al-Qaeda operational commander or group of militants who might form the next active cell in the West.

What was missing, some argued, was 'over-the-hill' strategic intelligence: that is, a glimpse at more than was immediately visible, that would allow decision-makers to better understand the causes of the continuing support for militant Islam and to identify other threats. These were what MI5 used to call its 'horizon watchers'.

A decade on from the attacks of 11 September, while bin Laden was dead and al-Qaeda, as a movement, weakened, it was hard to argue that the jihadist cause and the threat it posed to the West were diminished. Little had been done to address the causes of terrorism and anti-Western feeling generally. Extreme Islamists had established safe havens along the Afghan–Pakistan border, in Yemen, Somalia and parts of West Africa. Meanwhile, there had been no progress in ameliorating the enduring Arab–Israeli conflict, which inspired such anger across the Middle East. By the end of 2011, US troops withdrew from Iraq but without defeating the Sunni radicals they had fought for over eight years. Across the border in Syria, an uprising was under way against the regime of President Bashar al-Assad; Sunni radicals played a significant part in that revolution from the beginning.

In essence, the terrorism movement that bin Laden came to embody was a global insurgency, fuelled by a brushfire of rage against hated regimes and the Western foreign policies which kept them in power. The latest recruits could be tracked, prosecuted and locked up – or assassinated in a far-off country by a drone. But others would find a way to carry out their plot undetected, even if the risks of this were being reduced. Most counterterrorism work was essentially defensive. It did not take the fight to the cause of the problem. As Stanley Baldwin, the British prime minister, had said in 1932 regarding the emerging threat of air raids, however good the air defences, 'the bomber will always get through'.

To change analogy, terrorism was like a bacterial infection. It could certainly be tackled with strong drugs, like antibiotics. But the use of such drugs encouraged a resistance to develop, allowing the infection to mutate and take on a new form. Perhaps only a vaccination – the creation of effective antibodies – in the form of opposing home-grown movements within the communities from which terrorism had sprung, had a hope of permanently ending the menace.

As they flew home from their raid with bin Laden on board their helicopter in a body bag, the Navy Seals and the CIA left behind not only his wives but also their own agent, Dr Afridi. He was soon arrested by the Pakistani authorities and sentenced to a long prison term. Despite a campaign in the US Congress, at the time of writing he remains in prison and has repeatedly gone on hunger strike. Although he was accused of being a traitor, his prison sentence for treason related to alleged membership of a militant group, Lashkar-e-Islam. In August 2013 a retrial was ordered, but that November he was also charged with the murder of a patient eight years earlier. His lawyer fled the country soon after, citing threats to his life.

There was a wider and more devastating consequence to his recruitment, particularly as the CIA operation had wrongly been reported to be offering a polio vaccination (it was in fact hepatitis B). In 2012, tens of thousands of children along the north-west frontier of Pakistan were due to be vaccinated against polio (Pakistan was one of only three countries in the world where the disease was still endemic[41]), but the Taliban banned the campaign and families refused to let their children take part. The governor of Khyber Province blamed the CIA's 'fake vaccine' programme. In February 2012, a group of 200 American non-governmental organizations wrote to the CIA, accusing the agency of 'undermining the international humanitarian community's efforts to eradicate polio' and saying reports of the CIA's actions might have contributed 'to an uptick in targeted violence against humanitarian workers'.[42]

On 16 October 2012, a volunteer in the vaccination programme was shot dead in Quetta – one among dozens of polio workers who were to be killed or injured in the following two years. In unconnected incidents on 13 December 2013, two policemen responsible for guarding polio workers were murdered, together with a polio vaccinator, in north-west Pakistan.[43]

Spying is never costless or risk-free.

PART FOUR

Where Next?

Chapter 12
The Good Spy

'If you know the enemy and know yourself, you need not
fear the results of a hundred battles'

– Sun Tzu, *The Art of War*[1]

On 13 May 2013, a glum-looking American diplomat was sitting on a wooden chair in the carpeted office of a Russian ministry in Moscow. Behind him was a desk on which an array of objects was laid out. All of them had been found in his rucksack and were, it was claimed, the tools of a modern spy.

Ryan Christopher Fogle had been wearing a blond wig at the time of his arrest and he carried a spare black one. Among other items were three pairs of sunglasses, a Moscow atlas, a compass, a knife and a Bic lighter, envelopes with €500 notes amounting to $100,000, as well as what the Russians described as 'special technical equipment'. This included a metal shield for credit cards which prevented their data being read automatically.[2]

He also carried a letter that he wanted to deliver to a Russian FSB officer:

Dear friend,

This is a down-payment from someone who is very impressed with your professionalism and who would greatly appreciate your cooperation in the future. Your security means a lot to us. This is why we chose this way of contacting you. We will make sure our correspondence remains safe and secret.

We are ready to offer you $100,000 to discuss your experience, expertise and cooperation. The reward may be much greater if you are willing to answer specific questions. In addition to that, we can offer up to $1million a year for long-term cooperation, with extra bonuses if we receive some helpful information.

To get back to us, please go to an internet cafe, or a coffee shop that has Wi-Fi, and open a new Gmail account which you will use exclusively to contact us. As you register, do not provide any personal info that can help identify you or your new account. Don't provide any real contacts, e.g. your phone number or other email addresses.

If Gmail ask you for personal info, start the registration process again and avoid providing such data. Once you register this new account, use it to send a message to unbacggdA@gmail.com. In exactly one week, check this mailbox for a response from us.

(If you use a network or any other device (e.g. a tablet) to open the account at a coffee shop, please don't use a personal device with personal data on it. If possible, buy a new device (paying in cash) which you will use to contact us. We will reimburse you for this purchase.)

Thank you for reading this letter. We look forward to working with you in the nearest future.[3]

Accounts on Google's Gmail? Was this the new face of spying? Fogle, who was accredited as a third secretary at the US Embassy, was branded persona non grata and ejected from Russia.

The country's foreign ministry made a statement: 'At a time when the presidents of our countries have reaffirmed their readiness to broaden our bilateral relations, including special service [cooperation] in the battle with international terrorism, such provocative actions in the spirit of the "Cold War" do not facilitate a strengthening of mutual trust.'[4]

Of course those words were tongue-in-cheek. Russia was just as busy trying to spy on its rivals.

In this account of modern spying, I have tried to detail useful examples that provide raw material to help answer three particular questions. How has spying changed? When is it valuable? Who are the spies we need? As evidenced throughout, within spying there is much that remains constant – such as spying in Russia – and much that has evolved, often in quite subtle ways. In the light of these experiences, then, how should we answer these questions?

How Spying Has Changed

The Fogle case emphasized once more that the old games were still being played, albeit with less vigour. While we have focused on what is different about modern espionage, some themes endured. Foremost among them were the basics of human psychology and the efforts of major states to spy on each other. As Milton Bearden said, 'About the only difference in the handling of the ambush of Fogle by the Russian security service was that the photographic record of his arrest was in sharp, digital colour, rather than grainy black and white. It was a textbook takedown.'[5]

The motive to spy on another state comes from concern about that state's intentions. However much relations between the US and Russia relaxed following the Cold War, neither side's guard was entirely lowered. The same was true of relations between Russia and Great Britain, particularly after Vladimir Putin, himself a former KGB officer, became Russian president in 2000. Things were not helped by the poisoning in London in 2006 of Alexander Litvinenko, an ex-KGB officer who, according to family and friends, was an agent for Britain's SIS. The British blamed Russian operatives for killing him with a cup of tea laced with radioactive polonium.

Yet, despite the accusations, neither Great Britain and the US nor Russia wanted the confrontation to intensify beyond control. When an inquest was opened into Litvinenko's killing, the British government won a court order to keep evidence of Russia's involvement in the crime, as well as of Britain's relationship with Litvinenko, secret. Only when Russia invaded and seized the Crimean region of Ukraine in 2014 did Britain announce an official inquiry into Litvinenko's death, to examine in particular if Russia was responsible. But crucial parts of the evidence were likely to be heard behind closed doors.[6]

Russia, then, remained a threat, capable and prepared to challenge US global power. It still tried to run secret agents in the West and the West still tried to run secret agents in Russia. But neither the clash of interests nor the threat reached anything like Cold War proportions, so the effort expended to spy on each other never came close to what it had been. Wild as it was, Russia was now mixed up, in its own quixotic way, with the global capitalist economy. The wealth of the elite was tied up in bank accounts across the world. It had no interest in outright confrontation. On the flipside, the West wanted Russia's support to confront non-state issues like terrorism and organized crime. When the Boston Marathon was attacked by two immigrants from the Russian north Caucasus, killing three and injuring 170, the US needed Russia's help to learn about the men's background.[7] This was just a month before Fogle's arrest. So while

Russia remained an expansionary and corrupt power, pragmatic politics put a limit on hostilities. Cooperation was more important. The same was true of policy towards communist-ruled China, where despite aggressive Chinese espionage, particularly in cyberspace, and growing domestic repression, the West chose to avoid confrontation.

Beyond the continuation of state-on-state spying, another immutable was the steady expansion of the spy bureaucracy, as a chart of MI5's staffing levels illustrates. The total numbers may strike some as surprisingly small, revealing the relative modesty of Britain's secret establishment. But apart from a blip in the early 1990s, when staff numbers fell, they also show the agency's inexorable rise.

In the US, the intelligence bureaucracy had become a monster. By 2013, as a leak of the 'black budget' revealed, the CIA had a total annual budget to spend of $14.7 billion – more than the GDP of Iceland or seventy smaller countries. It employed 21,459 out of 83,500 civilians in the US intelligence community. Of its budget, $6.28 billion was allocated to three human intelligence categories: human intelligence enabling ($2.53 billion), human intelligence operations ($2.34 billion) and human intelligence technical tools ($1.41 billion). More broadly, technical intelligence still clearly absorbed the lion's share of intelligence spending, with the three main technical collection agencies taking up half of the whole intelligence budget between them.[8] The total 'black budget' was $52.6 billion, about the equivalent of the GDP of a small country such as Bulgaria.[9]

As their budgets indicate, the modern intelligence agencies are firmly entrenched. But though they have made their case for a permanent role, this is not to say that they remain as they once were. So, for example, recruitment has changed: their staff are no longer the exclusive preserve of the privileged white male. And attitudes and policies have altered. Whether in the CIA, the SVR (the former KGB) or SIS, the former high priests of the Cold War have had to adapt.

In Britain, an Establishment elite had always run the intelligence services, said former SIS officer Alastair Crooke, but that elite had changed: 'The "one of us" is not what it used to be. It's a different group who have come up through Oxford and Cambridge that are now the sort of Cabinet members and the political elite . . . But the entry price is [as before] that you don't criticize certain things.'

In the US, too, the agencies employed new types of people, but they clung to their influence. 'They became like any other middle-aged

Security Service (MI5) strength, 1909–2009

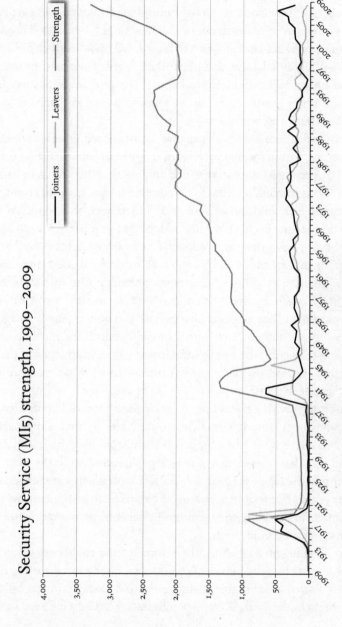

Source: Christopher Andrews, *The Defence of the Realm: The Authorized History of MI5*, updated edition (London, Penguin, 2010), Appendix 2

bureaucracy, they defend themselves ferociously,' said one former senior CIA executive.

Spies and spymasters had to become a different breed because the world was changing. The biggest change in espionage since 1989 was the refocusing of efforts in order to target non-state groups and, in particular, terrorist gangs. In my assessment of this new target, I described the view that human intelligence might be a dying art and that the 'flock of birds' – the diffuse, highly adaptive and networked form of terrorist group that al-Qaeda and its offshoots became after 9/11 – would not be as susceptible to penetration by human agents as the monolithic and hierarchical targets of old, like the Soviet secret service.

In fact, while there is no evidence that any major secret service has been able to recruit within the highest level of terrorist groups such as al-Qaeda, the goal of getting a 'man on the rock' was partly achieved: many agents have been run inside al-Qaeda, for example, sent for training among the militant groups in Pakistan or Yemen, and then been able to return with information about specific plots in development or leaders' location.

Recruiting spies in terror groups did not turn out to be the hardest problem. As in the Cold War, volunteers came forward and many deliberate recruitment operations, often exploiting the opportunities afforded by the arrest of a terror suspect or an interrogation at border control, have proved successful. The bigger challenge has been how to run these agents: not only how to stay in touch with them and control their activities, but also having to decide whether to shut down an operation to avoid the risk of a terrorist attack succeeding or to continue to allow an agent to function and get deeper inside.

As interviews with intelligence officers actively involved in such recruitments indicate, the solution has been to take a precautionary approach: to close down terror plots when there was any danger they might otherwise go ahead. This has altered the typical lifespan of an agent: rather than, say, a mole inside the Chinese Communist Party who might have remained in place for years, the modern agent might complete an assignment within a few months, but in doing so find himself unable to get alongside the very senior level of an organization.

Through concentrated effort, then, some of the challenges of recruiting such agents have been met. When the hierarchy of terrorist groups began to flatten and fragment, using the old, long-term, painstaking approaches against them became pointless. Instead, intelligence services began to mirror the terrorist groups by becoming faster, nimbler in their attitude to recruitment.

One former senior SIS officer recalled how, in contrast to the huge efforts and great time once expended to try to find a single Soviet recruit, the key quality of modern espionage was its remarkable speed and efficiency.

As we have just described, the recruitment process has been aided by a fusion of technical and human methods, as well as enhanced cooperation between agencies. With the use of intrusive digital surveillance and interception, for example, an intelligence officer can rapidly access an unparalleled amount of information about a recruitment target before approaching them. Preparation for a 'pitch' can be accelerated and there is a better chance of success.

While the debate over technical versus human methods of intelligence is not finished, it is impossible to regard, say, signals and human intelligence as either/or options. Consumers of intelligence – the military, for example – will insist that one form be corroborated by another. If a highly important agent is travelling to a dangerous place it is almost inconceivable that a major secret service would not use technical methods to track his progress and ensure that he has not been compromised, whether by bugging and tracking his mobile phone or by watching his movements from a spy satellite or drone. Conversely, when signals intelligence is relied upon without good backup from human sources – as witnessed with the assassination of Zabet Amanullah in Afghanistan – great errors can result.

Another blurring among the New Spies is the boundary between espionage and covert action. When an agent works inside a group plotting murder, the focus of effort by intelligence services has to be to defeat or disrupt those plots. There are great incentives to intervene, whether because an agency may be legally bound to prevent a known terrorist attack or because of political pressure to avoid the slightest risk of an attack succeeding. Ideally, an agent can pass information to a secret service, which can then use other means (for example, an arrest operation) to foil a plot. But it may not be so simple. An agent may be the only person able to intervene (for example, by planting a tracking device) to stop the attack.

The drawback of these successful counterterrorist operations is that so many are short-term in objective, tactical in scope and always designed to minimize risk. Secret services can intervene to disrupt a plot or scheme, but they rarely have the time or agent in place long enough to develop a broader understanding of the target. In fighting the terrorist, they have become one component in a global action-orientated secret police dedicated to catching or eliminating the 'bad guy'. The risk is that, while successfully stopping one potential attack after another, they do little to prevent these attacks from recurring.

The Value of Spying

One official at the top of government, formerly responsible for liaison with secret agencies, put it like this: 'If only people could know what plots have been aborted, what spying has achieved.' It was a fairly typical, and sincere, point of view espoused by insiders in the intelligence world. Given the inherent secrecy involved in good human intelligence, estimating the true value of modern spying is difficult. Because the activities of agents remain cloaked in secrecy in order to protect the identity and safety of the individuals involved, only much later will the true impact of their work be calculable. Indeed, it could be argued that if you know what really happened you cannot report it, and if you do not know you are in no position to judge.

This, however, is defeatist thinking, particularly given the great many examples of operations that have been exposed, as well as the great many insiders from the secret world able to give insight into where spying has been valuable or counterproductive. Although it has usually been impossible to name sources in this account, I can safely say that, adding their years of service together, the sources interviewed have collectively had more than a thousand years' experience of human intelligence. Let me try to sum up, then, what has emerged from interviews with them and from publicly available material, and discuss where this might lead us.

Spying's Limitations

No estimation of the value of spying makes sense without first considering its limitations. Modern spying, just like ancient spying, never offers unqualified benefits. It can easily go wrong and is not without distinct and costly trade-offs. These trade-offs are important, because without knowing in advance what will succeed or fail, the decision to use a spy must always be a risk calculation, weighing up the potential benefit of success with the potential fallout from failure. It is not enough to point to one great success and imagine this justifies everything that follows.

The first trade-off, to borrow from science, may be called the 'observer effect', which is the term used to explain that the act of observation alters the object under observation. Roughly applied to human espionage, it means that the act of spying cannot be neutral. At some point it involves taking actions, any one of which carries the risk of discovery that may induce a hostile and counterproductive reaction. For instance, the inducements offered in spying – such as paying agents large amounts of money – may not only be seen as evidence of hostile intent if discovered, but also incentivize agents to cause events that would never otherwise have happened, in other words to act as provocateurs.

One major advantage of signals intelligence over human intelligence is that the observer effect has tended to be much weaker. A signals intelligence satellite in orbit 22,000 miles into space could hoover up signals even from friendly states with almost zero chance of anyone working out who is being listened to. This calculation is altering, however. The diplomatic fallout from Edward Snowden's revelations about whose phone calls the US was listening to, including the German chancellor's and the UN secretary general's, showed that signals intelligence is not without risk of blowback. The widespread use of strong encryption also alters the calculation, since formerly passive signals intelligence agencies may need to take active measures, such as burglary, to steal the passwords used by their targets.

Another trade-off is the 'action effect', by which I mean that the use of intelligence tends to undermine its collection. This is because, consciously or unconsciously, an enemy will begin to notice when his secrets are turned against him. To take an extreme example, if an agent passes on details of a terrorist's murderous plot and that plot is defeated, the terrorist may then suspect the agent of betrayal, tell him no more secrets or even kill him. As the British Army demonstrated in its handling of the agent Steak Knife in the IRA, there are many clever ways to muddy the waters and misdirect suspicions about who leaked information. But it cannot always be done. And even when no one knows who the traitor is, over the long term, by an evolutionary process, those who are more security-conscious and do not leak secrets to the agent are likely to rise in importance. The result of all this is that secret services, even when they have very good agents and good information, tend to be very cautious about encouraging anyone to make use of that information.

The third major trade-off could be called the 'rogue effect', which is the tendency of secret operators to go off the rails, the risk being that spying's intrinsic secrecy divorces those involved from the norms of society. They lack the usual means of self-regulation in public life, notably judgement and scrutiny by the public.

In order to protect their tactics and the identity of their sources, spymasters remain cloistered in a kind of private club, in an isolated environment that can, without care, lead to rogue behaviour. Basic assumptions within this club can lie unchallenged, as can the veracity of their agents' reports. Apparently, if their activities are kept secret, usually ordinary and decent people will do irrational and indecent things. Or as one British intelligence officer put it crudely, 'Intelligence agencies whose operations are pursued without strict outside scrutiny invariably f*** up in the end.'

An example of this rogue behaviour was exhibited by the leadership of the CIA after the 9/11 attacks. They might have had their sign-off from the president and indeed reflected the vindictive public mood, but in countenancing systematic torture and a chain of secret detention places, they strayed far from the broader values of their society, or even the law. They had failed what should be called the 'flap test': that is, would a secret action be judged publicly acceptable if it were no longer secret? A less dramatic, but equally clear, example of aberrant behaviour was the Special Demonstration Squad (SDS) in London's Metropolitan Police, which, over the course of four decades, believed it acceptable – in the name of quelling protests by environmental activists, for example – for their agents to sleep with their surveillance targets and even father children (some of whom, it is alleged, they abandoned).

This was a genuine rogue unit. An investigation by the *Guardian* found that of nine undercover policemen identified, 'eight are believed to have slept with the people they were spying on'.[10] But, when ten women sued the Metropolitan Police, claiming they had been deceived, a judge came to the conclusion that so-called sexspionage was not unusual. Mr Justice Tugendhat, a High Court judge, said examples came to mind from the realms of fiction.

James Bond is the most famous fictional example of a member of the intelligence services who used relationships with women to obtain information, or access to persons or property. Since he was writing a light entertainment, Ian Fleming did not dwell on the extent to which his hero used deception, still less upon the psychological harm he might have done to the women concerned. But fictional accounts (and there are others) lend credence to the view that the intelligence and police services have for many years deployed both men and women officers to form personal relationships of an intimate sexual nature (whether or not they were physical relationships) in order to obtain information or access.[11]

How far should a spy go? It was an open question. But certainly not that far to deal with such a small threat. The SDS had been formed largely of uniformed policemen with training as neither detectives nor undercover agents, in stark contrast to Scotland Yard's professional undercover unit, for a long time designated SO10. 'It isn't normal to sleep with a target. If you have to, it means you are not in control,' said one former operative.

The Misuse of Spies

Pure spying, then, has many weaknesses, tending to undermine its value. But the biggest drawback of all comes not from intelligence collection itself but rather from the temptation to intervene and misuse that intelligence too readily. Modern society has developed great techniques to pry into the lives of others – the challenge is how we make use of these.

Society has faced these dilemmas before, but they were of a different character. In the Cold War, the issue was civil liberties. A substantial amount of spying was done by East and West against their own citizens, with the object of preventing subversion. But this information collected secretly was also used by the state to take pre-emptive action. So, for example, the careers of East Germans discovered to have contacts with the West were secretly hindered. And in the West, those with suspected communist sympathies were secretly blacklisted from taking up certain jobs and radical organizations were secretly subverted if they were seen as communist fronts. In essence, this spying was objectionable because it was an affront to natural justice and an open society in which someone's faults or blessings could be debated openly and fairly.

In the twenty-first century, the threat to civil liberties continues, even if it has altered. Intelligence collection is – contrary to some reports – far more tightly focused on those who are suspected of posing a violent threat to society and rarely directed against domestic 'subversives'. But when violent threats are identified, political leaders continue to look for a convenient and secret response. If a group of Britons in Pakistan are heard discussing bombing a shopping mall in New York, it might be tempting to think a convenient explosive dropped from a drone would deal with the problem. Or if, as in Britain, assassination is ruled out but the only evidence of the plot is secret intelligence, then it might be tempting to lock the plotters in jail using secret court procedures. As before, this poses a threat to natural justice. Supposing the intelligence is wrong? Is this action fair and proportionate?

But taking preventive action in this way also enlarges the role of secret services, moving intelligence into the uncomfortable and rarely accurate world of prediction. How often do people plan to commit a crime that may never come off or that they may, in the end, decide not to commit? We have found very powerful ways to reach into people's thoughts. The dilemma for society is when it is right to intervene and punish those intentions.

Judging When Spies Are Effective

While, as we have discussed, spying today has its limits and can be abused, one reason it persists is that mechanisms have been put in place to compensate for those weaknesses. A tendency to go rogue, for example, is prevented by strict political accountability.

Four observations on the effectiveness of spying were outlined earlier, drawn from experience in the Cold War: that activity is not the same as achievement; that human intelligence offers the most when it is corroborated or, better still, verified; that spying proves itself valuable when it is highly focused and politically directed; and that spying has to be a weapon of last resort. These principles apply equally to modern spying.

First, as before, the mere existence of a spy in the enemy camp is not sufficient to be of value. Modern technology and techniques can make spying more efficient than it has been before. Some spy missions are really successful and make a genuine difference in changing government policy or averting some crisis or crime, as, say, when the UK's agent in Yemen prevented an attack on an airline in 2012. But these successes are rare, even if, given the scale of potential security threats, it seems worthwhile to persist.

Second, it also remains true that many of spying's limitations – the potential weakness of information provided by a serial betrayer, the risk of a source being exposed and the effects of acting on intelligence – are all less worrisome when that intelligence can be corroborated. One former intelligence officer described how in Afghanistan, for instance, the military wisely ignored reports from secret agents that a Taliban group were in this village or that village, but when that report was corroborated by signal intelligence – for instance, by locating the mobile phones of identified Taliban fighters in that village – then they were willing to commit forces to attack the group. The HUMINT could not be trusted alone, but it helped to narrow the target for surveillance and thus, in the end, to locate the enemy with reasonable certainty.

Third, political direction and a tight focus remain key to successful HUMINT. As neither Sunni extremism nor Iraq's weapons programme was a focus in the early to mid-1990s, policymakers paid the price later when they found they had no spies in place where they needed them. The US, with its aim to remain a superpower and have global influence, has a particular problem with such focus. It tries to collect intelligence from too many places and, despite its huge resources, tends to underperform. But with strong political direction and by concentrating spying resources on key threats, agencies have a chance to make the recruitments they need.

Political direction also means political accountability. In most democracies, to guard against the tendency to go rogue, secret services require political approval for their operations. In the US, most covert actions are signed off by the White House, if not the president himself. In Britain, all non-trivial actions by SIS, anything likely to have repercussions, are signed off by the foreign secretary. And the system does work, even if successive scandals appear to show these mechanisms are still far too weak.

Finally, spying remains useful and successful when used as a last resort. It is a hostile act: always invaluable during warfare, but often counterproductive and always to be used sparingly in peacetime.

Spying on the enemy has been seen as crucial to military strategy on the battlefield since ancient times, with the resulting intelligence being used for tactics of surprise and ruse. 'All warfare is based on deception,' wrote

Sun Tzu in 400 BC. 'There is no place where espionage is not used.'[12] But in modern warfare, intelligence is even more valued, particularly as a means of replacing the grinding war of attrition – as seen in the trenches of the First World War – with victory based on the concentration of overwhelming force on the enemy's weak spots. Such an approach depends on both mobility and good information about the enemy and their plans.

Whether it is war in ancient China or against al-Qaeda, running human spies is just one way of filling in the canvas of a broad intelligence picture. But war fundamentally changes the risk calculation in espionage. In the Second World War, an agent who parachuted behind enemy lines faced a very high chance of capture or death, or both. But when good intelligence might save hundreds of lives, as, for example, in the D-day landings in Normandy, the risks to the agent were worth taking.

Because the Cold War was 'cold', the risk of death was usually remote. The Soviet Union executed its traitors, and so the West's recruited agents always risked their lives. But the intelligence officers who handled these agents were much safer. By tacit agreement, the superpowers never tried to assassinate each other or take reprisals. These safety guarantees, however, were of little value when the West got embroiled in 'hot' conflicts in the developing world. The war in Vietnam in the 1960s and 1970s brought mortal danger for US field operatives, as did the civil war in Lebanon in the 1980s. In each conflict, both CIA officers and agents were killed. The bombing of the US Embassy in Beirut in 1983 caused what is still the biggest CIA loss of life, with eight officers killed. In recent years, the War on Terror and the conflicts in Iraq and Afghanistan have brought new dangers.

Britain's SIS has always operated with great caution. No British officers have lost their lives in action since the Second World War. However, according to insiders, the lives of a series of agents working for the British have been lost while infiltrating Islamic militant groups. Given al-Qaeda's callous willingness to shed innocent blood, though, spying on them was, in principle, worth that sacrifice.

In peacetime, spying has had a very mixed record. In the fight against crime or domestic extremism, it coexists poorly with a criminal justice system that guarantees a fair and open trial, and it is hard to stop agents provoking crime. It should be used, but sparingly and only with great expertise. It may, for example, be essential as a means of tracing the hidden hand of the powerful gangsters who are the instigators and beneficiaries of serious crime.

Between peaceful nations spying is automatically dubious. The unmasking of a traitor or any attempt to recruit a spy tends to sow enmity. Where secret agencies have survived and grown in peacetime, it is because the fear of war is ever present. In particular, since the US detonated the atom bomb over Japan in 1945, the fear of nuclear conflict has made their existence, particularly in nations that possess nuclear weapons, hard to contest. Spying might often be expensive, inefficient and ineffective, but not always. Set against the prospects of nuclear war, that distinction makes all the difference. However much politicians might deride the tit-bits that their spies serve up, none of them could risk not having an intelligence service.

From our look at the Cold War, it is clear – with hindsight – that spying could raise the tension at times but also lower it, helping deal with paranoia about the other side's intentions. And if a scorecard existed, it would have to record that both the KGB and the CIA proved their ability to steal military secrets and to develop great systems of early warning. Military spying evened out the contest; early warning helped calm the nerves. And together they did, in their small and highly expensive way, help to keep the peace. Neither agency was ever a great success at political spying in the other's homeland. The West never noticed that the East was collapsing and the East never realized that it was failing. Up to a point, this same story of tactical brilliance and strategic myopia has continued.

In the new world of espionage, despite initial doubts after the fall of the Berlin Wall, the secret services won a partial reprieve by shifting the case for spying into a struggle against other non-state threats. The threats were not nuclear holocaust but dirty bombs; not invasion by Warsaw Pact troops but a massacre of the innocents, whether by warring tribes or a bomb in a shopping centre. Though less of a threat to the state, the damage they could cause was real and tangible to the public, and so the need for intelligence – and for spies – was arguably unassailable. And in declaring War on Drugs and then War on Terror, US politicians were beginning conflicts that might conceivably never end.

Whether or not combating terrorism is really a 'war', it still demands a proportionate response, but one in which spying remains a powerful weapon of last resort. As John MacGaffin, a thoughtful former senior CIA operations officer, wrote, 'Clandestine collection of HUMINT must be employed only in pursuit of information that is truly essential to the most critical tasks of civilian and military national security affairs and only when that information cannot be acquired in any other way. When either of these two conditions is missing, the outcome almost always suffers.'[13]

The results of spying first creak and then fall apart when they are relied upon too heavily and become the sole means of supporting critical actions. The use of military and intelligence methods to round up al-Qaeda prisoners and send them to Guantanamo Bay after 9/11, for example, may have seemed to make sense at the time. But it was counterproductive in the long term. The evidence collected against these men was usually secret intelligence and so was no use in a court of law. That has made it very hard for the US to decide what to do with them, and to justify their continued, indefinite detention.

Messy but Useful

As was the case in the twentieth century, it has been tempting for politicians to view human intelligence as the messy end of spying where, in comparison with digital techniques, the drawbacks come to the fore. But, as we have seen, snippets of bugged conversations, intercepted emails or stolen digital files can take you only so far. They are usually meaningless without context. If Putin is heard to say, 'Let's invade Ukraine' or 'Let's kill Obama,' does he really mean it? When an elderly Afghan warlord repeatedly calls a member of the Taliban and speaks to him with the utmost respect, does that mean he is also a Taliban supporter? Zabet Amanullah's killing illustrates how misunderstandings from technical leads can have disastrous consequences. Human beings can provide the cultural context that allows you to judge if what someone says needs to be taken seriously, together with background knowledge about their ambitions, friends and enemies.

Most of that background knowledge is not secret intelligence. It can be gleaned from ordinary human engagement, whether it is scholarship, journalism, diplomacy or popular entertainment. But some of the most threatening adversaries – whether heads of state or terrorist leaders – are private, remote individuals who rarely disclose their intentions and who, even if they speak in public, mostly tell lies. In these cases, only a source from within the leader's circle – a spy – will be able to pass on and interpret his intentions.

As Edward Snowden, the whistle-blower from the National Security

Agency, disclosed, state eavesdroppers like the NSA and Britain's GCHQ view the world by means of what they call 'selectors', approved targets for interception. While there may be thousands of these selectors, only a portion of them can be closely monitored: not every phone can be listened to, every conversation replayed and studied in depth. Spy agencies, however, do store great volumes of information about calls and emails and connections. According to the *Guardian*, 'One NSA report from 2007 estimated that there were 850bn "call events" collected and stored in the NSA databases, and close to 150bn internet records. Each day, the document says, 1–2bn records were added.'[14] But the point often missed in the controversy was that most of this was valuable only with hindsight: only after a target had been identified could the information be used to investigate his history. The most difficult intelligence problem, then, is to identify the target, before homing in on what is important among the blizzard of signals.

So how should a 'selector' be chosen? This is ultimately a policy decision based on a broad understanding of threats and possible sources of valuable information. There are many sources of open information that can be used to judge who should be placed under surveillance. But, again, only a spy may be in a position to identify some of the secret people and places that are important. Unlike a mobile phone, for instance, or a camera on a drone, a spy also talks back. Running a spy is a two-way process and an agent can challenge the wisdom of the questions he is being asked or the direction of intelligence gathering. 'If you are listening to the wrong person; if you're focusing on the wrong target, they can tell you,' said one former recruiter. Another intelligence officer said, 'While policy-makers will tell us where to spy, that doesn't mean we tell them what they want to hear.' This is above all the value of the 'human factor': spies are not just another 'ear' at the table, a stealer of secrets, but sentient beings who convey understanding.

The Spies We Need

So spies really can be useful if carefully deployed as a last resort against a threat that matters, and the nature of the spies we need depends on what that threat is and, in consequence, what secrets are really worth stealing. Judging the future state of the planet, and all the issues that will confront society, is a subject of its own, but there are some macro trends worth mentioning that point to the role that spying could and should play.

The most striking trend that impacts on security is globalization: the way that powerful groups, whether political movements or commercial companies, are increasingly able to span national borders, making use of cheap and easy communications (through direct messages and phone calls between individuals or by posting propaganda on the Internet); easy travel (because of ever-decreasing restrictions on international freedom of movement and ever-decreasing prices of aircraft travel); freedom of capital movement (driven by reduced state regulations and also high-speed digital money movements); and a breakdown of cultural differences (with the increased dominance of major languages and spread of international entertainment, be it Hollywood or Egyptian soap operas). All of these factors are drivers of global networking and challenge our nation-based preconceptions and state institutions. These tendencies may be as varied as al-Qaeda propaganda, the incredible worldwide popularity of a computer game or the power of a hedge fund that operates worldwide with little regulation. Ideas, money and people always spread internationally – consider the rise of major religions. What is different about the twenty-first century is the speed with which this can happen.

Obviously, the threats posed by transnational networks do not come from violent extremists alone, but also from other groups whose actions may have damaging consequences. An important target of intelligence should be not only Islamist extremism but also the multinational corporations, and in particular the world of plutocrats and international financiers, upon whose actions the jobs and livelihoods of millions of people depend. At the time of writing, the largest 307 US firms held $1.95 trillion in accumulated profits offshore to avoid paying corporation tax. Their decisions on where to move that cash pile and their production centres will determine the fate of nations.[15]

There are two main consequences of the increased power of globalized, non-state groups for spying. First, it creates an intelligence deficit, a requirement to monitor and understand events and people often thousands of miles away that may, through global networks, come to have a local impact. Second, it creates a more dangerous 'action imperative', an impetus to intervene across borders to influence those foreign events which have an increasing domestic impact. This imperative applies as much to citizens – for example, those taking action unilaterally across borders through a non-governmental group like Greenpeace – as it does to government policymakers who direct the activities of their diplomats or secret services. While durable solutions will only emerge from open collaboration across borders, when that cooperation breaks down or is non-existent, it will always be tempting to take some form of covert action. This may be secret cooperation, such as Pakistan's acquiescence in drone strikes on militant groups within its borders, or unilateral action, such as the raid on bin Laden's compound. Both have damaging side effects, undermining legitimate institutions in the foreign country and risking a backlash if the covert action is discovered. As they roam like buffalo across the world, tracking or even attacking the latest extremist group to threaten to bomb or hack computers in New York or London, it can be a little too easy for secret services to knock down the fences. In extremis, they may need to do so. But all this secret work is just a stop-gap solution that is no substitute for effective global cooperation.

The threat from non-state groups should be kept in proportion. Soviet leader Joseph Stalin once asked, 'The Pope! How many divisions has he got?'[16] And it is obvious that when it comes to raw military power, the most dangerous weapons in the world are still in the hands of major countries, which must remain a major target of intelligence. While the nuclear arsenals of Russia and the US are reduced, they continue to exist. And bomb technology is still slowly spreading (with programmes in Pakistan, India, North Korea, Iran and Israel). With the US and Russia holding 1,800 nuclear warheads at high alert (meaning capable of being launched within fifteen minutes), good intelligence about nuclear capabilities and intentions is still more important than dealing with any other threat, certainly including terrorism.[17]

The Intelligence Gap

When intelligence is absent, spying and spies are always the last thing you need, unless the missing piece to the puzzle is something very secret. Most so-called 'intelligence errors' come down to a failure of analysis, not a failure to collect intelligence. This was true of the rise of Sunni extremism in the 1990s (which led to al-Qaeda), as it was with the consequences of the US encouraging rebellion in Syria in the 2010s (which led to the rise of the murderous Islamic State, spanning Syria and Iraq). The errors could be blamed as much on journalists, diplomats, politicians and academics as it could on intelligence officials. The missing element was not a secret: the extremists involved were completely open in both their objectives and their violent tactics. The broader failure was in not recognizing the potential threat and taking it seriously early enough.

Having a spy in al-Qaeda's ranks who could have provided vital secret intelligence, such as specific details of plots like the attack of 9/11, would have made a huge difference. But, as will now be apparent, human intelligence needs to be targeted. To obtain such agents, the analysis and the appreciation of the threat have to come first.

What makes the world more dangerous is that just when domestic events in Western countries are more driven by other events far away, we have seen a degradation in knowledge about international affairs. Globalization has been combined, fatally, with an increased reluctance in the West to explore or learn about foreign cultures and opinions. The spread of Hollywood and US television programmes has encouraged the world to understand the West and discouraged the West from understanding the world. Language learning has slowly increased (in the US, particularly since 2001), but there are still woefully few who speak foreign tongues. Newspapers and television have lived through major cutbacks and foreign-based newspaper correspondents have become a rarity. Data moves everywhere across the Internet, but it rarely carries interpretation. People travel constantly, but when they visit strange places they usually come unprepared, are shocked by what they find and may walk away with prejudice rather than understanding. Contrary to belief, travel often narrows the mind.

Meanwhile, diplomacy has been scaled back. Ambassadors are prisoners of instant feedback and are micro-managed from their home capitals. They are sent to 'message' their government's policies, not to relay back the intuitions they gather.

There is no shortage of people who think they understand the world, but too many project their own thought processes on to others, or replace cautious analysis with wishful thinking. An example was the disastrous wave of neo-conservative ideology that held sway under President George W. Bush. A small Washington elite believed they could remake the Middle East and impose democracy, beginning with the invasion of Iraq. Such men turned diplomacy into a one-way process, trying to impose Western values and only listening to intelligence that accorded with their existing views.

To summarize, we have created a world of global consequence without global knowledge, and spying is not a remedy for this problem. The wars of the early twenty-first century, whether in Afghanistan, Iraq or Syria, were not lost or the cause dishonoured by a failure to collect particular intelligence; they were failures of a much broader nature: our inability to understand the world at large.

But while even good spies cannot prevent strategic ignorance, strategic ignorance can prevent good espionage. This is because effective spying needs to be focused on what really matters. Viewed any way, good spying depends on the deployment of tremendous resources: not so much money as concentrated effort, the deployment of finely honed tactics and the use of great and rare talent. This is as true for those involved with the skilful handling of volunteer agents as it is for those who have been targeted for recruitment. In more traditional spy work, such as has been used against the IRA, the Soviets and the Chinese, for instance, direct recruitment was an art requiring patience and time. The nimbler twenty-first century has brought in some new techniques to speed up the process, but only at the cost of many failures and by establishing great 'fusion teams' to develop targets rapidly, stage recruitment attempts and then actively monitor a potential agent's progress.

Imagine spying as a very powerful telescope observing an object on a far-off planet from Earth. There are great skills involved in moving the telescope to point at the chosen target and in making that telescope show us a clear, bright and enlarged picture, but none of those efforts is worthwhile unless the telescope is pointed at the right object. So, which way should that telescope be pointed?

Intelligence agencies do often try to spread their resources, the CIA especially. They monitor more than one thing at once, but with limited success. We've seen how the attempt to direct human espionage at terrorism – to find that elusive 'man on the rock' inside al-Qaeda in particular – has been fraught with challenges, and there is no indication that such a spy has been found so far. But spying tactics have adapted and al-Qaeda members have grown disillusioned. Time is the spymaster's best friend. Spy agencies are finding ways to get agents in among the militants.

As I write, al-Qaeda is fragmented, but new powerful terrorist groups such as Islamic State are looming equally dangerous. After the next great intelligence shock, after the Next Attack, the spy we wish we had had – the next-generation 'man on the rock', sitting next to some other as yet unidentified enemy – will be absent not because of the latest tactical blunders by the spymasters, but more likely because of our much wider myopia about where trouble is brewing in our world.

Secrets and Understanding

The intelligence gap that exists about our rapidly changing world needs to be filled in many ways. More important than acquiring certain secret information will be a greater effort to widen our engagement with other lands and cultures. Before trying to spy, we should reach first for almost every other person who is prepared, as the military say, to 'step outside of the wire', to leave the comfort of their surroundings and enter unfamiliar territory. Such explorers might be academics, journalists, backpackers, missionaries, diplomats, mobile phone salesmen, climbers or soldiers. We need them to understand foreign cultures intimately and to explain them to us.

But secret services can play an important role too, in areas where their special skills might be useful and when there is a really important secret that cannot be teased out by open means. A diplomat or journalist might be able to talk to an ordinary whistle-blower, but if the individual's job was so sensitive that his life would be in danger by talking or if his greatest value would come from remaining in his job while secretly informing, then sometimes only an intelligence agency has the capability to handle such a source.

At times direct, open engagement with a certain person or group is impossible. On occasion you need to wear a disguise, to lie and cheat to come close to someone. You may need to employ every trick in the book to get an insider's account of what is happening. The secret servant should be deployed to tackle the really tough nut. He should be the gifted talker who sneaks in where few dare and fewer are capable, then charms the feared foe into opening his soul and revealing his disposition. That may involve 'recruitment'; it may require some loose cash; it will most likely involve a few lies, a bit of pressure. But not always.

If spying is the only way to get a secret, what secrets are really worth stealing? While they are always much sought after and exciting for senior politicians and others with clearance to read them, they tend to be overrated. 'From infancy on, we are all spies,' John Updike once wrote, 'the shame is not this but that the secrets to be discovered are so paltry and few.'[18] He was not far wrong.

From a military standpoint, an obsession with secrets can be counter-productive. As John Robb, a former Special Forces operator and technology entrepreneur, noted, much of current and future low-intensity conflict – terrorist attacks or rebellions short of all-out war – will increasingly be characterized by 'open source warfare' where (borrowing from the software industry) almost all plans, orders and lessons learned are debated publicly. Overly secretive organizations, like most modern militaries, tend to hoard information and thus alter their plans far too slowly. On the other hand, open-source fighters can be incredibly flexible, are devolved and tend to evolve rapidly. Spies are not required to discover their plans.[19]

Those modern secrets that are important often lie in unexpected places. As recent counterintelligence research for the US Office of the Director for National Intelligence argued, the nation's most valuable secrets lay primarily not in governments but in the hands of private corporations, whether software codes or medical formulas, for example. Stealing the dull secrets of another country's state bureaucracy may simply be a waste of effort.

Insights into the motivating forces and intentions of powerful and influential people and groups, whether inside or outside government, are what is needed. Politicians and senior business leaders, after all, lie endlessly about their intentions. A spy may not be required to figure that out, but sometimes he may be, particularly if that leader is especially secretive as well as powerful or dangerous.

Spies may sometimes supply insights that are merely tactical (as opposed to strategic), meaning that they are only valuable in the context of a short-term battle. For example, a spy can tell his handler where the Russian president is planning to send his armoured columns, or reveal the location of a terrorist training camp or a specific bomb plot in a Western city or a Czech oligarch's plan to bet billions of dollars against the pound sterling. Such information may be helpful, may save lives on one side of a conflict (and also – don't forget – cost lives on the other side) or, when it is a matter of economic secrets, may protect the livelihoods of millions.

But far too often the tactical side is overrated. Under intense round-the-clock scrutiny by the media, twenty-first-century political leaders have become infected with a control-room mentality where, seduced by powerful communications and the ability to project precision power at great distance – for example, with missiles, drones or Special Forces – they can overestimate their ability to influence events in faraway places. Rather like looking through a drinking straw at one part of a big landscape, the US president in his situation room may follow the events in Osama bin Laden's compound in Pakistan, but that is only at the expense of ignoring everything else happening on a larger scale.

The biggest and most important secret worth a spy's efforts may therefore be not the specific plan or detail but rather the broader insight that conveys understanding. As one of Britain's most experienced operatives summed it up, 'Understanding that encapsulates intention is everything.' Those who dealt with Britain's most famous spy against the Russians, Oleg Gordievsky, recount his greatest value was in helping Margaret Thatcher understand the last Soviet leader Mikhail Gorbachev's peaceful intentions. Gordievsky's treachery, if discovered, would have led to his certain execution. But his actions ultimately assisted his country's leader.

According to those who have dealt directly with some of the more important secret agents, quite often the boundary between espionage – a secret and treacherous relationship with the enemy – and direct and honest engagement can be quite blurred. Behaving rather like whistle-blowers, while leaking information and breaking their organization's rules – and risking sanctions as severe as death – many of the best intelligence sources would never have called themselves 'secret agents' and would have argued that rather than being under the control of some foreign power, they were serving their own country's best interests. Some key sources in the IRA were just like this – for example, the Irish businessman Brendan Duddy, who served as a go-between with SIS. So are many liaison sources inside other countries' intelligence services. One former CIA operative said, 'The best and most reliable agent is the person with access to extraordinarily valuable intelligence who actually wants to pass it on and to collaborate with the agency or government that his handler represents.'

Where it counts, a spy inside the enemy's camp can have tactical value and provide deeper insight. But in Iraq and Afghanistan HUMINT agencies sometimes expended too much energy trying to recruit fully paid-up and loyal agents, when it would have been better to put the effort into seeking a higher-level intelligence source who, though unwilling to cross the line and betray his cause, could provide more insight.

One intelligence official said of Afghanistan, 'Our mission was not to understand the enemy but to defeat it.' And he was right. But, as another equally well-placed diplomat put it, perhaps the politicians had given the spymasters the wrong mission. In a war fought among the people and with no obvious 'good guys', working out who was really the enemy was an equally important mission. The diplomat added, 'And what if we cannot win, what if we cannot defeat an enemy, then having a real understanding of the enemy, and having contacts in the heart of their leadership, becomes all-important.'

As these conflicts showed, the more that intelligence officers were mere adjuncts to the war machine, serving up targets for air and drone strikes, for example, the more reluctant well-placed people in the enemy camp were to engage with them and help them to understand the conflict.

None of this was trivial. For a Taliban leader, any unsanctioned contact with foreigners could lead to instant execution, whether he passed over secrets or not. And on the Western side, such contacts needed political approval and risked public exposure. But having discreet contacts with an enemy is a given for spymasters. Past experience shows that covert ambassadors like SIS's Mark Allen in Libya and Michael Oatley in Northern Ireland can engage in ways that would be difficult for ordinary diplomats.

Some object to this role, deriding the notion of the spymaster as quasi-ambassador as a kind of 'secret state department'. One CIA veteran said, 'Look, we are an espionage agency. Do they just want to be an intelligence service? If so they can save a lot of money and subscribe to Reuters.'

But, as always, the secret service has to be the weapon of last resort. While organizing talks with an enemy is something that diplomats should be equipped to do, at certain times only the discretion and personal skills of an intelligence officer will engender sufficient trust to make an unlikely contact likely. And if such discreet contacts help to provide broader intelligence, they could make a far greater contribution to solving a conflict and protecting security than another cheap exercise in 'stealing secrets'.

The twenty-first-century secret service is far more than a spy service. In the field it performs many roles, as I saw in practice when I reported on the war in Afghanistan in 2008. It was clear that SIS and the enormous CIA station had a multitude of functions. They were members of a 'war cabinet', chaired by President Karzai, that directed the war; they were mentoring the local intelligence agency, the NDS, and Karzai himself; they were conducting secret missions to talk to the Taliban and other warlords; and they were also trying to help kill some Taliban and al-Qaeda members. In all, then, it was a mixed bag.

The agencies also have very different approaches. While the UK's focus has been on secret intelligence gathering, the CIA in particular has always been as much about covert action, the art of secret intervention. The itch to change the world by secret means is hard to resist for a powerful country and, though attempts to do so are often counterproductive, it is unquestionably one function of a secret agency, and one that may clash with pure-as-can-be observation.

There are many discussions about organizational structure and who does what. British and US intelligence agencies are organized very differently. For instance, SIS is almost entirely focused on secret HUMINT and does not even have a capacity for analysis. The CIA has a clandestine service, comprised of both spy runners and covert action warriors, which is only one division within a broader all-source agency. There were always calls for another reorganization. But what matters more than how a bureaucracy is structured is what role the organization performs.

Secret services, rather like nuclear missiles, need a dual-key control. Their actions need to be in strict and loyal accordance with both the orders of their country's elected leadership and their society's values. In spying, they need to be a vehicle to deliver uncomfortable truths to those in power. And, while adhering to instructions about what targets to spy on, they must have the courage to point out when the target and the enemy are poorly chosen.

The spy and spymasters we need cannot be mavericks. They must be trusted not to go rogue and embarrass either a people or its government. But they must be nonconformists, iconoclasts. They must be patriots but that patriotism should be rooted in serving their society's and humanity's wider values – agents who serve a better purpose than just supplying target data but instead strive to obtain insights about the thoughts and intentions of those abroad who are really shaping our world, whether these people be inside or outside government.

In short, what is most needed is total independence of thought, allied to accountability of action.

A Modern Betrayal

It might be asked what virtue there is in all of this. We have talked of the valuable information from spies, but does that really justify a spy's betrayal of his friends, colleagues or country – his treachery?

There are those who suggest that spying is a fundamentally immoral profession. The novelist John le Carré believes that the British made great spies because duplicity was built into their country's class culture. In a newspaper interview, he argued that the work of intelligence officers was to 'fine-tune the aptitude for duplicity into an art form'. And in Britain there were always appropriate recruits. 'We have never lacked in this country for people with larcenous instincts and charming manners.'[20] Markus Wolf, the former director of East German foreign intelligence, went further, saying, 'Every director of an intelligence service, including those in the West, would be in the wrong position if he said, "I have to be scrupulous about it – is that in line with my ethical conduct?" Intelligence methods are not moral things.'[21]

But le Carré's depiction of ruthless tactics in the service of some greater good, however dubious that objective might sometimes be, is not identical to Wolf's suggestion that in essence anything is acceptable in espionage; that somehow there is a moral equivalence to each side of a spy war, as if the need for rough tactics in war makes everyone equally bad. It does not. Wolf may have been a master tactician, but he was also the heartless servant of a bankrupt, oppressive regime.

As Oleg Gordievsky put it when justifying his treachery, 'The betrayal question is pointless because it [the Soviet Union] was a criminal state. The most criminal element of the criminal state was the KGB. It was a gang of bandits. To betray bandits . . . was very good for the soul.'[22]

The invocation of a higher cause is what helps spies live with themselves after they have betrayed their friends (even if it is, perhaps, some other motive, such as money, that has really lured them into betrayal). But where the real contradiction arises is not between moral purpose and sordid tactic (war is messy), but between this higher purpose and the much narrower interest of the modern state's secret service.

To justify what they do among their own people, intelligence services are fiercely patriotic, but at the same time they constantly ask foreigners to betray their flag. In his pitch, the spymaster asks a potential agent to think about betraying his group or country or co-religionists 'to save lives' or 'for peace'. The recruiter may honestly believe that. But the intelligence agency's appeal to universal values is disingenuous. When the situation is reversed, when an insider from the secret services or military blows the whistle (someone like Bradley Manning, the soldier who went to Wikileaks, or the NSA contractor Edward Snowden) for what they regard as equally high principles, they are treated not as heroes but as loathsome traitors.

Those among the very exclusive club of intelligence officers who have successfully recruited an important spy testify to feeling first-hand another, more personal contradiction with the state's purposes. Betrayal, as they have recounted, is not a trivial thing. It is not provoked from a brief, chance conversation but must usually be cultivated, which demands prolonged access to the potential secret agent. Those involved in recruitment often talk of its subtlety: the need to establish a real friendship, the creation of real emotional bonds. They were often fiercely loyal to their agents, even long after they had been passed across to another 'handler'. It was like a marriage, or, according to a retired officer, 'like giving away a child'. After all, said one legendary CIA recruiter, you needed thick skin: 'You have to be able to deal with ambiguity – with people's lives.' And give away their children they did: the friendship was a device, an emotional twist used in the service of a cause, a country they believed in.

Not every spy requires a good cause. Plenty will betray secrets for money, even to the dark side. Plenty also were just consumed by the love of the game. But in order to attract people who will betray their secrets to you, the cause must be important. And in a world of globalized threats and common interests that transcend borders, and where the actions of intelligence services are under ever-greater scrutiny, the contradiction between the greater good, espoused by secret services, and the narrow interests of the nation-state may come to look increasingly untenable.

What great cause, for instance, could motivate and justify spying between states that are moral equivalents: for example, for one ethnic group against another, or for France against Germany? Or take economic espionage: when multinational corporations, for instance, abandon all loyalties to individual states (and are quite willing to transfer jobs, cash hoards and tax liabilities from their nation), what would be the moral basis for a nation-state to assist them to win contracts? In contrast, when a transnational company is polluting the seas across the globe, then betraying its secrets seems perfectly justified.

When the threats to security faced by free citizens across the world are broadly similar – whether it is the spread of religiously motivated violence or the struggle against dictatorship, concentration of economic power and unregulated capital flows – then serving one state or another may begin to look petty. In those circumstances, a nation's ability to secure friends in other countries – whether spies or simply allies – may depend on how obviously its foreign policy matches its clear obligations as a global citizen.

When the CIA was exposed for its extraordinary renditions, secret jails and harsh torture of mainly Arab prisoners, for instance, what right-thinking Arab would really want to betray their secrets to such an organization? As Sir Richard Dearlove, the former British spy chief, indicated in a speech in July 2006, one of the reasons that intelligence organizations attracted willing agents from other countries, was 'because the West unequivocally, at the end of the Cold War, did occupy the moral high ground'. And, he went on to say, 'We are not on it at the moment.'[23]

Spying and secret service activity should continue to be nationally controlled. No international or non-government spy agency could be relied upon to protect vital secrets and keep alive the most sensitive agents. This is what the best intelligence agencies, through a century of experience, excel at. Nevertheless, intelligence agencies can rarely operate unilaterally as they confront global threats. In future, they will be expected to work constantly with other services and help serve wider interests. Their success, and their ability to recruit the spies we need to protect us all from the next big threat, will depend on the values by which they live, and the extent to which those values are shared not just by their government masters but also by all right-thinking people.

Notes

Introduction: The Exploding Spy

1 Milan Kundera, *The Unbearable Lightness of Being* (London/Boston, Faber and Faber, 1985), p. 250.

2 George Friedman and Scott Stewart, 'The Khost Attack and the Intelligence War Challenge', published by Stratfor, a private intelligence firm, in its *Geopolitical Weekly*, 11 January 2010.

3 See CIA Officers Memorial Foundation, *Washington Post* and www.cia.gov.

4 Confidential author interview with retired senior SIS officer.

5 Edward Luttwak, 'Thousands of Spooks, No One to Spy On', *Sunday Times*, 20 April 2014.

6 James Adams, *New Spies: Exploring the Frontiers of Espionage* (London, Pimlico, 1995), p. 149.

7 Stansfield Turner, 'Intelligence for a New World Order', *Foreign Affairs*, Vol. 70, No. 4, Fall 1991.

8 Martin Pengelly and agencies, 'Merkel Doubts Whether US Will Stop Spying on Germany', *Guardian*, 12 July 2014.

9 The New York City Office of Chief Medical Examiner, WTC Repository, 'World Trade Center Operational Statistics' document, last updated 20 June 2011: available at http://www.nyc.gov/html/ocme/downloads/pdf/public_affairs_ocme_pr_WTC_Operational_Statistics.pdf.

10 Gordon Corera, interview with Sir Colin McColl for *MI6: A Century in the Shadows*, BBC Radio 4, July–August 2009.

11 Congressional Record, House of Representatives debate on the National Security Act 1992, 5 February 1992, p. H382, courtesy of fas.org: fas.org/irp/congress/1992_cr/h920205-reform.htm.

12 William Pfaff, 'We Need Intelligence, Not Spies', *International Herald Tribune*, 21 July 1994.

13 Christopher Andrew, *The Defence of the Realm: The Authorized History of MI5*, updated edition (London, Penguin, 2010), p. 787.

14 Ibid.

15 Michael Smith, *New Cloak, Old Dagger: How Britain's Spies Came in from the Cold* (London, Victor Gollancz, 1996), p. 13.

16 Tony Blair, 'Doctrine of the International Community', speech to the Chicago Economic Club, 24 April 1999.

17 Walter Pincus, 'White House Labors to Redefine Role of Intelligence Community', *Washington Post*, 13 June 1994.

18 'America's Intelligence Services: Time for a Rethink,' *The Economist*, 18 April 2002.

19 T. J. Waters, *Class 11: My Story Inside the CIA's First Post-9/11 Spy Class* (New York, Dutton, 2006), cover.

20 Sir Richard Dearlove, 'Ten Years After 9/11: What Are the Priorities for the Intelligence Service in 21st Century Britain?', lecture to Global Strategy Forum, 5 July 2011.

21 Waters, *Class 11*, pp. 63–4.

22 Stephen Grey, *Ghost Plane: The True Story of the CIA Torture Program* (New York, St Martin's Press, 2006).

23 Josh Gerstein, 'Tenet: Aggressive Interrogations Brought U. S. Valuable Information', *New York Sun*, 26 April 2007.

24 Thomas Joscelyn, 'Cheney on the Value of Interrogations and Human Intelligence', *Weekly Standard*, 16 December 2008.

25 Author interview with Tyler Drumheller for 'Extraordinary Rendition', *Frontline*, PBS, 4 November 2007.

26 Sir David Omand, author interview and correspondence, 2008 and 2014.

27 Nick Hopkins and Julian Borger, 'Exclusive: NSA Pays £100m in Secret Funding for GCHQ', *Guardian*, 1 August 2013.

Chapter 1: The Secret Agent

1 George A. Hill, *Go Spy the Land* (London, Cassell, 1932), p. 3.

2 At the time, the DSO was given to junior officers for distinguished service or acts of gallantry against the enemy. Cromie's was in recognition of his 'service in command of British submarines operating in the Baltic Sea': see supplement to the *London Gazette*, 31 May 1916.

3 Report from Major Scale, Stockholm, 19 November 1918, with testimony of H. T. Hall, who was present with Cromie, National Archives file ADM 223/637, document 83.

Notes

4 Details of the Cromie incident from Nathalie Bucknall's eyewitness statement, National Archives file FO 337/87; Mary Britnieva, *One Woman's Story* (London, Barker, 1934); and Roy Bainton, *Honoured by Strangers: The Life of Captain Francis Cromie CB DSO RN, 1882–1918* (London, Constable, 2002).

5 Phillip Knightley, *The Second Oldest Profession: Spies and Spying in the Twentieth Century* (London, Pimlico, 2003), p. 3.

6 See, for instance, Michael Durey, 'William Wickham, the Christ Church Connection and the Rise and Fall of the Security Service in Britain, 1793–1801', *English Historical Review*, Vol. 121, No. 492, June 2006, pp. 714–45.

7 Thomas Erskine May, *Constitutional History of England: Vol. II, 1760–1860* (London, Longman, Green, Longman, Roberts and Green, 1863), Kindle location 5539.

8 From a history of 'British Military Intelligence in France during the latter part of the war' by Colonel Reginald Drake, quoted in Keith Jeffery, *MI6: The History of the Secret Intelligence Service 1909–1949* (London, Bloomsbury, 2010), p. 73.

9 Ibid., p. 87.

10 The Cheka (1917–29) became the NKVD (1934–46), then the MGB (1946–53) and KGB (1954–91). Since 1991, the old KGB has been split into the FSB (internal intelligence service) and the SVR (external intelligence service).

11 Spencer Tucker, *The Great War, 1914–1918* (New York, Routledge, 1997), p. 157.

12 Cromie telegram to the Admiralty, 24 June 1918, National Archives file FO 371/3286.

13 Report from Major Scale, 19 November 1918, National Archives file ADM 223/637, document 83.

14 Figures from www.westernfrontassociation.com and the National Army Museum's Western Front online exhibition at www.nam.ac.uk.

15 The London *Times* correspondent in Petrograd, George Dobson, quoted in 'Imprisoned in Russia. Barbarous Treatment. Englishman's Experiences', *New Zealand Herald*, Vol. LV, issue 17061, 17 January 1919, p. 8.

16 Report from Major Scale, 19 November 1918, National Archives file ADM 223/637, document 83.

17 The London *Times* correspondent in Petrograd, George Dobson, quoted in 'Imprisoned in Russia. Barbarous Treatment. Englishman's Experiences', *New Zealand Herald*, Vol. LV, issue 17061, 17 January 1919, p. 8.

18 Jonathan D. Smele, *The Russian Revolution and Civil War 1917-1921: An Annotated Bibliography* (London/New York: Continuum, 2006), p. 276.

19 Jeffery, *MI6*, pp. 134–8.

20 Andrew Cook, *Ace of Spies: The True Story of Sidney Reilly* (Stroud, The History Press, 2011), Kindle locations 1718–19.

21 Author telephone interview with Andrew Cook, 2013.

22 Cook, *Ace of Spies*, Kindle location 2302.

23 Ibid., Kindle location 2329.

24 National Archives file KV2 827. Referring to an 'Original enquiry from "C"', the response received by MI5 from 'H.Q. Irish Command' on 2 April 1918 states, 'No record of the birth of REILLY, Sydney T. in the Register in Clonmel'.

25 Cook, *Ace of Spies*, Kindle location 2363.

26 Ibid., Kindle location 2418, citing telegram CX 027753 of 16 April 1918 in Reilly's SIS file CX 2616.

27 Reilly telegram reports to London of his meetings with Bonch-Bruevich, May and June 1918, National Archives file WO 32/5669.

28 Lockhart's report to Foreign Secretary Arthur Balfour, dated 5 November 1918, National Archives file FO 371/3348.

29 R. H. Bruce Lockhart, *Memoirs of a British Agent* (London, Putnam, 1932), p. 316.

30 Cook, *Ace of Spies*, Kindle location 3817.

31 Lockhart's report to Foreign Secretary Arthur Balfour, dated 5 November 1918, National Archives file FO 371/3348.

32 Captain Hill's report to the Director of Military Intelligence, dated 26 November 1918, National Archives file FO 371/3350.

33 Lockhart's report to Foreign Secretary Arthur Balfour, dated 5 November 1918, National Archives file FO 371/3348.

34 Captain Hill's report to the Director of Military Intelligence, dated 26 November 1918, National Archives file FO 371/3350.

35 Ibid.

36 See scanned pamphlet at http://chroniclingamerica.loc.gov/lccn/sn83030214/1919-04-20/ed-1/seq-85.pdf.

37 Lockhart's report to Foreign Secretary Arthur Balfour, dated 5 November 1918, National Archives file FO 371/3348.

38 There are no exact figures, but estimated executions of between 50,000 and 200,000 are given at necrometrics.com. The source is Norman Lowe, *Mastering Twentieth Century Russian History* (London, Palgrave Macmillan, 2002), though many more tens of thousands, possibly hundreds of thousands, may have died in revolts and prison camps.

39 Winston Churchill, *The World Crisis: The Aftermath* (London, Macmillan, 1929), p. 235.

40 Cook, *Ace of Spies*, Kindle location 3296, citing Reilly's SIS file CX 2616.

41 Ibid., File No. 302330, Vol. 37, p. 241, Central Archives of the Federal Security Service in Moscow.

42 Captain Hill's report to the Director of Military Intelligence, dated 26 November 1918, National Archives file FO 371/3350.

43 Hill, *Go Spy the Land*, p. 3.

44 Details on the foundation of the Passport Control Office and its profits are given in Jeffery, *MI6*, pp. 153–4. The lack of immunity in such cover emerged in the public debate over the status of Frank Foley, SIS chief of station in the 1920s and 1930s, who saved many Jews by issuing them with visas to come to Britain.

45 The late John Hart, former CIA officer, in his testimony to the House Select Committee on Assassinations, 15 September 1978.

46 Howard Hart in a talk given to the Miller Center for Public Affairs, University of Virginia, on 3 December 2004. Hart was Islamabad chief of station during the CIA's efforts to arm and support the mujahideen in Afghanistan.

47 CIA FAQs at www.cia.gov.

48 Ian Fleming quoted in Ben Macintyre, 'Was Ian Fleming the Real 007?', *The Times*, 5 April 2008.

49 Leonard Moseley's recollections of his conversation with Ian Fleming are in a jacket review for Edward Van Der Rhoer's *Master Spy: A True Story of Allied Espionage in Bolshevik Russia* (New York, Scribner, 1981).

50 Cook, *Ace of Spies*, Kindle locations 136–9.

51 'Remarks by Deputy Director for Operations James L. Pavitt at the Foreign Policy Association', 21 June 2004: available at cia.gov (the extract is from *Kim*, Chapter 9).

Chapter 2: The Best-Ever Liars

1 Author interview with Milton Bearden, 2009.

2 Bickham Sweet-Escott, *Baker Street Irregular* (London, Methuen & Co. Ltd, 1965), p. 19. As described by Sweet-Escott, himself a recruit to Section D, the chief would take a new recruit up to the fourth floor of St Ermin's hotel and say to the officer guarding the entrance, 'This is X. Take a good look at him because he is now going to be one of us.'

3 Christopher Andrew, *The Defence of the Realm: The Authorized History of MI5*, updated edition (London, Penguin, 2010), p. 168. Philby was recruited in June 1934.

4 Jeffrey T. Richelson, *A Century of Spies: Intelligence in the Twentieth Century* (New York/Oxford, Oxford University Press, 1997), p. 136.

5 Andrew, *The Defence of the Realm*, p. 420.

6 Although operating under many different names, the Soviet and Russian secret services have been headquartered at the Lubyanka from 1920 to this day.

7 She worked in the Information Service of the Intelligence Directorate of the GUGB – the Main Directorate of State Security – which was part of the NKVD structure.

8 Andrew, *The Defence of the Realm*, p. 272.

9 Genrikh Borovik, *The Philby Files: The Secret Life of the Master Spy – KGB Archives Revealed* (London, Time Warner Paperbacks, 1995), p. xiv.

10 Ibid., p. 212.

11 Andrew, *The Defence of the Realm*, p. 272.

12 Borovik, *The Philby Files*, Introduction by Phillip Knightley, p. xiv.

13 Ibid., p. 216.

14 Ibid., p. 217.

15 Andrew, *The Defence of the Realm*, p. 342.

16 Telegram from Sorge to GRU, as detailed in Robert Whymant, *Stalin's Spy: Richard Sorge and the Tokyo Espionage Ring* (London, I. B. Tauris, 2006), p. 167.

17 Niall Ferguson, *The War of the World: History's Age of Hatred* (London, Penguin, 2009), pp. 432–3.

18 Both quotes from Whymant, *Stalin's Spy*, p. 184.

19 John le Carré, 'The Spy to End Spies: On Richard Sorge', *Encounter*, November 1966.

20 Borovik, *The Philby Files*, pp. x–xi.

21 The CIA officer involved requested anonymity.

22 Phillip Knightley, *The Second Oldest Profession: Spies and Spying in the Twentieth Century* (London, Pimlico, 2003), p. 433.

23 Ibid., p. 431, and John Prados, *Lost Crusader: The Secret Wars of CIA Director William Colby* (Oxford, Oxford University Press, 2003), p. 270: 'As Colby believed the primary task of counterintelligence was to place the CIA's own spies within the Russian intelligence apparatus, he asked Angleton what his staff had done to fulfill this goal. He learned that the CIA had no such agents.'

24 Andrew, *The Defence of the Realm*, p. 364.

25 Ibid., p. 385.

26 Hans Bethe to journalist, author and historian Richard Rhodes, quoted in *Race for the Superbomb*, PBS, January 1999.

27 Neil Tweedie, 'Kim Philby: Father, Husband, Traitor, Spy', *Telegraph*, 23 January 2013.

28 Ben Macintyre, *A Spy Among Friends: Kim Philby and the Great Betrayal* (London, Bloomsbury, 2014), Kindle location 2302. See also Yuri Modin, *My Five Cambridge Friends* (New York, Farrar, Straus and Giroux, 1994), p. 201.

29 Albert Lulushi, 'Interview with Voice of America about Operation Valuable Fiend', 14 June 2014: available at www.albertlulushi.com.

30 Remarks by Deputy Director for Operations James L. Pavitt at the Foreign Policy Association, 21 June 2004: available at www.cia.gov.

31 Interview with Sandy Grimes, episode 21, 'Spies', *Cold War*, George Washington University's National Security Archive, 30 January 1998: available at www2.gwu.edu/~nsarchiv/.

32 Among the coups was the acquisition by the CIA in the 1970s of an intact MiG-23 fighter jet with its documentation from Egypt. According to a person briefed, as a result of getting the MiG to the US, the Pentagon was able to scrap $8 billion it had set aside for research into its capabilities. The US Air Force could actually fly the plane to discover its qualities and faults.

33 Various sources, including Markus Wolf (with Anne McElvoy), *Man Without a Face: The Autobiography of Communism's Greatest Spymaster* (New York, Public-Affairs, 1997) and Christopher Andrew and Vasili Mitrokhin, *The Sword and the Shield: The Mitrokhin Archive and the Secret History of the KGB* (New York, Basic Books, 2000).

34 'Even though they had Mr. Guillaume under investigation, they did not warn Mr. Brandt against taking him that summer, as his sole aide, on a vacation trip to Norway. Mr. Guillaume later said that he filled an entire briefcase with secret documents, including letters to the Chancellor from President Richard M. Nixon about the NATO alliance's nuclear strategy': Craig R. Whitney, 'Gunter Guillaume, 68, is Dead: Spy Caused Willy Brandt's Fall', *New York Times*, 12 April 1995.

35 Wolf, *Man Without a Face*, p. xii.

36 Klaus Wiegrefe, 'Ostpolitik: How East Germany Tried to Undermine Willy Brandt', *Spiegel Online International*, 8 July 2010. Günter and Christel Guillaume were found guilty of espionage and sentenced to thirteen and eight years respectively. They were eventually freed in a 'spy swap' and returned as heroes.

37 Imre Karacs, 'US Keeps Its Stasi Secrets Locked Up', *Independent*, 6 March 1999.

38 James Adams, *New Spies: Exploring the Frontiers of Espionage* (London, Pimlico, 1995), p. vii.

39 Barry G. Royden, 'Tolkachev, a Worthy Successor to Penkovsky', *Studies in Intelligence*, Vol. 47, No. 3, 2003: available at www.cia.gov.

40 Widely reported, with specific reference to David Wise, *Nightmover: How Aldrich Ames Sold the CIA to the KGB for $4.6 Million* (New York, HarperCollins, 1995). Also Rupert Cornwell, 'Jeanne Vertefeuille: CIA Officer Who Unmasked the Spy Aldrich Ames', *Independent*, 16 January 2013.

41 Senate Select Committee on Intelligence, 'An Assessment of the Aldrich H. Ames Espionage Case and Its Implications for U.S. Intelligence', 1 November 1994: available at www.fas.org/irp/congress/1994_rpt/ssci_ames.htm.

42 CIA statement on 'Legacy of Ashes', 6 August 2007: available at www.cia.gov.

43 Tony Rennell, 'September 26th, 1983: The Day the World Almost Died', *Daily Mail*, 29 December 2007.

Chapter 3: Friendship

1 'IRA Questions Bemuse McGuinness', *Irish Times*, 29 September 2011.

2 Matt Born, 'What is the Truth behind the Story of Stakeknife', *Daily Telegraph*, 16 May 2003; 'Alleged Agent Statements in Full', BBC News website, 14 May 2003.

3 Talk at Reuters security seminar, 2011.

4 Owen Bowcott, 'Gerry Adams Reveals Family's Abuse by His Father', *Guardian*, 20 December 2009.

5 Henry McDonald, 'Gerry Adams Faces Investigation for Failing to Report Sexual Abuse by Brother', *Guardian*, 7 October 2013.

6 Stephen Grey and John Goetz, 'Target Britain', *Sunday Times*, 26 November 2000.

7 From FRU sources, plus Henry McDonald, 'Spy Says McGuinness Did Not Fire on Bloody Sunday', *Observer*, 6 May 2001.

8 Martin Ingram and Greg Harkin, *Stakeknife: Britain's Secret Agents in Ireland* (Madison, University of Wisconsin Press, 2005), p. 59.

9 Neil Mackay, 'Exclusive: Confessions of a Secret Agent Turned Terrorist', *Sunday Herald*, 23 June 2002.

10 Ibid.

11 'Report of the Tribunal of Inquiry into Suggestions That Members of An Garda Síochána or Other Employees of the State Colluded in the Fatal Shootings of RUC Chief Superintendent Harry Breen and RUC Superintendent

Robert Buchanan on the 20th March 1989', by His Honour Judge Peter Smithwick, 21 November 2013, p. 278, para 15.11.10.

12 Martin McGartland, *Fifty Dead Men Walking* (London, John Blake, 2009), pp. 164–5.

13 Ibid., pp. 251–2.

14 Stevens Inquiry 3, Overview and Recommendations, 17 April 2003, p. 16, pt 4.9.

15 Cory Collusion Inquiry Report: Patrick Finucane, 1 April 2004, p. 62, pt 1.178.

16 Prime Minister David Cameron statement on Patrick Finucane, 12 December 2012: available at www.gov.uk.

17 Hansard, House of Commons Debate on Facilities of the House, 18 December 2001, Vol. 377, cc. 151–262: available at http://hansard.millbanksystems.com.

18 William Scholes, 'Informer "Murdered on Orders of SF Man"', *Irish News*, 27 May 1986.

19 'IRA Questions Bemuse McGuinness', *Irish Times*, 29 September 2011.

20 All quotes from tape and Scappaticci response from Ulster Television *Insight* programme, 'Scappaticci', aired 15 March 2004.

21 Transcript of the Ulster TV programme.

22 Transcript of oral evidence from Lord Stevens of Kirkwhelpington and Andy Hayman, House of Commons, Joint Committee on the Draft Detention of Terrorist Suspects (Temporary Extension) Bills, 3 May 2011, p. 13.

23 Liam Clarke, 'Dark World of Agents is Not Black and White', *Belfast Telegraph*, 23 December 2011.

24 R. James Woolsey, testimony before the US Senate Select Committee on Intelligence, 2 February 1993, quoted, inter alia, in Douglas F. Garthoff, *Directors of Central Intelligence as Leaders of the U.S. Intelligence Community 1946–2005* (Washington, DC, Potomac Books, 2007), p. 221.

Chapter 4: Thunderbolt

1 Quoted in Stephen Dorril, *MI6: Inside the Covert World of Her Majesty's Secret Intelligence Service* (New York, Touchstone, 2000), p. 774.

2 Taken from Zanina Hollowday's diary, courtesy of her daughter-in-law (hereafter Hollowday diary).

3 Hollowday diary.

4 Author interviews with Antoniades, 2011–14, and his former commander, Renos Kyriakides, 2013.

5 Intelligence Services Act 1994, s 1.2c.

6 Hollowday diary.

7 Lionel Savery obituary, *Daily Telegraph*, 10 April 2012.

8 'Officer's Tribute to Accused Men', *The Times*, 5 November 1959.

9 HM Customs & Excise (HMCE) was merged with the Inland Revenue in 2005, becoming HM Revenue & Customs (HMRC).

10 Denise Lavoie, 'James "Whitey" Bulger's Capture Could Cause Trouble inside the FBI', *Washington Post*, 25 June 2011.

11 Author interview with Collins in 'The Heroin Connection', *File on 4*, BBC Radio 4, 6 March 2007.

12 'Thai Drug Trafficking Suspect Loses Diplomatic Immunity', *Bangkok Post*, 26 August 1991.

13 Specialist lawyer Simon McKay, explained in a letter: 'There is no legislative basis to authorise participation in criminality. There is an ability to authorise the use and conduct of informers and undercover officers (there is no distinction between intelligence agencies and police). Where they may engage in criminality this can be "approved" in advance. This is not strictly speaking authorising criminality but its effect is that it is unlikely a prosecution will follow assuming of course the level of criminality is confined to that approved.'

14 He died on 7 June 1967 in Cascais, Portugal.

Chapter 5: Jihad

1 Michael Scheuer, 'Inside Out', *Atlantic*, 1 April 2005.

2 Interview by Gordon Corera, *Newsnight*, BBC Two, 16 November 2006.

3 Author interview with Nasiri, May 2013.

4 Interview by Gordon Corera, *Newsnight*, BBC Two, 16 November 2006.

5 Ibid.

6 Omar Nasiri, *Inside the Global Jihad: How I Infiltrated Al Qaeda and Was Abandoned by Western Intelligence* (London, Hurst & Co., 2006), p. 59.

7 Author interview with Nasiri, May 2013.

8 'The Rise of the Islamist Terrorist Threat', www.mi5.gov.uk.

9 Author interview with Jack Devine, 2009.

10 'Menaces Terroristes', www.risques.gouv.fr.

11 Article 421-2-1 of the Penal Code, added in 22 July 1996: 'The participation in any group formed or association established with a view to the preparation, marked by one or more material actions, of any of the acts of terrorism provided for under the previous articles shall in addition be an act of terrorism.'

12 Interview by Gordon Corera, *Newsnight*, BBC Two, 16 November 2006.

13 Ibid.

14 Ibid.

15 Nasiri, *Inside the Global Jihad*, p. 48.

16 Ibid., p. 52.

17 Interview by Gordon Corera, *Newsnight*, BBC Two, 16 November 2006.

18 Henry A. Crumpton, *The Art of Intelligence: Lessons from a Life in the CIA's Clandestine Service* (New York, Penguin, 2012), p. 133.

19 Ibid., p. 134.

20 Nasiri, *Inside the Global Jihad*, p. 99.

21 Author interview with Nasiri, May 2013.

22 Ibid.

23 Bin Laden had fled to Sudan from Saudi Arabia following his opposition to the Saudi regime's alliance with the US to drive Iraq out of Kuwait.

24 Andrew Staniforth and Fraser Sampson (eds.), *The Routledge Companion to UK Counter-Terrorism* (Oxford, Routledge, 2012), p. 136.

25 Interview by Gordon Corera, *Newsnight*, BBC Two, 16 November 2006.

26 Author interview with Nasiri, May 2013.

27 Overheard by an ex-prisoner, interviewed by the author in Yemen, who had been in the cell next to al-Libi's in Afghanistan.

28 Nasiri, *Inside the Global Jihad*, p. 152.

29 Ibid., p. 165.

30 Tony Jones in conversation with the former CIA analyst, Australian Broadcasting Corporation, 17 November 2006. Scheuer also told the *New York Times*, 'I've never seen anything from that period that was so complete and rang so true': Mark Landler, 'Jihadist Double Agent Writes of Derring-Do,' 16 November 2006.

31 Author interview with Nasiri, May 2013.

32 Nasiri, *Inside the Global Jihad*, p. 250.

33 Ibid., p. 252.

34 Author interview with Nasiri, May 2013.

35 From the declassified version of 'Joint Inquiry into Intelligence Community Activities before and after the Terrorist Attacks of September 11, 2001', December 2002, Finding no. 11, p 90.

36 Interview by Gordon Corera, *Newsnight*, BBC Two, 16 November 2006.

37 Craig Whitlock, 'After a Decade at War with West, Al-Qaeda Still Impervious to Spies', *Washington Post*, 20 March 2008.

38 Michael Scheuer, 'Why It's So Hard to Infiltrate al-Qaeda', *Atlantic*, 1 April 2005.

Chapter 6: Caveat Emptor

1 Peter Taylor, 'The Spies Who Fooled the World', *Panorama*, BBC Two, 31 May 2013.

2 The Commission on the Intelligence Capabilities of the United States Regarding Weapons of Mass Destruction, Report to the President, 31 March 2005, official edition, pp. 11, 48 (hereafter WMD Commission report).

3 Bob Drogin, *Curveball: Spies, Lies and the Con Man Who Caused a War* (New York, Random House, 2007), Author's Note, p. xi.

4 Robert Dreyfuss and Jason Vest, 'The Lie Factory', *Mother Jones*, January–February 2004.

5 'Lexington', 'The Power behind the Throne', *The Economist*, 21 December 2000.

6 Andrew Gilligan, 'I Asked My Intelligence Source Why Blair Misled Us . . .', *Mail on Sunday*, 1 June 2003.

7 WMD Commission report, p. 48.

8 George J. Tenet, statement on his website: www.georgejtenet.com/CURVEBALL.html.

9 Butler Report, Point 330, p. 80.

10 Gordon Corera, *MI6: Life and Death in the British Secret Service* (London, Phoenix Paperbacks e-book, 2012), Kindle location 7388.

11 Hauptstelle für Befragungswesen (HBW).

12 Footnotes to WMD Commission report: 'Defense HUMINT confirmed that it had disseminated 95 reports from Curveball. DIA, *Memorandum from Director, DIA Re: Curveball Background* (Jan. 14, 2005)'.

13 Martin Chulov and Helen Pidd, 'Defector Admits to WMD Lies That Triggered Iraq War', *Guardian*, 15 February 2011.

14 Secretary of State Colin Powell's Remarks to the United Nations Security Council, 5 February 2003: transcript available at http://2001-2009.state.gov/secretary/former/powell/remarks/2003/17300.htm.

15 Martin Chulov and Helen Pidd, 'Defector Admits to WMD Lies That Triggered Iraq War', *Guardian*, 15 February 2011.

16 Peter Taylor, 'The Spies Who Fooled the World', *Panorama*, BBC Two, 31 May 2013.

17 WMD Commission report, note 274 of Chapter 1, p. 217.

18 US Senate Select Committee on Intelligence, 'Report on the U.S. Intelligence Community's Prewar Intelligence Assessments on Iraq', 7 July 2004, p. 154.

19 Les's email is described ibid., pp. 155–6.

20 Report by Stephen Grey, 'Iraq War Intelligence Probed', *Newsnight*, BBC Two, 30 March 2008.

21 WMD Commission report, pp. 91–2, and notes 292 and 293, Chapter 1.

22 Ibid., p. 93.

23 Ibid.

24 Telephone interviews and email exchanges with the author.

25 WMD Commission report, p. 85, with further detail in note 258, Chapter 1.

26 Ibid., note 242.

27 Notes provided by senior retired SIS officer.

28 Chilcot evidence from SIS1, p. 18.

29 Sir Richard Dearlove's evidence to the Chilcot Inquiry on 16 June 2010, pp. 87–9.

30 Chilcot evidence from SIS3, p. 17.

Chapter 7: Cover Blown

1 José María Irujo, 'Si atacamos el metro de Barcelona los servicios de urgencia no pueden llegar' ['If We Attack the Barcelona Metro, the Emergency Services Will Be Unable to Get Down There], *El País*, 26 January 2008. The description of Asim's journey to and movements in Barcelona is taken from police documents, F1's court testimony and the author's retracing of F1's steps in 2013.

2 F1's court testimony, audio provided to the author.

3 Tablighi Jamaat is proscribed in Iran, Russia, Tajikistan, Turkmenistan and Uzbekistan. Source: Igor Rotar, 'The Tablighi Jamaat: A Soft Islamization from the Ferghana Valley to Russia's Turkic Regions?', *Eurasia Daily Monitor*, Vol. 10, Issue 12, 23 January 2013.

4 Graham Keeley and Paul Haven, 'Spain, France at Odds over Terror Probe', *USA Today* online, 8 February 2008.

5 Since the end of 2005; F1 court testimony, notes p. 21.

6 F1 court testimony, notes p. 30.

7 José María Irujo, 'Si atacamos el metro de Barcelona los servicios de urgencia no pueden llegar' ['If We Attack the Barcelona Metro, the Emergency Services Will Be Unable to Get Down There], *El País*, 26 January 2008.

8 Guardia Civil application for search warrant, 18 January 2008, courtesy of Rastros de Dixan: http://rastrosdedixan.wordpress.com.

9 Court Ruling no. 1.140/2010, Appeal no. 10256/2010 P, Spanish Supreme Court, Madrid, 29 December 2010 (hereafter Appeal document), p. 5.

10 Appeal document, p. 5.

11 Ibid., p. 32.

12 Ibid., pp. 6 and 32.

13 F1 court testimony.

14 See Glossary.

15 Europa Press, 'El servicio secreto francés convocó de urgencia al CNI en Navidad para informarle de la trama terrorista' [The French secret service urgently summoned the CNI at Christmas to inform them of the terrorist plot], 2 February 2008. The existence of a protected informant had emerged when the suspects appeared in court on 23 January and was reported in *El Mundo* and *20minutos*, after the judge ordered they remain in custody on 23 January. *El País* also covered it on 24 January.

16 First Guardia Civil official report, 23 January 2008, p. 4.

17 Antonio Baquero and Jordi Corachán, 'Abortado en BCN un gran atentado de Al Qaeda' [A big al-Qaeda terrorist attack thwarted in Barcelona], *El Periódico de Catalunya*, 20 January 2008.

18 Garzón and McConnell were both quoted in Elaine Sciolino, 'Terror Threat from Pakistan Said to Expand', *New York Times*, 10 February 2008.

19 Graham Keeley and Paul Haven, 'Spain, France at Odds over Terror Probe', *USA Today* online, 8 February 2008.

20 Elaine Sciolino, 'Terror Threat from Pakistan Said to Expand', *New York Times*, 10 February 2008.

21 Craig Whitlock, 'After a Decade at War with West, Al-Qaeda Still Impervious to Spies', *Washington Post*, 20 March 2008.

22 Graham Keeley and Paul Haven, 'Spain, France at Odds over Terror Probe', *USA Today* online, 8 February 2008.

23 'Al-Qaeda's White Army of Terror', *Scotsman*, 12 January 2008.

24 Morten Storm, with Tim Lister and Paul Cruickshank, *Agent Storm: My Life Inside Al-Qaeda* (London, Viking, 2014).

25 Wikileaks: cable ID 10MADRID78, ID #245306, dated 25 January 2010.

26 Roshan Jamal Khan, testimony at his trial.

27 Blog maintained by Roshan Jamal Khan's brother and family: roshan-jamal-khan.blogspot.co.uk/2009/12/motive-for-association.html.

28 Graham Keeley and Paul Haven, 'Spain, France at Odds over Terror Probe', *USA Today* online, 8 February 2008.

29 Appeal document, pp. 116, 121–122.

Chapter 8: Allah Has Plans

1 Koran, 8:30, Surat Al-'Anfāl (The Spoils of War): available at http://quran. com/8/30.

2 President Obama's Inaugural Address: available at www.whitehouse.gov/ the_press_office/President_Barack_Obamas_Inaugural_Address.

3 'The Appearance of the Mahdi', *Sunan Ibn Majah*, Vol. 1, Book 36, Hadith 4084.

4 'When Will My Words Drink from My Blood?': available at www.ummah. com and first published on militant websites on 27 December 2008.

5 As-Sahab Foundation for Islamic Media, a jihadist website, interview with Humam al-Balawi, posted 27 September 2009 (hereafter As-Sahab interview).

6 As-Sahab interview.

7 Ibid.

8 Wikileaks: cable ID 07ISLAMABAD5283, 'PAKISTAN: ATTEMPTED INTERCEPTS OF COALITION AIRCRAFT', dated 14 December 2007.

9 New America Foundation: available at http://counterterrorism.newamerica. net/drones.

10 F. M. Begoum, 'Observations on the Double Agent', *Studies in Intelligence Journal*, 1962; declassified and released 18 September 1995: available at www.cia.gov.

11 Steve Coll, *Ghost Wars* (London, Penguin, 2005), p. 87.

12 Ibid.

13 Omar Nasiri, *Inside the Global Jihad: How I Infiltrated Al Qaeda and Was Abandoned by Western Intelligence* (London, Hurst & Co., 2006), p. 234.

14 'The al-Qaeda Manual, Part 19'. Retrieved 1 November 2013 from www.us-borderpatrol.com/Border_Patrol1803_19.htm.

15 Ibid.

16 Brian Fishman, 'Al-Qa'ida's Spymaster Analyzes the U.S. Intelligence Community', 6 November 2006: available at www.ctc.usma.edu.

17 'The Myth of Delusion': available from a variety of sources, including http:// counterterrorismblog.org/site-resources/images/Myth-of-Delusion.

18 As-Sahab interview.

19 Joby Warrick, The *Triple Agent: The Al-Qaeda Mole Who Infiltrated the CIA* (New York, Doubleday, 2011), Kindle locations 813–20.

20 As-Sahab interview.

21 Ibid.

22 Ibid.

23 'Difference Engine: Unblinking Eye in the Sky', *The Economist*, 13 January 2012.

24 Warrick, *The Triple Agent*, Kindle location 1409. Mehsud was killed on the night of 5–6 August and Humam appeared in late August.

25 As-Sahab interview.

26 Ibid.

27 'Interview with Brother Abu Dujanah al-Khorasani, a Well-Known Blogger in Jihadi Forums, and a Newcomer to the Land of Khorasan', published in English translation on *Vanguards of Khorasan*, Issue 15, 26 September 2009.

28 Ibid.

29 As-Sahab interview.

30 Ibid.

31 F. M. Begoum, 'Observations on the Double Agent', *Studies in Intelligence Journal*, 1962; declassified and released 18 September 1995: available at www.cia.gov.

32 Warrick, *The Triple Agent*, Kindle location 1840. Panetta was CIA director from 2009 to 2011.

33 Ibid., Kindle location 1999.

34 As-Sahab interview.

35 F. M. Begoum, 'Observations on the Double Agent', *Studies in Intelligence Journal*, 1962; declassified and released 18 September 1995: available at www.cia.gov.

36 As revealed in the military logs published by Wikileaks. See, for instance, www.theguardian.com/world/datablog/2010/jul/25/wikileaks-afghanistan-war-logs-glossary.

37 First mentioned in Bob Woodward, *Obama's Wars* (New York, Simon & Schuster, 2010) and articles relating to the book. See, inter alia, Steve Luxenberg, 'Bob Woodward Book Details Obama Battles with Advisers over Exit Plan for Afghan War', *Washington Post*, 22 September 2010.

38 Ian Shapira, 'For CIA Family, a Deadly Suicide Bombing Leads to Painful Divisions', *Washington Post*, 28 January 2012.

39 Joby Warrick, 'CIA: Systemic Failures Led to Suicide Attack', *Washington Post*, 20 October 2010.

40 As-Sahab interview.

41 Video broadcast in Peter Taylor, *The Secret War on Terror*, BBC Two, 14 March 2011.

42 'Prompting the Dying Person', *Sunan Abi Dawud*, Book 20, Hadith 3110.

43 As-Sahab interview.

44 Ian Shapira, 'For CIA Family, a Deadly Suicide Bombing Leads to Painful Divisions', *Washington Post*, 28 January 2012.

45 Ibid.

46 Blackwater was the name of a major private security and training business which operated in various war zones, including Iraq and Afghanistan. In 2009, Blackwater was renamed Xe Services, followed in 2011 by another new name, Academi.

47 Courtesy of Dr Jarret Brachman, expert in extremist thought and militancy. The poem was posted on the English sub-forum of the Al-Faloja forum in early January 2010.

Chapter 9: Faith in the Machine

1 Robert Baer, *See No Evil* (London, Arrow Books, 2002), p. 310.

2 Jane Mayer, 'The Predator War', *New Yorker*, 26 October 2009.

3 Interviewed for 'Kill/Capture', *Frontline*, PBS, written and produced by Dan Edge and Stephen Grey, 10 May 2011.

4 Video obtained by 'Kill/Capture', *Frontline*, PBS.

5 'Afghan Election Campaign Workers "Killed in Air Strike" ', BBC News website, 2 September 2010.

6 NATO ISAF News Release no. 2010-09-CA-027, 'Coalition Forces Conduct Precision Strike against Senior IMU Member in Takhar Province', 2 September 2010.

7 'Afghan Election Campaign Workers "Killed in Air Strike" ', BBC News website, 2 September 2010.

8 NATO ISAF News Release no. 2010-08-CA-134, 'Assessment of Civilian Casualties in Takhar Complete', 12 September 2010.

9 Ian S. Livingston and Michael O'Hanlon, 'Afghanistan Index', Brookings Institution, 10 January 2014.

10 Major General Michael T. Flynn, Captain Matt Pottinger and Paul D. Batchelor, 'Fixing Intel: A Blueprint for Making Intelligence Relevant in Afghanistan', Voice from the Field publication, January 2010, Center for New American Security.

11 Author interview with John Nagl for PBS *Frontline*.

12 The story of Semple's dialogue with the Taliban in Helmand and his expulsion from Afghanistan is described in Stephen Grey, *Operation Snakebite* (London, Viking, 2009).

13 'Will the Real Mohammad Amin Please Stand Up: A Case Study in the Practical Difficulties of Using Network Analysis as a Tool for Targeting', Eclipse Group. Supplied to the author by its director, Duane Clarridge, and first published on Eclipse's website in March 2011 (hereafter Eclipse report).

14 Eclipse report.

15 Kate Clark, 'The Takhar Attack, Targeted Killings and the Parallel Worlds of US Intelligence and Afghanistan', report for the Afghan Analysts Network, May 2011, p. 12.

16 Author interview with Duane Clarridge, November 2013.

17 Author interview with General David Petraeus for PBS *Frontline*.

18 A US official told me, 'Mohamed Amin was identified as our target. He is the uncle of Abdul Rahman and the father of Jamil and Feda Rahman.' His real family was not in Kabul but in Pakistan. 'He maintains a home with his wife in Shamsattu, in Peshawar agency,' the official said.

19 Interview by producer Shoaib Sharifi for PBS *Frontline*. The elder also confirmed that Aalem, whom he called 'Maulavi Aalem', had a home in Pakistan and his father was Abdul Waseh, a mujahid who was killed by the Russians. He correctly said that the nephew was in the custody of the NDS, the Afghan national security service.

20 'Afghanistan: Suicide Blast Kills Top Police Commander', BBC News website, 29 May 2011.

21 Author interview with Michael Semple for PBS *Frontline*.

Chapter 10: *The Peacemaker Spy*

1 'Obituary: Nicholas Elliott', *Independent*, 18 April 1994.

2 Michael Weiss, 'Useful Idiots', *New Criterion*, 12 August 2010.

3 The information about Alastair Crooke that follows comes from author interviews in Beirut, March 2013.

4 Frederick Montague Warren Crooke was the son of Robert Warren Crooke, born 1860 (physician and surgeon).

5 Letter from Warren Crooke, dated 7 February 1918, referenced in Nathan Wise, 'Playing Soldiers: Sydney Private School Cadet Corps and the Great War', *Journal of the Royal Australian Historical Society*, Vol. 96, No. 2, December 2010, p. 197. On 31 December 1919, the *Sydney Morning Herald* records Warren's brief return home: 'Lieutenant Warren Crooke (M. M.), of the Gurkha Rifles, India, only son of Dr. Warren Crooke, of Cordeaux, has returned to Australia. He left as a sergeant in 1915, fought through Egypt, Gallipoli, and France, and gained the Military Medal and his commission. He is now an officer in the Indian Army, and is on eight months' furlough.'

6 Vladimir Putin, *First Person: An Astonishingly Frank Self-Portrait by Russia's President* (New York, PublicAffairs, 2000), p. 23.

7 David McKittrick (ed.), *Lost Lives: The Stories of the Men, Women and Children Who Died as a Result of the Northern Ireland Troubles* (Edinburgh, Mainstream Publishing, 2008), p. 663.

8 James Harkin, 'Middleman in the Middle East', *Financial Times*, 2 January 2009.

9 Author interview with Milton Bearden for 'Mint Tea with the Terrorists', *New Statesman*, 11 April 2005.

10 Stephen Grey, 'Let's Talk: Ex-MI6 Man Plans Terror Summit', *Sunday Times*, 12 December 2004.

11 Alan J. Kuperman, 'The Stinger Missile and U.S. Intervention in Afghanistan', *Political Science Quarterly*, Vol. 114, No. 2, Summer 1999. His study was quoted in Peter Dale Scott, *Drugs, Oil, and War: The United States in Afghanistan, Colombia, and Indochina* (Maryland, Rowman & Littlefield, 2004), p. 5.

12 Suzanne Goldenberg, 'Rioting as Sharon Visits Islam Holy Site', *Guardian*, 29 September 2000.

13 Peter Beaumont, 'How a British Coup Ended Siege', *Observer*, 12 May 2002.

14 Many details from Beaumont, as before.

15 'Document Seized in (November 2002) in the Palestinian Authority Preventive Security Compound in Gaza', issued 2 September 2005, the Meir Amit Intelligence and Terrorism Information Center, Israel: available at www. terrorism-info.org.il/en/article/19270.

16 Alastair Crooke, 'Permanent Temporariness', *London Review of Books*, Vol. 3, No. 5, 3 March 2011 (hereafter Crooke, *LRB* article).

17 Documents leaked to the Arabic TV channel Al Jazeera, which they named 'The Palestine Papers'.

18 Crooke *LRB* article.

19 Inigo Gilmore, 'Ex-MI6 Officer Acts as Broker in Hamas Talks', *Daily Telegraph*, 1 September 2002.

20 Chris McGreal, 'UK Recalls MI6 Link to Palestinian Militants', *Guardian*, 24 September 2003.

21 Sir Richard Dearlove, testimony to the Chilcot Inquiry, 13 July 2010, p. 55.

Chapter 11: Vaccination

1 Hansard, House of Commons Debate on International Affairs, 10 November 1932, Vol. 270, cc. 525–641: available at http://hansard.millbanksystems. com.

Notes

2 Compound details and diagrams provided by US Department of Defense: available at www.pbs.org/wnet/need-to-know/security/seen-from-the-sky-where-bin-laden-was-killed/9013.

3 Interview with Admiral William McRaven, *The Situation Room*, CNN, 28 July 2012.

4 Peter L. Bergen, *Manhunt: The Ten-Year Search for Bin Laden – From 9/11 to Abbottabad* (New York, Crown Publishers, 2012), p. 230.

5 Mark Bowden, *The Finish: The Killing of Osama bin Laden* (Grove Press UK, 2012), Kindle location 1511.

6 This was first told in the unauthorized account of the raid by the Navy SEAL Mark Owen, *No Easy Day* (New York, Penguin, 2012), but the scene also featured in *Zero Dark Thirty*.

7 As described by Gary Schroen, the leader of one of the CIA's 'Jawbreaker' teams that was dispatched to Afghanistan, in his book *First In* (New York, Presidio Press, 2005), p. 38.

8 Senate Select Committee on Intelligence, 'Committee Study of the CIA's Detention and Interrogation Program' (hereafter Senate Torture report), declassified 3 December 2013, pp. 378–400.

9 Quoted by Nada Bakos, a former CIA analyst, in '"ZDT" Gets the CIA Wrong', *Salon*, 18 January 2013.

10 Bergen, *Manhunt*, p. 90.

11 Ibid., p. 100.

12 Bowden, *The Finish*, Kindle location 1680.

13 Senator John McCain, Congressional Record (Senate), 12 May 2011: available at www.fas.org/irp/congress/2011_cr/torture.html.

14 Senate Torture report, p. 384.

15 Senator John McCain, Congressional Record (Senate), 12 May 2011: available at www.fas.org/irp/congress/2011_cr/torture.html.

16 Senate Torture report, p. 399.

17 Ibid., p. 382.

18 Bowden, *The Killing*, Kindle location 1794.

19 As detailed by former CIA Counterterrorism Center officers Gary Schroen and Hank Crumpton in separate interviews. Schroen was interviewed for PBS *Frontline*'s 'The Dark Side', June 2006. Crumpton was interviewed for CBS's *60 Minutes*, 13 May 2012.

20 Bergen, *Manhunt*, p. 131.

21 Both quotes from Nada Bakos, '"ZDT" Gets the CIA Wrong', *Salon*, 18 January 2013.

22 Henry A. Crumpton, *The Art of Intelligence: Lessons from a Life in the CIA's Clandestine Service* (New York, Penguin, 2012), p. 71.

23 Ibid., p. 70.

24 Author interview with Paul Pillar, November 2013.

25 Author interview and email exchange with Sir David Omand, 2010 and 2014.

26 Ibid.

27 BBC News website, 19 December 2013: available at www.bbc.co.uk/news/uk-25450555.

28 Jason Bennetto, 'British Terrorist Plotted Wave of Attacks to Emulate 11 September', *Independent*, 7 November 2006.

29 Patricia Hurtado, 'Afzali, Alleged Terror Ally, Says He's "Perjury Trap" Victim', *Bloomberg.com*, 12 December 2009.

30 Karen DeYoung, 'Obama to Get Report on Intelligence Failures in Abdulmutallab Case', *Washington Post*, 31 December 2009.

31 William E. Burrows, author of *Deep Black: Space Espionage and National Security*, quoted in Jeffrey T. Richelson, 'The Spies in Space', *Air and Space* magazine, reprinted in the Congressional Record, 26 November 1991.

32 Vernon Loeb, 'Test of Strength', *Washington Post*, 29 July 2001.

33 Author's notes of speech by Michael Sheehan to a conference, 'Intelligence in the Age of National Security', 1 February 2008, organized by New York University's Center on Law and Security.

34 Robert Verkaik, 'How MI5 Blackmails British Muslims', *Independent*, 21 May 2009.

35 Richard Watson interview with Abu Nusaybah, *Newsnight*, BBC Two, 24 May 2013.

36 Michael Adebolajo was given a whole-life term; Michael Adebowale was sentenced to life with a minimum term of forty-five years.

37 Morten Storm, with Tim Lister and Paul Cruickshank, *Agent Storm: My Life Inside Al-Qaeda* (London, Viking, 2014), p. 268.

38 Charlie Savage, 'Former F.B.I. Agent to Plead Guilty in Press Leak', *New York Times*, 23 September 2013.

39 Mark Hosenball, 'Did White House "Spin" Tip a Covert Op?', *Reuters*, 18 May 2012.

40 This JSOC operation to support drone strikes in Pakistan emerged from reporting for 'Kill/Capture', *Frontline*, PBS, written and produced by Dan Edge and Stephen Grey, May 2011. Some details were first published by the author in an interview with the PBS website: http://www.pbs.org/wgbh/pages/frontline/afghanistan-pakistan/secret-war/jsoc-using-captured-militants-to-analyze-intel/.

41 'In 2013, only three countries (Afghanistan, Nigeria and Pakistan) remain polio-endemic, down from more than 125 in 1988': WHO Fact Sheet No. 114, Poliomyelitis, April 2013.

42 InterAction letter, 21 February 2012: available at s3.documentcloud.org/documents/322222/interaction-afridi-letter.pdf.

43 Zulfiqar Ali and Mark Magnier, 'Polio Worker, 2 Police Officers Slain in Pakistan', *Los Angeles Times*, 13 December 2013.

Chapter 12: The Good Spy

1 Sun Tzu, *The Art of War*, Chapter III, Verse 18, translation by Lionel Giles: available at http://classics.mit.edu/Tzu/artwar.html.

2 'Cloak, Dagger and a Blond Wig? FSB Says CIA Agent Nabbed in Moscow', *RT.com*, 14 May 2013.

3 Ibid.

4 Ibid.

5 Milton Bearden, 'The Moscow Rules Still Rule', *Foreign Policy*, 17 May 2013.

6 'Alexander Litvinenko Death: UK Announces Public Inquiry', BBC News website, 22 July 2014.

7 Eric Schmitt, Michael S. Schmidt and Ellen Barry, 'Bombing Inquiry Turns to Motive and Russian Trip', *New York Times*, 20 April 2013.

8 The National Reconnaissance Office, National Security Agency and National Geospatial-Intelligence Agency combined budgets equal $26 billion.

9 Wilson Andrews and Todd Lindeman, '$52.6 Billion: The Black Budget', *Washington Post*, published 29 August 2013: available at www.washingtonpost.com/wp-srv/special/national/black-budget/.

10 Paul Lewis and Rob Evans, 'Police Spies Court Case Suggests Sexual Relations with Activists Were Routine', *Guardian*, 17 January 2013.

11 Judgment in [2013] EWHC 32 (QB), Case No. HQ11X03952, 17 January 2013: available at www.bailii.org/ew/cases/EWHC/QB/2013/32.html.

12 Sun Tzu, *The Art of War*, Chapter 1, 'Laying Plans', point 18, and Chapter 13, 'The Use of Spies', point 18.

13 Jennifer E. Sims and Burton L. Gerber (eds), *Transforming U.S. Intelligence* (Washington, DC, Georgetown University Press, 2005), p. 86.

14 See http://www.theguardian.com/world/2013/jul/31/nsa-top-secret-program-online-data.

15 Richard Rubin, 'Cash Abroad Rises $206 Billion as Apple to IBM Avoid Tax', *Bloomberg News*, 12 March 2014.

16 Winston Churchill, *The Second World War: Vol. 1, The Gathering Storm* (London, Cassell & Co., 1948), p. 105.

17 Status of World Nuclear Forces 2013, Federation of American Scientists: available at www.fas.org/programs/ssp/nukes/nuclearweapons/nukestatus.html.

18 John Updike, *The Complete Henry Bech* (London, Penguin, 2006), Kindle location 148.

19 He expounded these ideas in John Robb, *Brave New War: The Next Stage of Terrorism and the End of Globalization. How They Organize and Operate in Iraq and Beyond* (New Jersey, Wiley & Sons, 2007).

20 Jake Kerridge, 'Hay Festival 2013: John le Carré on His New Novel, *A Delicate Truth*', *Daily Telegraph*, 25 May 2013.

21 Markus Wolf in a 1998 interview for CNN Special 'Cold War': available at http://archive.is/LI9N8.

22 Gordon Corera interview with Oleg Gordievsky, quoted in Gordon Corera, *MI6: Life and Death in the British Secret Service* (London, Phoenix Paperbacks e-book), Kindle location 5473.

23 Sir Richard Dearlove, interviewed as part of 'The Global Threat of Terror' panel at the 2006 Aspen Ideas Festival: available at www.aspenideas.org/session/global-threat-terror.

Bibliography

Adams, James, *New Spies: Exploring the Frontiers of Espionage* (London, Pimlico, 1995)

Agee, Philip, *Inside the Company: CIA Diary* (Harmondsworth, Penguin, 1975)

Ahmed, Nafeez Mosaddeq, *The London Bombings: An Independent Inquiry* (London, Gerald Duckworth and Co. Ltd, 2006)

Aldrich, Richard J., *GCHQ: The Uncensored Story of Britain's Most Secret Intelligence Agency* (London, HarperPress, 2011)

Andrew, Christopher, *The Defence of the Realm: The Authorized History of MI5*, updated edition (London, Penguin, 2010)

Andrew, Christopher, and Gordievsky, Oleg, *Instructions from the Centre: Top Secret Files on KGB Global Operations 1975–1985* (London, Hodder and Stoughton, 1993)

Andrew, Christopher, and Mitrokhin, Vasili, *The Mitrokhin Archive: The KGB in Europe and the West* (London, Penguin, 2000)

Andrew, Christopher, and Mitrokhin, Vasili, *The Sword and the Shield: The Mitrokhin Archive and the Secret History of the KGB* (New York, Basic Books, 2000)

Baer, Robert, *See No Evil* (London, Arrow Books, 2002)

Bainton, Roy, *Honoured by Strangers: The Life of Captain Francis Cromie CB, DSO, RN, 1882–1918* (Shrewsbury, Airlife, 2002)

Bamford, James, *Body of Secrets: How America's NSA and Britain's GCHQ Eavesdrop on the World* (London, Arrow Books, 2002)

Bamford, James, *The Shadow Factory: The Ultra-Secret NSA from 9/11 to the Eavesdropping on America* (New York, Anchor Books, 2009)

Bearden, Milton, and Risen, James, *The Main Enemy: The CIA's Battle with the Soviet Union, Told by the Mastermind Behind It* (London, Century, 2003)

Benjamin, Daniel, and Simon, Steven, *The Age of Sacred Terror: Radical Islam's War Against America* (New York, Random House, 2003)

Bergen, Peter L., *Manhunt: The Ten-Year Search for Bin Laden – From 9/11 to Abbottabad* (New York, Crown, 2012)

Berntsen, Gary, and Pezzullo, Ralph, *Jawbreaker: The Attack on Bin Laden and Al-Qaeda – A Personal Account by the CIA's Field Commander* (New York, Crown, 2005)

Berry, Colin, *The Deniable Agent: Undercover in Afghanistan* (Edinburgh, Mainstream Publishing, 2006)

Billingsley, Roger (ed.), *Covert Human Intelligence Sources: The 'Unlovely' Face of Police Work* (Hook, Hampshire, Waterside Press, 2009)

Blake, George, *No Other Choice* (London, Jonathan Cape, 1990)

Borovik, Genrikh, *The Philby Files: The Secret Life of the Master Spy – KGB Archives Revealed* (London, Time Warner Paperbacks, 1995)

Bowden, Mark, *The Finish: The Killing of Osama bin Laden*, Kindle edition (London, Grove Press UK, 2012)

Britnieva, Mary, *One Woman's Story* (London, Barker, 1934)

Cherkashin, Victor, and Feifer, Gregory, *Spy Handler: The True Story of the Man Who Recruited Robert Hanssen and Aldrich Ames* (New York, Basic Books, 2005)

Childers, Erskine, *The Riddle of the Sands: A Record of Secret Service Recently Achieved* (London, CRW Publishing, 2008)

Childs, David, and Popplewell, Richard, *The Stasi: The East German Intelligence and Security Service* (London, Macmillan, 1999)

Churchill, Winston, *The World Crisis: The Aftermath* (London, Macmillan, 1929)

Clarridge, Duane R., *A Spy for All Seasons* (New York, Scribner, 1997)

Coll, Steve, *Ghost Wars* (London, Penguin, 2005)

Collins, Catherine, and Frantz, Douglas, *Fallout: The True Story of the CIA's Secret War on Nuclear Trafficking* (New York, Free Press, 2011)

Cook, Andrew, *Ace of Spies: The True Story of Sidney Reilly*, Kindle edition (Stroud, The History Press, 2011)

Corera, Gordon, *Shopping for Bombs: Nuclear Proliferation, Global Insecurity and the Rise and Fall of the A. Q. Khan Network* (London, Hurst & Co., 2006)

Corera, Gordon, *MI6: Life and Death in the British Secret Service* (London, Phoenix Paperbacks e-book, 2012)

Crowdy, Terry, *The Enemy Within: A History of Spies, Spymasters, and Espionage* (Oxford, Osprey Publishing, 2006)

Crumpton, Henry A., *The Art of Intelligence: Lessons from a Life in the CIA's Clandestine Service* (New York, Penguin, 2012)

Davies, Philip H. J., *MI6 and the Machinery of Spying* (London, Frank Cass, 2004)

Desmaret, Gérard, *Le Renseignement Humain* (Paris, Chiron, 2004)

Devine, Jack, with Vernon Loeb, *Good Hunting: An American Spymaster's Story* (New York, Farrar, Straus and Giroux, 2014)

Devlin, Larry, *Chief of Station, Congo: A Memoir of 1960–67* (New York, PublicAffairs, 2007)

Bibliography

Dorril, Stephen, *MI6: Inside the Covert World of Her Majesty's Secret Intelligence Service* (New York, Touchstone, 2000)

Drogin, Bob, *Curveball: Spies, Lies, and the Con Man Who Caused a War* (New York, Random House, 2007)

Drumheller, Tyler, with Elaine Monaghan, *On the Brink: An Insider's Account of How the White House Compromised American Intelligence* (New York, Carroll & Graf, 2006)

Ferguson, Niall, *The War of the World: History's Age of Hatred* (London, Penguin, 2009)

Gartstein-Ross, Daveed, *My Year Inside Radical Islam: A Memoir* (London, Penguin, 2007)

Glees, Anthony, *The Stasi Files: East Germany's Secret Operations Against Britain* (London, Simon & Schuster, 2003)

Gordievsky, Oleg, *Next Stop Execution: The Autobiography of Oleg Gordievsky* (London, Macmillan, 1995)

Grey, Stephen, *Ghost Plane: The True Story of the CIA Torture Program* (New York, St Martin's Press, 2006)

Grose, Peter, *Gentleman Spy: The Life of Allen Dulles* (Boston, Houghton Mifflin, 1996)

Halevy, Efraim, *Man in the Shadows: Inside the Middle East Crisis with a Man Who Led the Mossad* (New York, St Martin's Press, 2006)

Harris, Shane, *The Watchers: The Rise of America's Surveillance State* (New York, Penguin, 2010)

Helm, Sarah, *A Life in Secrets: The Story of Vera Atkins and the Lost Agents of SOE* (London, Little, Brown, 2005)

Helms, Richard, with William Hood, *A Look Over My Shoulder: A Life in the Central Intelligence Agency* (New York, Random House, 2003)

Hennessy, Peter, and Herman, Michael, *Intelligence Services in the Information Age: Theory and Practice* (London, Frank Cass, 2001)

Hewitt, Steve, *Snitch! A History of the Modern Intelligence Informer* (London, Bloomsbury, 2010)

Hill, George A., *Go Spy the Land* (London, Cassell, 1932)

Hitz, Frederick P., *The Great Game: The Myths and Realities of Espionage* (New York, Vintage, 2005)

Hollingsworth, Mark, and Fielding, Nick, *Defending the Realm: Inside MI5 and the War on Terrorism* (London, André Deutsch, 2003)

Hopkirk, Peter, *Quest for Kim: In Search of Kipling's Great Game* (Oxford, Oxford University Press 1996)

Bibliography

Ignatius, David, *Agents of Innocence* (New York, W. W. Norton, 1987)

Ingram, Martin, and Harkin, Greg, *Stakeknife: Britain's Secret Agents in Ireland* (Madison, University of Wisconsin Press, 2005)

Jeffery, Keith, *MI6: The History of the Secret Intelligence Service 1909–1949* (London, Bloomsbury, 2010)

Judd, Alan, *The Quest for 'C': Mansfield Cumming and the Making of the British Secret Service* (London, HarperCollins, 1999)

Kalugin, Oleg, with Fen Montaigne, *The First Directorate: My 32 Years in Intelligence and Counterintelligence Against the West* (New York, St Martin's Press, 1994)

Keefe, Patrick Radden, *Chatter: Dispatches from the Secret World of Global Eavesdropping* (New York, Random House, 2005)

Knight, Amy, *Spies Without Cloaks: The KGB's Successors* (Princeton, Princeton University Press, 1996)

Knightley, Phillip, *The Second Oldest Profession: Spies and Spying in the Twentieth Century* (London, Pimlico, 2003)

Lockhart, R. H. Bruce, *Memoirs of a British Agent* (London, Putnam, 1932)

Lowe, Norman, *Mastering Twentieth Century Russian History* (London, Palgrave Macmillan, 2002)

Lycett, Andrew, *Ian Fleming* (London, Weidenfeld & Nicolson, 1995)

McGartland, Martin, *Fifty Dead Men Walking* (London, John Blake, 2009)

Macintyre, Ben, *A Spy Among Friends: Kim Philby and the Great Betrayal* (London, Bloomsbury, 2014)

Maclean, Fitzroy, *Eastern Approaches* (London, Penguin, 1991)

Madelin, Philippe, *Dans le Secret des Services* (Paris, Éditions Denoël, 2007)

Mallet du Pan, Jacques, *Considerations on the Nature of the French Revolution: And on the Causes Which Prolong Its Duration* (London, J. Owen, 1793)

May, Thomas Erskine, *Constitutional History of England: Vol. II, 1760–1860* (London, Longman, Green, Longman, Roberts and Green, 1863)

Melman, Yossi, and Raviv, Dan, *Spies Against Armageddon: Inside Israel's Secret Wars* (Beirut, Levant Books, 2012)

Milne, Tim, *Kim Philby: The Unknown Story of the KGB's Master Spy* (London, Biteback Publishing, 2014)

Modin, Yuri, *My Five Cambridge Friends* (New York, Farrar, Straus and Giroux, 1994)

Moran, Christopher, *Classified: Secrecy and the State in Modern Britain* (Cambridge, Cambridge University Press, 2012)

Moran, Lindsay, *Blowing My Cover: My Life as a CIA Spy* (New York, Berkley Books, 2005)

Bibliography

Nasiri, Omar, *Inside the Global Jihad: How I Infiltrated Al Qaeda and Was Abandoned by Western Intelligence* (London, Hurst & Co., 2006)

Olson, James M., *Fair Play: The Moral Dilemmas of Spying* (Nebraska, Potomac Books, 2006)

Page, Bruce, Leitch, David, Knightley, Phillip, and Le Carré, John, *Philby: The Spy Who Betrayed a Generation* (London, Sphere, 1978)

Pearson, John, *The Life of Ian Fleming, Creator of James Bond* (London, Coronet Books, 1989)

Philby, Kim, *My Silent War: The Autobiography of a Spy* (London, HarperCollins, 1999, and Cornerstone Publishing, 2010)

Post, Jerrold M., *The Mind of the Terrorist: The Psychology of Terrorism from the IRA to Al-Qaeda* (New York, Palgrave Macmillan, 2007)

Prados, John, *Lost Crusader: The Secret Wars of CIA Director William Colby* (Oxford, Oxford University Press, 2003)

Reilly, Sidney George, and Bobadilla, Pepita, *Britain's Master Spy: The Adventures of Sidney Reilly, An Autobiography* (New York, Carroll & Graf Publishers, 1986)

Richelson, Jeffrey T., *A Century of Spies: Intelligence in the Twentieth Century* (New York/Oxford, Oxford University Press, 1997)

Richelson, Jeffrey T., *The U.S. Intelligence Community* (Boulder, CO, Westview Press, 1999)

Rimington, Stella, *Open Secret: The Autobiography of the Former Director-General of MI5* (London, Arrow Books, 2002)

Sayers, Michael, and Kahn, Albert E., *The Great Conspiracy Against Russia* (London, Collet's Holdings Ltd, 1946)

Schroen, Gary C., *First In: An Insider's Account of How the CIA Spearheaded the War on Terror in Afghanistan* (New York, Presidio Press, 2005)

Sims, Jennifer E., and Gerber, Burton (eds), *Transforming U.S. Intelligence* (Washington, DC, Georgetown University Press, 2005)

Smele, Jonathan D., *The Russian Revolution and Civil War 1917–1921: An Annotated Bibliography* (London/New York, Continuum, 2006)

Smith, Michael, *New Cloak, Old Dagger: How Britain's Spies Came in from the Cold* (London, Victor Gollancz, 1996)

Staniforth, Andrew, and Sampson, Fraser (eds), *The Routledge Companion to UK Counter-Terrorism* (Oxford, Routledge, 2012)

Storm, Morten, with Tim Lister and Paul Cruickshank, *Agent Storm: My Life Inside Al-Qaeda* (London, Viking, 2014)

Sweet-Escott, Bickham, *Baker Street Irregular* (London, Methuen & Co., 1965)

Bibliography

Tenet, George, with Bill Harlow, *At the Center of the Storm: My Years at the CIA* (New York, HarperLuxe, 2007)

Tucker, Spencer, *The Great War, 1914–1918* (New York, Routledge, 1997)

Tzu, Sun, *The Art of War* (Boston, Shambala, 1991)

Urban, Mark, *UK Eyes Alpha: The Inside Story of British Intelligence* (London, Faber and Faber, 1996)

Van Der Rhoer, Edward, *Master Spy: A True Story of Allied Espionage in Bolshevik Russia* (New York, Scribner, 1981)

Vincent, David, *The Culture of Secrecy: Britain, 1832–1998* (Oxford, Oxford University Press, 1999)

Warrick, Joby, *The Triple Agent: The Al-Qaeda Mole Who Infiltrated the CIA*, Kindle edition (New York, Doubleday, 2011)

Waters, T. J., *Class 11: My Story Inside the CIA's First Post-9/11 Spy Class* (New York, Dutton, 2006)

Weiner, Tim, *Legacy of Ashes: The History of the CIA* (London, Penguin/Allen Lane, 2007)

Whymant, Robert, *Stalin's Spy: Richard Sorge and the Tokyo Espionage Ring* (London, I. B. Tauris, 2006)

Wise, David, *Nightmover: How Aldrich Ames Sold the CIA to the KGB for $4.6 Million* (New York, HarperCollins, 1995)

Wolf, Markus, with Anne McElvoy, *Man Without a Face: The Autobiography of Communism's Greatest Spymaster* (New York, PublicAffairs, 1997)

Woodward, Bob, *Obama's Wars* (New York, Simon & Schuster, 2010)

Wright, Lawrence, *The Looming Tower: Al-Qaeda and the Road to 9/11* (New York, Alfred A. Knopf, 2006)

Wright, Peter, with Paul Greengrass, *Spycatcher: The Candid Autobiography of a Senior Intelligence Officer* (New York, Viking, 1987)

Zegart, Amy B., *Spying Blind: The CIA, the FBI, and the Origins of 9/11* (Princeton/Oxford, Princeton University Press, 2007)

Acknowledgements

This is a book about secret intelligence and, as such, obviously very few of the dozens who assisted me will thank me for mentioning them here, or highlighting their particular role in the book. You know who you are and I thank you for your patience, your trust that I would try my best to portray your profession faithfully and your tolerance of my criticisms. I beg forgiveness if, despite your best efforts, I have failed to grasp the point. There is, of course, a warm beer behind the bar for you – preferably at the Gandamack Lodge, when it reopens.

There are some, however, who must be thanked publicly. With me throughout, as she was with *Ghost Plane* and *Operation Snakebite*, has been the unstoppable and razor-sharp researcher Christina Czapiewska, who had a lot to contribute too from her own personal knowledge and contacts. At different times, I also had tremendous additional research help from Lucy Bond, Jerome Taylor and Daniel Douglas. Particular thanks to my old friend John Goetz, who helped me explore the world of German espionage. And also to Stelios Orphanides, who helped track down EOKA fighters, and thank you to Susan Hollowday for sharing Zanina Hollowday's beautiful diary of her time in Cyprus. Thanks to Spanish investigative journalist Marco García Rey for his great assistance on the F1 case in Barcelona: I hope we shall keep digging into that one. I must also thank the hyper-generous Philippe Madelin, who helped set up interviews in Paris but sadly died in 2010. I also appreciate the help of the group of cage-prisoners in arranging several interviews.

Thanks too to colleagues who shared some of their adventures, enabling me to learn more about the intelligence world, and to those who have encouraged and funded these trips, in particular David Fanning and Dan Edge at PBS *Frontline* (Dan, I thank you unforgivably late for proofreading my last book); Dorothy Byrne and Kevin Sutcliffe of Channel 4; Kate Clark of the Afghan Analysts Network and Afghan producer Shoaib Sharifi; Sean Ryan at the *Sunday Times*; Michael Williams and Simon Robinson at Reuters. Thanks to all at Reuters for giving me time to finish this project. And I would especially like to thank my friend Mark Hosenball,

Acknowledgements

Washington intelligence correspondent, who advised me throughout and introduced me to some of his key contacts. Thanks too to Gordon Corera and David Loyn at the BBC.

This book had many inspirations, but it only came to be thanks to an idea and commission from Penguin's Tony Lacey and Jon Elek (now working at a leading London literary agency), after an introduction by my old friend Jason Burke. Michael Flamini at St Martin's Press in New York was an enthusiastic and wise supporter throughout, as was Joel Rickett, who took over the project at Penguin and reinvigorated it – and me! In production, Lesley Levene and Emma Brown carefully took the project to the finish line. Thanks too to my agents, first Emma Parry and then Grainne Fox, for their constant encouragement. Thank you all for bearing with me.

Thanks too to those who took the time and trouble to read the manuscript and make suggestions, including J and J, two wise ex-professionals from different sides of the Atlantic, my dear friend Rupert Chetwynd and of course my wife, Rebecca, for her suggestions and, above all, her steadfast loving support.

As ever, the errors are mine alone.

Index

In Arabic names the definite article (al-), used as a prefix, is ignored in the ordering of entries.